REVOLUTION BY CONSENT

REVOLUTION BY CONSENT

DHIRENDRANATH SEN

GYAN

Published by

Gyan Publishing House
5, Ansari Road
Daryaganj, New Delhi-110002
Phone: 011-47034999, 9811692060
E-mail: books@gyanbooks.com

Distribution Network
gyanbooks.com
India, USA, Canada, UK, Australia

ISBN: 978-93-7447-529-4 (PB)

First Published, 1942

2nd Impression 2026

Printed at: Gyan Press, Delhi.

REVOLUTION BY CONSENT
Author: DHIRENDRANATH SEN

REVOLUTION

By Consent ?

BY

DHIRENDRANATH SEN, M.A., Ph.D.

Lecturer in Constitutional and Administrative Law, Public Administration and Journalism, University College of Arts, Calcutta; Ex-editor, *Hindusthan Standard* and *Advance*; and lately, Member, Editorial Board, *Amrita Bazar Patrika*

VIDYODAYA LIBRARY PRIVATE LTD.

72 MAHATMA GANDHI ROAD :: CALCUTTA 9

PREFACE

The title of this book calls for a few words of explanation. Revolution is a much too abused and hackneyed term. Sometimes people use it in the context of organised violence. That to my mind is a superficial way of looking at the great movements of social and political emancipation which have stirred humanity in different historical epochs. A revolution is not necessarily an armed uprising, although in most cases struggles of the oppressed peoples have been accompanied by violent and extra-legal activities. That being so, it may be contended that revolution by consent is a contradiction in terms. There are, however, recorded instances of history showing that far-reaching social changes have taken place without resort to armed insurrections. These come about particularly when the upholders and beneficiaries of vested interests are unable to summon to their aid the energy and drive essential to the carrying on with any prospect of success of a life-and-death struggle for maintaining the *status quo*. By the compulsion of events they just give way to a superior and more dynamic social force.

I believe that the entire period between the two world wars has shaken to its foundations Britain's gigantic colonial structure. Indeed, the maturing crisis of capitalism brought about by its irreconcilable inner contradictions led to a series of "incidents" and wars which in their latest phase transformed the conflict into an international civil war. For the moment at least the hostilities on an international scale have been officially brought to an end, but with the increasing disequilibrium between the forces of production and the relations of production and sharpening of conflict between the "haves" and the "have-nots" civil war is becoming more and more intense and acute. This is revealed in the new wave of strikes and lockouts in all parts of the world. Men must change their social relations in accordance with material productivity. The ideas and categories about which there is so much metaphysical chatter are only the expressions of these social relations.

So far as the Indian problem is concerned, it has two aspects, namely, (1) internal and (2) external. British imperialism has almost ceased to exist as a vital force. It is in a decadent stage. It can not show its fight and resist effectively the Indian movement for national liberation. It has reconciled itself to the liquidation of its old form and, accordingly, it stands committed to the transference of power to responsible Indian hands on the basis of agreement, although there is some difference in emphasis between the Conservative reaction to new developments in colonial countries and the Socialist approach. Perhaps just a slight push may be necessary before the deed of transfer is completed, but it is now a patent fact that British imperialism can no longer play a dominant role in the mechanism of the social apparatus. That fact is demonstrated by the rapid transformation of the racial composition of the capitalistic structure in India. The process started after the First World War and the pace has been quickened by the historic forces released by its successor.

In its external aspect, therefore, revolution by consent, that is, the transfer of power from British to Indian hands through the ordinary legal process, is not outside the realm of practical politics. By this, however, I do not mean that the beneficiaries of British colonial rule will not strive by all possible means to maintain their hold over certain strategic positions in the sphere of defence as well as in that of economic exploitation. To these ends they have sought during the past few years to enter into secret trade and commercial deals and alliances with the rising Indian bourgeoisie and to maintain, maybe in a vague and distant way, friendly relations with the Indian Princes by a singularly astounding and historically unsupportable twist of the doctrine of the Crown's paramountcy. The struggle is thus beginning to shift from the familiar scene of Indo-British conflict to that of bitter and relentless class antagonism.

Despite the ugly manifestations of the present communal clashes which derive their sustenance from India's medieval social patterns and those irritants called Pakistan and Akhand Hindusthan, the deeper and more powerful undercurrents of class conflict are bound with the passage of time to produce a more abiding effect on the unfolding of the Indian drama. Even if the events tend to point to the peaceful and orderly liquidation of Britain's imperialist rule, the internal aspect of the Indian Revolution will, in all probability, provoke struggles on a vast and extensive scale. The rising Indian bourgeoisie is a force to reckon with and there are no indications that this class and the Indian Princes would yield without a stubborn fight.

Nevertheless it is no use trying to oversimplify the complex and vexed communal problem in the context of events that are taking place to-day. In the earlier stages of the impending change that problem may give a good deal of headache to the builders of India's future. It seems to me that with the progressive weakening of the British colonial system the Indian movement for national liberation has in the higher social strata taken forms of a provocative character. A progressive and liberating movement is being utilised to set a common cultural pattern in complete disregard of the trends of India's historical development. There is blind and dogged insistence on what I call morbid nationalism which in the Indian context is more or less synonymous with Hindu revivalism. The result is Muslim reaction in the shape of an organised agitation for Pakistan. The latter in its turn has naturally given rise to the demand in the Punjab and Bengal for the division of these strategic Provinces of mixed populations on the basis of religion. It is a vicious circle and what is amazing is that responsible leaders of great political parties should have allowed themselves to be hustled into policies which lead nowhere.

The solution, as I have pointed out in the book, lies in the redistribution of the Provinces and States on the basis of cultural and linguistic homogeneity with the right of self-determination for each individual unit, subject to its conformity in broad principles to Socialist democracy. A move in this direction is likely to lead to the evolution of India into a voluntary Union of Socialist Republics and I suggest that this is the only practical way out of what looks for the moment like an interminable communal conflict. It may be necessary in certain cases for the purposes of cultural development and protection of minorities to divide these republics into smaller constituent units such as autonomous republics, autonomous regions and national areas. These units shall, however, exercise powers vested in them by the laws of the Federal Union and of the republics concerned. A theocratic State, whether it is based on the Muslim Shariat or whether it seeks to derive its spiritual sustenance from the so-called idyllic bliss of the epic age, must be discarded as an instrument of counter-revolution. But there is hardly any doubt that we in this country are proceeding rapidly from the epoch of British imperialism with all that it implies to an epoch of class chauvinism. A new chapter of our history is opening with what consequences time alone will show.

This book is in no sense an attempt at a comparative study of the constitutions in all their substantive or procedural details. I have sought instead to focus attention on those specific problems which are agitating the public mind. A bird's eye view has been given of the changes in British policy since the famous declaration that Edwin Samuel Montagu made in Parliament in 1917, and an attempt has been made to throw light on the complicated issues which the capitalistic crisis has brought in its wake with reference to certain wellknown historical precedents. The views expressed in these pages are mine, and in no way connected with any public position which I may hold for the time being. They should, I submit, be taken for what they are worth. I claim no originality, but I do hope that the observations made in these pages supported, as they have been, by documentary evidence may provoke thought among those with whom rests the power to make or mar the future of this great and ancient land and its proud peoples. In order that the observations made or the views expressed in the book may be tested by reference to relevant documents I have given a selected number of appendices. They are illustrative and in no sense exhaustive ; and in selecting the documents care has been taken to find room for every important section of representative opinion.

I am indebted to Sree Saraswaty Press Ltd. for its prompt execution of work entrusted to it ; to my colleague Sri Sachindra Lal Ghosh for his going through the proofs ; and to my old friend Sri Basuda Chakravarti for the index. I must also acknowledge the help rendered to me in the preparation of this work by my younger brother, Professor Susil Kumar Sen, M.A., City College, and my colleague, Sri Siva Sankar Mitra. I regret very much that certain typographical errors have crept in despite our best efforts to eliminate them. I crave the indulgence of those who may care to go through these pages for these irritating lapses in view of the disturbed conditions in Calcutta and suburbs which upset my programme and interfered with the normal working of the Press.

DHIRENDRANATH SEN

CONTENTS

APPENDICES

CHAPTER I

THE BASIS OF BRITISH RULE

1. Dominion Status as a juridical concept

British rule in India, as in all the Crown's dominions and possessions, has been based since its inception upon the doctrine of sovereignty of the King-in-Parliament. That sovereignty has been exercised through instruments created from time to time by competent authorities to suit local conditions or developments in political or constitutional advance. The British Commonwealth and Empire is composed of widely scattered parts which differ from one another in their racial or religious characteristics, evolution of their histories, stages of their social and political development, the social basis of the systems of government which they have set up and their ideological or other proximity to the typically British pattern of parliamentary democracy. These wide and extensive territories have been brought together under one single allegiance by settlement, conquest, or cession. The group of self-governing communities constituted of Britain and the Dominions has now come to represent an element which, from a strictly constitutional point of view, has for historical, racial and other reasons reached a stage of development more or less uniform and similar in its bias, emphasis and technique of collective expression. Their position and mutual relations have thus been defined:

> They are autonomous communities within the British Empire, equal in status, in no way subordinate one to another in any aspect of their domestic or external affairs, though united by a common allegiance to the Crown, and freely associated as members of the British Commonwealth of Nations.[1]

The formula referred to above was presented in the Report of the Inter-Imperial Relations Committee set up by the Imperial

[1] This term was explained by the Solicitor-General on November, 24, 1931, as denoting only the Dominions. That interpretation, it is submitted, was not correct. Professor A. B. Keith took the view that

change in the basic structure of the State in any of the Dominions. The Dominions experiment with what is known as British Parliamentary democracy which in ultimate analysis is democracy without democratic content. In form, it is a democracy ; in substance, it is a plutocracy in the sense that even now power to do good or evil vests mainly in the propertied and privileged few. Dominion freedom is freedom for the Dominion bourgeoisie. It is not freedom for the toiling masses, far less for the natives and Asiatic peoples, as has been demonstrated by the recent happenings in the Union of South Africa. The Statute of Westminster is in a sense a deed of transfer, based as it is on class collaboration.

2. Indo-British Political Relations

In form as well as in substance, the course of Indo-British history has naturally been different. In the report of the Inter-Imperial Relations Committee already referred to it was stated that in the paragraphs seeking to define the status of Dominions there was no mention of India for the reason that "the position of India in the Empire is already defined by the Government of India Act, 1919". Right up to 1940, when Lord Linlithgow as India's Viceroy made a declaration to which we shall presently refer, the Government of India had been treated as a subordinate branch of the British administration and constitutional changes introduced from time to time had in no way affected the ultimate authority of the British Parliament to legislate for India or any part thereof.[1] These have been in conception and design essentially measures of devolution with responsibility retained for the Secretary of State in Council or, at a subsequent stage, for the Secretary of State. Leaving aside the earlier statutes, even the Government of India Acts of 1919 and 1935 have asserted in unmistakable terms the British claim to rule India and judge finally whether the peoples can be depended upon to exercise self-government and, if so, to what extent. British policy in this regard was enunciated by the late Mr. Edwin S. Montagu in 1917 in the later phase of the First World War. It was incorporated as the Preamble to the Government of India Act, 1919.[2] The statement of policy reads as follows:

[1] 26 Geo. 5. C. 2: s. 110(a). [2] 9 & 10 Geo. 5. C. 101.

> Whereas it is the declared policy of Parliament to provide for the increasing association of Indians in every branch of the Indian administration, and for the gradual development of self-governing institutions with a view to the progressive realisation of responsible government in British India as an integral part of the Empire:
>
> And whereas progress in giving effect to this policy can only be achieved by successive stages, and it is expedient that substantial steps in this direction should be taken:
>
> And whereas the time and manner of each advance can be determined only by Parliament, upon whom responsibility lies for the welfare and advancement of the Indian peoples:
>
> And whereas the action of Parliament in such matters must be guided by the co-operation received from those on whom new opportunities of service will be conferred, and by the extent to which it is found that confidence can be reposed in their sense of responsibility:
>
> And whereas concurrently with the gradual development of self-governing institutions in the Provinces of India, it is expedient to give to those Provinces in Provincial matters the largest measure of independence of the Government of India which is compatible with the due discharge by the latter of its own responsibilities,
>
> Be it therefore enacted by the King's Most Excellent Majesty etc., etc., etc.

The points that emerge from this preamble are (i) that Indian advance must be gradual and by stages ; (ii) that the time and manner of each advance must be determined by Parliament which holds itself responsible for the welfare and advancement of the Indian peoples ; (iii) that Parliament must be guided in this respect by the co-operation received from the peoples concerned and the extent to which confidence may be reposed in their sense of responsibility ; (iv) that along with the development of self-governing institutions a measure of independence is to be exercised by the Provinces without prejudice to the basic responsibility of the Government of India thereby envisaging Ministerial responsibility in respect of subjects transferred under devolution rules to the Provinces ; and (v) that even in 1919 Parliament had in mind the "peoples of India" as distinguished from the Indian nation or people.

Legally, the Indian States and their Rulers were left outside the scope of the Act of 1919. Their position, status and functions remained as before. The Act was intended to apply to British

India and the legislatures and administrations were set up for British India. It was nevertheless recognised that the Rulers of States were profoundly disturbed over the increasing uncertainty about their future in view of the projected changes in the administrative set-up of British India and the fluid character of paramountcy. Earlier Lord Hardinge had inaugurated a system of consultation with the Princes—a step pursued a little more energetically by Lord Chelmsford. That system was placed on a regular basis by establishing, in accordance with the recommendations of the Mont-Ford Report, a Chamber of Princes to meet the Viceroy annually for the discussion of problems of common interest. It was stipulated that there would be mutual consultation between the Standing Committee of the Chamber and the Political Department.[1]

The only significant innovation effected under the new Act was the setting up of Ministerial government in the Provinces with power defined within the ambit of the Act. A certain measure of relaxation of superintendence, direction and control by the Secretary of State was also introduced as a corollary. Otherwise there was no change in the main structure of the State. The "peoples of India" referred to in the Preamble means implicitly as well as by necessary intendment the propertied classes of India divided for legislative or administrative purposes in religious and racial communities such as Mohammadans, non-Mohammadans, Europeans, Anglo-Indians, Sikhs and Indian Christians. I say "propertied classes" because franchise was restricted to persons possessing high property qualifications or fulfilling educational and other analogous tests both for the Central Legislature and the Provincial Legislative Councils.

The Government of India Act, 1935, reproduced the preamble to the Act of 1919, thereby asserting once again the authority of the British Parliament to legislate for India[2], and preside over the destiny of its "peoples". Certain new features, however, were introduced by this measure. First, it envisaged for the first time a Federation for India.[3] Secondly, it sought to bring within the purview of the Indian Federation the Indian States in certain circumstances and under certain conditions.[4] Thirdly, it granted the Governors' Provinces by statutory provisions, as distinguished from rules, a large measure of autonomy with exclusive juris-

[1] The minor States were excluded from the Chamber.

[2] ss. 110 and 321. [3] s. 5. [4] ss. 5 & 6.

diction over certain subjects and concurrent jurisdiction over some others.[1] Fourthly, it extended the franchise to persons both in urban and rural areas who had, by and under earlier statutes, been denied these political rights. In the main, however, it was a scheme of Indo-British class collaboration with the British playing the rôle of the dominant partner inasmuch as it repudiated popular sovereignty and sought to bring the Rulers of States within the orbit without provision for democratic representation.

Partly for opposition led by the Rulers and mainly for the threatened hostility on the part of different political organisations of India the Federal Part of the Act had to be abandoned on the outbreak of war in 1939. The result has been that since April, 1937, when the Act came into operation the Governors' Provinces have been ruled under its provisions with or without Ministers while matters relating to the Centre have been legislated upon or administered under the provisions of the Act of 1919 with such modifications and adjustments[2] as have been deemed necessary in this extraordinary situation.

3. 1940—A Landmark

Perhaps for the first time in the long and chequered history of Indo-British relations Britain's claim to judge about India's fitness for self-government and to frame her constitution, asserted repeatedly and practically at all the successive stages of constitutional development, was withdrawn in August 1940, when Lord Linlithgow made a declaration of policy with the approval of the British Government. That declaration was presented to Parliament in a White Paper entitled "India and the War" by Mr. L. S. Amery, Secretary of State for India. The issues involved in the War and the British Government's increasing awareness of India's importance as the eastern bastion of defence and of the short-term and long-term requirements of strategy played no small part in this reorientation of Britain's India policy. Recalling the October pronouncement of 1939, in which Dominion Status had been declared the British Government's objective for India, the Viceroy laid stress on two points. The first was that the British Government would assent, after the conclusion of the War, to the setting

[1] s. 100 and the Seventh Schedule.

[2] Ninth Schedule to the Act of 1935.

up, with the least possible delay, of a body representative of the "prinsipal elements in India's national life" in order to devise the framework of a constitution. The framing of the scheme, it was conceded, should primarily be the responsibility of Indians themselves and should originate from Indian conceptions of the social, economic and political structure of Indian life. The second was that full weight should be given to the views of minorities in any revision of the country's constitutional arrangements.

The August declaration of 1940 was in no sense an offer of independence. Nor was it Dominion Status of the Statute of Westminster variety on the basis of the most recent interpretation put upon it. The expression "Dominion Status" was vaguely used by Lord Linlithgow. That is evident from the fact that the supreme quality of free association implicit in the Statute, namely, the right to secession, was clearly lacking. India was, on the face of it, intended to be a new variant of the type subject to all manner of safeguards and reservations. The British Government made it plain that they would not be a party to the transfer of their responsibilities for the peace and welfare of India to any system of indigenous Government whose authority was challenged by large and powerful elements in her national life. What by "large and powerful elements" they precisely meant was, however, left deliberately vague. But obviously they had in mind the Muslims, the scheduled castes and the Sikhs, though not necessarily the smaller racial or religious minorities. It was further stated that no prospect for reconstruction of Government along lines indicated in the declaration would be accepted without an adequate guarantee as to the discharge of Britain's imperial obligations. These, of course, referred to the business and trade interests of the British community in India, the rights hitherto exercised by the States under the doctrine of imperial paramountcy, protection of civil and other services recruited by the Secretary of State and the British Empire's strategic and operational requirements in war as well as in peace.

Subject to all these, the British Government expressed their desire that representative Indians should labour to reach a basis of friendly agreement, first, upon the form of the post-war constitution-making machinery and the method and procedure by which it should fulfil its task ; and secondly, upon the principles and outlines of the constitution itself. They offered their cooperation and assistance in any earnest effort to evolve a just and fair settlement in this regard. By far the most significant change foreshadowed in the declaration was recognition for the first time by the British Government of the right of Indians to frame the constitution of the land, thereby abrogating the main principles of British rule as embodied in the Montagu declaration of 1917 and the Government of India Acts of 1919 and 1935, although it was hedged in by so many restrictions.

For the duration of war the British offer of 1940 extended invitation to a certain number of representative Indians to join the Governor-General's Executive Council and proposed the setting up of a War Advisory Council representative alike of the Indian States and other interests in the national life of India as a whole. The object was to associate India more closely with the conduct of war. It was a move for expansion of the Governor-General's Council without any change in the 1919 structure of Government —a fact which together with certain other considerations weighed with the principal political parties in rejecting the offer. The Executive Council was subsequently reorganised in personnel but not in the quality of its representative character. The War Advisory Council, such as the one that came to be formed, was uninspiring.

4. The Cripps Offer and its Background

Two events of world-wide significance occurred. In June, 1941 Hitler invaded the Soviet Union and in December Japan launched an attack upon Britain and America in what was known as the Far Eastern theatre, which by its boldness of conception and execution no less than by its terrific swiftness gave a violent shaking to the Allied Command and almost paralysed it. An Axis pincer movement threatened to overwhelm the entire area from the the Caucasus to the Persian Gulf. The position to which the Allies were reduced, especially in the Pacific region, was desperate and Generalissimo Chiang Kai-Sheik's sudden visit to India in the spring of 1942 was significant. It is an open secret that a certain measure of diplomatic pressure was exerted by the Generalissimo and President Roosevelt in support of an immediate Indo-British settlement so that both psychologically and from the military point of view India could be used as a safe and powerful base of operations against Japan. The British Government appeared from the very beginning to treat India as their domestic problem thus countering, if with due courtesy, the suggestion from across the Atlantic and war-shattered China. Nevertheless Mr. Winston Churchill, who then was the head of Britain's National Government, made some response to the constant pressure of events and the friendly hints of his gallant American and Chinese allies by agreeing to send out the then Privy Seal and Leader of the House of Commons, Sir Stafford Cripps, on a mission to negotiate a settlement with India.

Both these considerations were emphasised by Mr. Churchill in the course of his Commons statement on March 11, 1942, announcing the British Government's decision as to the Mission and the task entrusted to it. "The crisis in the affairs of India arising out of the Japanese advance," observed the Prime Minister, "has made Britain wish to rally all the forces of Indian life to guard their land from the menace of the invader." Again, "we must remember that India has a great part to play in the world struggle for freedom and that her helping hand must be extended in loyal comradeship to the valiant Chinese people, who have fought so long. We must remember also that India is one of the bases from which the strongest counterblows must be struck at the advance of tyranny and aggression".

Even in his speech on the India debate in the Commons on July 20, 1946, Mr. Churchill was at pains to prove that his Government in 1942 had been moved, in making the Cripps offer, by the perils of war. "That offer," he pointed out, "was made at a moment when the Japanese held full naval command of the Bay of Bengal and it seemed that India might be invaded and ravaged by a large Japanese army." Proceeding, the ex-Premier continued, "As Prime Minister I take my full share of the responsibility for making the offer of 1942. Those days of peril are gone, although we received no assistance from the Congress party of India." The suggestion contained in these observations seems to be, first, that Mr. Churchill and his Government would not have made the gesture had not the war situation reached a critical stage along the Indian border ; secondly, that the Congress not only remained neutral but in a way injured the Allied war effort, thereby demonstrating lack of its influence and authority with India's vast masses ; and thirdly, that by its conduct during the War the Congress forfeited its title to be considered a major factor in connection with any settlement of the Indian problem by friendly negotiations.

It is difficult to say whether these sentiments expressed so vigorously by no less a person than the Prime Minister, apart from the inadequacy and dilatoriness of the Cripps Plan itself, had anything to do with its eventual rejection by the Congress after protracted negotiations for about three weeks and the August rebellion of 1942. But psychologically at least Mr. Churchill's speech was a damper and in a large measure undermined public confidence in the Cripps Mission and the then Lord Privy Seal's exhortations to Indian leaders to make up with Britain in those perilous weeks of the spring of 1942. Even today Mr. Churchill's broadside may darken counsel and raise doubts as to the intentions of Britain's Socialist Government.

In this perspective I consider the speech of Mr. Albert Alexander, First Lord of the Admiralty, in reply to the India debate on July 20, 1946, a timely and appropriate rejoinder. Mr. Alexander, who had come out as a member of the Cabinet Mission, regretted that Mr. Churchill had sought to create the impression that the 1942 offer had been made only when the enemy was at the gates. He said that that was exactly the complaint Indians had made in their expressions of doubt about British bonafides. He repudiated the suggestion that all the members of the Government in 1942 had associated themselves with the Cripps offer on the basis indicated by Mr. Churchill.

The Cripps scheme, like the earlier declaration of Lord Linlithgow, divided itself into two parts, the first giving in general outline a picture of post-war India, and the second dealing with the interim period. Both these plans, again, proceeded on the basis that so far as the post-war future was concerned, it was primarily for Indians to frame their own organic laws subject to certain reservations. To Mr. Churchill the Cripps offer involved no major change of policy as laid down in 1940 ; the one was complementary to the other inasmuch as the subsequent pronouncement was calculated "to clothe these general declarations with precision and to convince all classes, races and creeds in India of our sincere resolve . . . .". The Cripps offer differed, however, from the Linlithgow declaration in broad principles as well as in specific details despite Mr. Churchill's pleading to the contrary. But the differences, whatever their range and extent, applied not so much to the projected interim arrangements as to the long-term plans.

As to the interim proposals, leaders of the principal sections of the Indian people were invited, as in 1940, to participate in the counsels of their country, of the Commonwealth and of the United Nations. Subject to the British Government's final responsibility for the control and direction of the defence of India as part of their World War effort, Indian leaders were assured that it was for the Government of India in co-operation with the peoples of India to organise to the full her military, moral and material resources. It was, again, a proposal for change only in the personnel of the Central Government. The Government as proposed to be set up to replace the then existing machinery were to function mainly in terms of the Government of India Act, 1919. In form at least no important change was contemplated ; it was at best a scheme for expansion or enlargement. The Linlithgow declaration had to all intents and purposes pursued the same line.

In regard to the post-war future, however, the 1942 offer was more substantial. It was less vague and the general outline was bolder and far more distinct. For one thing, whereas in 1940 Dominion Status had been proclaimed to be the objective of Britain's India policy, Sir Stafford was authorised two years later to reproduce in effect the text of the Imperial Conference formula of 1926 as well as of the preamble to the Statute of Westminster as governing the relations between India and Britain. For another, the power of the proposed Indian Union to decide *in future* to sever connection with the member-States of the British Commonwealth and Empire was conceded. Again, there was a definite proposal for a treaty to be negotiated between the British Government and the constitution-making body of India to cover matters arising out of the complete transfer of responsibilities from British to Indian hands. Furthermore, there was a clear intimation to the Rulers of Indian States that whether or not any of them elected to adhere to the constitution that might be framed on Indian soil by Indians themselves it would be necessary to negotiate a revision of the so-called treaty rights and the doctrine of paramountcy as might be called for in the new situation. In these respects the Cripps Plan marked an advance on the vague and inadequate generalisations contained in Lord Linlithgow's declaration.

As to the precision of form and procedure of the Cripps Plan, in which the 1940 scheme lacked, reference is invited to the structure of the constitution-making body, the provision for participation of the Indian States in that body, the right of non-accession accorded to the British Indian Provinces along with the States, the arrangement contemplated for the non-acceding Provinces, if any, and the British promise to accept and implement forthwith the constitution as might be laid down. The door was left open to the non-acceding Province or Provinces to go into the Union subsequently should it or they so decide. The structure of the constitution-making body as envisaged in the Plan could be modified or altered if the leaders of Indian opinion in the principal communities so decided by agreement before the end of hostilities. The Congress rejected the offer on the ground, amongst others, that it did not transfer real power to the Interim Government, that it framed the long-term plan on the basis of division of India community-wise in disregard of the claims of cultural and linguistic units to political and administrative homogeneity and that there was no guarantee as to popular representation by a democratic process of the States in the constitution-making body. The Muslim League rejected it mainly in the ground that it did not concede the demand made in its Council resolution adopted at Lahore in 1940 for sovereign and independent Muslim zones in the North-west and the North-east separate from the rest of India. One has, however, reasons to believe that had the Congress at that time decided to work the Plan for what it was worth the League would have joined the Interim Government. But the broad fact remains that the trend of events on the Indo-Burma front which undermined public confidence in the British power to resist the invading Japanese forces appeared to weigh considerably with both these political organisations in coming to the decisions they eventually arrived at.

Constitutionally the process of readjustment promised in 1940 came to a dead stop. There was no move on the part of the British Government. The position virtually remained static for the entire period from the failure of the Cripps mission in April, 1942, right up to the Wavell move in June, 1945, for political reconstruction of the Governor-General's Executive Council. The idea underlying the Simla palaver was to proceed with the formation of a Coalition Government at the Centre without prejudice to the issues involved in a long-term settlement. It broke down on the question of parity of representation between the Congress and the League or between the Muslim League, purporting to represent the entire Muslim community, and Hindus, including the scheduled castes, for whom it was proposed to provide additional representation. So far as the Congress was concerned, the status, functions and powers of the Interim Government were an issue too, upon which, however, Lord Wavell failed to satisfy Gandhiji and members of the Working Committee. Incidentally it should be noted that the Congress agreed to associate itself with the prosecution of war against Japan provided that on other points the British Government came to an understanding with it. Once again, the failure led to another spell of "nothing doing" in the field of constitutional palaver or negotiations.

5. New Developments in the Process—the Labour Government's Move in 1946

Meanwhile the War came to an end. With the cessation of hostilities new problems emerged or old problems took a new form. An atmosphere of uncertainty and restiveness was created. There was a challenge to old forms, constitutions and the traditional type of productive relations. There were new, almost irresistible urges, and a clarion call for reconstruction and rehabilitation. Promises, pledges and solemn declarations of statesmen came to be scrutinised and put to the acid test of solid achievement. The whole world was in a state of flux and the world in our time is indivisible. In this potentially revolutionary setting of events the Government of India decided to stage at New Delhi a series of I.N.A. trials which only served to expose the hand-to-mouth tactics of British policy and to foster a spirit of hatred, suspicion and conflict. Across the border in Burma and particularly in Indonesia there were uprisings against foreign domination and exploitation. Nearer home the Indian ratings mutinied. This challenging mood affected, if on a minor scale, considerable sections of the armed forces and other organs of the coercive apparatus. All this assumed the general character of an open revolt of the East against the supremacy of the West.

In Britain, America and the Soviet Union among wide circles of the politically conscious peoples there were doubts, suspicions and questionings. "What next?" was constantly on their lips.

"Where is the end and how far?" was the question asked everywhere. In these circumstances and under the pressure of a revolutionary situation Mr. Clement Attlee announced in Parliament on March 15, 1946, the British Government's decision to send out a Cabinet Mission with the Secretary of State for India as leader, and the President of the Board of Trade and the First Lord of the Admiralty as members to negotiate a settlement with Indian leaders both as to how best Indians could by agreement evolve their country's organic laws and the manner in which they proposed to undertake the responsibilities of Government during the interim period and assist in promoting the objective aimed at in any long-term plan. It is natural that in winding up the India debate in Parliament in July after the Mission's return to London Mr. Alexander should have reminded Mr. Churchill of the vast changes in the Indian landscape that the War had brought about in the context of a new and rejuvenated East emerging from this terrible holocaust. Earlier on March 15 Mr. Attlee had given expression to similar sentiments and said :

> "Nothing increases the pace and movement of public opinion more than a great war . . . The tide, that runs comparatively slowly in peace, in war time becomes vastly accelerated . . . . . I am quite certain that at the present time the tide of nationalism is running very fast in India and indeed all over Asia. One always has to remember that India is affected by what happens elsewhere in Asia . . . I remember that in the Simon Commission Report although there were great differences in expression of the nationalistic sentiment between what were called extremists and moderates and although in many instances there might be such stress of communal claims as may seem almost to exclude the conception of nationalism, yet we found that among Hindus, Muslims, Sikhs and Maratthas, politicians or civil servants—among all of them the conception of nationalism had been growing stronger and stronger—and to-day I think that the national idea has spread right through, not the least perhaps among some of those soldiers who had done such wonderful services in the war."

CHAPTER II

THE BRITISH CABINET MISSION, 1946

1. Failure of Agreement and New Formula

On their arrival in India the Cabinet Mission, aided and assisted by the Viceroy, commenced work by starting negotiations, almost along lines tried without success since 1940, with the leaders of political parties and communities with a view to securing, if possible, an agreed settlement on the main issues in dispute. By the process of elimination in the course of these negotiations the two parties that remained on the scene, as on previous occasions, were the Congress and the Muslim League. The Mission and the Viceroy realised after crowded and anxious weeks of continuous palaver, again as in the recent past, that left to themselves the leaders of these two organisations would not find it possible to agree as to a common basis of approach to the problems with which they were confronted. In defence of the procedure they finally adopted on May 16 the Mission stated:

> It is not our object to lay down the details of a constitution . . ., but to set in motion the machinery whereby a constitution can be settled by Indians for Indians.
>
> It has been necessary, however, for us to make this recommendation as to the broad basis of the future constitution because it became clear to us in the course of our negotiations that not until that had been done was there any hope of getting the two major communities to join in the setting up of the constitution-making machinery.

Accordingly the Mission issued on May 16, a long statement containing proposals which they described as "recommendations" as distinguished from an award. These proposals dealt in the main with long-term arrangements, although in the last but one paragraph[1] of their statement they made it plain that they attached the greatest importance "to the setting up at once of an Interim Government having the support of the major political parties."

[1] Para. 23.

Except as to the political and communal complexion of the proposed Interim Government the Mission refrained, perhaps deliberately, from giving a detailed picture of that Government, its status and power and authority. Nevertheless they said that the British Government "recognising the significance of the changes in the Government of India, will give the fullest measure of co-operation to the Government so formed in the accomplishment of its tasks of administration and bringing about as rapid and smooth a transition as possible". This was, on the face of it, in the nature of an understanding on the point repeatedly urged by Congress leaders, as is evident from Maulana Abul Kalam Azad's letter to the Viceroy, dated May 25, that there must be a legal and constitutional change in order to give the Interim Government the status of a truly National Government.

Asked at a Press Conference on May 17, what precisely would be the powers of the Interim Government and whether the Governor-General would have the right to overrule its decisions, the Secretary of State replied that it was a matter for the Viceroy to settle up and decide. It was thus clear that, whatever position might emerge from actual working of the machinery, the Cabinet Mission did not comtemplate any legal change to take effect in this regard during the transition. This was confirmed in Lord Wavell's reply to the Congress President, dated May 30. He stated that he had never given the impression that "the Interim Government would have the same powers as a Dominion Cabinet". Continuing, the Viceroy reminded the Congress President of the Cabinet Mission's assurance of co-operation given with the approval of the British Government and intimated his intention to carry out faithfully what he called the British Government's "undertaking". He added that if the Congress trusted him, the Viceroy and the Interim Government would "be able to co-operate in a manner which will give India a sense of freedom from external control and will prepare for complete freedom as soon as the new constitution is made".

In his letter to the Viceroy on June 14, Maulana Azad, while repeating the suggestion earlier made that even though no legal change might be made at that stage, independence in practice might be recognised, appreciated "the friendly tone" of the Viceroy's letter and accepted the latter's "assurance" in this matter. For the reasons set out above the Congress waived its objection to the interim machinery which in law at least was intended to operate under the provisions of the Act of 1919. To the Muslim League, however, it was no issue with the Cabinet Mission ; implicit in its stand, on the contrary, was the demand that for the transition there must be no such change in the structure as might enable the majority in the Government to force a decision or place the entire Executive Government, after the British or Dominion pattern, on the vote of the Central Legislative Assembly or of the joint session of both Houses of the Legislature.

2. The Interim Government—the Ratio of Representation

The question, then, was about the ratio of representation of parties and interests in the Interim Government and the hope was expressed in the Mission's statement that the Viceroy, who had already started discussions, would succeed in forming a Government in which all the portfolios,[1] including that of the War Member, would be taken charge of by representative Indian leaders. It appears from the correspondence that passed between Lord Wavell and Mr. Jinnah that the Viceroy first suggested as a basis for discussion—no assurance or undertaking could be given at that stage—a formula of 5: 5: 2, five on behalf of the Congress, five to represent the Muslim League, one Sikh and one Indian Christian or Anglo-Indian. Apparently it was not acceptable to the Congress and the Viceroy proposed a revised formula of 5: 5: 3. To that, too, the Congress raised an objection on the ground that while it sought to inflate the League it was not fair to the other communities concerned and, on a long view, harmful to the interests of the country as a whole. Accordingly in concurrence with the Cabinet Mission the Viceroy undertook the responsibility of presenting in specific form his own scheme and it was incorporated in the Mission's statement of June 16.

The proposal put forward was for a Cabinet of 14 members, of whom 6 were to come from the Congress, including a Scheduled Caste member ; 5 from the Muslim League ; 1 Sikh ; 1 Parsi ; and 1 Indian Christian. This, however, was more in the nature of an award than a recommendation. For care was taken by the Viceroy to warn the parties concerned to the effect: "In the event of

[1] Para 23.

the two major parties or either of them proving unwilling to join in the setting up of a Coalition Government on the above lines it is the intention of the Viceroy to proceed with the formation of an Interim Government which will be as representative as possible of those willing to accept the statement of May 16." It looked like an intimation to the Congress that should it choose to stay out the League would be called upon to form the Government ; to the League that should it decide to withhold its co-operation the Congress might dominate the show. Both these parties at first inclined, if reluctantly, to working out the plan for what it was worth with minor adjustments.

Then suddenly disclosures were made of certain contents of the letters that had been exchanged between Lord Wavell and Mr. Jinnah and the Congress asked for and received the relevant portions of the documents in question.[1] The Congress at once insisted on the inclusion of a Muslim member out of its allotted quota of representation in the Government and practically pinned down the Viceroy to this important point of principle by reminding the latter of his refusal, as intimated through his letter, dated June 15, to Maulana Azad to uphold the Congress objection to names put forward by the Muslim League, and of his promise not to entertain similar objections from the other side. The test laid down by the Viceroy on that occasion was one of ability. The Viceroy had no reply to this beyond vaguely suggesting in his letter of June 27 to Maulana Azad that "it would not be possible to force through issues of this kind in the face of the opposition of either of the main parties." From the beginning the Cabinet Mission and the Viceroy seemed fencing in the matter of inclusion in the Interim Government of a non-Leaguer or nationalist Muslim. One finds it difficult to reconcile Lord Wavell's proposition laid down in his letter to Maulana Azad, dated June 15, with the statement made in his letter of June 22, intimating his and the Mission's inability to accede to the Congress President's demand for inclusion of a Muslim of their choice among the representatives of the Congress in the Interim Government. To put it mildly, it was politics of a sort at the highest level which did no credit to these top-ranking British statesmen.

[1] Cf. Maulana Azad's letter to the Viceroy, dated June 20, and the latter's reply thereto dated June 21.

It should be borne in mind that at no time did the Congress agree to parity of representation and the principle involved therein. On the contrary, in his letter to the Viceroy, dated June 13, Maulana Azad reiterated most emphatically the Congress opposition to parity in any shape or form. In reply to the Cabinet Mission's and the Viceroy's proposition that the proposed ratio of representation was a temporary expedient and must not be taken as a precedent the Congress President told the Viceroy in the same letter that in his view, which was shared by his colleagues, even the immediate results of any such provision would be harmful. Further, with reference to the parity formula canvassed at the first Simla Conference in June-July, 1945, Maulana Azad pointed out in his letter to the Viceroy, dated June 16, that the Congress had agreed to accept it on that occasion in view of the war emergency and under conditions then existing. It was also subject to the inclusion of at least one nationalist Muslim in the Interim Government. The circumstances of 1945 did no longer apply and the whole issue, the Congress President urged, must be approached from an entirely different angle.

Of course the Viceroy had earlier called the Congress President's attention, in his letter of June 15, to the proceedings of the Simla Conference and denied that what had been proposed was any kind of parity. The proposed Interim Government would be based, it was contended, on the basis of parties and not communities. The theory evolved by the Viceroy was interesting, if rather ingenious. It was not party parity because there were 6 Congressmen against 5 Muslim Leaguers. Nor was it parity community-wise because there were 6 Hindus against 5 Muslims. Writing to Lord Wavell on June 19, Mr. Jinnah, however, raised his preliminary objections to the new formula. He objected in particular to the withdrawal of parity between the Congress and the Muslims and the substitution for it of parity between the Muslim League and caste Hindus, the proposed inclusion in the Interim Government of a Congress Scheduled Caste member and the addition to the Council of a fourth representative of the minorities, namely, a Parsi. The League Working Committee deferred their decision in the matter of the formation of the Interim Government until the Congress intimated its final reactions to the proposals. Meanwhile Mr. Jinnah sought clarification of certain points to which the Viceroy replied on June 20.

It is on record[1] that in the evening of June 25 the Cabinet Mission and the Viceroy had, before the League Working Committee accepted the proposals in the statement of June 16, intimated to Mr. Jinnah the Congress acceptance of the statement of May 16 and its rejection of the statement of June 16. The Viceroy's letter further claims that Mr. Jinnah was definitely told then that in the circumstances a situation had been produced in which Paragraph 8 of the June 16 statement took effect. It adds that it was made clear to the League President that since the Congress and the Muslim League had both accepted the May 16 statement it was his intention to form a Coalition Government, including both these parties, thereby suggesting that the specific offer of an Interim Government made in the June 16 statement fell to the ground.

It is not altogether unnatural that there should have been such a bitter controversy over the interpretation of that fateful or, shall I say, fatal paragraph. What then does Paragraph 8 of the June 16 statement convey to the lay public? The Cabinet Mission and the Viceroy assumed that the specific interim set-up as proposed in the relevant statement was to come into existence if both the Congress and the Muslim League accepted it. It lapsed if both the parties or either of them stood out. The Congress as the larger of the two major parties having rejected the offer, it was for the Viceroy to reconsider the whole situation with a view to the formation of an Interim Government which would be as representative as possible of those willing to accept the statement of May 16. Since the Congress accepted that statement it was along with the League eligible for inclusion in the Interim Government. The Viceroy promised to reopen negotiations to that end.

Mr. Jinnah, on the other hand, assumed that by the statement they made the Cabinet Mission and the Viceroy stood committed to the setting up of an Interim Government immediately as part of their basic plan to transfer power and resolve the deadlock, no matter whether or not the Congress came in. If, as was clear, the Congress refused to join the Interim Government at that stage, the Viceroy was required, in fulfilment of his undertaking, to proceed without further negotiations with its formation with the Muslim League and others who accepted the statement of May 16

[1] Cf. the Viceroy's letter to Mr. Jinnah dated June 28.

and were willing to take part in it. The Cabinet Mission and the Viceroy contended that by accepting the May 16 statement the Congress voted itself into any interim picture not necessarily of the type presented on June 16, while Mr. Jinnah held that by rejecting the statement of June 16 the Congress went into political wilderness. The result was that Mr. Jinnah alleged a flagrant breach of faith against the Cabinet Mission and the Viceroy whereas the latter suggested that in persuading the League Working Committee to work the scheme presented on June 16 after having heard from the Cabinet Mission and the Viceroy of the Congress rejection of that scheme and their own decision accordingly to drop it Mr. Jinnah wanted to score a tactical point over the Ministers and the Viceroy. This is oath against oath. It is a case in which charges are sought to be repelled by insinuations.

Speaking for myself, I incline according to the ordinary and grammatical meaning of words and the accepted rules of construction to the interpretation put upon the relevant clause of the statement by Mr. Jinnah. The language of Paragraph 8 may, however, be stretched to yield the meaning which has been attributed to it by the Mission and the Viceroy in justification of their sudden but seemingly inexplicable withdrawal of their offer of June 16. It becomes then a matter of emphasis. Obviously the Mission's and the Viceroy's emphasis was more on acceptance of the long-term project than on that of the interim machinery envisaged in their statement of June 16. I think—it is just possible I am wrong—that without properly sizing up their moral and physical adequacy and in a hurry the Mission and the Viceroy presented their scheme almost in the form of an ultimatum. They soon realised that they were mistaken and the Congress forced them to withdraw it. They felt that Mr. Jinnah alone could not "deliver the goods" and, further, that the setting up of an Interim Government with the Congress in hostile opposition would defeat the purpose of the Mission.

But the Viceroy wrote to Mr. Jinnah on August 8, saying that the basic representation suggested finally to both the Congress and the League Presidents on July 22 "is the same as the one that the Muslim League Working Committee accepted at the end of June, namely, 6: 5: 3". Technically the Viceroy was correct because the total strength of 14 was retained and the communal ratios as specified in the 16th June formula were not disturbed. But politically the Viceroy's statement is half-truth. If there was no change in the position, how could the Congress agree to make proposals for an Interim Government on the basis of a formula which it had rejected? The offer of July 22 involved an important change in principle. For one thing, the Viceroy took special care to emphasise that it would not be open to either the Congress or the Muslim League to object to names submitted by the other party, provided they were accepted by him. For another, although it was stated that the three representatives of minorities would be nominated by the Viceroy, the clear implication was that the Congress proposals in this regard would not be overruled. At any rate, the promise of consultation earlier given Mr. Jinnah was withdrawn. While opposing Mr. Jinnah's unreasonable demand one need not approve of the Viceroy's sheer political opportunism. It was not a clean game. The Cabinet Mission and the Viceroy have so clumsily involved themselves in the intricacies of Indian politics that the British Government would find it exceedingly difficult, if not impossible, to extricate themselves from them today or in the near or distant future.

Further complication was added to the Indian situation by the Muslim League Council's resolution of July 29, withdrawing its acceptance of the long-term proposals. The step taken by the League Council, by the way, deprived its President of the right to be consulted along with the Congress President in connection with the formation of the Interim Government. That point was stressed by the Viceroy in his letter to Mr. Jinnah, dated August 8, in which he intimated to the latter his decision to invite the Congress to make proposals. In constitutional politics it was a tactical error on the part of the League because at once the Viceroy seized the opportunity to place it in a position of subordination to the Congress. The League Council's resolution deals at length with the circumstances which weighed with that body in taking this drastic step after elections to the Constituent Assembly in the British Indian Provinces had been completed and the States' Negotiating Committee set up to negotiate terms with a corresponding Committee that might be formed by the representatives of Provinces. The League Council accused the British Government of a breach of faith not only in respect of the Interim Government but also in regard to what it called the basic form of the constitution-making body. It also took the view, in the light of statements made by Congress leaders, notably Pandit Jawaharlal Nehru, and the mandate given to its representatives by the Assam Legislative Assembly at the instance of the Congress in the matter of "sectional grouping", that the Congress was out to nullify the plan by its "brute majority" in the Union Constituent Assembly. To the League Council's resolution and Mr. Jinnah's speech at its Bombay session Sardar Vallabhbhai Patel replied that there was no basis for agreement between the Congress and the Muslim League, suggesting at the same time that it was now for the British Government to proceed with their scheme without the Muslim League and in spite of its opposition.

To a certain extent and in spirit Sardar Patel was overruled by the Congress Working Committee which adopted a resolution on August 10, appealing to the Muslim League and all others concerned for cooperation "in the wider interests of the nation as well as of their own". The resolution, however, looked like a compromise between Pandit Nehru and Maulana Azad on the one hand and Sardar Patel on the other, for the Committee left no room for doubt that in their view "there are differences in the outlook and the objective of the Congress and the Muslim League". To Mr. Jinnah's charge that the Congress acceptance of the statement of May 16 was "conditional" they stated that while they did not approve of all the proposals contained in the statement they "accepted the scheme in its entirety". They reiterated, however, their previous view that "provincial autonomy is a basic provision and each province has the right to decide whether to form or join a group or not". The question of interpretation, it was maintained, would be decided by the procedure indicated in the statement itself. Evidently Mr. Jinnah did not deem this resolution adequate or satisfactory. In his broadcast on September 2, Lord Wavell sought to elucidate the point by insisting that any dispute regarding interpretation might be referred to the Federal Court. This was followed up on September 7, by Pandit Nehru in his first broadcast as the political head of the Interim Government. Pandit Nehru pointed out that the Congress would go into "sections", that sitting in "sections" its representatives would consider the question of grouping and that, if necessary, recourse might be had to the federal judiciary for rulings on questions of interpretation. He further held out the assurance that the Congress would not by its majority coerce any community or group but would instead seek "agreed and integrated solutions". The outlook nevertheless is dark and gloomy. The development in the situation and the repeated failures of efforts for a working agreement between the Congress and the League to provide the basis for the transfer of power only tend to underline the inherent weakness of the British approach and its lack of realism.

The reconstruction of the Interim Government with 14 members, excluding the Viceroy, in consequence of the Muslim League's participation in it, does not seem to have improved matters materially.[1] That conflicts persist will be evident from the correspondence that passed between Pandit Nehru and Mr. Jinnah and has been released to the Press. The points in dispute concern (i) the representative character of the League *vis-à-vis* the Congress ; (ii) the status and functions of the Interim Government ; (iii) the position of the two major parties (the Congress and the League) in relation to the minorities ; (iv) restrictions or limitations in regard to decisions involving communal questions ; and (v) the League's attitude towards the constitution-making body. On none of these issues is there any understanding between the Congress and the League, although both these bodies represent the main elements in the reconstituted Central Government. The Congress has accepted office on the Viceroy's invitation and after a good deal of hesitation the League has followed suit. The basis on which the Interim Government was first formed in consultation with Pandit Nehru has both in form and substance been altered by the manner in which the new appointments have been made and the reconstruction consequently effected.

Mr. Jinnah has waived his opposition to the appointment, on the recommendation of the Congress, of a non-League Muslim. He has further withdrawn his protest against the retention of the three members supposed to represent the Sikhs, Indian Christians and Parsis. But these he has not done by agreement with the Congress or in recognition of the principle that the Congress represents all sections of the Indian people except the followers and adherents of the Muslim League. There is, on the contrary, reason to be-

[1] The reconstituted Interim Government is composed as follows: Four Caste Hindus (Congress) ; one Scheduled Caste member (Congress) ; one Muslim (Congress) ; one Sikh ; one Indian Christian ; one Parsi (all these three recommended by Congress) ; four Muslims (Muslim League) ; and one Scheduled Caste member (nominated by League).

lieve that Mr. Jinnah was persuaded to waive his objections to the present arrangements without prejudice to his fundamental principles by the Viceroy's assurances in other respects or that he realised in the course of his talks with the Viceroy that the latter would not disturb them as a price for the League's co-operation in the Interim Government. If anybody has triumphed in these negotiations, it is neither the League nor the Congress but the Viceroy who by astute manœuvres has succeeded in roping in the Congress and the League with a definite swing in favour of his veto and extraordinary powers. Again, if the League finally decides to join the Constituent Assembly or Assemblies, it will rely on British guarantees in respect of Sections and groupings. Whatever might have been their intention, it is unfortunate that the League and its leader should have in effect strengthened the hands of the British Government and their Viceroy by the reiteration of certain demands which were essentially reactionary and held up the progress registered by the Congress under Pandit Nehru's leadership since its assumption of office at the Centre.

We have now at New Delhi virtually a new type of two-party Government with the Viceroy as the final referee in controversial matters, the parties concerned pulling the delicate machine in opposite directions and leaning more and more in pathetic confusion, if not in a spirit of party revenge, on British stewardship or the Viceregal veto. By these ill-advised and short-sighted tactics Mr. Jinnah has done positive disservice, as the leader of a great and growing political party, to India and Muslims alike. I do not, however, agree with Pandit Nehru and his colleagues that Gandhiji's formula accepted by Mr. Jinnah "is not happily worded". That they did not, as is clear from Pandit Nehru's letter to Mr. Jinnah, dated October 8, 1946, accept the formula is, of course, a different matter. The formula as agreed to by Mr. Jinnah was to the following effect:

> The Congress does not challenge and accepts that the Muslim League now is the authoritative representative of an overwhelming majority of the Muslims of India. As such and in accordance with democratic principles they alone have today the unquestionable right to represent the Muslims of India. But the Congress cannot agree that any restriction or limitation should be put upon the Congress to choose such representatives as they think proper from amongst the members of the Congress as their representatives.

The formula, I admit, appears self-contradictory. For if the League is "the authoritative representative of an overwhelming majority of the Muslims of India" the implication is that there are Muslims, whatever their number, who do not own allegiance to that body. How then can it "alone" claim to represent the Muslim of India ? If, again, the League alone has the "unquestionable right to represent the Muslims of India", how is the Congress free to choose its representatives, as is implied in the formula, from amongst its Muslim adherents? But the contradiction is rather apparent than real. What the formula meant was that the League would, in the exercise of its democratic right, nominate Muslims in the Interim Government. If, however, the Congress desired to include in its quota of representation persons other than Caste Hindus, there was to be no restriction or limitation on its freedom of choice. But such persons must be members of the Congress. It meant, to put it in a different way, that the Congress was free to nominate Caste Hindus, members of the Scheduled Castes, Sikhs, Indian Christians, Parsis, Muslims or members of any other community provided they belonged to the Congress. Pandit Nehru and his colleagues did not agree to this formula obviously because it debarred the Congress from claiming the right to represent Muslims and the smaller communities as such.

Pandit Nehru did not hesitate to stress the point in his letter to Mr. Jinnah, dated October 8, in which he wrote that "the Congress has the right to appoint a Muslim out of its quota" and further that "the Congress position in regard to the nationalist Muslims and the smaller minorities should not be challenged by you". Accordingly Pandit Nehru in concurrence with his colleagues proposed modification of the formula which went beyond Gandhiji's terms and was not acceptable to Mr. Jinnah. Pandit Nehru insisted in his letter of October 6, that he and his colleagues were prepared to commit themselves to "the purpose" of Gandhiji's formula provided that "for identical reasons the League recognises the Congress as the authoritative organisation representing all non-Muslims and such Muslims as have thrown in their lot with the Congress". Gandhiji's formula was disapproved by Pandit Nehru and his colleagues not because it was "not happily worded" but because it did not meet what they regarded as the legitimate Congress claims. The proviso suggested by them was not withdrawn in Pandit Nehru's letter of October 8, and in that view of the matter it was not correct to state, as Pandit Nehru stated, that he and his colleagues were prepared, for the sake of settlement, to "accept the whole of it. . . .".

Pandit Nehru's insistence on the inclusion of the paragraph left out in Mr. Jinnah's letter to him dated October 7, however, concerned an issue which had little or nothing to do with the representative character of the Congress. The paragraph referred to reads:

> It is understood that all the Ministers of the Interim Government will work as a team for the good of the whole of India and will never invoke the intervention of the Governor-General in any case.

In the absence of precise and adequate details about the Nawab of Bhopal's negotiations with Gandhiji and Mr. Jinnah it is neither possible nor fair to pronounce any opinion on the question as to whether this paragraph was an integral part of the formula or whether this was merely a point, as Mr. Jinnah wrote in his letter of October 12, for further discussion between the parties concerned. But Mr. Jinnah's refusal to agree to the paragraph shows clearly that he was anxious to leave the last and decisive say with the Viceroy—a stand fundamentally pro-British and reactionary and not in conformity with the spirit of the changes contemplated in the Cabinet Mission's long-term and interim plans. A Provisional Government with a British Viceroy as its head having the right to veto its decisions is quite out of place in a scheme envisaging vast and sweeping changes in the constitution of the land. Against this background and in view of Congress-League differences on important and vital questions the League's entry into the Interim Government is, on the face of it, a brake on progress rather than a step forward towards a peaceful liquidation of Britain's imperialist rule in India. The responsibility in this regard is entirely Mr. Jinnah's and it is rather surprising that the sturdy and valiant Muslims of India should have apparently acquiesced in it and been a party to the retention of a foreign authority as the final determining factor in the internal political situation.

The hope has, however, been expressed in certain circles that by working together in the Interim Government the Congress and the League would each cultivate an attitude of mutual help and accommodation and thus find a basis for an enduring Hindu-Muslim or inter-communal settlement. I do not dispute that things may shape in this fashion, but the commitments of these two political organisations and the social affiliations of their active leaders point to developments in the opposite direction. It seems that settlement is to come, if at all, from the base and not to originate at the top, however distant it may be in the circumstances of today. Incidentally the Muslim League's admission into the Interim Government without withdrawal of its Council's resolution of July 29, needs explaining having regard to the interpretation put by the British Government and the Viceroy on the impugned paragraph of the Cabinet Mission's statement of June 16.

3. Independence or Dominion Status

The point that strikes one at the outset in connection with the Cabinet Mission's entire project is certain reorientation of the British Government's India policy. Unlike the Cripps offer which starts with Dominion Status of the Statute of Westminster variety, they assume this time Indian independence to be the basis upon which representatives of the Provinces and the States in the Constituent Assembly may frame the constitution. The Cripps scheme starts with a recital of the Balfour formula as reproduced in essence in the Preamble to the Statute of Westminster, 1931. Complete independence of India is envisaged as a possible *future* event and not offered as an *immediate* prospect. It is laid down that the treaty to be negotiated between the British Government and the constitution-making body to cover matters arising out of the changes contemplated "will not impose any restriction on the power of the Indian Union to decide in future its relationship to other Member States of the British Commonwealth".[1] Reference may be made in this connection, by way of contrast, to Mr. Clement Attlee's declaration in Parliament of March 15, announcing the appointment of the Cabinet Mission, in which the Prime Minister made it clear that although he hoped that India would elect to remain within the British Commonwealth and Empire, it was for her to take the final decision. It was for her, that is, to remain within or opt out of the Commonwealth and Empire and if she decided in favour of independence, the British Government had no more to do than "to help to make the transition as smooth as

[1] The Cripps Plan, art. (c) (ii).

possible." Taking their stand on that declaration, the Cabinet Mission express the hope that the "new independent India may choose to be a member of the British Commonwealth" but repeat that it is a matter for the free choice of the Indian people.[1] Again, in their appeal to "the leaders and people of India" the Mission take care to remind them of "the opportunity of complete independence" which their scheme offers. In 1940 Dominion Status is a distant goal ; in 1942 Dominion Status is the immediate objective with independence as a future event ; in 1946 the issue is left open to "the people" of India.

4. Basis of Representation in Constituent Assembly

There are, of course, other differences between the abortive Coalition effort of 1942, and the Socialist venture of 1946. But these are, more or less, over matters of detail or of internal adjustment. For instance, the basis of representation in the Constituent Assembly is altered. In 1942, the constitution-making body was proposed to be elected by the entire membership of the Lower Houses of the Provincial Legislatures created under the Government of India Act, 1935, as a single electoral college by the method of proportional representation. There was thus no provision in specific terms for representation province-wise or community-wise or with reference to population. In 1946, however, provisions as to form and content are more precise with entrenched safeguards for Provinces, communities and, in a vague and distant way, in regard to population country-wise. The Constituent Assembly is in form a three-decker machine corresponding in substance to its threefold division into Provinces as constituent units, Groups conceived as a comparatively larger whole and at the top the Union Centre charged with limited and defined responsibilities. More of division than of unity, more of separatism than of collective massiveness, more of confederal looseness than of federal compactness—these are the special features of the Cabinet Mission's Plan as compared to the Cripps outline. In neither case is adult franchise the basis of representation. It is rejected by the Cabinet Mission on the ground that it "would lead to a wholly unacceptable delay in the formation of the new Constitution." Surprisingly indeed, the theory is not seriously challenged by the two

[1] The Mission's statement of May 16, Para 24.

major political parties. The Provincial Assemblies are accepted as the primary units of representation but not in the exact form devised in the Cripps scheme—the Provincial Assemblies separately and not as merged into one single electoral college.

Two difficulties are anticipated and sought to be solved in a manner deemed appropriate in the circumstances. First, the numerical strengths of the Provincial Assemblies do not bear the same proportion to the total population in each Province. Thus, as the authors of the Plan put it, Assam with a population of 10 millions has a Legislative Assembly of 108 members while Bengal with a population six times as large has an Assembly of 250. Secondly, the strengths of the several communities in each Provincial Legislative Assembly are not in proportion to their numbers in the Province concerned. Thus, according to the Cabinet Mission, the number of territorial seats reserved for Muslims in the Bengal Assembly is 48% of the total, although on the basis of the latest census figures they constitute 55% of the total population of the Province. Adjustment is sought to be effected by

(a) allocation to each Province of seats in proportion to its population, roughtly in the ratio of one to a million ;

(b) distribution of the seats allocated to each Province between the main communities in each Province in proportion to their population ; and

(c) provision for election of representatives reserved for each such community in a Province by the members of that community in the Legislative Assembly concerned.

The communities referred to in this context are "General", Muslim and Sikh, the "General" community including all persons other than Muslims or Sikhs.

It was proposed in the Cripps scheme that the constitution-making body would be in number one-tenth of the total membership of the electoral college. To that number was to be added the quota allotted to the States in the same proportion to their total population as in the case of the Provinces. The total number of members of the Provisional Assemblies being 1585,[1] the Provincial share of representation was to be 158 or 159 and the

[1] Cf. the Table in the Fifth Schedule to the Government of India Act, 1935.

States' share in the neighbourhood of 40-45. As against this the Cabinet Mission put the figures at 292 for the Governor's Provinces, the maximum of 93 for the States, 3 for the Chief Commissioner's Provinces and 1 for British Baluchistan—in all 389 members. Apart from widening the base of representation which marks a considerable advance on the restricted scope of the Cripps scheme in this regard, the Cabinet Mission's Plan proceeds at the initial stage to ensure that both the Provinces and the communities concerned are represented in separate blocs in proportion as approximately as possible to their numerical strengths. The device adopted leaves no room within a Province for the control of Hindu seats by Muslims and *vice versa* and in the Indian context of seats allocated to one Province by the pressure of votes in another. The communities, that is, "General", Muslims and Sikhs come in the exercise of the right separately conferred upon them. So do the Provinces.

Implicit in this scheme, by contrast with the Cripps offer, is the division of India into semi-independent Provinces or Groups and States and the peoples of India into three major communities. In conception and design it is a concession to the League case for separatism, although it must be recognised that it offers a better and more effective guarantee for the protection of minorities. The Cripps scheme and the Mission's Plan, however, alike recommend the same method of voting even though the latter, unlike the earlier effort, refers to proportional representation with emphasis on what is known as the single transferable vote. But evidently in 1942 the authors of the scheme had no other type of proportional representation in mind.

5. Proportional Representation

I think I should briefly explain this method not merely because it involves certain complications which at first sight puzzle the lay public but because, helpful as it is to the growth and development of small and minor groups within the legislature, it is, on every showing, a device which perhaps is more effective than any other to secure fair and equitable representation of parties and interests in given circumstances. The method, as the name implies, is proportional representation which is sought to be secured by means of the single transferable vote. It is a single vote as opposed to a multiple vote which may either be cumulative or distributive. Of the latter category the typical example is furnished by elections in the multiple-member "General" constituencies, say, to the Bengal Legislative Assembly. In such a constituency every elector has as many votes as there are seats or vacancies to be filled which he can distribute among his "most favoured" candidates or, if he so chooses, concentrate on one particular candidate. Under proportional representation with the single transferable vote no such voting is permissible. An elector has one single vote which is variously termed as the first preference or the primary vote or the original vote. In addition, of course, he is entitled to mark his preferences according as there are seats or vacancies to be filled. No vote is valid unless the voter has marked the figure 1 in his ballot paper in the space opposite the name of the candidate of his first preference. The other preferences, according to the number of seats or vacancies, may either be distributed or withheld, or partly distributed and partly withheld.

The practice is that the total number of valid papers, that is to say, the papers on which the figure 1 has been correctly marked are arranged in separate parcels in the names of the candidates marked with the figure 1. Each separate parcel is then counted, and each candidate is credited with one vote in respect of each paper on which the figure 1 or the first preference has been recorded for him. All these first preference votes as recorded in separate parcels are counted. Then the total is divided by a number exceeding by one the number of seats or vacancies, and the result added by one, disregarding any fractional remainder, is the quota which secures the return of a candidate. Take a three-member constituency. The result of counting of the figure 1-marked papers, let it be assumed, is as follows:

Candidates	Votes
A	25
B	15
C	10
D	5
E	2
F	12
Total	69

This number (69) is divided by 4 (exceeding by 1 the number of seats), and the quota or the number of votes sufficient for the return of a candidate in this case is 18 (the quotient 17 disregarding the fraction, increased by 1). Now the votes recorded for A exceed the quota, and A is declared elected. A has 7 surplus votes (A's total 25 less the quota 18). All his 25 papers are examined and arranged in separate sub-parcels and according to the second preferences indicated thereon. The result is found to be as follows:

The figure 2 is marked against B on A's 10 papers.

Do F 15 ,,

It is clear that the total number of transferable or second preference papers (25) exceeds the surplus (7). Thus only a portion of each sub-parcel (for B and F) is to be transferred. Now, if B gets 10 in 25, how much will he get in 7? Similarly, if F gets 15 in 25, how much will he get in 7? It is simple rule of three. The number of papers to be transferred in each of these two cases must accordingly bear the same proportion to the total number of papers in each sub-parcel as that which the surplus bears to the total number of transferable papers. The position is ascertained by multiplying the number of transferable papers in each sub-parcel (10 for B and 15 for F) by the surplus (7) and dividing the result by the total number of transferable papers, that is, for B $\frac{7 \times 10}{25} = 2\frac{4}{5}$ and for F $\frac{7 \times 15}{25} = 4\frac{1}{5}$. As the fractional remainder in each case has for the obvious reason to be taken into account and the first fraction being nearer the unit than the second, B gets 3 and F 4 out of A's surplus 7. In the result the candidates stand thus:

A	...	...	...	25 (elected).
B	15+3=	...	...	18 ,,
F	12+4=	...	...	16
C	...	...	...	10
D	...	...	...	5
E	...	...	...	2

One more seat has yet to be filled up. And how?

The last candidate E's parcel of 2 papers is now examined. It is found that the next preference is marked on each of these papers against F who has already got 16 votes. Adding 2 to this number, the candidate is declared elected. It should be noted in passing that the last candidate's parcel is to be taken up for scrutiny only when there is no surplus to the credit of any successful candidate or when the surplus is less than the difference between the lowest two candidates on the poll so that the relative position of these two candidates could not be altered even if the whole surplus were transferred to the last candidate. There are, again, cases in which candidates are declared elected even if they failed to reach the quota through "originals" or transfers or both taken together. These occur when the number of "continuing"[1] candidates is reduced to the number of seats or vacancies to be filled or when no quota is obtainable by transfers.

In the case of a tie between two candidates for one vacancy that candidate is to be preferred who has obtained a larger number of "originals" or "primaries". Where there is a tie between two candidates who have secured an equal number of "originals" or "primaries" that candidate is preferred against whom preferences are marked even though they may not be transferred, as in the recent Sind case in connection with elections to the Constituent Assembly. If more than one candidate has a surplus, the highest one is to be taken up first. Where, further, more than one candidate has the same surplus, that of the candidate who has the largest number of original votes is first to be disposed of.[2] Now voting under this system is done either in singles or in blocs. In bloc voting there are obvious risks for "marginal" cases, first, for the reason that in the case of a tie they are pushed aside by candidates with "primaries" and, secondly, because there is an unnecessary waste of votes in the process of transfers in pursuit of the quota for each "continuing" candidate.

Proportional voting, as distinguished from voting on the simple majority principle, tends to reflect more or less accurately in actual results the juxtaposition of parties, groups or interests in the constituencies. Under this system it is quite evident that the

[1] "Continuing" candidates are candidates other than those who have been elected or excluded from the poll.

[2] For further treatment of the subject read the author's *The Problem of Minorities*, pp. 455-490.

Congress in the "General" constituencies and the League in the Muslim constituencies would have lost to other parties a larger number of seats in the general election of 1946 than they have lost under the system now in vogue. Conversely with voting on the simple majority principle the Congress would not have lost 9 seats out of 216 "General" seats in the Constituent Assembly and the Muslim League would have captured all the 78 Muslim seats barring 3 seats reserved for the North-West Frontier Province where the League is in a minority in the Assembly, instead of 73 (now 74) which is its present strength. Thus in Bengal the Communists and Dr. B. R. Ambedkar's Scheduled Castes Federation in the "General" and the non-League Muslims under Mr. A. K. Fazlul Huq in the Muslim constituency would have gone unrepresented. Mr. Huq has since returned to the League. Elsewhere Mr. Rafi Ahmed Kidwai and a Unionist Muslim from the Punjab for Muslim seats and Sir Jwala Prasad Srivastava, Sir Padampat Singhania and the Maharajah of Darbhanga for "General" seats owe their return to the Constituent Assembly to the single transferable vote. Furthermore, the simple majority principle without reservation countrywise would in the present composition of the Provincial Legislative Assemblies have completely eliminated non-Congress and non-League parties respectively in the Hindu-majority and the Muslim-majority Provinces save in the North-West Frontier Province which is predominantly Congress and yet non-Hindu.

Quantitatively the communities recognised for the purposes of elections to the Constituent Assembly have contracted to a considerable extent under the Cabinet Mission's Plan as compared to the Table of Seats under the Government of India Act, 1935. Qualitatively, however, they have gained a great deal. The communities entitled to separate representation through separate electorates in terms of that Act are (i) "General," including the scheduled castes; (ii) representatives of backward areas and tribes; (iii) Sikhs; (iv) Muslims ; (v) Anglo-Indians ; (vi) Europeans ; and (vii) Indian Christians. The scheduled castes have been given separate representation through joint electorates with reservation of seats. The Cabinet Mission's Plan accords separate representation under separate electoral registers only to (i) "General", including all communities other than Sikhs and Muslims ; (ii) Sikhs ; and (iii) Muslims. Thus "General" has been made to appear as a huge "merger" with Hindus as the dominant partner. Certain sections of the scheduled castes and backward areas and tribes in particular have with plausible justification disapproved of this provision as having deprived them of proper and adequate representation in a machinery designed to determine their future, although the Congress which has come to dominate the "General" community has, on the whole, been fair in its choice in respect of both the quality and quantity of representation for these peoples. The other minorities have been given no separate recognition on the ground of population upon which seats in the Constituent Assembly have been earmarked.

6. Nationality and Alienage—Position of Europeans

The question of "Europeans" taking part as voters or candidates in elections to the Constituent Assembly as an element of the "General" community gave rise to misgivings among Congress leaders. These were expressed in unmistakable terms and as forcefully as possible in Maulana Azad's letter to the Viceroy, dated June 14. The Cabinet Mission were reminded of the two principles accepted by them in the composition of the Constituent Assembly. The first was that the constitution was to be framed by Indians for Indians.[1] The second was the allotment of seats in the Constituent Assembly roughly in the ratio of one seat to a million, on the basis of which representation was denied to 146,000 Muslims in Orissa and 180,000 Hindus and 58,000 Sikhs in the North-West Frontier Province. By these tests Europeans were not entitled to participate in, and influence the elections to, the Constituent Assembly. It was fantastic that Europeans in Bengal and Assam[2] with a population of only 21,000 should be enabled by the procedure laid down in the Cabinet Mission's Plan to obtain by their own votes 7 out of 34 seats reserved for "General" in these two Provinces, or to influence the elections in such a manner that

[1] Paragraphs 3 & 16 of the Mission's statement of May 16, and Mr. Clement Attlee's speech in Parliament on March 15, 1946.

[2] In Bengal the territorial seats for Europeans are 11 and Commerce, Industry etc. seats 14 in a House of 250. In Assam the territorial seat is 1 and Commerce, Industry etc. seats are 8 in a House of 108. See the Table of Seats for Provincial Legislative Assemblies in the Fifth Schedule to the Government of India Act, 1935.

the political, racial or social complexion of representation might be considerably affected. The Congress case on these points was without doubt unassailable. In his reply to the Congress President, dated June 15, the Viceroy expressed the hope that a "satisfactory solution of the problem will be found". That sentiment was reciprocated by Maulana Azad in his letter to the Viceroy on June 16.

The legal issue raised by the Congress President was, however, not free from ambiguity. While stating very clearly that the Congress had no objection to Englishmen or Europeans as such, it refused to be a party to the use of votes by foreigners and non-nationals as a ruling race for influencing representation in the Constituent Assembly, directly or indirectly. The Congress, it appears, was advised on expert legal opinion that participation by Europeans in voting on their choice of candidates for election to the Constituent Assembly from amongst members of their own race would be illegal and *ultra vires* of the scheme on the ground of their alleged alien status. Assuming that the Congress contention in this regard was correct, I do not see how any legal remedy could be effectively sought even if European members of the Provincial Assemblies had decided to reject the Congress demand. It is doubtful if the jurisdiction of any court could be invoked except perhaps in a purely declaratory pronouncement. The Mission's plan is not a statute and a breach of its provisions, it is submitted, involved no justiciable wrong unless a political inequity was interpreted as corresponding to it for the purposes of the existing substantive or procedural law.

Nor am I convinced, with respect to the Congress President and his legal advisers, that in terms of the present law all Europeans or Englishmen are foreigners or aliens. In law and in fact they are not. It must be clearly understood that my observations, for whatever they are worth, are confined to the law as it is and do not foreshadow the law as it should be. Further, my object is not to enunciate a political principle but to examine, as far as I can, the legal implications of the Congress President's proposition. Politically and on the broad principles underlying the State Paper of May 16, I am in complete agreement with him. Legally, that is, from the point of view of the English common law and statutory provisions I venture to differ from him, his colleagues and his legal advisers.

A "European," according to the Government of India Act, 1935, means a person whose father or any of whose other male progenitors in the male line is or was of European descent and who is not a native of India.[1] An "Anglo-Indian" is a "European" so defined except that he is a native of India.[2] The expression "native of India" includes any person born and domiciled within the dominions of His Majesty in India of parents habitually resident in India and not established here for temporary purposes. There is a difference between a "European" of this category and a "European British subject" in terms of the Criminal Procedure Code.[3] Under the Code a "European British subject" means (i) any subject of His Majesty of European descent in the male line born, naturalised, or domiciled in the British Islands or any Colony ; or (ii) any subject of His Majesty who is the child or grandchild of any such person by legitimate descent. Thus certain "Anglo-Indians" as defined by and under the Government of India Act, 1935, are for the purposes of the Code "European British subjects". If the Act of 1935 and the Code are read together, one finds that there are in India European aliens as well as European British subjects ; and so far as the latter are concerned, they are not foreigners in the purely legal sense of the term. That is evident from the relevant provisions of the Government of India Act, 1935. It is laid down, for example, that no person is qualified to be chosen to fill a seat in the British Indian Legislatures, Central and Provincial, or shall be included in the electoral roll unless he is either (a) a British subject ; (b) the Ruler or subject of a Federated State ; or (c) if and in so far as it is so prescribed with respect to any Province, and subject to any prescribed conditions, the Ruler or subject of any other Indian State.[4] Therefore, those Europeans whose names appear in the electoral roll of any constituency or who are members of any British Indian Legislature must be included, unless the contrary is proved, into the category of persons popularly known as European British subjects and as such cannot in law be treated as aliens or foreigners.

It seems there is some confusion between a "national" and a "native of India". These are not, from the point of view of

[1] First Schedule, clause 26(1) ; and Fifth Schedule, clause 19.

[2] Ibid.

[3] s. 4.

[4] First Schedule, clause 1 ; and Sixth Schedule, clause 3.

nationality meaning citizenship, synonymous terms. All "natives" of India" are "nationals" ; all "nationals" are not and need not necessarily be "natives" of India. The confusion seems to have been caused by the fact that "nationality" is a term in the English language with varying connotations. In a broad sense it is used to indicate the common consciousness based on race, language, traditions or other analogous ties and interests not necessarily limited to the municipal limits of a given State. It is symbolical of what may be called a psychological make-up manifested in a community ot culture. In this sense Europeans or Englishmen in India are not "nationals" of India as Indians on the whole are, although large sections of Muslims repudiate the latter proposition. In another and a more technical sense the term implies a definite connection with a definite State and Government. In the British Commonwealth and Empire it has been attended by ambiguity on account largely of its use for the purpose by mixing up this connection with the old, historical concept of allegiance to the Crown. In this sense Europeans or Englishmen, who are British subjects, are "nationals" as Indians other than the Rulers of States and their subjects are. In the latter context "nationality" means citizenship, an expression loosely used in this country. Save in Eire and partially in Canada and South Africa, where on the whole for internal as opposed to imperial or international purposes special arrangements, statutory and administrative, have been made, a "citizen" in different parts of the Commonwealth and Empire has no political status except as a subject of the Crown.

A "British subject" is a common-law concept. The term has further been defined in the Nationality and Status of Aliens Act, 1914, as amended in 1918, 1922 and 1933. Where, however, the common law has been modified or altered specifically by any statute of the British Parliament the statute supersedes the common law to the extent of repugnancy due to modification or alteration.[1] There are at the present moment at least three and possibly four categories of British subjects in the Commonwealth and Empire. There are, first, natural-born British subjects at common law or by the provisions of the Imperial Statutes and are treated as such in almost every part of the Crown's Dominions and possessions, although

[1] *Attorney-General* v. *De Keyser's Royal Hotel Limited* (1920 A.C. 508).

Eire has in effect repudiated it and in some Dominions doubt as to the automatic applicability of the Nationality and Status of Aliens Act, 1914, has been sought to be removed by local re-enactment of the relevant provisions. There are, secondly, naturalised British subjects as by or under the Imperial Statutes who enjoy the same status as natural-born British subjects. There are, thirdly, British subjects by local naturalisation who only within the territory concerned enjoy that status, for instance, aliens naturalised under the Indian Naturalisation Act, 1926,[1] enacted by the Indian Legislature. They are not British subjects in other parts of the Commonwealth and Empire but are entitled to British protection at international law. Lastly, there are Dominion nationals who must be assigned to any one of the above-mentioned three categories of British subjects.

British subjects of United Kingdom domicile in the service of the Crown in India or otherwise engaged belong to the first category and, according to the law as it stands, they cannot be treated as aliens or foreigners. They have, moreover, been given under the Government of India Act, 1935, certain protection in commercial and other matters which does not extend to British subjects from any other part of the Commonwealth and Empire.[2] What is of significance in this connection is the statutory provision as to complete saving, from the operation of any Act that may be passed by the Indian Central Legislature or any Provincial legislature, of the law of British nationality.[3] The present position in regard to Europeans of the United Kingdom domicile or Englishmen is that in India they are British subjects and not foreigners, that the imperial law has conferred upon them certain rights, privileges and immunities which do not apply to British subjects from any other part of the Commonwealth and Empire and that the status enjoyed by, or assigned to, them in India cannot be affected by any British Indian legislation.[4] What their position in future will be like is for the framers of the Indian constitution to decide. It is not clear, however, whether this falls within the unfettered scope of the proposed Constituent Assembly or is subject to the reservations in respect of the proposed treaty or the protection of minori-

[1] s. 7(1). [2] Chap. III, ss. 111-121.

[3] The Government of India Act, 1935, s. 110(b)(i).

[4] For further treatment of the subject read the author's *The Problem of Minorities*, Chapter XVII.

ties upon which stress was laid in the Cabinet Mission's statement of May 25, issued in elucidation of their proposals of May 16. I am glad, however, that members of the European community have, except in minor instances, voluntarily waived their undoubted legal right to vote in elections to the Constituent Assembly or to offer candidates from amongst themselves instead of provoking, by the exercise of an ill-gotten right, an atmosphere of countrywide hostility to the peaceful execution of a plan for the transfer of political power. I am also glad that Maulana Azad has left no room for doubt in anybody's mind that Congress objection to Europeans taking part in elections or setting up candidates was not prompted by racial considerations as such.

7. No Functional Representation

A glance at the Table of Seats for the Provincial Legislative Assemblies provided for in the relevant schedule[1] to the Government of India Act, 1935, shows that even more than ten years ago the British Parliament deemed it necessary that, in addition to territorial seats communitywise, a certain kind of functional representation[2] should be introduced to ensure protection, however inadequate, of the interests of Labour. The number of seats allocated to Labour is 38 out of the grand total of 1585 seats for all the Provinces taken together. This was niggardly and not at all commensurate with the importance of Labour as a potential force in the swiftly changing Indian situation. Even then on the basis of proportional representation by means of the single transferable vote Labour should have been entitled to 6 or 7 separate, independent seats out of the quota of 296 for the Provinces and British Baluchistan had there been reservation countrywise. Britain's Socialist Government, committed as they seemingly are in the domestic sphere to far-reaching social changes in the productive relations, have, curiously enough, assumed that it is only religious communities that needed protection and not interests which cut across such mediaeval divisions of the Indian peoples fostered alike by British policy and power-politics of certain political parties.

[1] Fifth Schedule.

[2] Commerce and Industry and Planting, Landholders, Universities and Labour are the interests recognised in the Act.

Apparently, however, the Cabinet Mission were largely influenced by two considerations. The first was that they were persuaded, on the basis of experience in their own country, that political parties tended ultimately to react to the social forces and to reconstruct their programmes accordingly. Some, they supposed, moved towards the *Right* upholding vested interest and privilege while others veered to the *Left* striving to abolish them. Indeed, the emergence of the Labour Party as a formidable force in British politics is a social phenomenon which cannot be completely lost sight of in appreciation of the general tendency in recent times towards the realignment of parties on other than purely territorial or political basis. The second was that the Cabinet Mission perhaps found, upon a rough and ready analysis of the results of elections to the Provincial Legislative Assemblies, that the Congress had captured an overwhelming majority of Labour seats,[1] thereby eliminating for all practical purposes Labour as an independent force to reckon with in the framing of a new constitution.

I do not suggest that these considerations are not at all substantial. Nevertheless it cannot be denied by any critical observer of events that the last general elections were held in an atmosphere which, thanks to hasty and ill-advised British policy, was charged with a kind of emotionalism not helpful to a correct and scientific perspective and that the results were not a sure index to the juxtaposition of social forces. Further, constitution-making being a long-term affair, the potentialities of Labour as distinguished from its immediate pull should not have been so callously disregarded by a Government which had won elections "at home" on a vital social security programme. It seems to me that either the Cabinet Mission for their lack of appreciation of the magnitude of the complicated problems of India sought to oversimplify the task with which they had been charged or that they thought that the major political parties alone could be relied upon in "delivering the goods" in the manner deemed appropriate by them both immediately and upon a long-term view. I suggest that this one or the other or both have been the major cause of failure which has marked the efforts of the British Government, whatever their political complexion, pursued since 1940 under Lord Linlithgow.

[1] Out of 38 seats reserved for Labour the Congress won 23, Communists 7, Independents 7, and Radical Democrats 1.

I am almost convinced that the dogged persistence in this short cut will yield no enduring results. There is need for a new approach. That approach must be social rather than purely political, political rather than narrowly communal, **Left** rather than **Right,** more realistic than abstract, more in tune with the mass urges than with class chauvinism and power-politics.

CHAPTER III

INDIAN STATES IN THE BRITISH COLONIAL SCHEME

1. Lessons of Imperialist Rule

An interesting and, in the peculiar context of British rule in India, instructive story is told of the Austrian Minister Beist who once summoned his Hungarian counterpart and delivered himself of a typical Machiavellian maxim: "Well, my dear fellow, you manage your hordes and I'll look after mine." When the factors and agents of the East India Company came to realise that sovereignty came steadily, if somewhat slowly, in the wake of trade they sat back quietly but with deliberation to profit by the lessons of history left as a legacy by the early founders and builders of empires. The Company divided India into British India and Indian India. In the first their word was law ; in the second they reigned, leaving India's feudal barons to rule. The system inaugurated by them has since been pursued with adaptations, modifications and changes in law and procedure which the tactics and strategy of colonial rule have demanded from time to time. It is a case of picking up one group and granting it rights, privileges and immunities, in order that the other groups may be ruled in comparative freedom from internal revolt or commotion without any serious challenge to the foundations of the system. The British Government have evolved what may be called a three-decker edifice—British India as a going colonial concern, Indian India as the base of its operations and the Paramount Power as the final and supreme arbiter of the destiny of each. It is easier and cheaper to bother with one unit or two or more than to involve oneself in the concerns of the whole. When one remembers this maxim and all that it implies one begins to appreciate the British Government's general policy in regard to the Indian States not only in the distant past but for the present and in the future as well.

After the Rebellion of 1857 Lord Canning said: "These patches of Native Government served as a breakwater to the storm which would otherwise have swept over us in one great wave." These Indian States have served as a "breakwater" all these years since. They are regarded as a "breakwater" even now despite all that is happening on the Indian political scene. We are grateful to Lady Minto for revealing the role of her distinguished husband as the formulator of the "counterpoise" doctrine. It was an important element in Lord Minto's applied Indian politics. Hindus were set against Muslims and Muslims against Hindus. This communal "counterpoise" is referred to in a subsequent chapter. But almost at the same time, that is, on May 28, 1906, he wrote to Lord Morley: "I have been thinking a good deal lately of a possible counterpoise to Congress aims. I think we may find a solution in the Council of Princes." Is the Chamber of Princes a variant of Lord Minto's "counterpoise"? Is not the present provision for States' representation in the Constituent Assembly just the kind of "solution" which Lord Minto envisaged four decades ago? In his evidence before the Joint Committee of Parliament on the Government of India Bill, 1935, Col. Wedgwood stated that the Princes had been brought into the proposed Federation for the purpose of making the Centre "conservative and pro-English." These statements made by responsible British statesmen in positions of authority and power furnish in a nutshell the background story of the alliance between the British ruling class and the Rulers of Indian States and should be kept in view in any objective study of the developments that are now taking place.

In status and character the Indian States differ basically from the British Indian Provinces. They are under personal rule of the Princes, though subject to the paramountcy of the Crown. It is not, therefore, surprising that, so far as the States are concerned, there is little or no material difference between the Cripps Scheme of 1942 and the State Paper of 1946, although the former had been initiated by a Tory-controlled National Government and the latter by a Socialist Government. In the Cripps plan the right remains with the Indian States to adhere or not to adhere to the projected Union ;[1] some revision of the old arrangements as called for in the new situation is contemplated ;[2] and representation in the constitution making body is offered in proportion to their population with

[1] Clauses (b) and (c) (ii).
[2] Ibid.

the same powers as the British Indian members."[1] In the Mission's scheme the quantum of States representation in the Constituent Assembly is increased proportionately to British Indian representation ;[2] a Negotiating Committee is envisaged at the preliminary stage of constitution-making to watch the interests of the States ; and the method of election of the States representatives is to be determined by consultation. This consultation may be between the British Government and the Rulers of States or between the latter and leaders of the major political parties in British India or between the Rulers and the States peoples' organisations wherever they exist or between the States' Negotiating Committee and the Corresponding Committee of the Constituent Assembly or a curious mixture of all these processes of consultation. No procedure is precisely laid down.

There is, however, little doubt that the project does not alter the position of vantage held by the Rulers in the present setting in the matter of unduly influencing, if not determining, the political character or the social basis of the quantum of representation assigned to the States. If, therefore, no machinery is devised to ensure. on a substantial and effective scale, representation of the States' subjects, the States' bloc in the Constituent Assembly with 93 members is bound to put such a tremendous pressure on its proceedings that it will be difficult, first, to evolve a free and democratic constitution for the Union Centre and, secondly, to place the States, should they continue to exist, outside the realm of their old traditional reaction pursued and fostered by the Paramount Power's outmoded "political" machinery. The only important point of departure in the Mission's scheme is that it seems to insist on the Union Centre embracing both British India and the States.[3] Evidently no discretion is left to the States to refuse accession to the Union, or it may as well mean that in the event of the States not adhering to the Union the entire scheme falls to the ground. In the terms of reference with which the States' Negotiating Committee have been charged the Chamber of Princes have stated that it is for each State to decide whether it should or should not accede to the Union. These provisions of the scheme, like many others, are susceptible of conflicting interpretations.

[1] Clause (d).
[2] Clause 19 (ii). The maximum number fixed is 93.
[3] Para 15 (i).

The Government of India Act, 1935, it may be noted, laid it down as a condition precedent to the setting up of an All-India Federation (i) that the States and groups of States acceding to the Federation shall be such as their Rulers are entitled to choose not less than 52 members of the States' total quota of not more than 104 members in the Upper House of the Federal Legislature[1] and (ii) that their aggregate population shall be at least one-half of the total population of the States.[2] Representatives of the States in both Houses of the Federal Legislature were to be chosen by the Rulers themselves[3]—a provision upon which the relevant clause of the Cabinet Mission's project, though couched in vague language, marks an advance inasmuch as it is now contemplated that the question of the States' proportion of representation in the Union Legislature and Executive and the method by which the representatives are to be chosen are matters to be decided by the Constituent Assembly or at the preliminary stage between the two Negotiating Committees. It is, however, laid down in the Mission's scheme that the States will retain all subjects and powers other than those ceded to the Union.[4]

The relevant clause relating to what are known as British Indian Provinces is differently worded perhaps mainly for the reason that from the time of the Company's rule onwards Provinces have developed along entirely different lines. There British authority has been complete while the States have been allowed, by sufferance or on strategic grounds, to enjoy some semblance of internal sovereignty. Previously the responsibility to decide whether or not Provinces should exercise powers in complete or partial freedom from Central interference and, if they should, in what form and by what method, was a matter of administrative rules or regulations. In the Act of 1919, they were given certain defined powers by devolution rules without prejudice to the unitary character of the constitution ; in the Act of 1935 they were accorded plenary powers within their defined field under a general federal structure. In either case, however, the final responsibility

[1] s. 5 (a) (b).

[2] The First Schedule, Part II. The total population in the Table is 78,981,912. In the States whose Rulers are Muslims there are only some 3,000,000 Muslims, with 8,000,000 in other States.

[3] The First Schedule, Part II, clause 6.

[4] Para 15 (4).

for decision was exercised by the British Parliament. Such is not the pattern of relations envisaged in the Mission's scheme or in the Cripps offer which preceded it. Provinces are treated in a way as federating units or, if one may say so, as originating authorities more or less like the States. In the Mission's Plan in particular it is stated that all subjects other than Union subjects and all residuary powers are to vest in Provinces ; and the Union subjects specified are Foreign Affairs, Defence and Communications and the subjects or powers required to raise finances for these purposes. In the case of the States it is a question of retaining what by their choice is not delegated or ceded. In the case of the Provinces the question is one of acquiring what they have hitherto not possessed and of retaining all the acquisitions save the specified Central subjects and powers. The difference is in the main to be traced to the fascinating story of two almost parallel developments that have taken place during the last two hundred years of Indo-British history.

2. Doctrine of Paramountcy

Connected with the proposed act of accession to the Union is the doctrine of paramountcy. The Cabinet Mission are of the opinion that with "the attainment of independence by British India, whether inside or outside the British Commonwealth, the relationship which has hitherto existed between the Rulers of the States and the British Crown will no longer be possible."[1] They add that paramountcy can be neither retained by the British Crown nor transferred to the new Indian Government. It means that the States or groups of States, as the case may be, become completely sovereign and independent entities except in so far as they accede to the Union, on British India becoming a Dominion of the Statute of Westminster variety or opting out of the British Commonwealth and Empire.

Legally, however, I do not agree to the proposition enunciated by the Cabinet Mission in this regard. It is open to the Crown on the advice of its Ministers to retain and exercise its paramountcy over the States. The effect of the Plan is the creation of a Princely Ulster standing in opposition to an Indian Dominion or a free,

[1] The Mission's statement of May 16, para 14.

independent and democratic Indian Union. It is equally open to the Crown on ministerial advice to transfer paramountcy to the new Indian Union in which the States are to have their due share of authority, power and responsibility. The effect of this upon a long view is the liquidation of these medieaval feudal autocracies which have throughout all recorded history been the base of reaction and arsenal of British imperialism in the East. The Mission seem to have disapproved of the Crown's retention of paramountcy in the hope of throwing the onus on the Rulers. They have rejected the case for its transfer to the Indian Union in their natural anxiety to ensure that in a certain eventuality or in some unforeseen contingencies all the reserves are not frittered away or exhausted in one single deal.

There is, however, nothing in the Mission's proposals of May 16, which from the legal standpoint overrules adoption of the one or the other process indicated above or the assumption of responsibility by the new Government to deal with the issue on its own initiative. I admit that in very competent and knowledgeable circles differing or even conflicting opinions have equally consistently been held. In 1928 the Indian States Enquiry Committee[1] insisted that without the States' agreement "the rights and obligations of the Paramount Power should not be assigned to persons who are not under its control, for instance, an Indian Government in British India responsible to an Indian Legislature." This demand was pressed "in view of the historical nature of the relationship between the Paramount Power and the Princes," and to counter any possible adverse effect of law and policy which might be pursued by the new Government "resting on a new and written constitution." The Rulers of States would rather continue under British control than assist in evolving a system in which paramountcy would either be abolished or transferred to a democratically controlled Indian Government.

A compromise formula was evolved as a result of discussions at the Round Table Conferences and informal negotiations, given legal shape and incorporated in the Government of India Act, 1935. It lays down that accession of a State to the Indian Federation is not to take effect otherwise than by the voluntary act of the Ruler concerned,[2] thus giving him free and unfettered discre-

[1] Cmd. 3302.

[2] s. 5.

tion to keep out and, jointly with a certain proportion of their order, to destroy the project. Power was further accorded to the acceding Rulers to decide in respect of what subjects they would accede. They could come into the Federation with such limitations and reservations as they desired to impose upon its powers. The Crown, however, reserved to itself the right to reject an Instrument of Accession if it considered that the terms of that Instrument were inconsistent with the scheme of the Federation.[1] The formula was a partial concession to the Rulers. The sovereignty to retain the *status quo* was preserved ; paramountcy interposed its authority only in the matter of determining finally the subjects of accession. It was a typical British compromise. But the question in law was whether the British Parliament was competent to enact legislation compelling the States to adhere to the Federation on its own terms, whether or not acceptable to them. Clearly the answer was "yes". Ethically and in fact, too, such a step would be perfectly correct and in accord with practice or usage.

3. The State under Company and Crown

Reliance has been placed by the Rulers of States on rights and immunities purporting to accrue from treaties, sanads and engagements which are construed in certain quarters as having determined for all time the nexus between the British paramount authority and the States. British relationship with the States may, broadly speaking, be divided into two periods: (i) the period under the Company's rule and (ii) the period under the Crown. Under the former regime the system was on the whole capricious with no meticulous regard for the treaties. The majority of the States, again, had no treaties ; only some forty States had some sort of compacts with the Paramount Power. Where they existed no uniform policy was followed. Lord Dalhousie, for instance, set his face resolutely against intervention in Hyderabad despite its gross misrule, although since 1811 there have been constant and, at times, provocative interferences.

In the eighteenth century, of course, many of the treaties had been conceived as concords between equals or allies. It had been

[1] s. 6.

held in 1712[1] by the Court of Chancery in the *Carnatic* v. *East India Company* that the relationship established between the parties was one between two independent States. Forms appropriate to treaties between independent sovereign States were retained long after equality had in fact been completely undermined. For example, in the Treaty concluded in 1800 between the East India Company and Hyderabad one finds:[2] "The peace, union, and friendship so long subsisting between the two States shall be perpetual ; the friends and enemies of either shall be friends and enemies of both." Again, in Lord Wellesley's treaty with Bharatput in 1805 the recital[3] starts thus: "A firm and permanent friendship is established between the Honourable the East India Company and Maharajah Sewaee Bahadur Ranjeet Singh Bahadur, and betwen their heirs and successors." It proceeds.[4] "As friendship has been established between the two States, the friends and enemies of one of the parties shall be considered the friends and enemies of both and an adherence to this condition shall be constantly observed by both States." Almost the same form is adopted in Lord Hastings' treaty with Mewar[5] concluded in 1818 and, further, in the same year in his treaty[6] with Bhopal.

But care was taken at the same time practically in every case despite the form to emphasise subordination of the States in their relationship with the Government of the Company. The States were required to acknowledge the Company's supremacy.[7] Negotiations with other States or Chiefs were prohibited save with the prior knowledge and consent of the British Government. The language employed in the case of Hyderabad or in that of Bharatpur in the subsequent clauses of the treaties in question is somewhat different. In the former in particular the Company's Government declared that "they have no manner of concern with any of His Highness's children, relatives, subjects or servants with respect to whom His Highness is absolute."[8] A like provision[9] was made in the treaty concluded with Holkar in 1818, although

[1] 2 Ves 60.
[2] art 1.
[3] art 1.
[4] art 2.
[5] art 1.
[6] art 1.
[7] The Treaty of Mewar, arts 3 & 4 ; The Treaty of Bhopal, arts 3 & 4.
[8] art 15.
[9] art 10.

paramountcy was asserted in respect of contracts with other States and of employment of Europeans or Americans.[1] The paramount power of the Company had clearly been recognised for a long time notwithstanding the fading remnants of Mogul sovereignty.

The manner and method of the exercise of paramountcy in the internal affairs of the States varied from time to time and depended more or less on the predilections of individual heads of the Company's Government. Thus while Lord Dalhousie, as has already been noted, repudiated in the case of Hyderabad all adhesion to the doctrine of interference which he considered "unwarranted and officious meddling," and went so far as to assert that the provisions of the treaties were obligations of international contracts, Lord Hastings had earlier[2] stated that the Company's object was "to render the British Government paramount in effect, if not declaredly so," holding the States "as vassals, in substance, though not in name." Paramountcy, however, was in fact in many cases exercised not only in the matter of succession, employment in the service of the States of white personnel and the assignment of the Company's agents as Residents to look after the internal concerns but also for the purposes of annexation and extension of the Company's dominion. Sir William Lee-Warner thought that from 1757 to the close of Lord Minto's Administration in 1813, the keynote of the Company's policy was one of non-intervention or limited liability. Annexations were sought to be avoided for these fiftysix years. From 1813 to 1857, on the other hand, the policy pursued was one of domestic intervention and, in certain cases, of territorial acquisitions. But there was no hard-and-fast line of demarcation. The author only indicated the general, broad tendencies.[3] In essence the dominant trend was more capricious than systematically planned. The fundamental point of departure from the chaotic policy associated with the Company's regime made on the assumption by the Crown in 1858, of direct rule was perhaps the solemn assurance that no acquisition or extension of territory was desired. In her Proclamation[4] taking upon the Crown the Government of India

[1] arts 9 & 13.
[2] Private Journal, Feb. 6, 1816.
[3] Lee-Warner's *The Native States of India*, pp. 53-58.
[4] November 1, 1858.

"heretofore administered in trust" by the East India Company Queen Victoria observed:

> "We desire no extension of our present territorial possessions; and while we will permit no aggression upon our Dominions or our Rights to be attempted with impunity, we shall sanction no encroachment on those of others. We shall respect the Rights, Dignity, and Honour of Native Princes as our own . . ."

Again,

> "We hereby announce to the Native Princes of India that all Treaties and Engagements made with them by or under the authority of the Honourable East India Company are by us accepted and will be scrupulously maintained; and we look for the like observance on their part . . ."

Earlier the sentiments expressed by the Queen had in effect been incorporated in the Government of India Act, 1858, passed in August of that year. It laid down:

> "All treaties made by the said Company should be binding on Her Majesty; and all contracts, covenants, liabilities and engagements of the said Company made, incurred or entered into before the commencement of this Act, may be enforced by and against the Secretary of State in like manner and in the same Courts as they might have been by and against the said Company if this Act had not been passed."[1]

4. Relationship Substantially Regularised

In pursuance of the new policy thus announced after the Mutiny instruments were issued in 1860, about 140 in all, known as Sanads. The Hindu Rulers were assured that adoptions made by them according to the law and custom observed by them would be recognised and the Muslim Rulers that any succession held valid under their law would be upheld. The object was to dispel the growing suspicion that had previously created an atmosphere of revolt and to rally the Princes in support of the Crown and its Government in India. In response the Princes acknowledged the Crown's supremacy and gave demonstrations of loyalty and allegiance to the person of the Throne. Their conduct left no room for doubt that they fully recognised that theirs was a subordinate status in no way equal to that of the British Government or of any independent sovereign State.

[1] 21 & 22 Vict., c. 106, s. 67.

Except in respect of territorial aggression by forcible annexation or on the doctrine of lapse the position remained as before. Foreign relations vested entirely in the British Government. Succession required their approval. The principle of isolation of each State from the others was as vigorously applied. Control was exercised over munitions and the armed forces while, on the other hand, the Rulers were bound by obligation to afford all facilities to the Indian Army whenever asked for. In a number of treaties the stipulation was made as to the States' co-operation in promoting economic schemes, if not in a declaredly coercive manner, at least by persuasive pressure which in effect meant the same thing. Paramountcy was exercised not only at successions but during minorities and on the alleged ground of misgovernment. In short, under the Crown's Government as under the Company's regime, the States lacked all the important attributes of independent sovereignty. But in purely internal affairs such, for instance, as the constitutions of the States, the relations between the Rulers and their subjects, separation of the Privy purse from the public revenue, organisation of the judiciary and the executive, measures designed to associate the subjects with formulation of policy, facilities for the exercise of civil liberties and the analogous matters the Crown and its Government refrained from interposing their authority.

The Paramount Power stood out as distant and apparently indifferent spectators so long as the Rulers just carried on, no matter whether their administration of internal affairs was good, bad or indifferent. They intervened only when British imperial interests were at stake or when the machinery was on the point of collapse or when gross barbarities were committed. Bad or poor government was a tolerable nuisance ; a government that became a menace to British sovereignty or proved otherwise undesirable was made to yield. The Rulers were in no sense royal sovereigns; the States were treated as loyal sovereignties. Throughout both the periods it was recognised that the Paramount Power was entitled to act in the interests of the Empire, in the interests of India and, what is of special significance, in the interests of the States themselves. If the treaty or sanad was no guide, necessity was the law. Where the treaty or sanad proved a handicap in the prosecution of the Paramount Power's policy in any given situation, it was no more than a mere scrap of paper.

It has been argued that since paramountcy is based, not on common law or statute, but upon treaties, engagements and sanads, supplemented by usage and practice of the Political Department, the relationship between the Crown and the States is *consensual*.[1] What the authors of this doctrine precisely mean by "consensual" is not clear. The view they have taken of the relationship seems rather *pro forma* than substantial. It is consensual in the sense that consent is presumed ; it is not consensual in the sense that the Ruler's consent must be given where it is essential to any desired or necessary modification of the compact. As Henry Maine wrote in 1864 in his minute on Kathiawar: "A sovereign who possesses the whole of this aggregate (the right to make war and peace, the right to administer civil and criminal justice, the right to legislate and so forth) is called an independent sovereign ; but there is not, nor has there been, anything in international law to prevent some of those rights being lodged with one possessor, and some with another . . . . Accordingly there may be found in India every shade and variety of sovereignty, but there is only one independent sovereign—the British Government."

Opportunity was taken in connection with the Baroda case (1873-75) by Lord Northbrook to intimate to the Gaekwar the considered view the British took of their relationship with the Rulers by way of reply to the Ruler's opposition to the setting up of a Commission to investigate serious complaints against his administration. The Viceroy reminded him that "this intervention, although amply justified by the language of treaties, rests on other foundations." The "other foundations" referred to evidently meant usage, practice and the requirements of a given situation. It was common ground, particularly after the assumption of direct sovereignty by the Crown, that "the British Government is undoubtedly the Paramount Power in India, and the existence and prosperity of the Native States depend upon its fostering favour and benign protection." The Ruler of Baroda was acknowledged, as generally in the case of every other Prince, as its sovereign, but was held responsible for exercising his sovereign powers, whatever their scope, "with proper regard to his duties and obligations alike to the British Government and to his subjects." Continuing, Lord Northbrook added: "If these obli-

[1] Eddy & Lawton: *India's New Constitution*, p. 22.

gations be not fulfilled, if gross misgovernment be permitted, if substantial justice be not done to the subjects of the Baroda State, if life and property be not protected, or if the general welfare of the country and people be persistently neglected, the British Government will assuredly intervene in the manner which in its judgment may be best calculated to remove these evils and to secure good Government." Although the Viceroy's letter was addressed to the Gaekwar on a specific issue which then arose, the principles enunciated in the document apply on the whole to the Princely Order.

"Good government" which, it was proclaimed, was one of the objects aimed at on that historic occasion must, however, be understood in its peculiar context. It was not intended to imply that what was sought to be secured must in its internal set-up conform strictly to the civilised standards attained elsewhere. That was left to the discretion of the Princes concerned without prejudice to the safety of the British Empire and the interests of India as a whole.

In 1926 Lord Reading, himself a lawyer of great eminence, further explained the position in his letter to the Nizam of Hyderabad in these words :

> "The sovereignty of the British Crown is supreme in India, and therefore no Ruler of an Indian State can justifiably claim to negotiate with the British Government on an equal footing. Its supremacy is not based only upon treaties and engagements, but exists independently of them and, quite apart from its prerogative in matters relating to foreign powers and policies, it is the right and duty of the British Government, while scrupulously respecting all treaties and engagements with the Indian States, to preserve peace and good order throughout India."[1]

In further support of the propositions laid down by Lord Reading reference may be invited to the Maharana of Udaipur's forced delegation of power to his son in 1921 ; the Maharaja of Nabha's abdication in 1922 and his internment in Kodaikanal in 1928 on charges of disloyalty and seditious associations ; the Paramount Power's refusal in 1926 to permit the late Maharaja of Kashmir to pass over the heir in descent in favour of his adopted son ; the Maharaja of Indore's handing over charge to his son in 1926 ; and the Ruler of Alwar's forced absence from his State and the temporary assignment to that State of a British officer in 1933.

[1] Cmd. 3302.

In all these instances paramountcy has been vigorously asserted even to the extent of controlling succession and securing transfer of allegiance of subjects from one ruler to another.

Normally British jurisdiction does not extend to the territory of an Indian State.[1] But there are exceptions. British subjects, Indian or other, as well as foreigners sometimes reside in the States and are engaged in trade, industry, business or otherwise employed. Right up to the inauguration of Reforms under the Government of India Act, 1935, the Governor-General in Council exercised jurisdiction over them to the total or partial exclusion of the States. I say "partial exclusion" because British Indian subjects, unless they are in the service of the Crown, are generally left to the jurisdiction of the States, although thereby the prerogative of the Crown is not disturbed or taken away. Today the power hitherto exerciseable by the Governor-General in Council vests in the Representative of the Crown in its relations with the States. In certain specified territories within a State the Crown's jurisdiction applies to all persons, whether British subjects or not. Such is the case in the Berars, the residencies, the cantonments, the Government of India's railway lands, and a number of civil stations such as Rajkote. In regard to railway lands the leading case is ***Muhammad Yusuf-ud-din*** v. *Empress*[2] in which the Judicial Committee of the Privy Council held that British jurisdiction over railway lands did not relate to offences not committed thereon nor in any manner connected with the administration of railway. There are, again, cases where the jurisdiction is shared between the Crown and the States concerned, for example, in Bihar and Orissa States.

Lee-Warner has classified the Crown's jurisdiction into (i) delegated jurisdiction, (ii) residuary jurisdiction and (iii) substituted jurisdiction. Delegated jurisdiction is traceable to the requirements of Imperial defence and to the States' lack of authority in foreign affairs. Residuary jurisdiction has arisen because "the residue of jurisdictory attributes which have not been left with the Native States are exercised for them by the British Government." Substituted jurisdiction is jurisdiction which the

[1] It is open to the Crown to decide what is British territory, although the issue may be debated in courts. *Empress* v. *Keshub Mahajan* (1882), I.L.R. 8 Cal. 985.

[2] I.L.R. 25 Cal. 20 (P.C.).

Paramount Power exercises when there is failure of the normal State machinery as in the case of grave disorders or legal disability due to minority. All these jurisdictions are exercised on behalf of the Crown by the Governor-General in Council (now by the Crown's representative in relation to the Indian States) in terms of the Foreign Jurisdiction Act, 1890, and of the Indian (Foreign Jurisdiction) Order in Council, 1902. These provisions are protected by s. 294(4) of the Government of India Act, 1935. There is no derogation from the Crown's right to determine by what courts British subjects or citizens of foreign countries shall be tried in respect of offences committed in the Indian States. But it is always within its competence to relinquish any power or jurisdiction in any Indian State.

5. Legal Status of Princes and their subjects

I do not propose in this book to go into the merits of each of the typical cases of intervention which have already been referred to. What is important to bear in mind is the extensive application of the doctrine of paramountcy in what may properly be regarded as the vital internal concerns of the States. Lord Reading, of course, held out the assurance that the provisions of the treaties and engagements would be scrupulously respected. That assurance, however, was vague and misleading. The issue is, first, whether in the case of any conflict as to treaties and engagements between the British Government and a Ruler the latter has access to an independent tribunal for relief and, secondly, whether in fact the provisions of treaties and engagements are upheld in given circumstances against the political requirements of the Paramount Power. To both these points the answer is in the negative. The Paramount Power is the final judge and its decision conclusive, not being open to challenge either in the municipal sphere or at international law. Strictly speaking, it is not a justiciable matter. The position of the Rulers is admittedly anomalous. They enjoy sovereignty without being sovereigns. They are, to all intents and purposes, rulers by sufferance. It has been consistently held that matters arising out of treaties, engagements or annexations, except in so far as they may involve claims based on a business contract, fall outside the jurisdiction of courts. It was ruled, for instance, that the court could give no relief in respect of the Government of India's action in removing from office the Maharaja of Panna.[1] Similarly the Privy Council took the view two years later that the jurisdiction of the Political Department in the Kathiawar States was political and could not be taken judicial notice of.[2]

The question has often been raised in regard to the legal status of the Rulers of States and their subjects. At international law they are entitled to British protection abroad.[3] The Rulers owe allegiance to the Crown and apart from treaties, engagements or sanads and the long-established usage which together determine the character and nature of relationship between the Crown and the Rulers, the latter have been recipients of honours conferred upon them as symbols of allegiance and loyalty. Since allegiance as a rule implies subjecthood the normal inference is that the Rulers are British subjects and so, if in a distant and indirect way, are their own subjects too. Here, again, there is an anomaly. The Rulers are immune from the jurisdiction of English courts.[4] In Scotland, however, no such immunity is extended to them in respect of torts committed by them in their personal as opposed to sovereign capacity.[5] In British India their position as to civil matters is governed by the Code of Civil Procedure.[6] Under certain conditions suits lie against them. They are liable to taxation under the Government of India Act, 1935, in respect of *private property* in British India, and of *public property* used for trade.[7] In criminal matters no exemption is given by the Indian Penal Code.[8] Thus in British India the immunity extended to the Rulers is more restricted than in England.

The Government of India Act, 1935, assumes that neither the Rulers nor their subjects are British subjects and as such are not normally entitled to political rights such as franchise and eligibility for membership of the legislatures and the Services under the Crown in British India. But not being aliens either, special provisions

[1] *Maharajah Madhaba Singh* V. *Secretary of State* (1904), L. R. 31 Ind. App. 239.

[2] *Hemchand Devchand* v. *Azam Sakarlal Chotamlal* (1906) A.C. 212.

[3] As to subjects, cf. 53 and 54 Vict., C. 37, s. 15.

[4] *Statham* v. *Statham and Gaekwar of Baroda*, (1912).

[5] *Ross* v. *Sir Bhagvat Sinhjee* (1891), 19 R. 31.

[6] s. 86.

[7] s. 155.

[8] *Baroda State Railway* v. *Habib Ullah* (1933), 56 All. 828.

have been made in these respects[1] for the Rulers of the Federated States and their subjects, and also by "declarations" by the Governor-General or the Governor, as the case may be, for the Ruler of any specified non-acceding State and his subjects. The Rulers and their subjects are for internal purposes in British India neither aliens nor the Crown's subjects. Their legal status is *sui generis* —surprisingly anomalous indeed but nonetheless in accord with the trend of historical evolution.

The Cabinet Mission's proposals made in their statement of May 16, concerning the States are, like many others, vague and misleading. On one point only they have been emphatic and it is that the relationship which has hitherto existed between the Crown and the Paramount Power must undergo a necessary change. Almost in every other respect the State Paper is a bare outline from which it is extremely difficult to deduce precise conclusions. The Mission have, of course, tried to explain why they have not examined matters bearing on the States in such detail as those in regard to the Provinces. But their explanation is by no means convincing. It seems to betray a conscious effort to leave gaps lest a fuller picture should, at one end, provoke opposition to their Plan on the ground of its reactionary character and, at the other end, cause disquiet among a class who had served the British imperialist cause in war as well as in peace loyally and with unflinching devotion.

It is not quite clear whether, for example, the States shall be an integral part of the proposed Union of India and, if so, whether it is open to them to keep out of it and thus in effect veto the whole scheme. It is not also clear whether the States' participation in the Constituent Assembly is essential and, if so, whether they can by non-co-operation hold up the progress of the Assembly. Certain observations are recorded in the memorandum issued on May 22, by the Cabinet Mission and the Viceroy as well as in the correspondence that passed between the Chancellor of the Chamber of Princes and the Viceroy during the Mission's negotiations. These are significant. In elucidation of the relevant paragraph[2] of their statement of May 16, the Mission, in concurrence with the Viceroy, repeat the Prime Minister's assurance that the Crown has

[1] Cf. 26 Geo. 5. C. 2, First Schedule, Part II, para 4; Fifth Schedule. para 1 (a); and s. 262 (1) (2) (4).

[2] Para 15.

no intention to initiate any change in its relationship with the Princes without their consent. Further, "the British Government could not and will not in any circumstances transfer paramountcy to an Indian Government". The Princes would be free in their own right to take any decisions they liked in regard to their relationship with the new Indian Union, whether of the Dominion type or enjoying full and complete independence outside the British Commonwealth and Empire. During the interim period, that is, the period between the coming into operation of a new constitutional structure and the present regime paramountcy shall, however, remain vested in the Crown and its representative.

It is, further, to be noted that the setting up of a Negotiating Committee by the Princes does not mean their unqualified and wholehearted co-operation in working out the Mission's project. The Nawab of Bhopal in his letter to the Viceroy, dated June 19, wrote to say that the decision on the question whether the States should or should not join the Constituent Assembly would be taken by a General Conference of Rulers and representatives of States and would depend on the result of the negotiations between the States' Negotiating Committee and a corresponding Committee formed by the representatives of British India in the Constituent Assembly.[1] The joint statement issued by the Nawab of Bhopal and Pandit Nehru on February 9, should not be construed as having solved the complicated problems of the States. Nothing is said in that statement except that "on the basis of a general understanding arrived at, it was decided to take up the question of representation of the States in the Constituent Assembly". The two Negotiating Committees "will consider the proposed allocation as well as the method of selection of the States' representatives". What the terms of the "general understanding" referred to are one canont say. But in view of the States' Negotiating Committee's terms of reference and Pandit Nehru's proclaimed social sympathies it will, I am afraid, be extremely difficult to reconcile the objectives of the Constituent Assembly and the claims of the Princes. The doctrine of Paramountcy, the Instrument of Accession, the internal sovereignty of the States, the relations between the Princes and their peoples and other analogous issues cannot but give rise to serious, if not bitter, con-

[1] Para 4.

troversies. It is much too early to conclude that an understanding has been reached in regard to these delicate matters.

The doctrine upon which it is held that the accession of a State to an Indian Union cannot take place otherwise than by the voluntary act of its Ruler is indeed interesting but somewhat novel. It follows from the theory that paramountcy is not based either on common law or statute, thus rendering the Crown and its advisers ineffective in the matter of altering the status by a unilateral act. Theoretically this is clearly repugnant to the whole conception of the structure of the British State which postulates the so-called omnipotence of the King in Parliament. There is nothing in the legal or extralegal nexus of any kind that cannot be touched either at common law and, where it fails, by statute. The issue, however, is not one of retention or transfer of paramountcy which as an instrument of intervention is in essence a historical category and came to be evolved out of the political necessity of those times. The question today is one of eliminating this outmoded doctrine and of setting a new pattern of structure of the State in accord with the increasing requirements of democracy.

Paramountcy is a term which does not seem susceptible of a precise definition. As the Butler Committee[1] wrote :

> We have endeavoured as others before us have endeavoured to find some formula which will cover the exercise of paramountcy and we have failed as others before us have failed to do so. The reason for such failure is not far to seek. Conditions alter rapidly in a changing world. Imperial necessity and new conditions may at any time raise unexpected situations. Paramountcy must remain paramount ; it must fulfil its obligations defining or adapting itself according to the shifting necessities of the time and the progressive development of the States. Nor need the States take alarm at this conclusion. Through paramountcy and paramountcy alone have grown up and flourished those strong benign relations between the Crown and the Princes on which at all times the States rely. On paramountcy and paramountcy alone can the States rely for their preservation though the generations that are to come. Through paramountcy is pushed aside the danger of destruction or annexation.

These words offer no guidance except that the Princes are asked to rely upon the "benign" imperial authority for their protection. They contain a hint, however, that paramountcy gathers

[1] Cmd. 3302.

new meanings in the light of "imperial necessity" and new conditions. What "imperial necessity" means is for the Imperial Crown and its Ministers to decide. What is implied by "new conditions" and how or when the exercise of paramountcy is to be adjusted to them are, again, matters within their sole discretion. Paramountcy is a curious amalgam of the Crown's of rights and obligations : rights which restrict the so-called sovereignty of the Rulers and obligations which the Crown owes them. In the rights are included intervention in cases of gross misrule, adjudication upon disputes between the States, the overthrow of a Ruler in certain circumstances and the determination of succession or adoption in disputed cases. The obligations extend to the protection of the States against foreign aggression and internal turmoil and the maintenance of their territorial integrity. But where a conflict arises between the exercise of prerogatives and the discharge of obligations the latter is superseded to the extent of conflict. That is the essence of paramountcy.

I know that Counsel engaged by some of the States to present their case before the Butler Committee took an entirely different view. They asserted that paramountcy was the result of agreement ; that the parties to the agreement were the Crown on one side and the States on the other ; that the States transferred to the Crown the conduct of their foreign relations and the responsibility of defence ; that in consideration of this the Crown undertook to protect the States and their Rulers against all internal and external dangers ; that paramountcy could not be transferred by the Crown without their consent. This doctrine of consensual relationship presumes, first, that the East Indian Company or the Crown negotiated treaties with independent sovereign States. That is not correct. Most of the States never held international status. "Nearly all of them," to quote the Butler Committee, "were subordinate to the Moghal Empire, the Mahratta supremacy or the Sikh kingdom and dependent on them." Further, "Some were rescued, others were created by the British." It presumes, secondly, that the Crown's prerogative in this regard cannot be modified or abolished by the British Government. That is not correct either. As a general rule paramountcy was exercised by the British Government in India through the Governor-General in Council until the coming into operation of the Government of India Act, 1935, by or under which the

Crown Representative in relation to the States acts in the name of the Crown either on his own responsibility or under instructions from the British Government. On the abolition or withdrawl of British sovereignty from India, which the Cabinet Mission's scheme envisages, paramountcy, I submit, goes to the Successor Government which in the present case will be the proposed Indian Union, whether or not the States accede to the Union. In any event, they do not become independent sovereign States at international law on the attainment by India of complete independence.

The Cabinet Mission might have thought that it was not their concern but that of the peoples of India and their representatives, if they so cared, to deal with the issue or that they had not the requisite moral or physical sanction, even if they had the will, to interpose their doubtful authority. If they really felt like that, the reservations they proposed in connection with the Constituent Assembly, especially those relating to the protection of minorities and the conclusion of a treaty to provide for matters arising out of the new situation were out of place and clearly impertinent. It is true that the Mission's proposals are refreshingly free from the jarring Churchillian phraseology about Great Britain's imperial obligations, but throughout the negotiations there was not the least suggestion that the so-called British obligations had lapsed or could not be pressed for consideration. Whatever might have been the historical necessity of the treaties with the States and the character of the obligations arising therefrom, it cannot be seriously claimed that they embody immutable principles which can neither be modified nor be completely abrogated except with the assent of the Princes. If the Paramount Power has any obligations today, these are not to the Rulers but to their subjects who constitute the human material for construction of a new democracy. In the conscientious discharge of these obligations the least the Cabinet Mission could do was to tell the Princes plainly that they were no longer entitled to protection and that their future depended entirely upon the peoples of India as a whole.

CHAPTER IV

THE CONSTITUENT ASSEMBLY—A CHALLENGE OR COMPROMISE ?

1. The Change of State-Power

It has already been shown that in abrogation of Britain's traditional India policy reserving to Parliament the unfettered right not only to frame India's constitution but, if need be, to legislate for India or any part thereof the British Government have since 1940 yielded to the pressure of public opinion and of events abroad by acknowledging that it is for Indians themselves to lay down their own fundamental laws. In Lord Linlithgow's time under Mr. Churchill's Tory-controlled Government this acknowledgment was recorded in vague, general terms.[1] Two years later, however, a machinery described as the constitution-making body was envisaged.[2] In the British Cabinet Mission's Statement of May 16, 1946, while repeating at the outset the expression "constitution-making machinery"[3] the Cabinet Mission have several times referred to it as the Constituent Assembly.[4] For the British Government this is new and hitherto forbidden *mantram*. It is, however, not without significance that the expressions vary almost from paragraph to paragraph. They use "constitution-making machinery", "Assembly to decide a new constitutional structure", "final Constituent Assembly", "Union Constituent Assembly", and then simply "Assembly", according as they seemingly fit in with different angles from which the problem is approached.

Before taking up this aspect of the problem which is of a technical nature, I propose to deal with the broad political issue. Is the machinery as envisaged in the State Paper, for instance, a Constituent Assembly in the real sense of the term? Is the convening of a Constituent Assembly necessarily and in terms of historical experience a revolutionary act? Is the devising of this machinery by

[1] Cf. Lord Linlithgow's statement of August 8, 1940.

[2] The Cripps proposals, clause (d).

[3] Para 17.

[4] Paras 19 (ii) (vii), 20 and 22.

the existing ruling authority as an instrument of transfer of power to a colonial people a feasible and practical proposition? Two conflicting views have been taken of the scope, functions and basic structure of the body proposed in the Mission's statement. The Congress leadership, on the one hand, has taken the Cabinet Mission at their word and interpreted their long-term plan as on the whole a genuine offer of independence to India, thereby reconciling itself to the possibility of a deed of transfer on the basis of agreement between the ruling class and the ruled. On the other hand, there are groups within the Congress and without and also individuals who tenaciously maintain that freedom cannot be achieved by compromise with the ruling class, especially when that class has no manner of affinity with the children of the soil. History tends to support the latter view, but on the other side it may be argued that times change and that history hardly ever, if at all, repeats itself.

In the Continent of Europe the State-power has as a normal rule changed hands by seizure of power as opposed to transfer by agreement through such instruments as the French Constituent Assembly convened in the wake of the Revolution of 1789, the February-March bourgeois-democratic experiment in Russia in 1917, and its transformation by a Bolshevik armed insurrection in October-November under Lenin's leadership. The Constituent Assembly is in a sense Europe's contribution to the ethics and technique of a definite phase of social revolution. It grows out of conflict, conflict between feudal autocracy and the rising bourgeoisie, between a dominant nation and oppressed and exploited nations or between an alien power and colonial peoples. Forms of this conflict vary; nor is its content always the same. In France the struggle mainly was between the monarchy and feudal barons on one side and the rising bourgeoisie, the lower middle classes and philosophers of the Revolution on the other. In Central and Eastern Europe it was a struggle between the dominant nations at the metropolis and the oppressed border nationalities. In India the conflict is primarily between an alien power and the subject peoples and also, on a relatively long view, between the alien power's allies, partners and agents in the States and in Big Business and the toiling masses in factory and field supported, sustained and inspired by a large body of "intellectuals" and others drawn from the so-called lower middle classes. Confusion admittedly exists as to the historic rôle of the Constituent Assembly. The reason, however, is not far to seek. In the typical cases dealt with at length below (France, Russia, U.S.A., the Dominions and Southern Ireland) the results yielded have not been similar in form or content ; the modes of approach have been different too.

2. French Revolution of 1789

In France as a result of the Revolution of 1789 the Constituent Assembly, without indigenous historical precedents to rely upon, as in Britain or the American Colonies, proceeded to frame a Charter of Rights in accordance with the principles enunciated by philosophers and political thinkers, particularly the stimulating social philosophy of the eighteenth century and Rousseau's *Contract Social*. Principles such as the sovereign right of the people and vindication of the ideal and dignity of mankind and the equalitarian slogans of Liberty, Fraternity and Equality at any time constitute a source of inspiration to the common man all the world over. It is not surprising that despite the failure of the Assembly and its accents of strife and conflict the Declaration of the Rights of Man should have made a deep and abiding impression upon all oppressed peoples and added a new chapter in the crowded but chequered history of human progress since written in different parts of the globe. The constitution formed in 1791, though essentially based on hatred of the *ancien regime*, contained certain durable elements ; and it is significant that for long eighty years from 1791 to 1870 during which France devised no less than eleven constitutions the fundamental principles of the Revolution of 1789 have served as the keynote of almost every instrument of the organic laws in its philosophical aspect, although there has been from time to time shifting of emphasis from monarchy to republicanism ; from republicanism to the consulate ; from the consulate to monarchy ; and again from monarchy to republicanism.

In 1875, however, a set of constitutional laws was framed with no logical basis or orderly completeness, which have, with consequential changes, endured right up to the end of the pre-war epoch. The Constitution of 1791 was nevertheless a middle-class organ of State-power directed principally against the King and privileged orders. At the initial stages, however, the King as such was not the target of attack. The States General was summered by him at Versailles on May 1, 1789, in response to the pblic demand. The election was not fought on the issue of abolition of the monarchy. In June the nobility and the clergy came to be associated with the Third Estate under the King's Command and the National Assembly so formed called itself the Constituent Assembly. The King remained even when the Bastille was stormed in July. The Constitution framed in 1791 was monarchical in form. In September the Assembly finished its work with Louis XVI as head of the State. Subsequently the King was overthrown and universal suffrage proclaimed. That was in August, 1792. In September the National Convention drafted a Republican Constitution by abolishing monarchy. Louis XVI was executed in January, 1793. It is important, however, to note that whatever the King's vicissitudes of fortune during this stormy period, it was fundamentally a class struggle. But the bourgeoisie who for the moment came to take charge of affairs refused to take any consistent stand on principles. Theirs was a tactic of expediency bordering on opportunism. They sought to devise a compromise between revolution and reaction, between principles and traditions, in their attempt to solve political and social problems with which they had been confronted. The so-called separation of the three powers over which many writers have since waxed eloquent led to suspicion and friction and, in the long run, to an increasing encroachment of the legislative upon the executive power. The artificial distinction between "active" and "passive" citizens made on the basis of a direct contribution equal to three days' labour violated the principle of equality of the Declaration of Rights in favour of the wealthier classes and destroyed for about half a century the solidarity of the middle classes and the proletariat.

It should be remembered that the French Constituent Assembly was in essence the fruit of a bourgeois-democratic revolution. It was not an instrument of proletarian dictatorship or even of social democracy. In 1789, the objective aimed at was the overthrow of absolutism and the nobility. The bourgeoisie had confidence in their strength and could afford to unite with the peasantry and in fact made common cause with them without grave menace to the stability of their rule. This alliance contributed to the victory of the revolution, although once firmly in the saddle the bourgeoisie betrayed their allies. By contrast in 1848, the issue was one of the proletariat overthrowing the bourgeoisie with the help of the petty-bourgeois strata whose betrayal brought about the defeat of the revolution. The Revolution of 1789, according to Karl Marx, proceeded in an ascending line whereas that of 1848 proceeded in a descending line. In 1789, the mass of the people, with the bourgeoisie at the top, swept away absolutism. In 1848, on the other hand, petty-bourgeois democracy sided with the bourgeoisie and betrayed the proletariat and helped defeat the revolution.[1]

3. Russian Revolutions of 1905 and 1917[2]

Far more interesting are the great experiments in Russia in revolutionary seizure of power. It must be admitted, however, that the philosophy of the Rationalists and Humanists of the eighteenth century which was the core of the French Revolution provided the background of the abortive Russian Revolution of 1905 and, to a large extent, of the February-March Revolution of 1917. The change from February-March to October-November marked a decisive step forward in the emancipation of the toiling masses. On January 22, 1905, there was a terrible blood-bath. The army vanquished the workers and others who had risen in revolt against the *Tsar* and his Government. There were shootings and firings and the Tsar's henchmen cynically exclaimed : "We have taught them a good lesson !" In a sense it was a lesson that the tormented peoples laid to heart. The revolution was spreading from city to city, from village to village. The Tsar and his men were shaking and then as some sort of a sop they offered certain economic concessions. Thousands of workers pledged themselves to the overthrow of the Tsarist Government. They said that "Bloody Sunday" must be avenged. They were not all Social Democrats. Among these thousands there were hundreds of people who had hitherto been loyal and devoted to the person of the Tsar. A wave of strikes swept the land. The number of

[1] For further treatment read Lenin's *Selected Works*, Vol 5. pp. 154-163.

[2] Cf. *The History of the Civil War in the U.S.S.R.* (Vol. Two). *The Great Proletarian Revolution* (October-November 1917).

strikers rose by leaps and bounds. These factory strikers were joined by railway workers and postal and telegraph employees. They stirred the whole country. The peasantry began to line up. There were military uprisings too.

In August, 1905, the Tsar offered popular representation, the so-called *Bulygin Duma,* on a restricted franchise. This legislative body was, however, to have no legislative powers. It was to be an Advisory Council. The offer was intended "to allay the unrest of the people, to force the revolutionary class to cease, or at least to slacken, its struggle". It was welcomed by the liberals but rejected by the people. The Social Democrats' reply to the Tsar was, "Down with the *Advisory Duma !* Down with the Tsarist Government! Not the Tsar, but a Provisional Revolutionary Government must convoke the first real popular Representative Assembly in Russia"! It was not a Constituent Assembly by agreement ; it presupposed seizure of power. It was not to be convened by the then ruling authority ; it was to be summoned instead by a Provisional Government formed by a revolutionary insurrection.

Like the French Revolution of 1789, the Russian Revolution of 1905 was in its social content a bourgeois-democratic revolution. It aimed at a democratic republic, an eight-hour day, confiscation of all the big estates of the nobility, civil liberties and universal and equal suffrage, in short, all those political and social measures for which the French revolutionaries had fought and which they had practically achieved. But unlike the French Revolution in which the bourgeoisie made common cause with petty-bourgeois democracy for the overthrow of the monarchy and the nobility, it was in the form and technique of struggle a proletarian revolution, first, because the proletariat was the vanguard of the movement and, secondly, because the economic and social strikes which soon developed with a mass political strike were deliberately employed for rousing the masses and paralysing the State-power and its apparatus. It differed materially from the revolutionary movement which for the first time in the history of Russia had been directed against Tsarism in 1825 in that the latter had been confined to noblemen.

From 1825 to 1881, when Alexander II was assassinated by the terrorists, the struggle was carried on and led by middel-class intellectuals. The experiment was more or less analogous to the heroic Bengal uprising from 1905 to 1919. From the latter year onwards Gandhiji evolved in his way a new technique of mass struggle in India, took charge of affairs and imparted a new tone to the tactical and credal foundations of the Indian movement for national liberation. As in Bengal, so in Russia, these determined and high-spirited fighters amazed the world by their heroic deeds in the dogged pursuit of "Liberty or Death". But in neither case was it a mass uprising or popular revolution like the Russian Revolution of 1905. In either case, again, the methods of struggle were rather romantic than scientifically planned.

The Russian experiment of 1905, however, sustained a temporary defeat: temporary because it was the prologue, as Lenin put it, to the coming European revolution. There is no doubt that it made a moving and passionate appeal to the oppressed peoples of both Europe and Asia, that its mass character, its driving force and its method of struggle in their irresistible sweep affected the broad masses of humanity and constituted alike a source of inspiration to the defenders of revolutionary uprisings all the world over and a challenge to the ruling classes, the exploiting bourgeoisie, the feudal tyrants and their allies in all grades of the reactionary social cadre.[1]

Efforts were subsequently made by the Tsar and his advisers after this reverse to clothe pure autocracy with democratic forms. A bicameral legislature was brought into being: the Imperial Council and the Duma. By manipulation of the electoral colleges franchise was restricted to the propertied classes in violation of the manifesto of 1905. The Council and the Duma enjoyed concurrent powers, the initiative to legislate being in fact exercised by the latter. All matters of defence were excluded from the jurisdiction of the Duma. A considerable portion of the budget was, as in India, non-voted or not open to discussion and modification. Even where it was subject to the vote the final authority vested in the Tsar's Ministers who could restore the rejected budget and impose new taxes. Ministers were responsible to the Tsar, and not to the Duma. The Tsar had power, again as in India, to promulgate ordinances when the Duma was not in session, and to prorogue or dissolve that body as often as he liked. He had the right in his sole discretion to suspend the constitution by declaring a state of

[1] Read Lenin's *The Beginning of the Revolution in Russia—Lecture on the 1905 Revolution* reproduced in *A Handbook of Marxism* (Victor Gallancz Ltd.), 1935, pp. 609-634.

siege. The system worked creakily and under the stress of war which broke out in 1914 it completely broke down.

In March the Tsarist Government was overthrown. Then a Committee of the Duma set up a Provisional Government. A succession of precarious and unstable Ministries followed. A large number of delegates belonging to the Socialist Party co-operated with the Provisional Government on the basis of coalition, but it was soon found that the coalition was only a makeshift. The Ministries continued the war against the Central Powers while pleading with the Allies for "peace without annexations or indemnities". The underlying motive was to secure peace not to build Russia anew but to suppress rebellion and restore the country's basic social structure. It was announced that arrangements would soon be made for the election of a Constituent Assembly to frame the constitution of the land.

Meanwhile the Soviet Councils which had taken the initiative in organising the rebellion of 1905 came out of their shell and began to function openly. In June, 1917, an All-Russian Congress of Soviets met at Petrograd. It agreed in September to the election of a Democratic Council to constitute a Provisional Parliament to which the Government would be held responsible. Once again it was a united democratic front and, what is important to note, a purely Socialist organisation itself, the Congress of Soviets for the moment acquiesced in this device. Within the Congress, however, there was conflict between Bolsheviks and Mensheviks and petty-bourgeois liberals. The former emerged as the more effective militant force. Their slogan was "All power to the Soviets." In pursuance of their programme they organised themselves, and on the night of November 6-7, 1917, by a sudden, surprise and lightning attack took possession of Petrograd and placed under arrest the members of the Provisional Government. Prime Minister Kerensky had already left the Winter Palace.

The elections to the Constituent Assembly were completed during the first week of the October-November Revolution. Even at the Second Congress of Soviets which closed on October 27, it was resolved that "for the purpose of administering the country, pending the convocation of the Constituent Assembly, a Provisional Workers' and Peasants' Government shall be formed to be known as the Council of People's Commissars. Thus came into being the Soviet Government. The Bolsheviks under Lenin's leadership took the line that in view of the rapid and far-reaching developments in the situation the Constituent Assembly had outlived its usefulness. Accordingly they dissolved the Assembly on the very first day of its meeting, that is, on January 18, 1918. On that day the Third All-Russian Congress of Soviets met and adopted the declaration of the rights of the working classes. Thus the Congress of Soviets which replaced the Constituent Assembly provided the nucleus of that gigantic Socialist machine which has alike been the pride of its peoples and a death-defying challenge to its enemies. Previously on November 30, 1917, a detachment of sailors had stopped the "unofficial conference" of the members of the Constituent Assembly sponsored by the Constituent Democratic Party.

The Bolshevik thesis on the two phases of the Russian Revolution of 1917 had been enunciated by Lenin in 1915. The proletariat would fight with determination for a democratic republic and confiscation of lands. They would utilise to the fullest extent the revolutionary potentialities and rally the "non-proletarian masses of the people" for the purpose of ridding Russia, by the capture of power, of military feudal imperialism represented by Tsarism. Opportunity must, immediately upon the victory of this bourgeois-democratic revolution, be taken to quicken the pace of the revolutionary tempo and achieve the Socialist revolution.[1] In the course of a report made to the Sixth Congress of the Bolshevik Party in August, 1917, Stalin dealt at length with the developments that had taken place since March, and made a moving appeal for driving the revolution forward to its completion. He wrote that a coalition of four forces had brought about the February-March Revolution: the proletariat, the peasantry, the liberal bourgeoisie and capitalists of the Allied countries. The latter two forces, as Stalin put it, wanted a little revolution for the sake of a big war[2]. The proletariat and the peasantry wanted to bring the imperialist war to an end and seize power by the overthrow of the big landlords and the bourgeoisie. A Coalition Government had emerged from the mass movement, but the bourgeoisie soon made use of it as an instrument for deceiving the masses and promoting their class interests.

[1] Read Lenin's *Selected Works*, vol. 5, pp. 162-63.

[2] Read *Preparing for October* (the Minutes of the VIth Congress of the Bolshevik Party), Modern Books Ltd., 1931.

Apropos of the revolutionary crisis in Russia, Lenin took care to examine the rôle of each class affected by the situation. The Tsar and the feudal landlords preferred an understanding with the German monarchy to the transfer of power to the liberal bourgeoisie. The liberal bourgeoisie wanted to frighten the Tsar and the nobility into sharing power with them. The revolutionary proletariat were determined to consummate the revolution by wresting power from the Tsarist Government and the bourgeoisie. These lines were clear. Confused and puzzled and deceived, however, the petty bourgeois strata of society did not know what precisely they were about in that crisis of history. They were driven forward and backward by two opposite tendencies. "The petty bourgeoisie, however, i.e., the vast mass of the barely awakened population of Russia," wrote Lenin, "is groping blindly in the wake of the bourgeoisie, a captive to nationalist prejudice, on the one hand driven to revolution by the unprecedented, unheard of horrors and miseries of war, the high cost of living, ruin, imprisonment and starvation, and on the other hand glancing back at every step to the idea of defence of the fatherland, or to the idea of the State integrity of Russia, or to the idea of small peasant prosperity, to be achieved by a victory over Tsarism and Germany, but without a victory over capitalism."[1]

Stalin followed up this thesis and observed: "Our misfortune is that Russia is a petty bourgeois country, who follows the lead of the Socialist-Revolutionaries, who are compromising with the cadets, so that until the peasantry is disillusioned with the idea of compromise between the upper and lower classes we shall suffer and the revolution will fail."[2] But both these Bolshevik leaders knew that the rapid sharpening of the crisis was an objective factor of the situation which was fraught with immense revolutionary possibilities. Lenin in particular called upon the proletariat to push forward the petty bourgeoisie and utilise all its forces in order to push forward, when life compelled it to move to the Left. Stalin energetically countered the theory that to talk of a Socialist revolution in Russia, when capitalism was only feebly developed, was Utopian chatter and asserted that the revolution started in February-March could not be stopped half-way. He

[1] Read Lenin's *Selected Works*, Vol. 5, p. 151.

[2] Read *Preparing for October* (the Minutes of the VIth Congress of the Bolshevik Party), Modern Books Ltd., 1931.

admitted that the defeatists and waverers "would be right if it were not for the war, if it were not for the devastation, if the foundations of national economy had not been shaken." But these factors, he argued, were bound to accelerate the transition from the bourgeois-democratic phase of the revolution to its socialist phase. He denounced the Provisional Government as a puppet, a wretched screen behind which stood "the cadets, the military clique and Allied capital, the three mainstays of the counter-revolution."

The question was not merely one of convening a Constituent Assembly. The question was: who was to convene it? The Bolsheviks were convinced that that historical rôle belonged to the proletariat in the interregnum between March and November. If followed that it was not for the bourgeois-democratic Constituent Assembly but for the Congress of Soviets to harness the fruits of the revolution in the task of setting the pattern of a new State. Thus from the democratic revolution of February-March and the Constituent Assembly they proceeded to the Socialist revolution of October-November and the Congress of Soviets. While maintaining that the demand for a Constituent Assembly in the given situation was a perfectly legitimate part of the programme of what he called the revolutionary social democracy Lenin made it clear from the beginning of the Revolution of 1917[1] that the republic of Soviets was a higher form of democracy than the ordinary bourgeois republic with a Constituent Assembly. He admitted, however, that in a bourgeois-controlled social order the Constituent Assembly constituted the highest form of democracy. The change from "All power to the Constituent Assembly" to "All power to the Soviets" had been planned in anticipation of the events that followed with a view to securing a wider and more enduring base for social emancipation.

4. The American War of Independence

I think that a rapid survey of the developments that led to the independence of the American colonies is not out of place here, although it was in form a new pattern of movement that the Americans evolved. There were three distinct phases of the

[1] Read Lenin's *Thesis on the Constituent Assembly* printed in *Pravda*, January 8, 1918.

struggle: (1) the Congress phase of 1774-76; (2) the Confederal phase of 1776-87; and (3) the Federal Convention phase of 1787-89. It is admitted that this is a rough classification. The first was one of revolt against the "mother-country". The second was one of consolidating the immediate achievements of the revolution by a loose compact of confederal relations as a war emergency measure. The third was one of projecting the general urge for national solidarity into the institutional structure without prejudice, however, to the "rights" of States. Except when by a successful revolution the American colonies wrested power from the British Crown and its Government and proclaimed themselves to be independent sovereign States, the changes effected were more or less formal and confined generally to the inter-State relations upon the basis either of a loose confederacy or of a more compact federation. In the peculiar context of the present Indian situation in which the main and primary conflict is directed towards the liquidation of British rule, the first of these three periods is far more important inasmuch as it offers lessons of experience in our struggle for national freedom either by seizure of power or, as has been proposed, by agreement between the ruling metropolitan power and the peoples of India. I do not suggest that the American example should be followed in this country in spirit and in letter. Nor do I presume the inevitability of the Indian struggle taking the shape or form of the American movement for independence. Yet I believe that it is useful to examine the British Cabinet Mission's proposals in a historical perspective.

I contend further that for the very simple and obvious reason that the American war was fought for the overthrow of British rule as distinguished from the French and Russian revolutions which aimed at the capture of power from the indigenous sources of tyrannical power the New World's revolutionary experiment may have its special appeal to us in India. The French and Russian revolutions were in the main class struggles whereas the American war of independence was the proud and rebellious child's overthrow of the parent and forcible possession of the inheritance. On a long view, however, the latter was, of course, fraught with far-reaching social potentialities not only by the impact of the "jerk" but also on account of the fundamental philosophy of the revolution. In India, however, the struggle is primarily, as in the American Colonies, national-*cum*-territorial and, in the final analysis, social in the broad sense of the term, as in France and Russia. Therefore, we in India may well learn a great deal from all these revolutions.

In the early sixties of the eighteenth century with increasing prosperity, political maturity and under new urges some two million colonists in America were impatient and became restless under restraint from across the other side of the Atlantic. They resented the encroachments of the Parliament at Westminster and began to challenge its right to tax and legislate for them without consent. The Stamp Act precipitated an open conflict. But even with the repeal of that Act the problem in a way remained. The Rockingham Government was succeeded by a new Ministry. It was a "mosaic" Ministry, as Edmund Burke called it ; a "curious show", as that great philosopher-statesman denounced it. This Ministry added fuel to the fire by its excessive cleverness, its indiscretion and its provocative stress on the sovereignty of Parliament.

New and other troubles were brewing. By 1774 progressives, radicals and advanced thinkers in the colonies were moving very fast indeed to a position of challenge. The Virginian colonists chose delegates to consider the situation. Thomas Jefferson wrote a "Summary View" of the rights of British America and presented it to the delegation. Apart from the immediate grievances, certain broad principles of social organisation rendered so popular by the seventeenth century rationalists were set forth in vivid and resonant language. That Government originated in consent, that when consent was lacking it lost its moral and legal basis, that the ruled had the inherent right to revolt against an intolerable tyranny—these and other analogous doctrines were enunciated.

In the summer of 1774 the Virginian call for a colonial Congress evoked a warm and almost instantaneous response and a Congress was ushered into existence. Delegates were chosen by committees of correspondence. The Congress was in effect "a meeting of the committees of correspondence of the several colonies". These committees were charged with the task of maintaining popular rights and, if need be, organising and leading a revolution. The Congress, however, did not aim at revolution immediately, but it was, to all intents and purposes, an extra-legal and, what is more important, revolutionary body. The delegates to the Congress were not chosen in the majority of cases in a normal manner by the colonial legislatures. Recourse to this procedure was avoided to circumvent the obstruction of Governors and the opposition of conservative elements of the population. In early September the Congress met at Philadelphia. The resolution adopted at the initial stage was in the nature of a compromise. But the tension was acute ; the spirit of revolt was in the air. For the time being, however, it was a revolt against abuses of the sovereign authority of Parliament, a revolt designed, in the first instance, within the Empire and under the Crown, to assert the rights of the colonies and their peoples on the basis of the Charters and the fundamental principles of English law.

In the meantime save in one or two cases were set up Governments within Governments or, more precisely, Governments outside of the purely legal authorities—committees, conventions and conferences. During this period of more than a year and a half these extra-legal bodies to a large extent paralysed the machinery as by "law" constituted. It was yet a rebellion of protest, if I may use that expression, and not a revolutionary act of secession from the Emipre. But revolution was in the air. The conflict between the King and his Government and the colonists was interminable and irreconcilable. It deepened. The base widened. In April, 1775, the peak was reached when the remnants of the British troops retreated to the protection of their men at Boston. Thus the war began. In May, 1775, the Congress again met at Philadelphia in the midst of the war. It demanded peace with honour. It would break off, if necessary, from Britain by war. Accordingly the Congress proceeded to organise an army, appointed George Washington Commander-in-Chief, and at the same time addressed a petition to King George III. No adequate response came. What was offered came much too late. What was more, the King and his Government were not prepared to abandon the right of Parliament to "bind the colonies and people of America . . . in all cases whatsoever". That was Lord North's "Conciliatory Resolution" passed in the Commons in February, 1775, and placed before the Congress in May. The gesture was rejected in July, and in the following month George III issued his historic "Proclamation of Rebellion".

It looks rather curious that the colonists continued the war against the King after the proclamation not as armed rebels owning no allegiance to the Crown, but as the latter's colonial subjects. The explanation, however, seems to be that the revolutionaries took the line that theirs was a revolt not against the Crown as such but against the Crown's flagrant violation of the cherished principles of government by compact. Even in the spring of 1776 there was no formal declaration of independence. But in fact the colonies were no longer dependencies, but independent sovereign States. In May a Virginian Convention convened without formal legal authority empowered its delegates in the Congress to sponsor a declaration of independence of the colonies. In June the following resolutions were moved and placed before the Congress:

> 1. That these United Colonies are, and of right ought to be, Free and Independent States, that they are Absolved from all Allegiance to the British Crown, and that all communication between them and the State of Great Britain is and ought to be totally dissolved; and that as Free and Independent States, they have full power to levy War, conclude Peace, contract Alliances, establish Commerce, and do all other Acts and things which Independent States may of right do.
>
> 2. That it is expedient forthwith to take the most effectual measures for forming foreign alliances.
>
> 3. That a plan of confederation be prepared and transmitted to the respective Colonies for their consideration and adoption

On July 1, 1776, the resolution proposing the declaration of independence was debated in a Committee of the whole House. The final vote was taken the next day, the result showing that only three delegates recorded their disapproval. On July 4, the declaration was formally adopted and on August 2, it was signed by members of the Congress.

The declaration shows that the American colonists, as in the case of leaders of the French Revolution, were largely influenced by the dominant political philosophy of those times. Rousseau, Locke and others inspired them. It was the philosophy of natural rights and compact. Man, they assumed, was born free and only by agreement was government set up with limitations, reservations and restraints for the common good. Where there was a breach of the compact the right to revolt was not only justified, but necessary and desirable. The authority of kings and kingdoms, of governors and governments, whatever its scope and sphere, was "derived", and not "original", a doctrine which is of pivotal importance in all institutional changes that have been brought about by revolutions, not to speak of the American constitution. The principles enunciated by the political philosophers were interpreted by leaders of the American Revolution thus: "We hold these truths as self-evident, that all men are created equal, that they are endowed by their Creator with certain inalienable Rights, that among these are Life, Liberty and the pursuit of Happiness."

While one must not disregard or reject these principles as lyrical effusions the broad fact cannot be ignored that the revolution was principally directed against the King and the tyranny of what the American colonists then began to look upon as an alien Government. It is a mistake to think that at that stage there was any serious attempt to evolve an elaborate and comprehensive scheme of government or give specific guarantees as to equality of economic competence or of political power among different classes of the community. It was not a movement for the establishment of social democracy as such or for projecting the desires, impulses and urges of the revolution into the organs of the State power. It was, again as in France in 1789, or as in Russia in 1905, a bourgeois-democratic revolution. It differed from both in that it was organised to capture power by the overthrow of a territorially alien authority. By contrast with its Russian counterpart of 1905, it was far more restricted in form and technique of struggle for the reason that the bourgeosie rather than the lower strata of society was the vanguard of the revolution and also because the instrument of military uprisings as distinguished from mass economic and political strikes was employed for the purpose of overthrowing the ruling power.

After formal severance of connection with the British Crown and Westminster the colonies proceeded to address themselves to inter-State relations and the structure upon which those relations were to be based. It may be recalled that in one of the resolutions sponsored at the Congress at the instance of a Virginian delegate it was proposed that steps should be taken for the formation of a confederation of the States. The impelling, urgent and immediate necessity was, of course, the war which had to be waged against a relentless and organised enemy. But there were problems of peace too, which had to be faced. So the articles of confederation were drafted and adopted by the Congress on November 15, 1777. The Congress being more in the nature of a constituent convention than a Constituent Assembly with requisite sanction to enforce its decisions, the articles were referred to the States for their consideration. They were endorsed and ratified by each of the thirteen States. The last to come into the confederacy was the State of Maryland which accorded its approval on March 1, 1787. The main principles underlying the Confederation were stated thus:

> *Art. I.* The style of this Confederation shall be "United States of America".
>
> *Art. II.* Each State retains its sovereignty, freedom and independence, and every Power, Jurisdiction and Right which is not by this Confederation expressly delegated to the United States in Congress assembled.
>
> *Art. III.* The said States hereby severally enter into a firm league of friendship with each other, for their common defence, the security of their liberties, and their mutual and general welfare, binding themselves to assist each other, against all force offered to, or attacks made upon them or any of them on account of religion, sovereignty, trade, or any other pretence whatever.

For the duration of the war no serious conflict arose naturally because all these thirteen States were determined to bring it to a successful end. On the cessation of hostilities, however, the institutional gaps in the machine revealed themselves in consequence of the inadequacy of the confederacy to tackle the complex problems of life and organisation that emerged from economic ruin and devastation. Alexander Hamilton went so far as to canvass energetically the merging of the State sovereignties into a strong unitary State. But the idea of a Central Leviathan was repugnant to the prevailing bias in favour of the State residuum. Accordingly the Congress decided on February 21, 1787, that "on the second Monday in May next a convention of delegates who shall have been appointed by the several States be held at Philadelphia for the sole and express purpose of revising the Articles of Confederation and reporting to Congress and several legislatures such alterations and provisions therein as shall, when agreed to in Congress and confirmed by the States, render the federal constitution adequate to the exigencies of government and the preservation of the Union".

George Washington, who was the Commander-in-Chief during the war, was chosen President of the Convention as proposed in the resolution of the Congress. Delegates attended from every State except Rhode Island. By agreement the Convention went beyond the terms of reference in two respects. First, it took upon itself the responsibility, contrary to the directives of the Congress, to draft a whole constitution instead of restricting itself to the revision of confederal relations. Secondly, it decided that the Draft Constitution should be referred, not as proposed by the Congress, to the Congress itself and the several legislatures, but to the people in each of the States. The convention by agreement seemed to have assumed sovereign powers *vis-a-vis* the Congress which had brought it into being and the legislatures of States ; it transformed itself into a Drafting Committee in relation to the peoples of the States.

The constitution as drawn up by the Convention, together with the resolution and the President's covering letter, was "transmitted to the several legislatures in order to be submitted to a Convention of Delegates chosen in each State by the people thereof, in conformity to the resolves of this Convention." It was ratified by eleven of the thirteen States before March 4, 1789, the day earlier fixed for the commencement of the new constitution. North Carolina and Rhode Island elected to keep out and there was no question of coercing the non-aceeding States into adhering to the Union against the express will of their peoples. In May, 1789, however, Rhode Island ratified the constitution and in November, 1789, North Carolina followed suit. The State of Vermont, which had originally been out of the Confederacy, was admitted by the Congress into the Union as a constituent unit in February, 1791 ; and gradually the number of federating units rose to forty-eight. It is clear that the right of non-accession as well as the right of post-federal accession were acknowledged and recognised.[1] While ratifying the draft constitution several of the States-Conventions proposed amendments. Some of these were incorporated in the constitution as the Ten Amendments of 1791. They were popularly known as the Bill of Rights. From time to time other amendments followed.

In a historical sense and from the point of view of procedure the American pattern was more Anglo-Saxon than Russian or even French. It was less disruptive of the traditional structure, save for its violent break with the "mother country", than its French or Russian counterpart. It was nevertheless the achievement of a national bourgeois revolution against a territorially alien

[1] art IV, sec. 3 (1).

monarchy and the fictitious omnipotence of its Parliament. The revolutionary fervour of the first two periods cooled down when the convention met to "revise" the Articles of Confederation in 1787. The dominant elements in that body were by tradition and social affiliations conservative and even reactionary. Of the fifty-five members[1] thirty-three were lawyers and eight businessmen who on the whole were upholders of the social *status quo*. Most of them were interested in public securities, land speculation, trade and manufactures and shipping and primitive slave labour. The small farmer and debtor classes virtually went without representation in the convention. The Bill of Rights embodied in the Ten Amendments was the prize of ratification, and its origin and elaboration must be traced state-wise to Massachusetts, Virginia and New York, and class-wise to the small farmer and the debtor.

It is not surprising in view of the prevailing social reaction and its influence as a major force that it should have taken seventy-eight years after the adoption of the federal constitution to forbid slavery throughout the United States at least partially ;[2] ninety-three years to abolish franchise discrimination on grounds of race, colour, or previous servitude ;[3] one hundred and thirty-six years to provide for the popular election of the senators ;[4] and one hundred and forty-three years to abolish franchise discrimination due to sex.[5] No other great revolution in history has been so much averse to any major social change and yet so sweetly amenable to the soft and subtle whispers of reaction.[6] It is on a gigantic continental scale and experiment in dualism : an interminable conflict between principle and practice, between precept and example, between political freedom and economic serfdom, between liberty and entreached property.

[1] Seventy-four delegates were elected to the Convention. Nineteen for some reason or other did not attend.

[2] Thirteenth Amendment, 1865.

[3] Fifteenth Amendment, 1870.

[4] Seventeenth Amendment, 1913.

[5] Nineteenth Amendment, 1920.

[6] For fuller treatment of the subject read Andrew C. Mclaughlin's *A Constitutional History of the United States* ; and T. M. Cooley's *The General Principles of Constitutional Law*.

5. British Dominions

A. Canada

I propose now to take up some of the British Dominions. It must be stated at the very outset that the term "Constituent Convention" has been loosely used or used in these cases in a context different from the categories I have already discussed, except perhaps to a certain extent with reference to Southern Ireland at present designated *Eire*. In the last, of course, the change that has taken place is the result of a nationalist revolt as distinguished from a social revolution. Elsewhere, however, whatever has been achieved is born out of compromise, agreement and, in a sense, devolution, although in South Africa some sort of an armed uprising preceded what has been described as orderly transfer of power from British to Dominion hands.

In the chronological order in the series comes the Dominion of Canada. Originally it had been founded as a French colony in 1608. In 1760 it came under British rule by conquest. First Quebec and then Montreal capitulated. The new acquisition came to be known as the Province of Quebec. Difficulties naturally arose. The French were in the majority but the British were persuaded that they alone were entitled to be taken into consultation in regard to the administration of affairs. Added to the conflict of race and religion was the conflict of language. The British Government could offer no formula to resolve these conflicts except that on the question of religion under the Treaty of Paris the British Crown gave the undertaking that "His new Roman Catholic subjects may profess the worship of their religion according to the rites of the Roman Church so far as the laws of Great Britain permitted."

A statute was enacted by the British Parliament known as the Quebec Act, 1774. By and under this Act all the territory held by the Provinces of Quebec and Ontario was included in the Province of Quebec without the assent of the peoples concerned and evidently in disregard of the general trend of opinion. Provision was made for the exercise of the religion of the Church of Rome, for the right of the clergy to collect their tithes and for release from "the oath of abjuration". Complete authority vested in the Governor who, however, was subject to the direction and control from Westminster. The first in a series of constitutional experiments under British auspices, this Act was an attempt at the unification of two hostile and diametrically opposed forces. The American War of Independence and the appearance on the scene of this North British colony of a number of "Unity Empire Loyalists", who had been opposed to secession from the British Crown but believed in representative government, gave rise to a new political outlook amongst the English settlers. The French settlers were opposed to popular institutions, first, probably because they were by tradition and temperament averse to change ; and, secondly, because they realised quite early that "popular" control meant, in the circumstances then prevailing, British domination to the exclusion of the French.

The internal controversy in the colony could not be adjusted locally. A representative of the British minority went to London in 1788 and urged the repeal of the Quebec Act and asked for the setting up of representative government with control over taxation. This representation was not unsuccessful. It led to the passing by Parliament of the Canada Act, 1791. It divided the entire territory into two Provinces: Upper Canada and Lower Canada. This separation was evidently effected for the purpose of adjusting the claims and interests of the two rival communities and affording them opportunities of development in their respective zones, however restricted in their scope and incidence. those opportunities might have been. Each Province was independent of the other, both, of course, being subject to the suzerainty of the British. In each Province the executive was appointed by the Governor and held office during his pleasure. The legislature was bicameral, the Upper House (Legislative Council) being nominated. Laws were ordinarily made by the legislature, but in financial matters the executive was independent of it so that it could draw upon the resources without appropriations being voted by the Assembly.

Constant friction occurred between the legislature and the executive in each Province. The Governor's dissolution of the Assembly on frequent occasions proved ineffective. In the English-majority Province (Upper Canada) the fight was between the ruling clique and other sections of the people who were outside of the charmed circle. In the French-majority Province (Lower Canada) apart from collision between the legislature and the executive, there was an additional complication due mainly to French dominance in the House of Assembly as opposed to perpetual British bias in the Council and the executive. Almost identical demands were, however, pressed in both the Provinces—elected Upper House, control of the purse and responsibility of the executive. The tension of the conflict which continued for about four decades became more and more acute and it burst into ill-organised insurrectionary uprisings in both Upper and Lower Canada. There was unrest also in the three coastal provinces, namely, Nova Scotia, New Brunswick and Prince Edward Island. In these Provinces, as in the two Canadas, the crisis was sharpening, although there was no actual uprising. The political demands made by them were not basically different from those that emanated from the two Canadas.

Then came the famous Durham Mission. On the basis of Lord Durham's recommendations the Union Act, 1840, was passed by the British Parliament. It sought to unite the two Canadas again with the result that the French were relegated to the background in the political life of the community. A statutory but powerful minority, they were not prepared to reconcile themselves to internal British domination. Thus the third Canadian experiment was a failure, having produced frequent deadlocks. From both the parties, however, came proposals for a change. In the Maritime Provinces, too, they did not rest idle. Delegates from these Provinces met at Charlottetown to explore the possibilities of a Maritime Union. A larger conference, which the Canadian Union joined, followed. This conference, known as the Quebec Convention, adopted 72 resolutions giving an outline of the constitutional structure which it wanted the British Parliament to set up. Broadly speaking, the proposals set out were : a Federal Union embracing Upper Canada, Lower Canada and the Maritime Provinces ; eligibility of the North-West territory, British Columbia, and Vancouver for subsequent admission to the Union ; and Provincial legislatures and executives with necessary powers. This conference was described as a Constituent Convention.

The resolutions were taken up by the Canadian Parliament in 1865. "Take it or leave it" was the procedure adopted by the sponsors of the resolutions and the Government. It has been suggested in certain quarters that the Quebec resolutions were treated as the terms of a treaty between Canada and Britain which could not be amended but accepted or rejected *en bloc*. The obvious implication is that there was a compact and that the parties thereto were the two countries named above. This interpretation is clearly wrong. At that stage Britain was not in the picture. It was, if at all, a compact between the several colonies and not between Canada and Britain. They were passed by both the Houses of the Canadian Legislature, but not without opposition. On reference being made to the Provincial Legislatures the decisions were finally agreed to after a good deal of bitter controversy, particularly in Nova Scotia. These proposals were carried over to London by a Canadian delegation and a Bill was accordingly drafted by the Law Officers of the Crown in consultation with the Secretary of State and the delegates. The Bill was passed into law in March, 1867. It is the famous British North America Act. Since then three important constitutional amendments have been made by the British Parliament and steps have been taken to adapt the relevant Royal Instructions and Letters Patent to the new constitutional set-up.

Now, certain points are clear. The Quebec Constituent Convention of 1864 was not a Constituent Assembly in the accepted sense of the term. It had no sovereign power. It did not emerge from any successful revolution. It did not seek to change the basis of the State power either socially or even formally. It acknowledged in law and in fact the sovereignty of the British Crown and Parliament. Only, under the Statute of Westminster, 1931, a change of a somewhat drastic nature has been recorded without any change in the social composition of different organs of the State. I call it "somewhat drastic" because the power to make laws in the municipal sphere or with extra-territorial effect has passed completely from Westminster to Canada with the consequential right to amend or abrogate British law or any Act passed by the British Parliament save those protected by or under the Statute of Westminster. For the reasons indicated earlier the British Parliament, and not any Dominion agency, is for all practical purposes the Dominion of Canada's Constituent Assembly. It held that position in 1867 ; it has held it since without interruption. That position may not be disturbed unless there is, by local Dominion agreement, abolition of this constituent right of the British Parliament.

B. *Australia*

Mutatis mutandis almost the same procedure was adopted in Australia in regard to its constitutional development. Like the

Canadian Provinces the Australian States were British colonies, more or less, functioning under British laws and completely subject to the British Crown. In Australia as in Canada Governors were agents of the British Government and both the legislatures and executives were creatures of the British statutes and Royal Instruments. But one or two points in connection with the Australian experiment in constitution-making cannot be ignored. In the case of Canada the delegation went to London with a series of resolutions and parleyed with the representatives of the British Government, and to some extent at any rate, the constitution that finally emerged was the result, as Mr. Joseph Chamberlain pointed out, of British advice and suggestion. In the case of Australia the States, through their representatives, worked out the plan without British assistance and advice and the Commonwealth Act of 1900 was, with few alterations of a verbal or technical nature, essentially the Bill presented to the British Government and Parliament by the Australian delegation. The first was a British-Canadian compromise ; the second was British ratification of an Australian charter. This explains to a certain extent the difference between Canadian constitutional savings and those for Australia under the Statute of Westminster, 1931. Constitutional changes need in Canada an Imperial Act and in Australia a referendum as provided for in chapter VIII of the constitution. Again, in Canada the result was to amalgamate the Provinces into one Dominion while in Australia the constitution created for certain defined and limited subjects a federation of a number of more or less sovereign States. This is explained by the fact that the Australian States had enjoyed for a much longer period than the Canadian Provinces complete self-governing existence.[1]

In both these instances, however, the units, that is, Provinces and States, were presumed to be sovereign entities when federation was explored and proposed. The right of non-accession on the part of the units was inherent in both the plans and provision was made in each case for post-federal adhesion.[2]

In Australia federation as a contrivance to reconcile State

[1] J. Chamberlain's speech on the Commonwealth Bill in the House of Commons, May 14, 1908..

[2] For Canada read the preamble to the British North America Act, 1867, and ss. 146 and 147 ; and for Australia the preamble to the Commonwealth of Australia Act, 1900, and ss. 121-124 of the schedule.

rights with national unity took a definite and concrete shape by gradual stages. The system inaugurated in America was not without its lessons. A comparatively more recent example was furnished by the Canadian Dominion. In 1847, when giving assent to the proposal of separating Victoria from New South Wales, Earl Grey envisaged "the ultimate necessity for some central authority in Australia". His effort to give it a practical shape three years later evoked no response. The idea was taken up and pursued by Sir Henry Parkes, Premier of New South Wales. In 1883, at his instance a conference of the colonies was called and it produced an Australian Federal Council which was sanctioned by the British Parliament.[1] It was an experimental measure, a kind of loose Advisory Council with restricted legislative powers and no executive authority. It was no effective instrument. Then there was the Russian scare and the colonies and their statesmen were very much exercised over the state of Australian defences. A conference was held at Melbourne in 1889 to consider a report made by Major-General Edwards on the problem. It was decided to request the several legislatures to appoint their representatives to a National Australian Convention. In 1891, this Convention met at Sydney and certain resolutions were adopted. They read:

(*a*) The powers and rights of existing colonies to remain intact excepting as regards any such powers at it may be necessary to hand over to the Federal Government.

(*b*) No alterations to be made in the States without the consent of the Legislatures of such States as well as of the Federal Parliament.

(*c*) Trade between the federated colonies to be absolutely free.

(*d*) Power to impose customs and excise duties to be vested in the Federal Government and Parliament.

(*e*) Military and naval defence forces to be under one command.

(*f*) The Federal Constitution to make provision to enable each State to make amendments in its constitution if necessary for the purposes of federation.

These resolutions were then referred to a committee of experts. With some alterations they were adopted by the committee. The draft Bill embodying these decisions was submitted to the legislatures of the colonies for ratification. It failed to gain wide popular support. A Federal League was set up to awaken the peoples to the necessity and urgency of a union at least for security and other analogous purposes. In 1895, Premiers of the States met

[1] 48 & 49 Vict. C. 60.

again and decided to sponsor enabling Bills in their respective legislatures providing for a convention of delegates to frame a constitution. It was decided that the constitution so framed would be submitted to the several legislatures, each legislature sitting as a committee of the whole House ; that the amendments which might be recommended by these legislatures would be referred back to the convention ; and that a final draft made by the convention after consideration of the amendments would be submitted to the peoples of the several States by way of a general referendum. The convention met at Adelaide in 1897. Queensland kept out, having declined to pass any enabling Bill. The convention drafted a constitution. The draft was forwarded to the legislatures of the colonies concerned. With their amendments it went back to the Sydney Convention. The draft as amended was passed by the convention held at Melbourne in 1898. On popular referendum being taken, it was approved and ratified by five of the six colonies again with certain changes, alterations and amendments, Western Australia standing out. That draft Bill was the basis of the Commonwealth of Australia Act, 1900. The Commonwealth Constitution was scheduled to the Imperial Act ; in form at least it was not a British enactment as such. Meanwhile Western Australia decided by a referendum to join the federation. Under a Royal Proclamation issued in September, 1900, the constitution came into operation in January, 1901. It has since been amended several times through the usual agency.

C. South Africa

The history of constitutional development in South Africa is interesting, if rather curious. It is curious because of the peculiar turn it took in the direction of a unitary government contrary to the earlier trend in the colonies. In Canada the powers of the Provinces were specified, the residuary being left to the Dominion Centre. In Australia, on the analogy of the United States, the scheme of distribution of powers left the States complete masters of the residuary field and gave the Commonwealth Centre defined, specified and delegated powers. It was not for nothing that the units in Canada were called Provinces and those in Australia States. The Union of South Africa Act, 1909, granted all the powers to the Union Centre except in one or two respects, and rendered the contracting colonies into self-governing local bodies.

It may be recalled that in 1872, full responsible government was conferred on Cape Colony and that Natal received it in 1893. In accordance with the undertaking given in the Treaty of Vereeniging concluded in May, 1902, after the Boer War the Campbell-Bannerman Government made proposals for the grant of responsible government to the Transvaal and Orange River Colonies in 1906. In commending those proposals to the approval of Parliament Mr. Winston Churchill, who then happened to be the Colonial Under-Secretary in the Liberal Administration of Sir Henry Campbell-Bannerman, made observations[1] which would sound strange, rather amusing, after these forty years, coming as they did from the present Tory Leader in Great Britain. Mr. Churchill said : "The system of representative government without responsible Ministers, without responsible powers, has led to endless friction and inconvenience wherever and whenever it has been employed. It has failed in Canada, it has failed in Natal and Cape Colony. It has been condemned by almost every high colonial authority who has studied this question." Dealing with the circumstances which then prevailed in these colonies, Mr. Churchill proceeded to add: "It is just for that reason that we should now step forward, and, taking occasion by the hand, make an advance in the system of government. How often in the history of nations has the golden opportunity been allowed to slip away! How often have rulers and Governments been forced to make in foul weather the very journey which they have refused to make prosperously in fair weather !"

What a change ! What a wide gulf between Mr. Churchill, the Colonial Under-Secretary in the Campbell-Bannerman Government of 1906 and Mr. Churchill, the accredited Tory leader of 1946! Is it a fall or a revenge of nature? But even then in 1906 as in 1946, Mr. Churchill was fully conscious of what he called imperial interests and the white man's burden. He would have set his face firmly against the proposals which he himself initiated had he not believed that the Boers had definitely abandoned their own ambition of creating in South Africa a united State independent of the British Crown and accepted instead that other political idea which was represented by the Dominion of Canada and the Commonwealth of Australia. Mr. Churchill rejoiced in the fact that

[1] A. B. Keith's *Speeches and Documents on Colonial Policy*, 1763-1917, vol. II, pp. 3-24.

for the first time in many years "the two white races dwelling together in South Africa have found a common foundation on which they can build . . . .".

So to Mr. Churchill, as to the British Government of which he was then a junior member, responsible self-government within the British Empire was a practical and acceptable proposition, and not a sovereign independent national State. To them in 1906, it was a prerogative of the white man, and not the inherent right of a coloured race. That is one of the reasons, it may be noted in passing, why large sections of Indians have viewed with suspicion the solemn declarations made in Parliament and the promises of British statesmen. For one thing, Indians are not a white people. For another, they have not been able to reconcile themselves to a place within the British Commonwealth and Empire, however advantageous that position may be, or to the doctrine of British or any other alien trusteeship. Therein lies the core of the Indo-British conflict which cannot be resolved by recourse to Dominion precedents or experiments in Dominion statehood.

Coming back to South Africa, there are two great motive forces which, according to the Earl of Crewe, moved the South African colonies towards a Union.[1] They realised that it would not be possible for them to take their place in the Empire beside the Dominion of Canada or the Commonwealth of Australia unless they formed themselves into a Union. They realised further that great difficulties and complications had arisen out of the railway systems of the different colonies and that they could not be solved except by devising a common machinery of supervision and control. Besides, it was evident that the administration of affairs concerning the colonies under a central union was less expensive, especially in the spheres of defence, communications, foreign relations and customs. Early in 1907, a communication was addressed from the Cape which led Lord Selborne to prepare a memorandum on the subject of Union. In 1908, a series of conferences followed and a convention was held first at Durban, then at Cape Town and lastly at Bloemfontein.

In 1909, the convention prepared a draft Bill and submitted it to the Colonial Legislatures. Amendments were proposed by all the legislatures with the exception of the Transvaal Parliament.

[1] A. B. Keith's *Speeches and Documents on Colonial Policy*, 1763-1917, vol. II, pp. 25-47.

At the Bloemfontein session of the convention those amendments were taken up and in deference thereto the draft Bill was revised. The revised draft was then referred back to the legislatures of the four colonies. In Natal the demand for a referendum was made. The draft was agreed to by an overwhelming majority. Thus in June it was accepted by each of the four colonies. Delegates were chosen from them to proceed to London to get it enacted into an Act by the British Parliament. The Act was passed in September, 1909.

In Canada, Australia and South Africa there was a certain amount of uniformity in the manner and method of approach. In each case the need for change was felt and given expression to locally. In each case the initiative in proposing and constituting a national convention was taken by the colonies themselves. In each case, again, the draft went from the convention back to the colonies and was ratified by them. In certain cases, as in Australia and, in one instance, in South Africa, a referendum was taken along with ratification by the legislatures. In each case, while the originating authority was local, the final sanctioning authority was the British Parliament. In each case finally the class structure of the State remained intact and the change was territorial or, if one likes, national in form and content rather than social. It follows that in all these Dominions the constituent conventions were drafting committees, and not sovereign bodies such as those convened, as in France, Russia and the United States, upon seizure of power. In the case of the Union of South Africa, however, there is no restriction under the Statute of Westminster, 1931, on its constituent powers as in Canada and, in a different sense, in Australia. In exercise of those powers the Union has passed two Acts of far-reaching constitutional importance.[1] These are decisive steps towards complete national independence, although the doctrine of allegiance to the British Crown has not yet been destroyed.

D. *Southern Ireland*

Perhaps the nearest approach to a Constituent Assembly, convened by a revolutionary Provisional Government on the capture

[1] Act of the Union Parliament to provide for the declaration of the Status of the Union and for the adoption of certain parts of the "The Statute of Westminster, 1931"—June 22, 1934; and Act of the Union Parliament to provide for the King's Acts as Head of the Executive and for the use of Royal seals in connection therewith—June, 22, 1934.

of power, was the machinery devised for framing the constitution of Ireland in 1921. That country had behind her centuries of bitter conflict. Dominantly racial and national in complexion, the conflict was not, upon a long and distant view, without social significance. As long ago as 1869 Karl Marx drafted a resolution on the relations between the Irish and English working classes which was adopted by the Council of the International Workingmen's Association.[1] The resolution sought to interpret the class character of the Irish agrarian revolution and the probable effect of its victory on the English landlords, the English army and the English bourgeoisie. If the Irish fortress of English landlordism fell, it would collapse in England too. The English landed aristocracy would not only be deprived of the spoils of exploitation, but its moral authority and prestige would be completely shattered. In England farmers and agricultural labourers would then find it easier to deal effectively with this idle and pampered and corrupt aristocracy.

That was about the landlords. What about the bourgeoisie? Its exploitation of Irish poverty by means of forced transplantation of impoverished Irish peasants resulted, on the one hand, in worsening the condition of the English working class and, on the other, dividing the Irish and English workers into hostile camps. Again, to the gullible and unsophisticated English people in field and factory Ireland was offered as "the only excuse of the English Government for maintaining a big standing army, which in case of need they send against the English workers". Therefore, by striking a decisive blow at English landlords in Ireland and the oppression of the English national-bourgeoisie the stage would be set for a democratic agrarian revolution in Ireland as well as for a social democratic revolution in England. Appeal was made to the English working class to make common cause with the discontented elements in Ireland, as the essential preliminary condition of its own emancipation, in turning the compulsory union of Ireland with England into "an equal and free union, if that is possible, or into full separation, if this is inevitable".

A national movement against an acquisitive, exploiting and ruling power should not be judged by the mechanical calculations of immediate gain or loss or from the point of view of the ascertain-

[1] Reprinted in *Marx, Engels & Lenin on the Irish Revolution*, Modern Books Ltd., 1933.

able achievements of the oppressed nationality or nationalities, but from the point of view of its immediate or long-term effect on the emancipation of mankind as a whole. Struggles carried on in isolation by forces propelled by mixed and sometimes undefined or ill-defined motives are fraught with potentialities on a world scale. Those who think that on getting up one fine morning they will find on one side of a front line an army shouting "We are for socialism" and on the other side another army replying "We are for imperialism" and then sit back quietly to persuade themselves that here is a "revolution" are only deceiving themselves or do not know what they talk about. Lenin ridiculed this fantastic idea. The occasion was provided by the Irish Rebellion of 1916, and Karl Radek's article thereon under the caption "A Played-Out Song" which appeared in the May issue of *Berner Tagwacht*. While describing the rebellion as a "putsch" the author wrote that the Irish question was an agrarian issue and that the nationalist movement was at that stage a "purely urban petty-bourgeois movement which, notwithstanding the sensation it caused, had not much social backing." Lenin rejected this analysis as a "monstrously doctronnaire and pedantic opinion".[1]

Revolutions take different lines at different stages of social evolution, but the essence is in revolt against oppression, tyranny and exploitation in any shape, or form. It may be bourgeois revolt against monarchy and nobility ; it may be a national revolt against alien domination ; it may be an agrarian revolt against landlords ; it may be a proletarian revolt against a native or foreign bourgeoisie. It may so happen that different discontented elements in revolt are somehow mixed up in a given situation and import into the movement "their prejudices, their reactionary fantasies, their weaknesses and errors". Nevertheless, they are sometimes, though not always, driven by the increasing tempo of the struggle to attack and assail the citadel of reaction. The century-old Irish revolt against England passed through various stages and combinations of class interests. The rebellion of 1916 was a movement for Irish independence, for the right of national self-determination. It was not a "putsch" ; a blow primarily aimed at British rule in Ireland, it was a movement which, objectively, was part of the world struggle for human liberation. So in the recent past has

[1] Cf. Lenin's *Collected Works*, Vol. XIX..

been India's struggle for independence. So it is today, although as a result of the Second World War, of the countrywide devastation it has wrought, of the suffering and privation that have followed in its wake, and of the virtual breakdown of the economic machinery the social conflict in the struggle has been amazingly sharpened with realignment of forces and new divisions and new alliances.

The Irish Easter rising was preceded by the great Dublin strike of 1913, which led to the establishment of the Irish citizen army. The army was pledged both to the cause of labour and to that of Irish unity and liberty. Many of these men drifted to the ranks of the Irish volunteers, an organisation which owed its inception to the Republican brotherhood. When the Easter rising came about the citizen army did not rest idle. It associated itself with the insurrection. Thus, in the course of that heroic struggle, the union between Republicans and Socialist labour was consolidated. The proclamation of the Irish Republic on Easter Monday, 1916, declared "the right of the people of Ireland to the ownership of land and to the unfettered control of Irish destinies to be sovereign and indefeasible". It is true that the proclamation was couched in vague and wide terms. Nothing more concrete was perhaps possible in the circumstances, but the basic character of the new order which the authors of the proclamation envisaged was not open very much to doubt. A sovereign republic in form, it was agrarian revolution in social content.

Sinn Fein as a party was not, relatively speaking, an active factor during that period. The course of events and the dramatic turn of the Easter rising and the method of its suppression brought about the amalgamation of different Irish parties. Sinn Fein and the Republican movement came to an understanding with each other. An overpowering sense of national liberation unified all sections of the people. In November, 1917, a Sinn Fein Convention met and adopted the Republican formula. It demanded the convention of a Constituent Assembly "comprising persons chosen by the Irish constituencies as the supreme national authority to speak and act in the name of the Irish people and to devise and formulate measures for the welfare of the whole people of Ireland." Sinn Fein came to the fore and asserted itself as the vanguard of the revolution during the last two years of the war. At the General Election held immediately after the

7

conclusion of the Armistice in December, 1918, it nominated candidates in all Irish constituencies. The candidates chosen were committed, according to the party mandate, not to attend Parliament at Westminster, but to form instead an Irish National Government. Labour did not contest the elections in order that the demand for national self-determination might be endorsed by an unequivocal national vote. Sinn Fein swept the polls. The members met at Dublin on January 21, 1919, and constituted themselves into Dail Eireann (Parliament of Ireland). It adopted a Declaration of Independence and reaffirmed the proclamation of the Irish Republic of 1916. A message to the free nations of the world was addressed in which the Irish nation's claim to freedom was reiterated.

Internally, a democratic programme was drawn up in collaboration with the Irish Labour Party. It proclaimed that the nation's sovereignty extended not only to all its citizens, but to all its natural possessions, the national wealth and wealth-producing processes. It further stated that the rights of private property must be subordinated to public welfare. To this programme set out in general and wide terms may be traced the more detailed and comprehensive declarations of fundamental rights which found place in the Irish constitution subsequently adopted.

At the first session of Dail Eireann the new State was given the official title "Saorstat Eireann" (Irish Republic), a name which has not been altered despite many drastic changes that have followed. Dail Eireann was not only the supreme legislative organ of the new State, but also the Government of the Irish Republic, a curious mixing-up, but warranted by the uncertainties of the situation. In practice, however, executive authority was exercised by a Cabinet consisting of a President elected by the Dail and certain members appointed by the President subject to confirmation by the Dail. In the spring of 1921, the British Government ordered elections to be held for "the Parliament of Southern Ireland" in accordance with the provisions of the Government of Ireland Act, 1920. Dail Eireann challenged the validity of that Act. It decided, nevertheless, that the elections announced to be held should be contested and that upon the elections the first Dail should stand dissolved and that in its place the members elected should form the Dail and then be summoned by the President.

Accordingly, the second Dail came into existence.. It proceeded to launch upon certain important schemes of agricultural and industrial development. In order to finance its projects the revolutionary Irish Government floated a national loan in Ireland and America. It was proscribed by the British Government. A violent conflict was thus precipitated. The country was in a state of active warfare. The Irish revolutionary Government was then declared illegal. The atmosphere created was one of terror by shootings, executions and reprisals. There was an unending competition in crime. On the British side the Cabinet found in the progressive deterioration of the Irish situation cause for grave anxiety. On the Irish side, British repression served in the end as the rallying point of a united anti-British Irish front. The whole of Ireland was in the fray. All sections of the Irish people were integrated, as it were, into a *union sacree* for the achievement of Republican independence and consolidation of the triumphs of the Revolutionary Government. It does not mean, however, that this sense of unity dawned upon the people all of a sudden. It was the result of a combination of circumstances. Nor would it be proper to ignore the schism that divided the Irish Nationalists who stood for complete independence and the Southern Unionists who counselled moderation, and the greater and more dangerous conflict between the Northern Unionists and the rest.

The Home Rule Act, 1914, which had sought to create a subordinate legislature for Ireland under British suzerainty in all important respects, naturally failed to conciliate sensitive Irish nationalist sentiment. It was followed by another British effort to rally Irish opinion in the shape of an Irish Convention held in 1917-18.[1] This convention was boycotted by Sinn Fein which in the meantime had emerged as the most powerful force after the Easter Rising. On the other hand, the Ulster Unionists who had taken part in the proceedings dissociated themselves from the convention's recommendations and repudiated the proposal that Ireland should have plenary powers of legislation and taxation without any British control and be treated as a sovereign independent national State. Instead they proposed permanent separation of Ulster[2] from any scheme of Irish self-government co-equal in

[1] Report of the Irish Convention, Dublin, 1918 (Cmd. 9019).

[2] The Province of Ulster consists of nine counties, of which six at present belong to Northern Ireland and the remaining three are incorporated in the Irish Free State.

power and authority with the British Government, and the maintenance of its association with the United Kingdom. The Southern Unionists, however, declined to line up with their counterpart in the north by pressing the general nationalist demand for self-government, making it clear at the same time that they would not go as far as the Irish nationalists. In the circumstances no compromise was possible. There is evidence to show that in certain Tory circles there was an attempt not to resolve the conflict, but to complicate the situation by fanning the flames in Northern Ireland.

The British authorities made yet another feeble and faint-hearted effort towards conciliation by getting through Parliament a measure known as the Government of Ireland Act, 1920.[1] The provisions of this Act are not important except for the fact that for the first time it recorded in effect British official acceptance of Ulster's case for partition on the basis of the two-nation theory. The project broke down as was evident from the developments that took place in Southern Ireland. The sentiment in the South was no longer a sectarian current ; it was now a national stream. The Provisional Revolutionary Government was in the saddle. The armed forces of the Crown, on the other hand, tried in vain to suppress the Government and the people by a reign of terror. Then Prime Minister David Lloyd George took the initiative in putting an end to this reckless British policy by starting negotiations with the Irish rebels to explore the possibilities of an Anglo-Irish settlement. Dail Eircann responded to Mr. Lloyd George's gesture, though not without considerable hesitation. It appointed plenipotentiaries to go to London to treat with the British Government. The articles of agreement for a treaty between Great Britain and Ireland were signed on December 6, 1921, by members of both the delegations. It was laid down that the instrument "shall be submitted forthwith by His Majesty's Government for the approval of Parliament and by the Irish signatories to a meeting summoned for the purpose of the members elected to sit in the House of Commons of Southern Ireland, and if approved, shall be ratified by the necessary legislation."[2]

In Great Britain at a special session of Parliament in December, 1922, the treaty was approved by an overwhelming majority, the

[1] 10 & 11 Geo. V. C. 67. [2] art. 18.

Ulster representatives and several of their Unionist sympathisers dissenting. It was accorded statutory recognition, in the teeth of bitter opposition from the same quarters, by the Irish Free State (Agreement) Act, 1922, passed on March 31, of that year. In Ireland the voting, however, was close. It was approved after two weeks of bitter controversy on January 7, 1922, by a majority of seven votes, sixty-four members of Dail Eireann voting for and fifty-seven against approval. In terms of the treaty it was submitted to a meeting of the members elected to the House of Commons of Southern Ireland convened on January 14, 1922. Only the Dail supporters of the treaty and four representatives of Dublin University attended this meeting and they unanimously approved of the treaty. This led to a split among members of the Sinn Fein party, with the result that Mr. de Velera and his Cabinet resigned. In consequence of the treaty[1] a Provisional Government under Mr. Michael Collins was set up on January 14, 1922, by members of the Southern Irish Parliament.

For our immediate purpose it is not necessary to go into the detailed provisions of this Anglo-Irish Treaty. What are particularly relevant in the present context are the procedure adopted for the convocation of the Constituent Assembly and the reservations in respect of the sovereignty of Ireland. The procedure referred to above was put in this form:

> By way of provisional arrangement for the administration of Southern Ireland during the interval which must elapse between the date hereof and the constitution of a Parliament and Government of the Irish Free State in accordance therewith, steps shall be taken forthwith for summoning a meeting of members of Parliament elected for constituencies in Southern Ireland since the passing of the Government of Ireland Act, 1920, and for constituting a provisional Government, and the British Government shall take the steps necessary to transfer to such provisional Government the powers and machinery requisite for the discharge of its duties, provided that every member of such provisional Government shall have signified in writing his or her acceptance of this instrument. . . "

In defending the treaty in Dail Eireann on December 6, 1922, and commending it to its approval Mr. A. Griffith, the first Irish signatory, made a speech which summed up the substance of the instrument. He claimed that it was the first treaty since 1172,

[1] art. 17.

signed on equal footing between the representatives of the Irish Government and those of the British Government. He claimed that it acknowledged the equality of Ireland ; that it recognised the free State of Ireland ; that it brought back the flag of Ireland, her full rights and powers of fiscal control and an equal voice with Great Britain, and the Dominions in the conduct and direction of foreign affairs in peace and in war ; that after 700 years it forced the withdrawal from her soil of the British troops and prepared the ground for the formation of an Irish army.

Mr. Griffith then proceeded to counter the suggestion that the oath[1] which was mandatory was a derogation from the sovereign status of the Irish Free State. He said that it was an oath of allegiance to the constitution of the free State of Ireland, to the country, to the treaty, and to the King as head of the British Commonwealth of Nations. If, however, a conflict of these allegiances arose by the abuse of authority by the King and his Government in the United Kingdom or in any of the other Dominions, then, added Mr. Griffith, the allegiance to the country would supersede the allegiance to the Crown even to the extent of resistance. Mr. Griffith read out to the Dail the text of a letter which Mr. Lloyd George had addressed him on December 13, 1921, in elucidation of the points covered by the treaty. This document stated *inter alia*:

> The framing of that Constitution will be in the hands of the Irish Government, subject, of course, to the terms of Agreement, and to the pledges given in respect of the minority by the head of the Irish Delegation. The establishment and composition of the Second Chamber is, therefore, in the discretion of the Irish people. There is nothing in the Articles of Agreement to suggest that Ireland is in this respect bound to the Canadian model.
> I may add that we propose to begin withdrawing the Military and Auxiliary Forces of the Crown in Southern Ireland when the Articles of Agreement are ratified.

In his House of Commons speech on December 14, 1921, Mr. Lloyd George referred, in addition, to two other important

[1] I . . . do solemnly swear true faith and allegiance to the Constitution of the Irish Free State as by law established and that I will be faithful to H. M. King George V, his heirs and successors by law, in virtue of the common citizenship of Ireland with Great Britain and her adherence to and membership of the group of nations forming the British Commonwealth of Nations (art. 4 of the treaty).

points which, it will be seen, were not seriously examined by Mr. Griffith in the Dail. It was a curious omission on the part of the head of the Irish Delegation. The points generally concerned (1) Ulster and its position in the project as contemplated in the treaty,[1] and (2) the reservations in respect of the ports,[2] the civil service personnel in the employ of the Crown in Ireland who might be discharged by the Irish Free State or who might retire in consequence of the change,[3] the limitation of armaments,[4] and harbour facilities[5] and coastal defences.[6]

As to Ulster, it was made clear that in no circumstances would the British Government agree to any proposals involving its coercion. A similar pledge had previously been given by Prime Minister Asquith, and his successor expressed his determination to stand by it. By coercion, as Mr. Lyod George explained, was meant not persuasion employed to bring Ulster within an All-Ireland Parliament or friendly discussion suggesting cooperation in a common endeavour to build a united Irish Free State, but a threat of armed intervention by the Crown's forces. Ulster was given the option either to join an All-Ireland Parliament or to keep out of it.[7] If it elected by an address to the Crown to remain where it was, no change in its constitutional position was contemplated in the treaty or intended by those on the British or the Irish side who had signed it. It was nevertheless pointed out that in the event of Ulster deciding to continue as a separate entity, there should be redistribution of boundaries. Provision for a Boundaries Commission was accordingly made in the treaty. It was to be composed of three persons, representative respectively of the British Government, the Free State Government and the Government of Northern Ireland with the British representative acting as the Chairman. The commission was to determine the boundaries between Northern Ireland and the rest of Ireland in accordance with the wishes of the inhabitants concerned and with due regard for economic and geographic conditions.[8] After the presentation of an address to the Crown by the Parliament of Northern Ireland in terms of the treaty a commission was set up. But the boundaries issue was disposed of by the agreement of December 3, 1925, signed

[1] art. 11.
[2] art. 10.
[3] art. 9.
[4] art. 8.
[5] art. 7.
[6] art. 6.
[7] arts. 11 & 12.
[8] art. 12.

by representatives of the three Governments, which was confirmed by appropriate legislative enactments.[1]

In regard to reservations and safeguards under point (2), a limitation was imposed upon the raising of armaments and the training of the armed men within the boundaries of Ireland. Mr. Lloyd George put the total strength of armed men for the whole of Ireland at 40,000 approximately and indicated that the share of each part of Ireland should roughly correspond to their respective population strengths. The relevant provision of the treaty was to the effect that the Free State's military establishments "shall not exceed in size such proportion of the military establishments maintained in Great Britain as that which the population of Ireland bears to the population of Great Britain".[2] Thus the military quota of each of these three parties—North, South and Britain—was to be in proportion to their respective populations. Of the navy Mr. Lloyd George stated rather bluntly that the British Government could not allow the working of Dominion Status to operate. Where the security and interests of the United Kingdom were concerned nothing was left to chance, nothing to "good will or the general interpretation of the vague conditions of the treaty". The naval defence was left to the British Navy. In the case of war[3] it was to have free access to all the Irish harbours and creeks. This was subject to no condition, no qualification. No consent of the Free State Government was required. In time of peace, however, such harbour and other facilities were to be given to the Imperial forces as were specified in the *annexe* to the treaty or such other facilities as might be agreed upon between the British Government and the Government of the Free State.[4]

These reservations designed primarily in imperial interests did not, however, prohibit the construction or maintenance by the Free State Government of such vessels as were necessary for the protection of the revenue or fisheries.[5] It was stipulated that on the expiry of five years a conference of representatives of both the Governments would be held to review these provisions in order that Ireland might have a share in her coastal defence. On the

[1] 15 & 16 Geo. 5 C. 77 & Irish Free State Act, No. 40 of 1925.
[2] art. 8.
[3] art. 7 (b).
[4] art. 7 (a).
[5] art. 6.

basis of reciprocity and on the payment of customary port and other dues the ships of both the countries were given access to their respective ports.[1] This provision was intended, on the admission of the British Prime Minister himself, to protect British ships against any future Irish legislation excluding them from the coastal trade with Ireland.

In accordance with the articles of agreement Dail Eireann, sitting as a Constituent Assembly, proclaimed the establishment of the Irish Free State (SAORSTAT EIREANN) and enacted a Constituent Act on October 25, 1922.[2] The Dail asserted that "all authority comes from God to the people", and expressed the confidence that "the national life and unity of Ireland shall thus be restored". The constitution of the Irish Free State was annexed to the Constituent Act as the First Schedule. On December 5, 1922, the British Parliament followed up by a corresponding Act[3] providing for the constitution of the Irish Free State. What is of special constitutional significance is the procedure adopted by the British Parliament. The Irish constitution as such formed no part of any enacting section or clause of the Imperial Act ; only the Irish schedule was adopted and given statutory recognition. It was enacted that the constitution would come into operation on the same being proclaimed by the King in accordance with Article 83 of the Constitution. Provision was further made that nothing in the Irish Constitution "shall be construed as prejudicing the power of Parliament to make laws affecting the Irish Free State in any case where, in accordance with constitutional practice. Parliament would make laws affecting other self-governing Dominions.[4]

Between 1921 and now drastic changes have taken place not only in the world generally but in particular in the relations between Britain and different parts of the Commonwealth and Empire. In Southern Ireland there has been a decisive impact of these changes. By the Constitution (Removal of Oath) Act, 1933, the oath of allegiance to the Crown has been abolished. On the validity of this measure being challenged the Privy Council rejected this contention in 1935, and held that it was *intra vires* of the Irish legislature apparently relying on the Free State's accretion

[1] art. 6.
[2] Act No. 1 of 1922.
[3] 13 Geo. 5. C. 1, Session 2.
[4] s. 4.

of power due to the Statute of Westminster.[1] What was eliminated was not the allegiance of Irish citizens as such to the Crown, but the oath taken by legislators and Ministers. The Free State was released from the obligation in respect of its share of the public debt of the United Kingdom[2] by a treaty between Great Britain and Ireland concluded on December 3, 1925.[3] Its liability to pay fair compensation to civil servants contemplated in the treaty of 1921[4] led to litigation[5] and the British Government were compelled to pay the extra compensation,[6] the Cosgrave Government refusing to pay a single penny. This was a preceding which caused disquiet among British investors in connection with the question of part or full repudiation of India's public debts canvassed several years ago. Incidentally, however, this question does not arise at present in view of the fact that the position has been reversed as a result of the financial effects of the Second World War. Today India is Britain's creditor with huge sterling balances standing to her credit. The provisions of the Anglo-Irish Treaty in regard to ports and other facilities were cancelled by agreement in 1938. No provision was made in the treaty as to Irish appeals to the Privy Council. The Irish Free State has, however, taken the earliest opportunity to abolish them,[7] and there can be no question as to the validity of this Irish legislation in terms of the Statute of Westminster. According to the latest position the decision of Eire's Supreme Court, which is the court of final appeal, is in all cases final and conclusive.[8]

In the debates in Parliament on the Irish constitution in 1922, certain points came up for discussion. Critics of the measure, for instance, alleged that the provisions relating to Irish citizenship[9] created a status unknown to the British constitution or to the constitution of any of the King's dominions or possessions. In particular it was asserted that the phrase "Irish citizen" was an innovation completely repugnant to the law and practice in Britain, Canada or any other self-governing Dominion. That was an erroneous idea. As long ago as 1910, the Dominion of Canada passed

Moore v. *Attorney General* (51 T.L.R.)
art. 5. [3] art. 2. [4] art. 10.
Wigg & Cochvane v. *A. G. of Irish Free State* (1927 A. C. 674); and *Irish Civil Servants, in re,* (1929 A.C. 242).
20 Geo. 5, C. 4. [7] Act 45 of 1933.
The Constitution Act, 1937, art. 34 (4). [9] art. 3.

an Immigration Act in which the phrase "Canadian citizen" was freely used for certain defined purposes. Therefore, there was no substance in the contention urged by critics of the constitution. It is true that "citizen" in English law is not what they call a term of art. The allegiance to the Crown is implied in subjecthood, but within a wider circle of "British subjects" local categories of "citizens" have been created in the Dominions. The Irish move in this regard created no precedent whatsoever. A common allegiance to the Crown or common subjecthood does not carry with it equality of rights or privileges in the Dominions. Its incidence varies from place to place and steps have been taken to restrict political and, in some cases, other rights to such British subjects as fulfil the requirements of Dominion Acts. British subjecthood as such does not in our time imply any common status or privilege except for the purposes of protection abroad.

The provision next attacked was to the effect: "Save in the case of actual invasion, the Irish Free State shall not be committed to active participation in any war without the assent of the Irish Parliament".[1] This, it was pointed out, was inconsistent with a corresponding treaty provision that the Irish Free State Government "shall afford to His Majesty's Imperial Forces in time of war, or of strained relations with a foreign Power, such harbour and other facilities as the British Government may require for the purposes of coastal defence".[2] The charge of repugnancy was untenable. As was explained by the Attorney-General on behalf of the British Government, the impugned clause did not mean that the Irish Free State would not give harbour or other facilities in certain circumstances. What it meant instead was that the Irish Free State was under no obligation to raise troops, or otherwise to get involved in the operations of a war, without its consent and approval. There was no conflict between the two clauses. Besides, it has long been a settled doctrine that the British Government cannot in their own right involve any Dominion in a war which has not been brought about by its own action. In the course of a speech in the Canadian House of Commons on February 1, 1923, Mr. Mackenzie King gave expression to this view in most emphatic terms. The difficulty, of course, arose in the case of the Irish Free State not theoretically, but from the standpoint of the practi-

[1] art. 49.

[2] art. 7(b).

cal bearing of its treaty liability in respect of harbour and other facilities because it was clear that no enemy State would regard this concession to the belligerent British armed forces on its soil as compatible with strict neutrality. But in 1938 the anomaly was removed by the cancellation by agreement of these reservations of the treaty.

In pursuance of its consistent policy directed towards liquidation of every vestige or symbol of British authority Southern Ireland proceeded to enact appropriate legislation to establish complete sovereignty of the people. By the Executive Authority (External Relations) Act, 1936, the *Oireachtas* (the Irish National Parliament) eliminated the Crown except in the sphere of external relations where, too, it was stipulated that so long as its association with the British Commonwealth was not terminated the Crown might act, as by law and practice it acted on behalf of any one of the Member-States, for the purposes of the appointment of diplomatic and consular representatives and the conclusion of international agreements and that in any event it was required to act on the advice of the Irish Executive Council.[1] It is, however, significant that the occasion of King Edward VIII's abdication on December 10, 1936, was utilised by the de Valera Government not for destroying but for acknowledging formally the allegiance to the Crown.[2] A further and more decisive step in this process of liquidation was taken by the Constitution Act, 1937. *Eire* is the new name given to the State,[3] thereby asserting the supremacy of the Irish language over English. The English language is recognised as a second official language.[4] Ireland has been declared a sovereign independent, democratic State.[5] All powers of Government, legislative, executive and judicial, it is affirmed, derive from the people, whose right it is to designate the rulers of the State and, in final appeal, to decide all questions of national policy.[6] The national flag is the tricolour of green, white and orange.[7] The constitution of Saorstat Eireann in force immediately before the coming into operation of this Act and the Constitution of the Irish Free State Act, 1922, have been repealed.[8]

[1] art. 3 (1).
[2] art. 3 (2).
[3] art. 4.
[4] art. 8 (2).
[5] art. 5.
[6] art. 6 (1).
[7] art. 7.
[8] art. 48.

The office of the Governor-General has been abolished and his place *mutatis mutandis* has been taken by a President elected by direct vote of the people.[1] The President is required to act on the advice of the Government except where otherwise empowered to act in his discretion or in consultation with the Council of State.[2] That body should not be confused with the Second Chamber. It is in design and structure only an advisory body with no legislative or executive powers.[3] The Government is to consist of not less than seven and not more than fifteen members appointed by the President and collectively held responsible to Dail Eireann.[4] The head of the Government is designated "The TASISEACH" or Prime Minister. The entire executive power of the State is vested in the Government both in internal affairs and external relations.[5] War cannot be declared and the State cannot participate in any war save with the assent of Dail Eireann[6] (the Lower House). In the case of actual invasion, however, the Government may take whatever steps they may deem necessary for the protection of the State. While every international agreement to which the State becomes a party shall be laid before Dail Eireann,[7] it shall form no part of the domestic law of the State save as may be determined by the Oireachtas.[8]

At the present moment there is no link between *Eire* and the British State except the precarious, uncertain and rapidly fading symbol of the Imperial Crown ; and there could be no better and more effective demonstration of this posture of affairs than the dogged and determined Irish resistance under Mr. de Valera's leadership against their involvement in the last Great War. It is not necessary to discuss here the ethics of *Eire's* strategy and the philosophy underlying that strategy from the point of view of wider human interests and what is so often called a historic necessity. But it cannot be denied that during the war and before Prime Minister de Valera had with amazing consistency and skill pursued the central objective of his struggle for complete national sovereignty. On one vital issue, however, his efforts have not yet met with success. He has not yet been able to unify South and North, although the constitution of 1937 provides, with

[1] art. 12.
[2] art. 13 (9).
[3] art. 31.
[4] art. 28.
[5] arts. 28 & 29.
[6] art. 28 (3).
[7] art. 29 (5).
[8] art. 29 (6).

reservations for the present as to the extent and scope of *Eire's* law,[1] that the national territory consists of the whole island of Ireland, its islands and territorial seas.[2]

Now, the Irish Constituent Assembly, which was provided for in the Anglo-Irish treaty, is typically Irish. It conforms neither to the French, Russian or American pattern nor to the Dominion category. It was the result of both revolution and compromise. It was the product of revolution in so far as the Irish people had already set up a Provisional Revolutionary Government in complete defiance of the British Government and their armed forces. It was the product of compromise inasmuch as with such a Provisional Government in the saddle their representatives proceeded at British request to London to parley with the representatives of the British Government with a view to evolving an agreed formula, and ultimately accepted and signed the articles of agreement for the treaty of 1921. The treaty was by no means Britain's recognition of Ireland's republican independence. In one or two respects, the position accorded to her fell short of Dominion status, as was pointed out by Mr. Lloyd George himself in the course of his Commons speech on December 14, 1921, commending the treaty to the approval of Parliament. The British Prime Minister stated that where the security of Britain and the Empire was concerned the Irish State was required to agree to certain reservations. Those reservations as specified in the treaty were not in conformity with "the ordinary working of Dominion status".

But slowly, steadily but, on occasion, with lightning speed Southern Ireland has utilised the treaty to nullify its provisions and to break the spinal column of British imperialism. The Statute of Westminster, 1931, supplied the requisite legal sanction. Politically other forces, both internal and external, were increasingly at work. *Eire* is now virtually an independent sovereign Republic. What remains of the Crown as under the Executive Authority (External Relations) Act, 1936, is no more than a slender thread which may at any moment give way. Because I maintain that in essence as well as in form, in the method of approach as well as in the procedure adopted, the Irish Constituent Assembly differs from the Constituent Conventions of the Canadian, Australian and South African colonies I think that Sir John

[1] art. 3. [2] art. 2.

(now Lord) Simon's picturesque analogy drawn in his Commons speech on November 27, 1922, on the Irish constitution framed in terms of the treaty was exaggerated and rather colourful. "As the Prime Minister pointed out", observed Sir John, "the constitutions under which different parts of our Empire are now working are in a very large measure constitutions which have been settled on the soil where they were to operate, by the people who were to live under them."[1] That is not true in the case of India, the colonies and possessions. It is a half-truth in the case of the Dominions. The very difference in nomenclature between "Constituent Convention" and "Constituent Assembly" means a great deal in a historical perspective. But apart from this difference, there was difference in content and form between the Irish pattern and the categories of the other Dominions.

[1] A. B. Keith's *Speeches and Documents on the British Dominions, 1918-1931*, pp. 120-121.

CHAPTER V

BRITAIN'S PROBLEM IN INDIA : CERTAIN BASIC ASSUMPTIONS

1. Procedural Basis of Constitution-Making Machinery

Britain's problem in India and, for that matter, in all colonial countries generally is based on certain assumptions which peoples of this country would do well to bear in mind in examining the scope of the Cabinet Mission's project and its political and social implications. The first assumption is that British imperialism has by its inner contradictions now become almost an anachronism in history and cannot hold what it had. Where it cannot, as at present, sustain itself by its own strength it must seek alliances in response to the urge of survival. It follows that the Mission's Plan is a continuation of that process of political adjustment by compromise necessitated by the forces released in the inter-war period and accentuated by the rapid transformation of the racial character of the capitalist enterprise due mainly to the last war. The second assumption is that the compromise arrived at must be one which, if it is to prove fruitful even for a temporary period for the decadent imperialist structure, must not alter fundamentally the basis of the State. To that end alliances must, if possible, be negotiated with those social classes that not only do not think in terms of revolution but would resist with all their might a decisive change in the relations of production. The third assumption is that the transfer or adjustment must be made with reference to religious communities because distribution of power on such basis is more likely in India in the present setting to ensure reaction than any other principle. The fourth assumption is that where a deed of transfer is based on compromise the final sanctioning authority is the party that makes the offer despite its historically determined precarious existence unless, of course, in the meantime forces are mobilised to remove the last vestige of its power and influence and prestige. The questions, therefore, are : Can the Constituent Assembly now in session or the three Sectional Assemblies and the Union Constituent Assembly as proposed in the Cabinet Mission's long-term plan resolve the conflict between India and Britain and that between the exploiting few and the exploited and oppressed and submerged many? Does the project at all contemplate a real, drastic and necessary change of the State-power? Or does it aim at some sort of an upper-class deal designed to preserve in the name of national freedom the essence of the existing structure with certain adjustments in the racial composition of the State and its organs?

The first point of importance that arises is not merely one of convening the Constituent Assembly or Assemblies but of who in fact is to convene them. It may be recalled that this very issue was raised in connection with the Russian revolutions. Indeed in every instance in which the Constituent Assembly in the real sense of the term was used as an instrument for determining the deed of transfer of power it was summoned by a Provisional Government representative of those for whom the transfer was intended. This procedure was in effect adopted even in the case of Ireland. The coming into existence of a Provisional Government prior to the convocation of the Assembly is, historically speaking, of the essence of any scheme of transfer of political power through this machinery. The British Cabinet Mission's Plan does not fulfil that requirement except in a vague way: in a vague way because the Mission state that they "attach the greatest importance . . . to the setting up at once of an Interim Government having the support of major political parties".[1] Not the slightest suggestion is made about the responsibilities of this Government in regard to the Constituent Assembly or Assemblies, although care is taken to lay stress on other functions of the Administration. This omission is not only significant; it is, on the face of it, deliberate.

The preliminary steps in connection with the Constituent Assembly or Assemblies have been taken by the Governors of Provinces in accordance with the Viceroy's directive, although after the summoning of the preliminary meeting the initiative has passed into the hands of its Chairman. The directive was issued in terms of the last paragraph of the Cabinet Mission's and the Viceroy's statement of June 16, which reads as follows :

[1] Para 22.

> The Viceroy is also directing the Governors of the Provinces to summon the Provincial Legislative Assemblies forthwith to proceed with the elections necessary for the setting up of the constitution-making machinery as put forward by the statement of May 16.

Apart from the broad political issue as to the suitability of this kind of action by representatives of the British Government in their sole discretion, it is not, I am afraid, free from certain technical errors. It is clear that the Assemblies were summoned by the Governors under s. 62 (2) of the Government of India Act, 1935. It is also clear that the Assemblies proceeded to the election of representatives in accordance with the Governors' message sent under s. 63 (2). So far there was no difficulty. But these were sessions of the Provincial Assemblies, and not meetings of members convened for a specific purpose. The proceedings of the sessions must be conducted in accordance with the provisions of the Act or the rules made thereunder. It is laid down that save as otherwise expressly provided all questions shall be determined by a majority of votes of the members present and voting.[1] Has Mr. Jinnah, Dr. Ahmedkar or Pandit Nehru, for instance, been elected by the majority of votes of members present and voting in the Assemblies concerned? Was not the procedure adopted repugnant to the statutory provision?

Indeed, proportional representation by means of the single transferable vote either in the Chamber taken as a whole or in communal compartments is not permissible under the Act except where special provisions in that behalf have been made, as in the case of election of a certain number of members of the Provincial Second Chamber, where it exists, by members of the Provincial Assembly. No such rule was made by the appropriate authorities in respect of elections to the Constituent Assembly or Assemblies. Even if it were made, it is doubtful if it would be valid except for members of the Assemblies meeting and transacting certain specified business as distinguished from sessions of the Assemblies. Nor can a directive issued by the Viceroy, or the authority given him by Ministers of the Crown in that behalf, abrogate the provisions of the governing statute and legalise proceedings which are otherwise invalid. The proceedings connected with the election of

[1] s. 66(1).

representatives to the Constituent Assembly or Assemblies seem to me irregular on the ground (1) that the decisions were not taken, as required by and under the statute, by the majority of votes of the members present and voting, and (2) that the method of voting adopted was not in these cases permissible as not being expressly provided for by rules within the scope of the Act. They could be legally sustained only by the general rule of interpretation that where there is no prohibition the whole field is open to a legislature exercising within its own ambit plenary powers. I submit that the provisions of s. 66 of the Government of Act, 1935, constitute a prohibition, if not expressly, at any rate by necessary intendment.

I think the Viceroy should have been advised to direct the Governors to summon members of the Provincial Assemblies for elections to the Constituent Assembly or Assemblies in accordance with the Cabinet Mission's scheme instead of summoning formally sessions of the Assemblies for the purpose. In order that the proceedings of the constitution-making body or bodies may not be held up by recourse to vexatious litigation the British Government should get through Parliament a Validating Act. I must point out, however, that where, as in Britain or in India, the final law-making authority is supreme, the question of constitutional or legal validity of statutes or executive acts is not of great practical importance as in the United States because, by simple and ordinary legislative process, the irregularities may be corrected or illegalities validated with retrospective effect. Things may be delayed or progress held up but not "killed" or vetoed by decrees or judgments of courts.

2. No Revolutionary Provisional Government

Coming back to the question of the Provisional Government without which the Constituent Assembly looks like a debating or drafting Committee, the Cabinet Mission and the Viceroy have throughout their negotiations and in their formal official documents avoided that expression. They have consistently referred to the executive authority that is to function between now and the formation of a Government under the new constitution as the Interim Government. In the *communique* issued from New Delhi on August 24, 1946, announcing the King's acceptance of the resignations of members of the Governor-General's Executive Council and his appointment of members of the new Government, the old form is retained, although in the *communique* itself and the Viceroy's broadcast of that date the expression "Interim Government" occurs. In the Press Note issued on August 31, in connection with the distribution of portfolios, mention is once again made of the "Interim Government". Politically and in constitutional practice "Interim Government", however, means nothing except that it is a stop-gap arrangement. It has acquired no specific meaning such as is attributed to "Provisional Government". Even the "Care-taker Government" manned by permanent members of the Civil Service, which has been replaced, may be called an "Interim Government" without any violence to English terminology. The exact form of the present Interim Government is clearly indicated in the announcement of the appointment of Mr. C. Rajagopalachariar made at New Delhi on September 10.[1] As usual members of the new Government have taken three oaths, namely, the oath of allegiance to the King, his successors and heirs by law ; the oath of office ; and the oath of secrecy. The first-named oath reaffirms the British Crown's sovereignty and, in the context of the present constitutional position, the British Government's paramountcy. The term "Interim Government" refers to time and not to functions and duties as such save in so far as every Government is required to discharge certain functions and duties. There is no emphasis on qualitative change. It is, of course, implied that the Interim Government will stand behind the Constituent Assembly or Assemblies and enforce their decisions in addition to its attending to the urgent and immediate calls of day-to-day executive business. But its moral and political adequacy must be commensurate with the grave responsibilities of a transition. Does the Mission's scheme contemplate such Government?

There is no difference in this regard between what was offered by Sir Stafford Cripps in 1942, and the Mission's proposals except that under the latter all the members of the Viceroy's Government,

[1] Government of India Home Department, New Delhi, the 10th Sept., 1946, No. 60/13/46-Public—Whereas His Majesty the King Emperor of India has been graciously pleased to appoint Sri C. Rajagopalachari to be a member of the Council of the Governor-General of India, it is hereby notified that the Honourable Sri Rajagopalachari has on the forenoon of this day taken upon himself the execution of his office.

including the Defence Member, are Indians. They differ from the administrative set-up of the 1919 Act in that members of the Government are mostly drawn or may all have been drawn from political parties on the basis of proposals made primarily on political grounds. There is no legal change in the status, functions and powers of the Interim Government barring what has been effected by the India (Central Government and Legislature) Act, 1946.[1] So far as the Central Executive is concerned, the relevant amendments apply to the composition of the Executive Council[2] and the powers of the Governor-General.[3] It is provided by sub-section (3) of section 36 of the Government of India Act, as continued in force by the Government of India Act, 1935,[4] that three at least of the members of the Council must be persons who have been for at least ten years in the service of the Crown in India, and that one must be a barrister of England or Ireland or a member of the Faculty of Advocates of Scotland, or a pleader of a High Court, of not less than ten years' standing. This is repealed so that the Viceroy's field of choice has been extended. But it indicates no new policy, for the implementation of the Cripps offer would have necessitated this amendment. As a matter of fact, Sir Stafford Cripps promised in 1942 that Mr. Churchill and his colleagues then in power would sponsor a short Bill for the purpose if the "major political parties" agreed to work the plan.

Then it is provided by section 18A of the Interpretation Act,[5] that the expression "Governor-General" in relation to the period between the commencement of Provincial Autonomy under the Government of India Act, 1935, and the inauguration of federation thereunder means the Governor-General in Council. This is amended and the Governor-General is authorised to exercise his powers under the amending legislation of 1946 in his discretion. That means that in very important matters of Central legislation affecting the law-making powers of the Provinces the initiative in law rests with the Viceroy, the Governor-General in Council being eliminated for these purposes. This certainly is a retrogade step inasmuch as it confers powers on a single person to the exclusion of a corporate body. These amendments apart, the administrative machinery remains intact.

[1] 9 & 10 Geo. 6, Ch. 39. [2] s. 1. [3] s. 6(1).
[4] Ninth Schedule. [5] 52 & 53 Vict. C. 63.

The relevant issue is one bearing on the position and powers of the Governor-General *vis-a-vis* his Executive Council, or the Interim Government. It is covered by provisions of sections 40 and 41 of the Consolidated Government of India Act[1] (not the Government of India Act, 1935). All orders and other proceedings of the Governor-General in Council, it is laid down, shall be expressed to be made by the Governor-General in Council, and shall be signed by a Secretary to the Government of India, or otherwise as the Governor-General in Council may direct. When so signed, they shall not be called into question in any legal proceeding on the ground that they were not duly made by the Governor-General in Council.[2] The Governor-General may make rules and orders for the more convenient transaction of business in his Executive Council, and every order made or act done, in accordance with such rules and orders, shall be treated as being the order or the act of the Governor-General in Council.[3] The difference between the two sub-sections should be carefully noted. The rule-making power for the transaction of business vests in the Governor-General, but once the rule is made or any order passed such rule or order binds the Governor-General in Council.

By this power the collective character of the corporate body known as the Governor-General in Council has been undermined, if not completely destroyed, and the Executive Council reduced to a loose conglomeration of the heads of departments with no sense of collective responsibility and no unity of purpose so as to compel the Viceroy, if need be, to listen to them. This process has been helped by the policy underlying appointments to the Council hitherto followed of which loyalty and attachment to British rule as opposed to progressive, if at times militant, political affiliations have been the primary consideration. The practice hitherto followed is the legacy of the Indian Councils Act, 1861.[4] The observations made in that year on January 26 by Lord Canning about the distribution of business among members in the course of a despatch to the Secretary of State are interesting. Lord Canning wrote: "A division of departments . . . has to some extent taken place,

[1] 5 & 6 Geo. 5, Ch. 61 ; 6 & 7 Geo. 5, Ch. 37 ; 9 & 10 Geo. 5, Ch. 101 ; and 12 & 13 Geo. 5, Ch. 20.

[2] s. 40(1).

[3] s. 40(2).

[4] 24 & 25 Vict. C, 67, s. 8.

and the result has been good. I would recognise this division by law, and I would carry it out more distinctly. For this purpose the law should declare that it shall be in the power of the Governor-General to charge each Member of the Council with the direction of such department of the Government as he may think fit. . . It is not possible, or desirable, to define by law what questions should be submitted to the whole Council. Subjects constantly arise upon which it is quite right that a Member of the Council should consult the Governor-General, but which it would be a waste of time to bring before every Member of the Council. . . There is no fear that important questions would be kept from the consideration of the whole Council. . ." But in his despatch of August 9, 1861, the Secretary of State remarked : "I need hardly impress upon your Lordship the necessity of caution in framing the rules and orders, so as not to exceed the limit of the discretion conferred upon the Governor-General. . . The object to be kept in view is the more convenient transaction of business. There is nothing in the provision of a nature to detract from the authority or responsibility of the Governor-General or the Council."

If opinion is divided on any question brought before a meeting of the Governor-General's Executive Council, the opinion and decision of the majority of those present shall bind the Governor-General in Council. In the case of a tie the Governor-General has a second or casting vote.[1] Should, however, the Governor-General differ from the majority in a matter which, in his judgment, affects or may affect the safety, tranquillity or interests of British India or any part of British India, he may on his own authority and responsibility take action otherwise than in accordance with the opinion or decision of the majority of the Council.[2] This reservation is not to be construed as empowering the Governor-General to do anything which he could not lawfully have done with the concurrence of his Council.[3] The Act presumes that the majority decision as a normal rule prevails ; only in exceptional circumstances recourse may be had to the Governor-General's reserve power. It has often been said that there have hardly been occasions in recent years, if at all, where the Governor-General deemed it necessary to overrule the Executive Council. Perhaps

[1] s. 41(1). [2] s. 41(2). [3] s. 41(4).

that is true. I do not know. It explains nothing except that the Executive Council lost its corporate character partly by the Governor-General's accretion of power and in part on account of the rules of business made from time to time.

As far as I have been able to gather, members of the Council were concerned mostly with their own departmental matters and normally did not address themselves to other questions as being outside their jurisdiction. In such atmosphere members inclined, apart from the statutory provisions, to look forward to the Governor-General for lead and guidance rather than to each other for collective decisions even on vital issues. It was not a case of the Governor-General's reserve power being rendered inoperative by political pressure from within or by his ready and enthusiastic response to the country's demands ; it was a case of the exercise of that power being rendered unnecessary by the members' easy adaptability to the seductive environments of the giant machine. I think that by this method Lord Linlithgow was able to secure a majority or unanimous decision of his Executive Council on the question of arrest of Gandhiji and members of the Congress Working Committee immediately after the A.-I.C.C.'s historic August decision of 1942, or the restraint of Mr. Sarat Chandra Bose by orders of the Government of India.

The announcement of the formation of an Interim Government on August 24, 1946, makes no change in the legal position. It is no new thing. In the Cripps offer of 1942, as well as during the Cabinet Mission's negotiations in 1946, the British Government and their representatives repeatedly stated that they did not intend to attack the basic structure of the Central Government. In his letter, dated May 30, to Maulana Abul Kalam Azad, the Viceroy wrote that he had not told him that "the Interim Government would have the same powers as a Dominion Cabinet", adding that the whole constitutional position was entirely different. Nevertheless an assurance was given that "His Majesty's Government would treat the new Interim Government with the same close consultation and consideration as a Dominion Government." That assurance was reaffirmed by Lord Wavell in his broadcast from New Delhi on August 24, in which it was stated that he would "implement fully H.M.G.'s policy of giving to the new Government the maximum freedom in the day-to-day administration of the country." But once again care was taken by the Viceroy to assert that "the new

Interim Government would operate under the existing constitution."[1] In regard to the change signalised by the appointment of an Indian for the first time as the Defence Member, it has been made clear that " the constitutional position of the Armed Forces is in no way changed".

An impression may have been created that the entire Central executive authority has passed into the hands of Pandit Nehru and his colleagues and that something like a Cabinet has in fact, though not in law, been set up with the Governor-General acting, like the King in England or the Dominion Governors-General, as the constitutional head. Nothing could be farther from truth. The practice initiated by Pandit Nehru of members of the Interim Government meeting in his office rooms in the New Delhi Secretariat at regular intervals, exchanging notes and taking stock of the day's or week's work was an informal affair. The Muslim League members' refusal to take part in these proceedings on their entry into the Government has upset it. Normally the meetings of the Governor-General in Council are held under the Governor-General's chairmanship or, in his absence, under that of the senior member in accordance with rules and at such meetings the main decisions on policy or programme are taken. Sanction attaches to these decisions, and not to any other. Then there is an extensive field of executive business which is held exclusively by the Viceroy. He works through a staff which is outside of the ordinary administrative machinery and is not in any way amenable to control by the Interim Government as such. This exclusive field extends to such matters as the relations between the Paramount Power and the States, those between the Governor-General and the Governors of Provinces and the safeguards for what are known as the Secretary of State's services. As to any appropriation of revenue or moneys relating to these subjects, the decision of the Governor-General is final.[2] In regard to the rest of executive business, of course, the Interim Government comes in, but there, too, as has been pointed out, the Governor-General may in certain circumstances interpose his authority. It is dualism in action. This, then, is the machinery which the Congress has agreed to use for the interim period. It may be asked, as already it has been asked in certain quarters,

The Viceroy's New Delhi broadcast of August, 24, 1946.
Ninth Schedule s. 67A(4).

that if this was the kind of the Provisional Government of India for which the country had fought so long and so ardently, what was all this pother about these years? What did "Quit India" really mean? Is it the type of Government which the Congress can utilise effectively for the purpose of investing the Constituent Assembly or Assemblies with requisite sanction to force decisions on the British Government?

In attempting to answer these questions certain points should be borne in mind. First, for the first time in the history of Indo-British connection the leader of the largest and most representative body had been officially invited, as in Britain and the Dominions, to aid and assist the Governor-General in recommending names for the new Government for the final approval of the King. It was by no means a formal proceeding, for it appears that the list of names given by Pandit Jawaharlal Nehru has in its entirety been accepted by the Viceroy and approved by the King. It is a definite acknowledgment by the British Government and the Viceroy of a principle on which the Congress has consistently taken its stand. I do not suggest that it is an act of self-abrogation on their part. This change in policy has been brought about by irresistible pressure from within and without and India's men and women may feel legitimately proud that they have played no mean part in shaping the course of events. Secondly, however deplorable the Muslim League's earlier decision to keep out, which it has since revised by joining the Interim Government, the British Government and the Viceroy were forced to implement Mr. Clement Attlee's assurance given in Parliament that they could not allow a minority to place their veto on the advance of a majority.[1] It should, however, be admitted that almost a similar sentiment had been expressed by Mr. Winston Churchill in Parliament while announcing the appointment of the Cripps Mission in 1942.[2] Mr. Churchill stated that "the War Cabinet have agreed unitedly upon conclusions for present and future action which, if accepted by India as a whole, would avoid the alternative dangers, either that the resistance of a powerful minority might impose an indefinite veto upon the wishes of the majority, or that

[1] Prime Minister Clement Attlee's Commons Speech on March 15, 1946.

[2] Prime Minister Winston Churchill's Commons Speech on March 11, 1942.

a majority decision might be taken, which would be resisted to a point destructive of internal harmony and fatal to the setting up of a new constitution." Obviously there is some difference in emphasis, but as a statement of principle it was a distinction without a difference, particularly in view of the fact that Mr. Attlee, too, was at pains to express his deep concern about the rights of minorities. In both the statements the minority's right to veto was overruled. The rejection in toto of the Cripps offer by the Congress and the Muslim League described by the British Government as the two major political parties left no opportunity to pin down Mr. Churchill to his proposition. But who can deny that these years of strife and conflict, of challenges and upheavals throughout the world awakened the British people to the progressive deterioration in Indo-British relations and the imminent peril to peace and security?

The step taken by Lord Wavell in inviting Pandit Nehru to make proposals for the formation of the Interim Government and setting it up on his advice seems to involve the transfer of responsibility to resolve internal conflicts or quarrels from British to Indian hands, although the British Government and their agents out here have not yet been completely eliminated from the picture. The policy hitherto followed has been that India can have her freedom for the mere taking provided she reports jointly to the British Government that she has made it up. Until then the latter are in the saddle and continue to discharge the obligations of their Indian trust without frown or favour ! That kind of patronising attitude was not only insulting to India's self-respect, but in a way an incitement to tactics of intransigence. It made certain groups or parties look for British support with the result that deadlock followed deadlock. Now the scene of action has been transferred, seemingly at least, and the initiative has changed hands. This is no small national gain, although it may for the moment involve grave internal disorders. But in view of the fact that the Muslim League's quota of five seats in the Interim Government was kept vacant and of the Viceroy's appointment of persons recommended by that body, including a Scheduled caste Hindu, it is wrong to call the Central Administration Pandit Nehru's Government. It is not, either in law or in fact. The selection of Pandit Nehru as Vice-President of the Interim Government does not give him the status of the Prime Minister as one acquainted with English constitutional history understands that office. Pandit Nehru is at best the first among equals, *primus inter pares,* as they put it, in the new administrative set-up. It is reasonable to assume, however, that the Muslim League responded to the Viceroy's appeal and joined the Government because it had reasons to suspect that its continued non-cooperation would not lead to the break-up of the machinery.

In addition to the considerations indicated above, there is another point which seems to have counted with the Congress President and his colleagues in agreeing to co-operate with Lord Wavell in the setting up of the Interim Government more or less along lines suggested in the statement of June 16, 1946, (6: 5: 3) which the Congress Working Committee had previously rejected by their decision of June 25. That is the Viceroy's special stress on the spirit in which he was prepared to work the new arrangement and which, according to him, is of much greater importance than any formal document and guarantee. It is true that usage and practice rather than statutes have played a decisive role in the evolution of English constitutional history. By gradual stages many a statutory provision have been rendered obsolete by accretion of popular power on the basis of principles enunciated by the eighteenth century Rationalists and Humanists. Thus a large body of what they call fictions of law has grown up. Nor can it be denied that there is substance in Lord Wavell's proposition that "the most liberal intentions may be almost unrecognisable when they have to be expressed in a formal document".

At the same time one cannot forget that the so-called constitutional conventions are typically British. Psychologically they make no appeal to the Indian mind. There is doubt about the applicability of such conventions to the conditions and environments in this country. What is more important, it is not because of their sincere, honest and implicit faith in the spirit of a constitution rather than in its letter that the British Government have refused to initiate legislation in Parliament to transform the transitional Government. Their final decision has aparently been influenced by Mr. Jinnah's insistence on the *status quo* being maintained for the interim period and by their long-term imperial strategy. Indeed Mr. Jinnah's fear, genuine or other, has been sought to be exploited in the British interest such as British interest is still viewed by the Labour Government, contrary to the lessons of history, on the advice of the War Office and the reactionary official hierarchy. They seem to have decided that no opportunity should be given to the energetic protagonists of *Quit India* or the left-wing Indian political parties to utilise the legal machinery of the Government of India to assail British suzerainty before they obtain a full and complete picture of India under the proposed treaty. The subordinate status of the Interim Government and the legal restraints are being maintained as a sort of a bargaining counter at the time when vital decisions will have to be taken on matters arising out of the transfer of responsibilities from British to Indian hands. Whether this will succeed is, however, a different matter. But it is in accord with the general verdict of history that vested interests in the process of liquidation, whatever their character and complexion, are impelled by the urge of survival to resort to every conceivable device. It does not matter whether or not it is sustainable by the principles of ethics or logic.

British policy in regard to Muslims generally and to the Muslim League in particular, followed during the last several years, brings into bold relief these clumsy, desperate and apparently self-contradictory tactics. These have been tactics of concession-cum-coercion, of appeasement coupled with repudiation. The British Government and the Viceroy, for instance, have shown no hesitation in rejecting Mr. Jinnah's case for Pakistan and, at the last stage of the Mission's negotiations, throwing him overboard, although the British Government and Lord Wavell have once again assured him that the provisions relating to Sections and Groups would be strictly adhered to and that the Interim Government would operate under the existing constitution. The text of correspondence that passed between Lord Wavell and Mr. Jinnah from July 22, 1946 to August 8, 1946, tends to show that all through it had not been a clean game. Mr. Jinnah is wrong that in the Mission's and the Viceroy's statement of June 16, the basis of representation was 5: 5: 4 ; the basis, as the Viceroy points out, was 6: 5: 3, from which there has been no departure. On the other hand, the Viceroy was not telling the truth and the whole truth when he sought to create the impression by his New Delhi broadcast that there had been no change of tactics on the part of the British Government. He should have made it clear that if, for lack of agreement, it was a case of one major political party being invited to advise him as regards the formation of the Interim Government, it was the Congress and not the League that was entitled to this right by its own strength and also for the confidence it commands among other sections of the community. He should have made it clear, too, that if it was a question not of the smaller minorities choosing their own representatives but of either of the major parties making recommendations it was, again, the Congress and not the League, to whom the right belonged.

In fairness to all the parties concerned, these principles should have been adequately emphasised by the Cabinet Mission at the beginning of the negotiations instead of raising false hopes in certain quarters. All these shady proceedings reinforce the argument urged earlier that Mr. Jinnah's authority, influence and weight count little or nothing where British interests, whatever they may be, are involved. It is not Mr. Jinnah's insistence that there must be no change in the constitutional machinery for the interim period that has finally influenced British policy in this regard. Nor was the time factor of any material importance. During the past several years, it may be noticed, important amendments to the Government of India Act, 1935, have been effected without any difficulty. Had the British Government honestly desired or favoured a change to adapt the legal framework to the political requirements they could have introduced it in the course of three or four weeks. That the Congress leaders' action in refraining from pressing their demand for amendment of the present Act in these circumstances should cause surprise is quite understandable.

With the Muslim League inside the Interim Government and determined to make the best of a bad bargain certain alternative developments are possible. There is, first, the possibility of a closer and more intimate alliance between the Congress and the British Government with positive leanings towards the Right for meeting the League's challenge. There is, secondly, the possibility of the British Government and their agents out here exploiting this internecine strife for the purpose of pushing the Congress back and reasserting their dominance in the administrative machinery on the plea of justice, equity and fair play. There is, thirdly, the possibility of the Congress precipitating conflict with its British partners in the joint enterprise and going out for what has so often been called the final struggle. There is, fourthly, the possibility, as a result of this interminable civil strife, of the leadership of either party being isolated and power being wrested from them by the combined efforts of the Indian masses with the left-wing middle strata of society and militant Workers' Councils assuming command. In any event the Interim Government is not going to prove a bed of roses. Nor is it the kind of Government that can function effectively behind the Constituent Assembly. I must concede, however, that for the immediate present between the British Government, the Congress, the Muslim League and the Princes they left no course open other than the one that has been adopted. I have my serious doubts if this set-up augurs well for the Constituent Assembly and a peaceful and orderly transition from the present state to Indian freedom and democracy. Whether the Interim Government will in this atmosphere be an Indian version of the pre-Soviet Kerensky Government of Russia, or of the pre-Nazi Hindenburg Government of Germany, or of the de Valera Government of Southern Ireland is a matter about which one cannot risk a prophecy at this stage. Anything may happen, but the times are exciting and we are in the midst of a crisis of history.

3. One Constituent Assembly or Three Assemblies?

I now proceed to examine, as fully as I can, the provisions relating to the Constituent Assembly and its "Sectional" auxiliaries which have provoked such a bitter controversy. At the outset attention is called to Field-Marshal Auchinleck's broadcast in Hindusthani to the Indian troops on May 17, 1946, the day following the announcement of the Cabinet Mission's long-term Plan, in the course of which the Commander-in-Chief stated that while the Interim Government "carries on the daily business of governing the country, it is proposed that there should be set up three assemblies composed of representatives of all parties and creeds and classes, and elected by the Provincial Legislatures". It is, of course, not expected of a military man that in his choice of diction or in the precision of language employed to convey a political idea he should cultivate the austerity of a trained lawyer or the judgment of a seasoned statesman. One is, however, entitled to assume that the Commander-in-Chief knew what he meant when he mentioned "three assemblies" with reference to the framing of India's constitution. It is, moreover, certain that his speech had been approved by the Cabinet Mission and the Viceroy upon a most vigorous and close scrutiny. Special significance attaches to his reference to "three assemblies" and Field-Marshal Auchinleck's assurance to the troops gives an indication of the creative or destructive minds of those responsible for the Mission's long-term project. The rest of his speech is not much important as being a pale and insipid paraphrase of the authorised version of the State Paper. Evidently by "three assemblies" the Commander-in-Chief had in mind the "assemblies" for Sections A, B, and C leaving out of account the Union Constituent Assembly mentioned in the Mission's Plan.[1] Perhaps it did not occur to him how these "three assemblies" would stand in relation to the Union Assembly or how these three regional currents could be merged in a national stream for the unity of India's defence upon which naturally this gallant gentleman laid so much stress.

The broad principles of British policy have been stated plainly in the Mission's statement. Negatively, there shall be no *Pakistan* of the League variety, or its revised version as in the now-famous C. R. formula, or the pattern into which it was finally evolved by the deft Gandhian touches, in other words, no independent sovereign States in north or south, east or west. Affirmatively, there shall be a Union Centre, the final repository of India's State-power, dealing with specified subjects, side by side with States and autonomous Provinces enjoying the residuaries and, if so decided, groups of Provinces in possession of powers delegated to them, in their common interest, by the Provinces concerned. After this first start, however, the mechanism of the machine begins to give trouble. It has no precedent in the known structures of States ; it is the post-war product of war-stricken mechanics.

The elected representatives of the Provinces meet at New Delhi on the summons of the Viceroy presumably acting in consultation with the Interim Government. At this stage the States are represented by a Negotiating Committee set up by the Princes.[2] This Negotiating Committee have, of course, no place in the preliminary meeting of the Provincial representatives, where the general

[1] Para 19 (VII). [2] Para 19 (II).

order of business is decided, a Chairman and the office-bearers elected and an Advisory Committee on the rights of citizens, minorities, and tribal and excluded areas set up.[1] There is no point in ousting the States representatives from such important proceedings unless it is assumed that the Princes may, if they so like, withdraw from the project. Thereafter the Provincial representatives divide up into three Sections. These Sections then proceed to settle the constitutions for the Provinces in question and also decide whether any Group constitution should be set up for those Provinces and, if so, with what provincial subjects the Group in each case should deal. Once the "Group" is formed there is no opting out by any of its constituent units except by a decision of the new legislature of the Province concerned created under the new constitution after first general election.[2] Then the representatives of the Sections (no longer the Provincial representatives) and the Indian States "reassemble" for the purpose of settling the Union constitution.[3] Thus the representatives elected by the Provincial Legislative Assemblies continue as such at the preliminary meeting without the States ; they become "Sectional" representatives when they divide up into the Sections and thereafter. It is an interesting study in the evolution of species by what may be called a "jerk" in constitution-making. If, as is clear, the representatives of the States have no place in the preliminary meeting, how subsequently do they and the Provincial representatives, transformed into Sectional representatives, "reassemble"? If they "reassemable", as it is proposed they will, is not the "preliminary" meeting of the Provincial representatives without the States' representatives a contradiction in terms?

Further complications arise. In the Union Constituent Assembly, where both the Sectional and States' representatives are present as integral parts of that body, the resolutions varying the provisions of paragraph 15 of the State Paper or raising any major communal issue are not in order unless approved by a majority of the representatives present and voting of the two major communities.[4] The Chairman of the Union Constituent Assembly decides which, if any, of the resolutions raise a major communal issue. Before giving his decision he consults the Federal Court, if so requested

[1] Para 19 (IV).
[2] Para 19 (V).
[3] Para 19 (VI).
[4] Para 19 (VII).

by a majority of the representatives of either of the major communities.[1] It is not stated whether or not the opinion of the Federal Court binds the Chairman. In the absence of a specific provision in this regard the Chairman is presumed to have the final say. In terms of the Act of 1935, the Federal Court as such can have no advisory jurisdiction in such matters unless the Chairman approaches it *via* the Governor-General who alone in his discretion can refer to it certain questions of law.[2] The Cabinet Mission "recommend" that the rough outline given in paragraph 15 is the "basic form" which the constitution should take. The term "constitution" here used seems to include the Union Constitution, the constitutions for the Provinces and the Group constitutions, if any. It means, in other words, the entire machinery of the Indian State under the new Plan. Otherwise it makes no sense. But the language of the State Paper should have been more precise regard being had to the contradictions it reveals from page to page. I call it the Indian State because the concept of more than one independent sovereign State for India is for the present rejected, subject to reservations for the Indian States.

4. Constitutional Unity of India Acknowledged

What, then, is the basic form of this new Indian State? It is the Union of India embracing both British India and the States. It deals with Foreign Affairs, Defence and Communications. It possesses the powers necessary to raise the finances required for these subjects.[3] It has a legislature constituted of representatives from the Provinces and the States, and an executive.[4] A question raising a major communal issue in the legislature requires for its decision the majority of the representatives present and voting of each of the two major communities as well as a majority of all the members present and voting. The "two major communities" referred to mean, as in paragraph 19, Hindus and Muslims. All subjects other than the Union subjects mentioned above and the residuaries vest in the Provinces[5], and the States retain all subjects

[1] Ibid. [2] s. 213. [3] Para 15 (1). [4] Para 15 (2). [5] Para 15 (3).

and powers except those ceded to the Union.[1] Provinces are free to form Groups with executives and legislatures and each Section determines the Provincial subjects to be taken in common.[2] The Union constitution and the Group constitutions shall contain a provision whereby any Province is entitled, by a majority vote of its Legislative Assembly, to call for a reconsideration of the entire constitutional structure after an initial period of ten years and at 10-yearly intervals thereafter.[3]

It has been suggested that the provision of paragraph 19(V) is repugnant to paragraph 15 (3), (5) and that the latter being the "basic form" it supersedes the former to the extent of repugnancy. I do not agree that there is repugnancy. Paragraph 15 states in broad terms the principles while paragraph 19 sets out the procedure to be followed in giving institutional forms to those principles. In interpreting a whole scheme it is an elementary rule that construction is to be made of all the parts together, and not of one part only by itself. The words of each clause, according to the dictum of Lord Watson, should be so interpreted as to bring them into harmony with the other provisions if that interpretation does no violence to the meanings of which they are naturally susceptible.[4] So interpreted, the language of paragraph 19 does no violence to that of paragraph 15 and the apparent conflict should be sought to be resolved by construing the document as a whole.

While rejecting the Muslim League's demand for Pakistan as well as the Congress scheme presented to them the Cabinet Mission have acknowledged what they call the very real Muslim apprehensions "that their culture and political and social life might become submerged in a purely unitary India in which the Hindus with their greatly superior numbers must be a dominating element".[5] They have expressed the view that the solution they have offered instead "would be just to the essential claims of all parties, and would at the same time be most likely to bring about a stable and practicable form of constitution for All-India".[6] Therefore, the basic form of the scheme is : (1) An Indian Union with defined and restricted powers for the Centre ; (2) Provinces and

[1] Para 15 (4). [2] Para 15 (5). [3] Para 15 (6).
[4] *North Eastern Ry.* v. *Hastings (Lord)*, 1900 A. C. 260 at p. 267.
[5] Para 12. [6] Para 15.

States as units with all powers for the Provinces other than those required for the defined and restricted Union subjects and for the States other than those ceded to the Union ; and (3) Groups of Provinces, if decided upon by the Sectional representatives concerned. The State Paper should be interpreted with reference to this basic form.

It is, however, asked that if the Sections are to settle the constitutions of the Provinces and, if they so like, also the Group constitutions, what is the point in stating that the "Provinces should be free to form groups"? The question, then, is whether the "sovereign" rights of the Provinces should be interpreted as superseding, in the case of repugnancy, the powers of the Sections or whether the latter overrule the former. I think the proper construction by way of reconciliation of this conflict is that until after the first general election under the new constitution the "sovereign" rights of the Provinces must be read subject to the powers of the Sections. The rights, say, of Bengal and Assam are for this specific purpose and for the limited period the rights of 70 representatives of these two Provinces meeting together in Section C and taking decisions. "Provinces" in paragraph 15 (5) means in this context the Provinces in the Section in question, and not each of the Provinces concerned, and this is confirmed by the phrase "each Group" used in the same sentence with reference to the determination of Provincial subjects that may be taken in common. If "each Province" had been intended, "each Province" would have been inserted when "each" occurs quite appropriately elsewhere in the same paragraph. If "singular" had been intended, "singular" would have been used in paragraph 19 (VIII). It is true that in a statute or document words in the singular include the plural and that words in the plural include the singular, but this holds good unless the contrary intention appears.[1] Only where the language of a document, in its ordinary meaning, leads to a contradiction of its purpose or to absurdity, a construction may be put on it which modifies the meaning of the words and even the structure of the sentence.[2] No such consideration applies to the present controversy. As a matter of fact, the Mission in their statement of May 25, in reply to the Congress and the League, left

[1] 52 & 53 Vict. C. 63 (Interpretation Act, 1889), s. 1 (1) (a).
[2] Maxwell's *The Interpretation of Statutes* (7th edition), p. 198.

no room for doubt as to what had been intended by them. They wrote:

> The interpretation put by the Congress resolution on paragraph 15 of the statement to the effect that the Provinces can in the first instance make the choice whether or not to belong to the Section in which they are placed does not accord with the Delegation's intentions. The reasons for the grouping of the Provinces are well known and this is an essential feature of the scheme and can only be modified by agreement between the parties. The right to opt out of the Groups after the constitution-making has been completed, will be exercised by the people themselves since at the first election under the new Provincial constitution, this question of opting out will obviously be a major issue and all those entitled to vote under the new franchise will be able to take their share in a truly democratic decision.

There appears to be some confusion between "Sections" and "Group constitutions". One is different from the other. For each and all the Provinces to go into "Sections" is mandatory along lines set out in the Table of Representation for the Constituent Assembly ; to form "Group constitutions" is, however, a matter of discretion not for each Province separately, but for all the Provinces in the relevant Section sitting together. There is no safeguard for decisions on major communal issues in meetings of the "Sectional representatives", as in the Union Constituent Assembly, and the Union Legislature that may be created under the new constitution. The decisions, whatever they may be, will be by a simple majority vote unless a different method is adopted by agreement. It is no use trying to read into words or sentences meanings which they do not bear, or to put into the mouth of the authors of the State Paper words which they have not used. As it is, in Section C there is the possibility, unless there is agreement, of Bengal Province-wise and Muslims community-wise dominating the proceedings. Similarly but on a more secure basis, the same privileged position is held by the Punjab and Muslims in Section B. I have no doubt in my mind that the Cabinet Mission's statement of May 16 bears the interpretation which has been put upon it by the British Government in their statement of December 6. They have made it plain that the decisions in the Sections "should, in the absence of agreement to the contrary, be taken by a simple majority vote of the representatives in the Sections". What is of special significance is that they regard the statement as so interpreted as "an essential part of the scheme" for enabling the Indian peoples to "formulate a constitution which H.M.G. would be prepared to submit to Parliament." The idea is that if the proceedings of the Constituent Assembly are conducted and decisions taken at any stage in violation of this "essential part of the scheme", the British Government's undertaking to get the decisions implemented falls to the ground.

So far there is no lack of clarity, but difficulty arises when one is confronted with the British Government's assurance that "should the constitution come to be framed by a Constituent Assembly in which a large section of the Indian population had not been represented, H.M.G. would not, of course, contemplate . . . forcing such a constitution upon any unwilling parts of the country." It is not clear what they mean by "a Constituent Assembly", "a large section of the Indian population" and "any unwilling parts of the country". It is evident from the resolution adopted by the Working Committee of the Muslim League on January 31, that that body has taken it for granted that the reference is to the absence of the Muslim League from the preliminary sittings of the Constituent Assembly and that any decisions at those sittings without the Muslim League's participation would be *ab initio* void, invalid and *ultra vires.* The matter is not so simple as the Muslim League Working Committee would have us believe.

The language in which the British Government's statement has been couched is open to different and conflicting interpretations. It may be construed as extending the immunity to Provinces, compact homogeneous groups in any specified zone or area or what the Muslim League's Working Committee may have in mind. As a matter of fact, in its resolution passed on January 6, while agreeing to advise action in accordance with the interpretation of the British Government in regard to the procedure to be followed in the Sections, the A.-I.C.C. has pointed out that "this must not involve any compulsion on a Province and that the rights of Sikhs in the Punjab should not be jeopardised". It goes further and says that in the event of any attempt at such compulsion "a province or part of the province has the right to take such action as may be deemed necessary in order to give effect to the wishes of the people concerned". There is, on the face of it, an apparent conflict between the first part of the A.-I.C.C.'s resolution and the second part. For once it is conceded, as it has been conceded, that the decisions in the Sections may be taken by a simple majority vote there is no point in insisting that the taking of such decisions involves compulsion on a Province or part of it.

The A.-I.C.C., however, might have meant one of these two things : it might have meant, that is, that as in the Union Constituent Assembly so in the Sections the decisions should be by agreement and not by a simple majority vote. It might have meant, secondly, that whether the decisions are by agreement or by a simple majority vote, the constitutions of the Provinces concerned or of the Groups, if any, should not be so framed as to render the Provinces' right to opt out null and void for all practical purposes. The second is to my mind a fairer and more reasonable approach than the first and Maulana Abul Kalam Azad appears to me to have taken this view in the course of a statement issued on the eve of the Karachi session of the Muslim League's Working Committee. But whatever may be the Congress approach or the Muslim League's interpretation, the British Government owe it to themselves and to the Indian peoples to throw light on what actuated them in inserting the last paragraph of their statement of December 6, before further progress is made in the matter of implementation of the Cabinet Mission's long-term project.

There is apprehension that once the smaller Provinces or the religious minorities are in the "Sections" it may not at all be possible for them to opt out in terms of paragraph 19 (VIII) of the Mission's Plan. I see no ground for such apprehension. It is laid down that as soon as as the new constitutional arrangements have come into operation it shall be open to *any* Province to come out of the Group in which it has been placed. The decision in this regard shall be taken by the new legislature of the Province after the first general election under the new constitution. It is intended that there shall be no restriction whatsoever on the exercise of this freedom to opt out on the part of a Province. Any device in the Provincial or Group constitution that may be set up by Sectional representatives, which may seek to limit, qualify or nullify this freedom, is repugnant to the provisions of the paragraph and to the basic form of the Mission's long-term Plan and should be summarily rejected by those on whom the responsibility may lie to accord final sanction to the constitutional arrangements made under the project.

But there is no denying the fact that theoretically at least provisions as to mandatory "Sectional" division and grouping are grossly unfair in Section C to Assam and Hindus, and in Section B to the North-west Frontier Province and Sind and to Hindus and Sikhs. They cut at the root of Provincial rights which are of the essence of contractual relations of a Federal compact. These are conceesions to Mr. Jinnah and the Muslim League, which should not have been made on the ground, amongst others, of their blatant repugnancy to the principles of self-determination, over which the League and its leaders wax so eloquent. It seems to me, however, that this controversy over Sections and Groups is unreal unless, of course, provisions are incorporated in the constitutions of Provinces or Groups by a simple majority vote in the Sections, which may nullify the right of the Provinces to opt out in terms of Paragraph 19 (VIII) of the Cabinet Mission's Plan. It is unreal because if the Provinces concerned so decide, they may have no occasion to go into Groups at all. It is common ground that the existing constitution operates at the Centre and in the Provinces until it is replaced by a new constitution or constitutions under the Cabinet Mission's Plan. It is laid down that after the first election under the new constitution or constitutions it will be open to the Assembly of any Province to take a decision to opt out. That being so, if a Province wants to keep out of its relevant Group, there is nothing to stop it or stand in its way. Therefore, there may be no Groups in B or C Sections. Difficulty, however, remains in the matter of constitutions of Provinces. They are to be framed by the Sections and not subject to alteration by the Provinces except perhaps after the expiry of the ten-year period. It comes to this that for ten years from the commencement of the new constitution or constitutions Assam may be governed under a constitution framed by the majority from Bengal or the Muslim majority in the Section. *Mutatis mutandis* in Section B for ten years the Punjab votes may decide the fate of Sind and the North-West Frontier Province or the Muslim majority may fashion the life of the non-Muslim minorities in the Punjab. But I maintain that the Cabinet Mission's Plan does not contemplate that what is fundamental to the life of a Province or a compact communal area of considerable size should be imposed upon them against their express will.

From the point of view of self-determination and Provincial rights and also, paradoxical as it may sound, in the interest of a strong Federal Union for India the Cripps formula was far better and much less cumbrous than the mechanism of the Cabinet Mission's project. The British Government then declared that their object was the creation of a new Indian Union. They undertook to accept and implement a constitution framed on that basis by a constitution-making body, "subject only to the right of any Province of British India that is not prepared to accept the new constitution to retain its constitutional position, provision being made for its subsequent accession if it so decides". With such non-acceding Provinces, if they so desired, the British Government were prepared to enter separate arrangements analogous to those contemplated for the Indian Union.[1] The starting point then was a Federal Union whose ambit of authority, power and jurisdiction in relation to the units was left to the decision of the constitution-making body without any restrictions. It was open to each Province either by decision of its legislature or through a popular referendum, if it so liked, to keep out of it at the initial stage and then, on further reflection, to accede to it subsequently. No coercion of Province by Province was involved as now. Community-wise, too, there was no reasonable ground for any serious objection because the decisive verdict in the last resort was that of the majority of the people in the Province. I wonder if these points at all occurred to the Congress President and his Working Committee. Or was it the old scare of the post-dated cheque that made people blind to the substantial assets of the Bank upon which in 1942 there had been a panicky run?

5. Modern Federal Trends

What is perplexing is not so much the apparent conflict between paragraph 15 (5) and paragraph 19 (IV) (V) of the Mission's statement as the projected delimitation of functions between the Union Centre and the Provinces or that between the former and the "Groups", if any. It will, I am afraid, be a breach of the terms of the Mission's Plan if the Chairman elected at the preliminary meeting of the Provincial representatives in the Constituent Assembly rules on his own responsibility or at the instance of any member or members that they shall not divide up into Sections or that each Province is free to go its own way in

[1] The Cripps Plan, clause (C) (1).

disregard of the decision of the appropriate sectional representatives. But surely it will be perfectly within the rights of the Union Constituent Assembly to take decisions, and of its Chairman to give rulings, which are pertinent to the defined functions of the Union Centre or the recommendations that may be made by the Advisory Committee as envisaged in paragraphs 19 (IV) and 20. The three subjects assigned to the Union are of such wide import in our time that it is difficult, if not almost impossible, to bring them within the limits of a precise definition. "Defence" both in war and peace may reasonably make demands upon Provinces which are almost destructive of their residuary sovereignty. Similarly "Communications" may with equal justification extend to what, as a normal rule, is regarded as the exclusive Provincial terrain. Again, obligations may arise or commitments may be made by the Union in respect of "Foreign Affairs" which will amount to encroachments on powers held, in the ordinary meaning of words, to be purely Provincial.

Where, then, is the boundary line? The art of most skilful draftsmanship or the ingenuity of phraseology may fail to draw it. It may as well lead to constant friction and expensive and prolonged litigation. It is worth while recalling in this connection an important Canadian case which was decided by the Privy Council in 1930. In *Attorney-General for Canada* v. *Attorney-General for British Columbia*[1] Lord Tomlin took special care to summarise the principles of construction which had been held by the Privy Council in a series of earlier decisions to apply to the Canadian Federation in particular, and generally to the contractual relations of a Federal compact. These are: (i) that the legislation of the Dominion, so long as it relates to subjects expressly enumerated in s. 91 (Dominion), is of paramount authority, even though it trenches upon subjects enumerated in s. 92 (Provincial) ; (ii) that it is within the competence of the Dominion Parliament to provide for matters which, though otherwise within the legislative competence of the Provincial legislatures, are necessarily incidental to effective legislation expressly enumerated in s. 91 ; and (iii) that mere overlapping does not invalidate either Federal or Provincial legislation if the field is clear, and where the field is not clear the Federal law supersedes the Provincial law to the extent of repugnancy.

[1] A. C. 111, 118 (1930).

It may be argued that the principles referred to above may apply to federations where, as in Canada, the residuum belongs to the Centre, and not, as in the United States or the Australian Commonwealth, to the units. While conceding that there is some force in this contention there is little doubt that they indicate a general trend of all federal compacts with or without statutory centripetal bias. What does one find in the United States, a different federal pattern from Canada? In a long catena of cases Chief Justice Marshall had by rules of construction of the implied powers extended the scope and sphere of federal legislation and consequently reduced the legislative authority of the States despite their residuaries.[1] "The American Republic", as Professor Kennedy so aptly put it, "began with a theory of State rights. Today we watch the ever-increasing growth of Federal Power".[2] The same trend governs the present relations between the Australian Federation and the States, whatever might have been the intentions of the authors of the compact. The result has been obtained in part by legislation and in part by judicial decisions. The exclusive powers assigned to the Centre are enumerated in s. 52. They extend impliedly, if not by express intendment, also to the duties of excise and bounties on the production or export of goods[3], to the naval or other armed forces, to the imposition of any tax on the property of any kind belonging to the Commonwealth,[4] and to the coinage and legal tender in payment of debts.[5] The powers exercisable by the Centre under s. 51 are, however, not exclusive "unless from the nature of power, or from the obvious results of its operation, a repugnancy must exist so as to lead to a necessary conclusion that the power was intended to be exclusive." In any other case, "the true rule of construction is that the power is merely concurrent."[6] Where, however, a repugnancy arises between a Commonwealth law and a State law in the concurrent field the latter is superseded to the extent of repugnancy.[7] Save in respect of subjects which are exclusively federal the onus of proof rests

[1] For further treatment read the author's *The Problem of Minorities*, Chapter XVIII.

[2] Kennedy's *Essays in Constitutional Law*, p. 84.

[3] s. 90. [4] s. 114. [5] s. 115.

[6] Quick and Garran: *The Annotated Constitution of the Australian Commonwealth*, p. 509.

[7] s. 109.

with the Commonwealth that it is competent to legislate as to a matter which, prior to the federation, belonged to the States.[1]

Like the Privy Council in respect of the Dominion of Canada the High Court of Australia has by its rulings enlarged the scope of the Federal power.[2] Of special relevance to the controversy that may arise in the Indian (Union) Constituent Assembly over the implications of Defence is the decision in *Victoria* v. *Commonwealth* in which the High Court held, contrary to the decision in *Commonwealth* v. *Australian Shipping Board,*[3] that "where a clothing factory was established to supply clothing for the military forces of the Commonwealth during the War, legislation authorising the supply of clothing to Commonwealth Government Departments other than the Department of Defence, to the Government of Victoria, and to the local authorities of the same State, was valid as incidental to defence power."[4] By a constitutional amendment in 1929[5], the Commonwealth has come to hold a position of dominant authority in financial matters. Leaving aside the statutory changes, the general trend of judicial interpretation has rendered the States' residuary power almost anæmic. New South Wales challenged the validity of the Financial Agreements Enforcement Act, 1932, enacted by the Commonwealth Legislature under s. 105A, and the matter was taken to the Court. The High Court held that the Act was in order.[6] The observations made by one of the judges are significant. Starke J. said :

> "The States are subjected by the constitution to the legislative power of the Commonwealth to enforce and execute the Agreement. The national power is paramount and may be exerted against the property, moneys, and revenues of the States, in whatever form they exist, and wherever found."

6. Possible Lines of Conflict in Indian (Union) Constituent Assembly

These tendencies apart, it is plain common sense that where there is responsibility there must be power commensurate with it

[1] *Attorney-General for Australia* v. *Colonial Sugar Refining Co.* A.C. 237 (1914).

[2] *Burkard* v. *Oakley*: 25 C.L.R. 422 (1918).

[3] 39 C.L.R. 1 (1926).

[4] 52 C.L.R. 533 (1935).

[5] s. 105A.

[6] *New South Wales* v. *Commonwealth*, 46 C.L.R. 246 & 264 (1932).

so that responsibility may not be reduced to a nullity. Hence honestly and in all seriousness those who stand for a federated India will try to make the powers assigned to the Indian Union, however restricted numerically they may be, as adequate and effective as required in the circumstances of to-day. On dividing up into Sections after the preliminary meeting the representatives of Provinces, let us assume, decide in Sections B and C to frame not only the constitutions for the Provinces but the Group constitutions as well and give them the widest measure of sovereignty apparently consistent with the terms of the Plan. Thereafter they reassemble with or without the States representatives in the Union Constituent Assembly and are confronted with far-reaching proposals, again apparently within the defined ambit of the Union, but obnoxious to the Provincial and Group constitutions earlier settled in B and C. Thus a conflict ensues. In this conflict do the Union Constituent Assembly's decisions supersede the Provincial and Group constitutions? Or do the latter prevail over the former? It is wrong to think that it is a hypothetical case. In the organisation of modern States of a federal type one cannot avoid this conflict.

In anticipation of conflict of this character the preliminary meeting has set up a Committee to report on the Union Centre subjects not later than April 15. This step has been taken evidently to demarcate clearly the fields of jurisdiction so that the authority of the Centre may not impinge upon that of a Province or a Group or that of a Province or a Group upon that of the Centre. Admittedly there may arise many points of detail in regard to the listing of subjects which may involve broad issues of principle. I agree with Mr. Rajagopalachariar, who sponsored this move, that there are lacunæ in the Cabinet Mission's scheme which have got to be filled up as far as possible at some stage or other. The point is whether this matter should be taken up at the plenary sitting or in the "Sectional" Assemblies or in the Union Constituent Assembly. Having regard to the specified agenda of business for the preliminary meeting and its limited scope it is reasonable to argue that the Cabinet Mission did not contemplate that a decision in this regard should be taken at the preliminary stage except by agreement. Mr. Rajagopalachariar's resolution may therefore be construed by the Muslim League and the Indian States as an attempt to forestall certain constitutional arrangements without their consent. Representatives of the Provinces might have stayed their hands for some time yet. Incidentally it should be remembered that in our time when there is a growing extension of the State's functions the statutory demarcation, however carefully defined in principle or however meticulous in detail, is apt in the nature of things to leave a wide residual field. The Mission's Plan, of course, offers no machinery for settlement of such disputes except where they involve major communal issues. There, too, the majority of either Hindus or Muslims can hold up progress because there can be no decision unless it is agreed to by the majority of either community.

Difficulty arises also regarding the Advisory Committee, which was intended by the Cabinet Mission to be set up at the preliminary meeting with due regard for full representation of the interests affected. Its function is to report to the Union Constituent Assembly upon the list of Fundamental Rights, the clauses for the protection of minorities, *and a scheme for the administration of the tribal*[1] *and excluded*[2] *areas*, and to advise whether these rights should be

[1] "*Tribal areas*" means the areas along the frontiers of India or in Baluchistan which are no part of British India or of Burma or of any Indian State or of any foreign State (Government of India Act, 1935, s. 311). The central executive authority extends to the exercise of such rights, authority and jurisdiction as are exercisable by His Majesty by treaty, grant, usage, sufferance, or otherwise in and in relation to the tribal areas, (s. 8). The functions of the Governor-General in this behalf are required to be exercised in his discretion (s. 11.) The discussion of, or the asking of questions on, any matter connected with the tribal areas is prohibited, save with the consent of the Governor-General in his discretion, in either Chamber of the Indian Legislature except in relation to estimates of expenditure. [s. 38 (d) (i).]

[2] Under the Government of India (Excluded and Partially Excluded Areas) Order, 1936, the excluded areas are in *Madras* the Laccadive Islands (including Minicoy) and the Amindiri Islands; in *Bengal* the Chittagong Hill Tracts; in the *Punjab* Spiti and Lahaul in the Kangra District; in *Assam* the North-East Frontier (Sadiya, Balipara and Lakhimpur) Tracts, the Naga Hills District, the Lushai Hills District and the North Cachar Hills Sub Division of the Cachar District; and in the *North-West Frontier Province* Upper Tanawal in the Hazara District. Power is reserved to His Majesty by Order in Council under the Government of India Act, 1935, (s. 91) to direct that the whole or any specified part of an excluded area shall become, or become part of, a partially excluded area; alter, but only by way of rectification of boundaries, any excluded or

incorporated in the Provincial, Group or Union constitution.[1] Where does the final decision lie? If it is the right of the Union Constituent Assembly to decide, then the Provincial and Group constitutions of Sections B and C may be materially and even, in fundamentals, altered in disregard of the Muslim minority in the Union Assembly. If, on the other hand, the Union Assembly's decision in this regard is subject to the provisions of the Provincial and Group constitutions already settled by the Sectional representatives, then reference to the Union Constituent Assembly is meaningless. No light is thrown in the Cabinet Mission's Plan on this issue.

Recourse to the federal judiciary has been suggested quite seriously in the case of such disputes. That procedure is not under the present Act available to the Union Constituent Assembly or its Chairman unless the Governor-General in his discretion seeks the opinion of the Court. Even if it were possible with or without the Governor-General's help, it is bound to delay or retard progress and expose the Union Constituent Assembly to frequent litigation of a mischievous, maybe, frivolous character. Besides, a Constituent Assembly does not function by resort to a judicial machinery or arbitration on issues of dispute between and among members. It is not in accord with dignity or swift dispatch of business.

The provision of paragraph 15(6) as to the insertion of a clause in the Union and Group constitutions empowering each Province to call for a reconsideration of the entire constitutional machinery after every ten years is, again, not free from ambiguity. It does not specifically state that it will be open to any Province to secede from the Union, although that right is implied. It does not necessarily mean that each Province will have power to amend

partially excluded area; and, on any alteration of the boundaries of a Province or the creation of a new Province, declare any territory not previously included in any Province to be, or to form part of, an excluded area or a partially excluded area. The executive authority of a Province, of course, extends to its excluded areas. That notwithstanding, no Act of the Central Legislature or of the appropriate Provincial Legislature applies to an excluded area unless the Governor by public notification so directs (s. 92). The Governor is required to exercise his functions in his discretion in respect of any area in a Province which is for the time being an excluded area.

[1] Para 20.

or alter its constitution in whatever manner it may like. It does not mean that immediately after a Province decides by a majority vote of its Legislative Assembly a machinery is brought into existence by some invisible authority and that the latter is at once and automatically in seisin of a countrywide dispute as to the basic principles and detailed provisions of the Provincial constitutions, the Group constitutions and the Union constitution. That would be a gigantic and provocative affair. What does it mean? With respect to the distinguished authors of the State Paper, I find in it nothing but a vague and nebulous idea rendered all the more cloudy and confusing by anæmic phrase-mongering. It may as well be that the Cabinet Mission deliberately left the paragraph in that chaotic stage in order that it might be given a concrete shape by representatives of the Indian peoples themselves in accordance with their own needs and requirements. Which of these bodies gives the shape—the Union Constituent Assembly or the Sectional representatives? If both, then who disposes of any repugnancy that might occur between the provisions made by the Union Constituent Assembly and those laid down by the Sectional representatives? Do they again go to the Federal Court for justice, equity and good sense?

7. What does the Proposed Indo-British Treaty Mean?

Equally vague, though far more sinister, is paragraph 22 of the State Paper which provides that a treaty is to be negotiated between the Union Constituent Assembly and the United Kingdom to cover certain matters arising out of the transfer of power. The procedure contemplated under this paragraph, it will be seen, is different from that adopted in 1921, in the case of Southern Ireland. In the latter instance the articles of agreement for a treaty had first been negotiated and signed by representatives of the Irish Revolutionary Provisional Government and the British Government. These articles gave a full and clear idea of the reservations which the British Government had demanded and to which the Irish Government after negotiations agreed. They then made appropriate provisions for the constitution-making machinery in regard to both its substantive and procedural aspects so that the framers of the Irish constitution were left in no doubt as to how far they could go and where they were to stop. In this, as in other respects, the British Government's India Plan lacks precision and courage. The treaty-making is not normally the function of such a large body as the Constituent Assembly or even of a properly constituted legislature. The initiative is taken by the Executive Government and its decision goes to the legislature for ratification, amendment or modification.

If it is intended, as has been suggested in certain British and Indian circles, that the Interim Government is not virtually the continuation of the East India Company's executive framework sustained, with certain modifications, under the constitution at present in operation, but a Provisional Government in the real sense of the term, then this task should have been assigned to the Interim Government, if not for its conformity to the general form, at least for the reason that the work of the Constituent Assembly might have been expedited and unnecessary delay avoided. At any rate, the Constituent Assembly might have known precisely where it stood in the matter of constitution-making.

It seems to me that this sensible and correct procedure was not acceptable to the Mission because, as the treaty involved questions affecting the Indian States, they were persuaded that the Interim Government, in which the Princes had no representation, were not competent to undertake this responsibility. There is another consideration that might have influenced British policy in this regard. Fear and anxiety dominated the Mission's negotiations from beginning to end : fear of the unknown and anxiety about their future in the new relation of forces. In an atmosphere of fear and anxiety vagueness and indecision are the traditional safety-first tactics. Time is relied upon pathetically, but not without hope, as a healer and it may be that the Cabinet Mission were advised that with the passage of time the situation internally and externally might by some miraculous turn of events put the British Government in a better bargaining position.

Now, what are those "certain matters" which are supposed to arise out of the transfer of power? The approach in the Cripps offer did not materially differ from that in the present Plan, but in the scheme of 1942, specific indications were given in two respects. First, it was stated that the treaty "will make provision, in accordance with undertakings given by His Majesty's Government, for the protection of racial and religious minorities. . . ." Secondly, it was laid down that whether or not "an Indian State elects to adhere to the constitution it will be necessary to negotiate a revision of its treaty arrangements so far as this may be required in the new situation".[1] In the course of his speech in Parliament on March 11, 1942, Prime Minister Winston Churchill went a little more in detail into the matters referred to in the Cripps Plan. Mr. Churchill observed that the framing of the constitution by the projected machinery was "subject to the fulfilment of our obligations for the protection of minorities, including the Depressed Classes, and our treaty obligations to the Indian States and to a settlement of certain lesser matters arising out of our long association with the fortunes of the Indian sub-continent". Similar indications had been given in the Linlithgow offer of 1940. There is nothing to show that British policy in this respect has undergone any substantial change since 1942 or even 1940 except in so far as it is open to the Constituent Assembly under the new scheme, if it so likes, to proceed with the framing of the constitution on the basis of complete independence. But independence, whatever shape or form it may eventually take, is subject to two reservations. This point was explained by the Cabinet Mission in their statement of may 25, 1946. They observed *inter alia :*

> Once the Constituent Assembly is formed and working on this basis, there is no intention of interfering with its discretion or questioning its labours. His Majesty's Government will recommend to Parliament such action as may be necessary for the cession of sovereignty to the Indian people, subject only to two matters which are mentioned in the statement (May 16) and which we believe are not controversial, namely, adequate provision for the protection of the minorities (paragraph 20 of the statement) and willingness to conclude a treaty with His Majesty's Government to cover matters arising out of the transfer of power (paragraph 22 of the statement).

The question of "nationalities" and "minorities" I propose to take up in the next chapter. The second reservation seems to extend to (i) the treaty rights of the Princes ; (ii) the question of Defence for internal and external purposes ; (iii) the commercial and trade interests of the British European community in their internal and external aspects ; and (iv) compensation to the personnel of the Army, Navy and Air Force and the Secretary of State's services, who may be called upon by the Union Government or the

[1] Clause C (ii).

Governments of Provinces to quit or who may themselves ask to be relieved of their responsibility under the new arrangements. With regard to the Princes I have already dealt with their position historically and in the light of the new constitutional developments as foreshadowed in the State Paper. The Crown will cease to exercise its paramountcy on the establishment of a free, independent Indian Union ; nor shall it be transferred to the Union by the Crown. The matter is left to be negotiated, in the first instance, between the States Negotiating Committee and a corresponding Committee of the Provincial representatives in the Constituent Assembly, and then to be dealt with at the Union Constituent Assembly, should the States agree to participate in its proceedings. Failing that, the issue may be fought out between an independent India and the States. Even the issue as to how the States representatives should be "selected" to the Constituent Assembly is a matter of negotiations in which the Cabinet Mission, if they are to be taken at their word, had no hand.[1] The question, first, is whether at that stage the British armed forces, wherever they may be stationed, would be employed to aid and assist these feudal autocracies. The question, secondly, is whether failure of agreement between the States and the Constituent Assembly would relieve the British Government of their obligation under the State Paper of May 16, read with the Mission's explanatory memorandum of May 25, to implement the constitution that may be framed in accordance with the procedure laid down.

Far more complicated is the question of defence. In connection with the Anglo-Irish Treaty of 1921, Mr. Lloyd George, it has been shown, addressed a letter to the head of the Irish Delegation in elucidation of the scope of its terms in which he held out the assurance on behalf of the British Government that they proposed "to begin withdrawing the military and auxiliary forces of the Crown in Southern Ireland when the articles of agreement are ratified." On this point the Mission's Plan is vague and misleading. No assurance of the kind given by the then Prime Minister in the Irish case has yet come from the present Socialist Prime Minister or any comparable British authority. All that the Cabinet Mission have said is that there is no intention on the part of the British Government of "retaining British troops against the wish of an

[1] The Mission's statement of May, 25, 1946.

independent India under the new constitution". They made it plain, however, that as under the present constitution, which the Congress has accepted as the major element in the Interim Government, the British Parliament has the ultimate responsibility for the security of India, the British troops would remain until other arrangements were made under the new constitution.[1] This was in reply to the Congress demand for the withdrawal of British troops from Indian soil and obviously the Congress Working Committee did not like to make it an issue in view of what they were persuaded to regard as more urgent and important problems awaiting immediate solution. Nevertheless there is a good deal of difference in spirit as well as in letter between the Mission's statement and Mr. Lloyd George's promise to Southern Ireland in 1921. So many precedents in support of the British effort to force or negotiate arrangements to maintain and protect the "life-lines" of the Empire, whatever their repugnancy to the sovereign status or the domestic requirements of the countries concerned. They did it in Egypt. They did it in Iraq. Are they going to follow a different a policy in India?

Professor R. Coupland is a name with which India has been very much familiar in recent years. It is reported that he had an assignment under Sir Stafford Cripps in 1942, in the capacity of a constitutional adviser. Earlier he had come out to this country on what then appeared to be a private study mission. On his return he produced a book[2] dealing exhaustively with different aspects of the Indian problem in their historical setting as well as in their immediate or future political bearings. *Apropos* of the question of the so-called British obligation in respect of defence Professor Coupland writes that when the transfer of power is effected Britain will naturally offer such assistance as India may require for the time being against external aggression. He develops his thesis with consummate skill and in mild but persuasive language. British aid will, according to him, meet India's first and primary need because she cannot on her own expect, for some time to come, to provide herself with an adequate system of modern defence. Then in the order of priority are the British interests, the Common-

[1] The Mission's statement of May 25, 1946.

[2] Professor R. Coupland's *The Constitutional Problem in India* (Oxford Press).

wealth interests and the interests of the United Nations. It is contended that the war has demonstrated more convincingly than ever before that the security of India is a strategic necessity for peace and freedom throughout the world. What is meant by peace the learned professor does not care to tell us. What kind of freedom he wants maintained and preserved he does not say either. But the world's peace and freedom cannot be maintained unless the security of India is guaranteed ! The security of India cannot be guaranteed at least for the present except with British military aid ! And why? On one side of India lie China, Burma, Malaya, the Dutch East Indies and the approaches to Australia and the Pacific ; on the other the middle East and the approaches to South Africa and the Suez Canal.

Of Professor Coupland's knowledge of the border terrain of this country there is no doubt. There is no doubt about her strategic importance in the event of any war. But who, according to Professor Coupland, are the potential disturbers of the world's peace and freedom? Who are India's possible enemies? What is the ground for preserving complete identity of Indian and British interests in all circumstances? Mark Professor Coupland's words. If, as he assumes, Britain, Australia, South Africa, the British Commonwealth and the United Nations are all our allies, who is the imaginary foe? Now that Japan has been crushed, who attacks us from north-east and south-east? Now that Hitler's Germany and Mussolini's Fascist Italy and Empire have been completely shattered, who attacks us accross the Middle East and the Suez? Are there any States of considerable size and importance outside of the United Nations Organisation that can challenge the united might of that body, of the British Commonwealth and Empire, of Britain or even of India? If there are, what are those States? Or does this learned professor of an ancient University and constitutional strategist of the British Commonwealth and Empire apprehend an early breakdown of the U.N.O. and its machinery of peaceful settlement of inter-State disputes? If he does, where does he expect attack on free and independent India from? Not, of course, from South Africa, for that Dominion is and will ever be our ally despite its atrocious anti-Indian legislation ! Not from Australia, for that Dominion, too, is and will ever be our ally despite its white Australian policy ! Not from Britain, for that country has been our trustee in the past, is our guardian angel for the present and in the near and distant future will be our friend and ally notwithstanding the consequences of British rule in India ! Is Professor Coupland anticipating a new polarisation of forces with Socialist revolution with its economy of abundance and social freedom on one side and the trans-Atlantic neo-plutocracy with its cartels, trusts, monopoly capital and economy of scarcity on the other? Is he trying to prepare the ground psychologically and by subtle propagation of a fear complex and the cult of survival for a new type of Indo-British alliance? I am afraid there is evidence that Professor Coupland's strenuous labours in this direction have not been altogether fruitless.

Now, Professor Coupland says that the geographical situation of India would necessitate in peacetime the stationing of British troops on Indian soil and their collaboration with Indian forces in a joint system of defence. Quoting with approval Sir Stafford Cripps' statement to a Press Conference at New Delhi in 1942 that "no Imperial troops will be retained in this country except at the request of, or by agreement with, the new Indian Union or Unions," he maintains that this is a matter that would be taken up in connection with the proposed treaty between India and Britain. He then cites as precedents South Africa, Southern Ireland and Egypt. Not only that: he goes farther and points out that the leasing by the British Government in 1940-41 to the United States of defence bases in Newfoundland, the British West Indian islands and British Guiana is the proof it affords that such collaboration is necessitated by modern conditions of defence and is in no sense a derogation from the sovereign status and dignity of an independent nation.

Professor Coupland has, of course, due regard for sensitive and suspicious Indian sentiment. He says that there is no question, as in Egypt, of the British troops remaining in India as forces of occupation or interfering with the country's internal security. That will exclusively be an Indian responsibility. But, as in Egypt again, they will be here to defend the frontiers of India. Naturally their location will lie in the neighbourhood of the north-west and north-east frontiers. That, however, is not enough. For the purpose of defence in depth aerodromes will be required at various distances from the frontiers right in the heart of this vast country and along all her strategic lines. For defence by sea, say, from the Persian Gulf, the Mediterranean and the Pacific facilities for British naval and coastal air forces will be needed at the major Indian ports.[1]

The familiar accents of the Anglo-Egyptian treaty breathe through Professor Coupland's proposals. That treaty was signed on August 26, and ratified by the Egyptian Chamber on November 14, 1936. It was based partly on Lord Curzon's declaration of 1922, and partly on the British Government's draft treaty of 1930. By the former the British protectorate over Egypt was terminated and Egypt declared to be an independent, sovereign State with certain security and military reservations. The provisions of the treaty of 1936, and the draft treaty of 1930, differ in respect of the property of "foreigners", the capitulatory regime and the immigration of the Egyptians into the Sudan. In these matters the treaty of 1936 has made more liberal concessions to the Egyptians while in regard to the military reservations the draft treaty of 1930 was less objectionable. Under the arrangements now in force all the outward and formal symbols of Egypt's independent sovereignty are acknowledged, including the termination of military occupation. In return the British Government are entitled to station forces in the Egyptian territory in the vicinity (both east and west) of the Suez Canal, "with a view to ensuring in co-operation with the Egyptian forces the defence of the Canal".[2] The number of such forces is not to exceed 10,000 land troops and 400 pilots of the air force, exclusive of auxiliary personnel. The Egyptian Government are required to construct and maintain roads, bridges, railways, etc. necessary for military operations, and to allow the British Air force to ply, wherever necessary, for training. In the event of war, imminent menace of war, or apprehended international emergency the King of Egypt must give aid to the British King on Egyptian territory, including the use of his ports, aerodromes and means of communication. If necessary, the Egyptian Government must proclaim martial law and take censorship measures to render their aid and assistance effective.[3]

The administration of the Sudan continues "to be that resulting from the agreements of January 17, and July 10, 1889". In the approved imperialist fashion the primary aim of the Condo-

[1] Read Professor Coupland's interesting Chapter (XIII) on *British Obligations*, pp. 156-171.

[2] art. 8

[3] art. 7.

minium is declared, in accordance with Art. II of the Anglo-Egyptian Treaty signed in August, 1936, in the wake of the Italian invasion of Abyssinia, to be the welfare of the Sudanese, but appointments and promotions of officials in the Sudan are made by the Governor-General in whom is vested the entire legislative and executive auhority. He is the supreme military commander of all the forces in the country. He is appointed by a decree of the King of Egypt on the recommendation of the British Government and may be removed from office in like manner. The Governor-General is assisted by a Council created on the analogy of the Executive Council of the Governor-General of India. The decisions of the Governor-General in Council are issued as Ordinances. These are to be notified to the Egyptian Government, but the latter have no power to amend or alter them. The Governor-General has power to overrule the Council in all matters. The Sudanese budget is, however, subject to the audit and approval of the Egyptian Government. In other respects, the Sudan is on the whole independent of Egypt. But for all practical purposes the British dominate the show. Negotiations for the revision of the Anglo-Egyptian treaty may be opened with the consent of the two contracting parties after the expiry of ten years from its commencement. After twenty years, however, the question of revision may be raised by either party. It is not at all surprising that the military concessions to Britain stipulated in the treaty and the financial obligations imposed upon the Egyptian Government in respect of construction works should have caused resentment in progressive Egyptian circles. It seems that for various reasons it will be difficult to reach a satisfactory settlement as a result of the conversations which have since seemingly broken down between Egypt and Britain over the treaty terms. By far the most difficult hurdle is perhaps the Sudan. It is reported that when Nokrashy Pasha's predecessor, Sidky Pasha, met the British Foreign Secretary in London in autumn last year they drew up what is widely known as the Sudan Protocol. The authentic text of the document has not been published, but it is understood that the Egyptian sovereignty over the Sudan was acknowledged with certain reservations. The first reservation was that the present Anglo-Egyptian administration as established by the Condominium Agreement of 1899 should continue for the time being as some sort of an interim arrangement. The second was that the Sudanese should be left free at an appropriate time to determine whether they should be completely independent or be linked with Egypt in accordance with the principle of self-determination. In view of the recriminations on either side it is difficult to obtain a full picture of the situation. While it is reasonable and fair that the Sudanese should have the right of national self-determination the British Government's insistence on maintenance of the *status quo* and their persistent plea for intervention in discharge of their so-called obligations may lead one to suspect that they are interested in preventing a friendly union betwen Egypt and the Sudan. The correct and democratic approach in the circumstances would be on the following lines:

(i) that there should be immediate withdrawal of all British troops from the Nile Valley ;
(ii) that the Sudanese should have the right of national self-determination ; and
(iii) that Britain must waive her claim to participate in any defence scheme or plan jointly with Egypt.

The Anglo-Iraqi treaty of 1930 took as its model the Anglo-Egyptian draft of the same year. In Iraq, as in Egypt, all the formal treaty forms are observed and maintained. The compact is declared to have been "concluded on terms of complete freedom, equality and independence". Peace and friendship are established between the two Governments, a close alliance solemnly affirmed and a full and frank consultation in all matters of foreign policy affecting their common interests provided for.[1] In the event of war, or imminent menace of war (on Egyptian analogy) the King of Iraq must aid Great Britain by giving on Iraq territory all facilities and assistance, including the use of railways, rivers, ports, aerodromes and means of communication.[2] The British Government are further authorised, of course, without prejudice to this treaty pattern of sovereign rights, to maintain air bases in the vicinity of Basra and west of the Euphrates as well as to station British troops in certain specified localities.[3] If foreign military instruction is necessary, it must necessarily be British and no other, especially along the vital "life-lines" of the Commonwealth and

[1] art. 1. [2] art. 4. [3] art. 5.

Empire ; and under the treaty Iraq undertakes to appoint British military instructors and offer the traditional immunities and privileges to the British armed forces. According to the British declaration of 1928 on the treaty of Paris for the renunciation of war the defence of Iraq, as that of Egypt, is treated for all practical purposes as a British responsibility. Egypt and Iraq are, in form, full-fledged independent sovereign States and these military concessions, forced or voluntarily given, are supposed not to derogate from their internal or external sovereignty.

Of the military reservations in the case of Southern Ireland previously dealt with at length nothing more need be said. They have been withdrawn. In South Africa, in terms of the Churchill-Smuts agreement of 1921, the British Government are permitted to use the port of Simonstown as a naval base and to maintain its own naval dockyard there, although the Union has since that year undertaken the entire responsibility for its defence, including approved coastal defences at Table Bay and at the naval base at Simon's Bay. Thus a new theory of Statehood is being evolved. Neither Dominion Status of the Statute of Westminster variety nor complete independence is in any way affected or prejudiced by the stationing of foreign troops, the maintenance of military bases by a foreign Power and the grant or extortion of concessions involving heavy financial and administrative liabilities. In support of this theory Britain's lending of certain bases to the United States during the War has been cited by Professor Coupland. It is not unlikely that the British Government will press for the insertion in the proposed treaty between India and Britain of military guarantees on the Egyptian or Iraqi model or on the Commonwealth analogy in Southern Ireland and South Africa.

The protection, if any, of the commercial and trade interests of the British European community may come under the general question of minorities or be covered by the treaty according as members thereof are treated as Indian nationals or aliens. At the present moment, as I have shown, they are not aliens. They are not only entitled to all the political and civil rights which are accessible to Indians but enjoy certain special privileges which are not accorded to British subjects other than Indians. It will be for the Constituent Assembly or Assemblies to investigate this matter and take decisions keeping in view the paramount interests of the country. The question of compensation to the members of the Secretary of State's services for termination of their jobs or premature retirement due to constitutional changes raises issues of a delicate nature. They entered, or were induced to enter, those services in expectation of certain amenities and prospects which the new system cannot offer. On the other hand, India was called upon to undertake obligations and liabilities without her consent and against her will. One's genuine sympathy for these men need not blind one to the fact that if the dismissal or forced retirement involves a breach of solemn undertakings or the terms of agreement, the responsibility attaches to the British Government and to nobody else, in any case not to the poor Indian taxpayer. Therefore, the best and most reasonable arrangement would be for the British Government to accept full financial liability. That may be deemed to arise appropriately from Britain's past policy. In no circumstances should India agree to more than a token share of this liability in view of the employment of these services primarily in imperial interests, and of the limited resources of the new Indian State in the initial period of the experiment.

Opportunity may be taken at the time of treaty-making by the British Government or their representatives to urge writing off or scaling down or diversion of India's sterling balances so that British finance-capital may to a certain extent avert the disaster that stares it in the face or make good at least a portion of the colossal loss sustained in the War. Certain questions and answers in Parliament on February 4, 1947, in connection with the sterling balances are revealing. Mr. Churchill succeeded in pinning down the Chancellor of the Exchequer to an admission, though somewhat grudging and halting, that the Governor-General had been notified at the time of the late Government that Britain reserved her full right to present a counter-claim on account of effective defence of India—land, sea, air and diplomacy—by which the freedom of India from foreign invasion had been secured. Dr. Hugh Dalton promised to bear this point in mind when the time would come for negotiating a final settlement. In the Lords the Secretary of State declared that through the part she had played in the War Britain had saved India, Egypt and many other countries from the horrors of conquest. Expressing its sympathy with India's desire to use her sterling balances to finance capital development *The Times* has written editorially more than once that payment in full to India and other creditors is impossible. It proceeds to add that only the most "dialectically minded" would deny outright that the War was India's cause as well as Britain's and that for that reason it would be proper and reasonable to accept the burden of some part of its cost. Then this influential British newspaper expresses its considered opinion that the liability has arisen out of an expenditure incurred on Indian goods and services at inflated prices. This, however, is a proposition which is repudiated by the Parliamentary Committee's survey which suggests, on the contrary, that while current market prices in India might have been high, the British and Indian Governments were able to secure favourable controlled rates for most of their purchases. The Committee found that over a wide range of stores Indian prices were seldom higher and were generally appreciably lower than the prices in Britain.

Members of the Constituent Assembly will have to resist the proposed scaling down with determination. They cannot afford to forget the fact that this credit has been literally built out of the sweat and toil, blood and tears of the country's ill-fed and half-naked millions. Industrialists, Indian or European, have made little or no sacrifice whatsoever for it ; they have, on the contrary, exploited the war emergency and the calls it made on the peoples to the fullest extent to build fortunes in complete disregard, on critical occasions, of the elementary decencies of social behaviour. The sterling balances are in no sense their assets. It should be the duty of the Constituent Assembly, if I may say so, not only to recover this credit from the British as quickly as possible and make provision for its use not for the benefit of the indigenous bourgeoisie who are out to have their finger in every pie, but for socialisation of such industries as are at the present stage of development susceptible of effective and, on the whole, remunerative public ownership and control.

7. Inter-Commonwealth Treaties at International Law

The use of the term "Treaty" in connection with the arrangements proposed to be negotiated between the Constituent Assembly and the United Kingdom may create some confusion. It does not necessarily imply an agreement between two High Contracting Parties on the basis of equality, freedom and independence. In fact, that position is not postulated in the Cabinet Mission's Plan because both expressly and by necessary implication the Constituent Assembly and its Sectional auxiliaries have been in law brought into existence by a dominant ruling power, for the pacific settlement of certain problems in a colonial country, subject to the final sanction of the ruling power itself. I may in this connection cite the Anglo-Irish treaty of 1921 as an instance, although the specific issue that had arisen between the British Government and the Irish Free State was not finally disposed of. The controversy was first raised by the British Government in a note addressed to the League of Nations on November 27, 1924. The document reads as follows:

> Since the Government of the League of Nations came into force, His Majesty's Government has consistently taken the view that neither it nor any conventions concluded under the auspices of the League are intended to govern relations *inter se* of various parts of the British Commonwealth. His Majesty's Government considers, therefore, that the terms of article 18 of the Covenant[1] are not applicable to the articles of agreement of December 6, 1921.

The reply to the British view came in the shape of a statement made on December 15, 1924, by the Irish Free State's Minister for External Affairs. It was to the following effect:

> The Covenant of the League of Nations sets out the duties undertaken by every Member of the League. There are no distinctions between the Members—none has special privileges and none is exempt from the obligations set forth in the Covenant. Article 18 means that every treaty and international engagement entered into after January, 1920, shall be registered. The Irish Free State as a Member of the League, as well as every other Member, is bound by this article. As the treaty is the basis of the Free State's relations with the other members of the British Commonwealth of Nations it was pre-eminently our duty to register. To have failed in this would have been to repudiate the Convent, which can be done neither by the Free State nor by any other Member of the League.

This was followed by a note addressed on December 18, 1924, to the League of Nations by the Free State Government. The note stated:

[1] Every Treaty or international engagement entered into hereafter by any Member of the League shall be forthwith registered with the Secretariat, and shall, as soon as possible, be published by it. No such Treaty or international engagement shall be binding until so registered.

> The Government of the Irish Free State cannot see that any useful purpose would be served by the initiation of a controversy as to the intention of any individual signatory to the Covenant. The obligations contained in article 18 are, in their opinion, imposed in the most specific terms on every Member of the League, and they are unable to accept the contention that the clear and unequivocal language of that article is susceptible of any interpretation compatible with the limitations which the British Government now seek to read into it. They accordingly dissent from the view expressed by the British Government that the terms of article 18 are not applicable to the Treaty of December 6, 1921.[1]

The controversy as to the implications of a treaty or an agreement concluded between the members of the British Commonwealth was bitterly pursued in connection with the signature of the optional clause of the Statute of the Permanent Court of International Justice. The relevant clause[2] provides as follows :

> The members of the League of Nations and the States mentioned in the Annex to the Convent may, either when signing or ratifying the protocol to which the present Statute is adjoined, or at a later moment declare that they recognise as compulsory, *ipso facto* and without special agreement, in relation to any other member or State accepting the same obligation, the jurisdiction of the Court in all or any of the classes of legal disputes concerning:
>
> (a) the interpretation of a Treaty;
> (b) any question of international law;
> (c) the existence of any fact which, if established, would constitute a breach of an international obligation;
> (d) the nature or extent of the reparations to be made for the breach of an international obligation.
>
> The declaration referred to above may be made unconditionally or on condition of reciprocity on the part of several or certain Members or States or for a certain time.

While accepting the jurisdiction of the Court the British Government excluded from the operation of the declaration of acceptance three classes of disputes. These were: (1) disputes in respect of which provision had been or might be made for some other method of peaceful settlement ; (2) disputes between the members of the British Commonwealth; and (3) disputes about matters which fell within what was called the domestic jurisdiction of a State. To these exceptions the Dominions generally agreed. As

[1] These three documents are published in A. B. Keith's *Speeches and Documents on the British Dominions*, 1918-1931, pp. 347-348.

[2] Article 36 of the Statute.

a subordinate branch of the British Administration India agreed too.

The Irish Free State, however, made a declaration in different terms. It refused to accept the proposition that disputes between the members of the British Commonwealth were not justiciable matters for the International Court. When the British Government made the declaration subject to those reservations, they included in the term "the British Commonwealth of Nations" India, and one of the reasons for the exclusion of the inter-Commonwealth disputes was, as was pointed out by Professor A. B. Keith, the objection of the Dominions to have their issues concerning immigration and treatment of resident Indians submitted to an International Court.[1] The British Government, however, claimed in the course of a memorandum submitted in 1929[2], that such disputes had been excluded because the members of the Commonwealth, though international units individually in the fullest sense of the term, were united by their common allegiance to the Crown. The view thus expressed was in accord with the doctrine laid down by the Legal Committee of the Arms Traffic Conference in 1925, to the effect that the terms of the League Conventions must not be regarded as regulating *inter se* the rights and obligations of various territories subject to the same sovereign. It was recommended by the Imperial Conference of 1926 that in any case where the terms of Conventions were to be made applicable between different parts of the Commonwealth and Empire the form of a treaty between Heads of States should be avoided.[3]

The Covenant of the League of Nations, which under the leadership of Mr. Woodrow Wilson, was evolved at the Conference of Paris in 1919, after the First World War, has been replaced by the Charter of the United Nations signed at the city of San Francisco on June 26, 1945. The position of India and, for that matter, members of the British Commonwealth of Nations should now be examined in the light of its provisions. Does the Charter recognise the sovereignty of each member and its equality of status with any other member at least for the specific purposes which it has professedly in view? Does it or does it not make any distinc-

[1] A. B. Keith's *Speeches and Documents on the British Dominions, 1918-1931*, p. 416.

[2] Ibid, pp. 410-17.

[3] Ibid, p. 382.

tion between Britain and other member-States all united by a common allegiance to the British Crown ? Can obligations arising out of a treaty or agreement between members of the British Commonwealth and Empire be treated as justiciable disputes or matters for the UNO's intervention in terms of the Charter?

The Charter lays down that the Organisation is based on the principle of the sovereign equality of all its members.[1] But it is subject to the provision that nothing contained in it shall authorise the United Nations to intervene in matters which are essentially within the domestic jurisdiction of any State, or shall require the members to submit such matters to settlement under it.[2] If in the context of Indo-British relations India is part of the British State, then any dispute between the two comes within the domestic jurisdiction of the latter and is, therefore, a matter in which no intervention under the Charter, except perhaps the application of enforcement measures with respect to threats to the peace, breaches of the peace, and acts of aggression as under Chapter VII, is contemplated. If, on the other hand, they are separate States the principle of "domestic jurisdiction" does not apply. To this question the answer, however, is simple. Membership of the Organisation is open only to States[3] and such are presumed to be States understood in their ordinary, general political meaning. Being already a member, India is not only acknowledged as a State, but her "sovereign equality" with any other Member-States is guaranteed. Accordingly any dispute that may arise as to the interpretation of the treaty that may be concluded between the Indian Constituent Assembly and the United Kingdom should be regarded as a justiciable matter for the purposes of the Charter.

But it is almost certain that unless the allegiance to the British Crown is replaced by a new allegiance the British Gov-be regarded as a justiciable matter for the purposes of the International Court on the basis of common allegiance, though admitting, as in 1929, that India is individually "an international unit in the fullest sense of the term". Logically, however, this doctrine is open to challenge in view of the other provisions of the Charter. All Members of the United Nations—and India is a

[1] art. 2(1). [2] art. 2(7). [3] arts. 3 & 4.

member—are *ipso facto* parties to the Statute of the International Court of Justice which forms an integral part of the Charter.[1] Every treaty and every international agreement entered into by any Member of the United Nations after this Charter comes into force shall as soon as posible be registered with the Secretariat of the Organisation and published by it.[2] It shall be open to any Member of the United Nations to bring any dispute, or any situation which might lead to international friction or give rise to a dispute to the attention of the Security Council or of the General Assembly.[3] Appropriate procedures or methods of adjustment, including reference, in the case of legal disputes, to the International Court in accordance with the provisions of the Statute of the Court may be recommended by the Security Council.[4]

I cannot see how in view of India's membership of the Organisation, the specific guarantee of the sovereign equality, and the express acknowledgement of her status as a State she can be prevented from getting any treaty or agreement concluded by her with the United Kingdom or any other Member-State registered with the U.N.O's Secretariat and invoking methods of adjustment or any other relevant procedure under the Charter, including reference to the International Court, for the pacific settlement of disputes. But it seems to me that the whole thing will turn on the allegiance to the Crown and it is a matter to which the Interim Government as well as the Constituent Assembly and its "Sectional" auxiliaries would be well advised in giving their earnest and most anxious consideration in order that friction of the kind which arose out of the Anglo-Irish Treaty of 1921 may be avoided.

8. Is The Union Constituent Assembly A Sovereign body ?

I have tried as fairly as possible to examine the Cabinet Mission's proposals in their immediate and long-term bearings. Both these aspects are important because they constitute a whole. You cannot separate the Interim Government from the constitution-making machinery. The British Government, the three Cabinet Ministers and the Viceroy have made statements which

[1] arts. 92 and 93.
[2] art. 102(1).
[3] art. 35.
[4] art. 36.

suggest that these two instruments have been devised for the purpose of making the transition as quick and orderly as the circumstances may permit. On the Indian side, particularly on behalf of the Congress and the Muslim League, indications have been given, despite Mr. Jinnah's recent faint disclaimer due to his disappointment, that they believe in the sincerity of the British promise to quit without coming into violent collision with the forces in a state of mobilisation for any struggle for Indian emancipation. Certain facts, however, must not be ignored. The Interim Government is legally the Viceroy's Executive Council, although in their statement issued on May 25, the Cabinet Mission claimed that this Government would have a new basis. That basis, as they put it, is that all portfolios, including that of the Defence Member, are to be held by Indians and that "the members will be selected in consultation with the Indian political parties". These, in their view, are very significant changes and mark a long step towards independence.

Whether or not the Interim Government will, as promised, enjoy the greatest possible freedom in the exercise of the day-to-day administration of India will depend on factors internal as well as external, all of which cannot be foreseen at the moment. The Muslim League's participation in this Government without revising its July resolution may give rise to problems which may be exploited for the exercise of British authority affecting, if not overruling, the decisions of the new Government. As regards the Constituent Assembly—and the Commander-in-Chief, be it noted, mentioned three Assemblies—Pandit Jawaharlal Nehru has been persuaded to think on legal advice and in the light of the Mission's statement of May 25, that in relation to the British Government it is a sovereign body. He is perhaps right in so far as the latter stand committed to implement its decisions provided they are satisfied with regard to the two reservations which the Cabinet Mission have set out. Pandit Nehru looks at the Constituent Assembly simultaneously from two points of view. Internally, of course, it is a matter between communities and interests. Externally he would not submit to any interference from the British Government. I am afraid, however, that this is a bit over-simplification of a very difficult and complicated problem. The final sanction, if we go by the British proposals, rests with the British Government.

What is still more disquieting is that it is not merely a question of formal sanction being given to, or withheld from, the constitution or constitutions that may be framed on Indian soil. The machinery has been so devised that on any question of policy as well as in matters of detail the British Government will have the right of ultimate decision. Mention has been made of reference being made in certain circumstances to the Federal Court on disputes that may arise in working out the machinery in terms of the Cabinet Mission's Plan. I have already shown that for obvious reasons the Federal Court is just not the forum where to fight decisively, and with dignity, political or social battles. Political issues such as those involved in this process of change of the State-power must be approached politically. They are not, ordinarily speaking, justiciable disputes susceptible of easy and amicable adjustment by recourse to this judicial procedure. In the last analysis it is going to be a conflict between the Indian movement for independent political existence and the British effort to retain as far as possible their authority and power. In that conflict the Indian movement can succeed only if it can rally the masses and mobilise them for the overthrow of the existing State and the system of judicious patronage which it has built up.

One should not forget that even if the Federal Court were an appropriate tribunal for adjudication, it is basically, if I may say so with due respect to the judges, a symbol of British paramountcy. The judges are not our own men. They have been appointed by the British Crown on the advice of its Ministers in the United Kingdom. Their knowledge, their experience and their impartiality as such are not open to question. A Constituent Assembly which sits to frame a free constitution of a free people does not seek adjudication from a court created by those whose authority is challenged by the Assembly. If the Constituent Assembly is not sovereign internally, it cannot assert its sovereignty externally. If, for instance, the Muslim representatives in B and C Sections frame proposals which are in the opinion of the Hindu and Sikh representatives repugnant to the terms of paragraph 15 or of paragraph 19 of the State Paper, who decides the issue finally? Is it decided by the Union Constituent Assembly or the Federal Court or the British Government ? In the first case, the Union Constituent Asembly is, of course, a sovereign body both internally and externally. In the latter two cases it is not, either in respect of internal arrangements or in relation to the British Government. In this struggle the Interim Government has no *locus standi* in terms of the Act by or under which it has been brought into existence. It cannot, unlike a revolutionary Provisional Government, defy the British Government and enforce the decisions of the Constituent Assembly.

Thus the machinery devised so ingeniously by the Cabinet Mission does not correspond in material points to the consistent Congress stand in this regard. At Faijpur for the first time in December, 1936, the Congress adopted a resolution stating that it "stands for a genuine democratic State in India where political power has been transferred to the people as a whole and the Government is under their effective control." It stated further that such "a State can only come into existence through a Constituent Assembly elected by adult suffrage and having the power to determine finally the constitution of the country." At Haripur in February, 1938, while rejecting the constitution of 1935, the Congress declared that "a constitution for India which can be accepted by the people must be based on independence and can only be framed by the people themselves by means of a Constituent Assembly without interference by any foreign authority." At Tripuri in March, 1939, that demand was reiterated by the Congress in equally emphatic terms. It declared afresh "its solemn resolve to achieve independence for the nation and to have a constitution framed for a free India through a Constituent Assembly elected by the people on the basis of the adult franchise and without any interference by a foreign authority." The position thus taken up by the Congress was made far more explicit both in procedure and in substance at the Ramgarh Session in March, 1940. It made it clear that "no permanent solution is possible except through a Constituent Assembly where the rights of all recognised minorities will be fully protected by agreement as far as possible between the elected representatives of various majority and minority groups or by arbitration, if agreement is not reached on any point." It was declared that "India's constitution must be based on independence, democracy and national unity . . . ."

Until its acceptance of the State Paper the Congress has all these years stood for a completely sovereign Constituent Assembly for the purpose of framing an Indian constitution on the basis of complete national independence and without any interference by a foreign authority. It was not only a slogan ; it envisaged a countrywise machinery for the capture of power so that conditions could be created in which it would be possible to convene a fully sovereign Constituent Assembly. Let us not deceive ourselves. The machinery devised by the Cabinet Mission differs materially from the Constituent Assembly that the Congress has had in view. It is not a sovereign body. The authority of the British Government in terms of formal definitions has neither been overthrown nor eliminated. The reservations for which provision has been made and to which the two major political parties in India have agreed are so cumbrous and complicated that the transition from the present position to full-fledged freedom may be exceedingly painful and difficult.

Pandit Nehru has indicated that this Constituent Assembly may be transformed into a revolutionary body. Lenin, it may be recalled, evolved the doctrine of revolutionary defeatism in his clarion call to the Russian workers and peasants in 1917, to strike from within. A new experiment in revolutionary constitutionalism in a different context, I admit, is not altogether outside the realm of practical politics. Is Pandit Nehru's resolution on objectives adopted at the preliminary meeting a move in that direction? The main points in that resolution are (i) the fundamental principles upon which the future State of India is to be based and (ii) the source of authority of that State. India according to the declaration shall be an independent sovereign Republic and all power and authority of the State and its constitutional units are presumed to be derived from the people. The Muslim League Working Committee's resolution passed at Karachi does not place on record its opposition to an independent Republic as such, but it objects to what it calls the "essentials of the constitution" which Pandit Nehru's resolution purports to lay down. It is not clear, however, on what specific point or points the Muslim League joins issue with the Congress. Far more definite and explicit in this regard are the terms for entry into the Indian Union adopted by the Chamber of Princes on January 29 at New Delhi. The Chamber has declared that the Princes' entry shall be on no other basis than negotiation and that the final decision shall rest with each State. The States reserve to themselves the right either to enter into a federal relationship with the Successor Government in British India or, failing that, to enter into particular political arrangements with it. Again, on its termination at the close of the interim period paramountcy is not to be transferred to, or inherited by the new India Government. All the rights surendered to the Paramount Power will return to the States and the Indian Union will accordingly exercise only such functions in relation to the States as are assigned or delegated by them to the Union. Obviously the Chamber's resolution is in the nature of a cautious warning to the representatives of Provinces that the States may keep out if the conditions laid down by them are not adhered to on the British Indian side. Contrary to what has been said by some distinguished members of the Constituent Assembly I maintain that the Princes' terms of reference for the States Negotiating Committee come definitely into conflict with Pandit Nehru's propositions.

Now, the expression "independent sovereign Republic" means hardly anything more than that India shall be completely free from British control and that the monarchial form of the State is to be discarded. A democratic Socialist Union of Republics, I suggest, should have fitted in more appropriate with Pandit Nehru's proclaimed political and social sympathies. An independent sovereign Republic is not necessarily a democratic State, far less a democratic Socialist State. All power and authority of the State being derived from the people smacks of formal parliamentary democracy or some kind of dictatorship with which the world has been familiar for so many decades unless means are provided for associating the people by democratic procedure with the tasks of law-making and administration at short, regular intervals particularly when the management of vital public affairs is involved. These points, however, need not be stressed unduly, for Pandit Nehru's resolution only gives a broad general outline of the principles. Things are expected to take a concrete shape when further progress is made in the framing of the constitution or constitutions.

Except perhaps in one or two procedural details the declaration of objectives as agreed to unanimously at the pleminary meeting does not in my view go outside the general framework of the State Paper. The Muslim League Working Committee's call for dissolution of the Constituent Assembly is in the circumstances utterly inappropriate and impertinent. Mr. Jinnah and his colleagues should hear in mind that the initiative has passed out of the hands of the British Government. Whatever may be their sympathy for the Muslim League's cause, it is not within their competence to dissolve the Constituent Assembly. The State Paper has made no provision for any action of this kind. All that the British Government can do is to advise Parliament not to implement the constitution or constitutions that may be framed by the constitution-making machinery if they are persuaded that the terms of the State Paper have been violated. If they do so, then they will have to face a conflict. Are they prepared for it? I have my doubts. The Muslim League Working Committee's appeal to the British Government is a counsel of despair. It is an invitation to the British to resume into their hands the control of affairs which in consequence of stirring world events has already passed to the Indian peoples and their representative leaders. It is a retrograde step and as such will evoke no effective response.

But this does not mean that the legitimate claims of the Muslim community and minorities should be disregarded by a majority of votes. No constitution can function except with the support and sanction of the peoples concerned and Muslims and minorities represent peoples whom it would be a mistake to ignore. If by "revolutionary constitutionalism" is meant elimination of the British as the major partner in the Indian Administration, we need not worry. But in the present context "revolution" must have a richer social content, and to the extent the Constituent Assembly succeeds in framing the constitution or constitutions on the basis of democracy and social freedom, on the reconciliation of the relations of production with the forces of production it will evolve a joint front for the broad masses of the Indian peoples irrespective of caste or religion and lay the foundations of what Pandit Nehru once called a coöperative Commonwealth. Revolution is not a slogan. It is not a metaphysical abstraction. It is a method of action which must seek to integrate the State machinery with the popular urges and project the needs and aspirations of the masses into the organisation of the State and its fundamental laws.

CHAPTER VI

NATIONS, NATIONALATIES AND MINORITIES

1. British Policy of Divide and Rule

Francis II of Australia is quoted by D. Parieu as having once addressed to the French ambassador a homily to this effect:

> My people are strangers to one another and yet it is for the better . . . . I have Hungarians in Italy and Italians in Hungary. Each suspects his neighbour; they never understand one another and in fact detest one another. Their antipathies, however, conduce to order and their mutual hate to the general peace.[1]

I shall not go so far as to contend that the statement expressed in the above question represents in every minute detail Britain's India policy. That was not possible in this country for the simple reason that there were no Hungarians in Italy and no Italians in Hungary. But "divide and rule" must of necessity be the historical basis of colonial rule in every country, and British rule in India has followed that traditional pattern despite the objectively progressive character of its early intervention in Indian affairs and the far-reaching political, educational and social reforms introduced from time to time, which have, on the one hand, given a new awakening to the peoples of this land and, on the other, imparted certain elements of stability to its political structure until today when the inner contradictions of capitalism and the capitalist crisis generally are shaking it to its foundations. In his article on "The British Rule in India" published in the *Tribune* of June, 25, 1853, Karl Marx wrote : "England, it is true, in causing a social revolution in Hindustan, was actuated only by the vilest interests and was stupid in her manner of enforcing them. But that is not the question. The question is, can mankind fulfil its destiny without a fundamental revolution in the social state of Asia? If not, whatever may have been the crimes of England, she was the unconscious tool of history in bringing about that revolution."[2] There was thus a conflict between the

[1] *Principles De la Science Politique*, p. 304.

[2] *A Handbook of Marxism*, p. 187.

objective role of British rule in its early phase and the motives of British policy.

From the very beginning the British created a division of the Indian territories into British India and Native India. Within British India the main division was between Hindus and Muslims. In the early stages of British rule Muslims had looked upon these new masters wth distrust and suspicion. To them the latter were no better than interlopers and their regime something like contraband. As a community they declined to assist the British in the consolidation of their gains of conquest. They refused to take advantage of the facilities of western liberal education offered by the British Government. The latter, on their part, leaned more and more upon Hindu support or loyalty in the carrying on of the administration. The first period was one of Anglo-Hindu collaboration with Hindus playing a very subordinate role on orders or under instructions from the dominant partner in whose hands the power to take final decisions lay. In administration, trade and industries Muslims had little or no share. Almost the same policy was pursued after the rebellion of 1857 despite the Queen's Proclamation declaring equal eligibility for public offices irrespective of caste, creed or colour, which was more or less a reiteration of the statutory provision of the Act of 1833 in this regard. European British subjects were preferred to Indians and Hindus to Muslims, except in those branches where Europeans were not available.

In 1885 the Indian National Congress came into existence. It was open to all sections of the community and, as a matter of fact, Hindus, Muslims, Parsis and Englishmen (not, of course, the ordinary masses) not only joined the movement but contributed their respective quotas of leadership to the organisation. Hume, Wedderburn, Bonnerjee, Naoroji and Tyabji are well-known names in the first Roll of Honours. In its early days it was an organisation of professional classes who asked for reforms. They asked for separation of the judiciary from the executive, increasing association of Indians in the higher branches of public administration, equality of rights for Indians with Europeans in criminal law and implementation of the Queen's Proclamation in letter and in spirit. In our time the resolutions embodying these demands read like petitions and memorials addressed in all humility to the final seat of supreme authority. Yet the British Government and their agents read into them, quite rightly, gestures of protest, whispers of deep discontent, yes, new challenges. What gave them cause for anxiety was not the charter of demands but the organised, collective stand which the Congress represented.

The tone of the Congress resolutions became more and more firm and assertive. In the beginning of this century the movement took a decisive turn with the approaching crisis of capitalism. The results of the Russo-Japanese war and the British policy of repression-*cum*-conciliation profoundly influenced Indian political thought. The leadership of the Congress was rapidly passing into the hands of what was then called the extremist wing while among the rank and file, particularly in Bengal, a party grew who believed in seizure of power by violent means. Ideologically and as a platform the Congress remained as before national in the sense that it was an organised Indian protest against alien rule and the injustice, inequity and repression it involved. Organisationally, however, it began to take a definite shape as a lower-middle class Hindu movement directed towards the achievement of Indian independence. The British Government turned round and inaugurated for the first time a policy of Muslim appeasement as a "counterpoise" of one religious community against another. Lady Minto's *Diary* contains extracts from a letter said to have been received from a high official by her husband in the evening of October 1, 1906, just after the Aga Khan Deputation's meeting with him, which throw light on the British bureaucracy's reaction to the "counterpoise" theory. "I must," wrote the official, "send your Excellency a line to say that a very big thing has happened today, a work of statesmanship that will affect India and Indian history for many a long year. It is nothing less than the pulling back of sixty-two millions of people from joining the ranks of the seditious opposition."[1] Muslim in increasing numbers became junior collaborators in the imperialist enterprise. Hindus were suspect, and where Hindu coöperation was unavoidable there was a good deal of picking and choosing.

It was left to Lord Morley, a liberal philosopher-statesman, to give expression to this policy in concrete terms under the Indian Councils Act, 1909[2]. Muslims were given separate representation in Provinces where they were in a minority. As Secretary

[1] Lady Minto's *Diary*, pp. 47—48.
[2] 9 Edw. 7, C. 4.

of State Lord Morley, however, suggested "the plan of a mixed or composite electoral college, in which Mahomedans and Hindus should pool their votes, so to say".[1] He expressed his belief that his plan of Hindus and Muslims voting together in a mixed and composite electorate "would have secured to the Mahomedan electors, wherever they were so minded, the chance of returning their own representatives in their due proportion." The idea was, as Lord Morley pointed out, that such composite action would bring the two great communities more closely together. That was a view which, on the Secretary of State's admission, was held by "men of very high Indian authority and experience who were among my advisers at the India Office."

Lord Morley's scheme was based on the principles of proportional representation. But Lord Minto's Government doubted whether the plan would work in India. A section of highly-placed Muslims also protested against it. It was abandoned and instead the system of separate electorates with weightage was adopted under the Indian Councils Act. Lord Minto's doctrine of "counterpoise" to Congress aims[2] was ruthlessly applied. The Muslim Deputation's "command performance"[3] and Lady Minto's entries in the *Diary* are recorded events of contemporaneous history. But subsequently Lord Morley sought to rationalise this scheme of religious registers. In his speech in the Lords on the Bill on February 23, 1909, the Secretary of State enunciated an interesting thesis in these words :

> Only let us not forget that the difference between Mahomedanism and Hinduism is not a mere difference of articles of religious faith. It is a difference in life, in tradition, in history, in all the social things as well as articles of belief that constitute a community. Do not forget that, in talking of Hindus and Mahomedans, we are dealing with and brought face to face with vast historic issues, dealing with some of the very mightiest forces that through all the centuries and ages have moulded the fortunes of great States and the destinies of countless millions of mankind.[4]

[1] A. B. Keith's *Speeches and Documents on Indian Policy*, Vol. II, p. 91.

[2] Lady Minto's *Diary*, pp. 28—29.

[3] The phrase was employed by Maulana Mahomed Ali in his Presidential address to the Cocanada Session of the Congress, 1923, to describe the Aga Khan Deputation that waited on Lord Minto on Oct. 1, 1906.

[4] A. B. Keith's *Speeches and Documents on Indian Policy*, Vol. II, pp 93—94.

The scheme enshrined in the Act of 1909 was expanded and consolidated under the Government of India Act. It was given a greater impetus under the British Government's communal decision popularly known as the MacDonald Award which is the basis of representation in the legislatures created by or under the Government of India Act, 1935. In fairness it must, however, be admitted that as long ago as 1915 Mr. G. K. Gokhale, an ex-President of the Indian National Congress, agreed to the principle of "special representation of Mahomedans" in the legislatures.[1] In the Scheme of Reforms adopted by the Indian National Congress at Lucknow on December 29, 1916, and accepted by the All-India Muslim League on December 31, 1916, the system of separate electorates for Muslim representation in the Provincial Legislative Councils with weightage was recommended. It was further recommended that "no Bill, nor any clause thereof, nor a resolution introduced by a non-official member affecting one or the other community which question is to be determined by the members of that community in the Legislative Council concerned shall be proceeded with, if three-fourths of the members of that community in the particular Council, Imperial or Provincial, oppose the Bill or any clause thereof or the resolution.[2]"

It is not, therefore, correct to say that the Congress and its leaders have since its inception in 1885 consistently opposed separate electorates as being obnoxious to the principles which they have so ardently cherished. Nor have they hesitated to propose what they considered effective safeguards against communal legislation being enacted to the prejudice of a religious community. It may be asked that if the Congress and a Congress leader of the eminence of Mr. Gokhale could approve of separate electorates for Muslims and weightage of representation in the legislatures, what ground is there for the charge that the British Government and their agents were out to create and perpetuate Hindu-Muslim division for the consolidation of imperialist rule by conceding the Muslim demand for separate, communal representation and weightage? It may be argued that the British Government agreed to what was rendered inevitable by the inexorable dynamics of history. To that the answer is that the fact of their support

[1] Read G. K. Gokhale's *Political Testament*, 1915, paragraph 3.

[2] A B. Keith's *Speeches and Documents on Indian Policy*, Vol. II, p. 125.

to separate representation on a religious basis by itself did not make them suspect. What was and is objected to is the manner of their emphasis on internal divisions and the technique employed to foster and promote them. Lady Minto's *Diary* and a British official's congratulations to Lord Minto, already quoted, bring into bold relief the motives of British policy.

To these may be added the policy deliberately pursued in the organisation of the army in India. Immediately after the rebellion of 1857 the Punjab Committee of 1858, which included Sir John Lawrence, it may be recalled, made recommendations which were calculated to "keep alive provincial, class and race separatism, so that the main elements of the Indian Army could not combine with each other in any joint movement against British rule."[1] The Punjab Committee observed :

> As we cannot do without a large Native Army in India, our main object is to make that army safe, and next to the grand counterpoise of a sufficient European force, comes a counterpoise of Natives against Natives . . . . . To preserve that distinctiveness (racial or territorial) which is so valuable, and which, while it lasts, makes the Muhammadan of one country despise, fear or dislike the Muhammadan of another, corps should in future be provincial, and adhere to the geographical limits within which differences and rivalries are strongly marked. By the system thus indicated, two great evils are avoided, firstly, that community of feeling throughout the Native Army and that mischievous political activity and intrigue which results from association with the races and travel in other Indian provinces; and secondly, that through discontent and alienation from the service which has udoubtedly sprung up since extended conquest has carried over Hindustani soldiers so far from their homes in India proper.

The "counterpoise" as recommended by the Punjab Committee was between races, that is, between Europeans and Indians, and territorial, that is, between Province and Province. It was not between Hindus and Muslims as such. That is explained by the fact that during that period, particularly after the rebellion of 1857, British policy was marked by fear and distrust of Muslims. But the doctrine of "counterpoise" was adhered to with special emphasis on the dominance of the British element in the organisation of the army. In consequence of the rebellion Indians were excluded from artillery and the scientific branches and restricted mainly to infantry and cavalry. To that must be traced

[1] The Sapru Committee's Constitutional Proposals, p. 271.

also the reduction of the ratio of Indian personnel to European personnel and the artificial distinction between the so-called martial and non-martial races ; consequences which, to a considerable extent, have been negatived by the requirements of the Second World War.

Divisions between the States and the other India, between Indians and Europeans, between Muslims and non-Muslims and between Province and Province have been relied upon by the British for the consolidation of their rule. Sometimes other new divisions have been created, fostered and nursed. There is, however, nothing surprising or unusual in the policy pursued by them. An alien imperialist power could not safely and with any measure of confidence adopt a different course among so many millions of human beings who were proud of a great and ancient past and a large body of whom, Muslims in particular, recalled with no less pride the glorious days of the Delhi Sultanate.

But the specific issue taken up in this chapter is the communal controversy of which the British have taken the fullest advantage. British Indian history in this context may roughly be divided into three periods. From the beginning of their rule right up to the end of the nineteenth century it was a period of patronage to Hindus in which Muslims were isolated as far as possible. From the beginning of this century to the end of the Second World War Muslims were given the priority in the scheme of distribution of patronage. The third period has just commenced ; it is a period of class collaboration in which the Hindu bourgeoisie, it seems, is going to play the role of the major partner in the enterprise. Not that class conflict was absent from the earlier epochs of British rule, but then it was in the background for the reason that those were years when the progressive character of capitalism had not yet been completely exhausted. The years between the two wars have released forces in which the capitalist structure such as the British assiduously built up and projected into their colonial rule cannot sustain itself whatever contrivance it may resort to. They have reconciled themselves to this phenomenon of history and without any qualms of liberal conscience they are disposed to make alliance with those who are in a position to "deliver the goods" and give them some share, however small, of the spoils of exploitation.

On the face of it, this new orientation of British policy under a Socialist Government may sound paradoxical. It is nevertheless true, so far as the main trend is concerned. Confusion seems to exist as to the role of the British Labour Party both "at home" and abroad and this explains to a certain extent the fact that we in this country are victims to a number of illusions. On the Right they nurse the illusion that the British have by a miraculous change of heart decided most gladly and willingly to go into liquidation and that their quitting the scene is only a question of time. That is a half-truth and, therefore, misleading. The victory of revolution, according to the practical application of the Marxian theory, never comes of its own accord ; it is achieved only by stern, stubborn and organised struggle.[1] On the Left the Communist Party of India appear to think that the imperialist structure almost remains intact having undergone no change in these inter-war years, especially in consequence of the last war. Their emphasis on the anti-imperialist front in the old sense seems to err on the side of excess. I do not suggest that imperialism is as dead as mutton. Nothing of the kind has yet happened. But I do maintain that British capitalists can no longer run their shop in this country except as junior partners. In the very nature of the case the struggle for freedom must evolve a new strategy to adjust it to the vast and sweeping changes that have been effected in the racial composition of the capitalist structure during the past five or six years. The struggle must be socio-political : social because a purely nationalist movement cannot but tend in the present setting to turn back to social reaction and political because the last vestige of British authority must be completely eliminated.

Taking his stand on what he calls radical democracy, Mr. M. N. Roy seems to suffer from the British Socialist complex. He thought that British democracy was such a great force that it could, if it so willed, join hands with the progressive forces in India and take the initiative in enforcing drastic measures of social reconstruction in complete disregard of the "upper class political parties" and the rising Indian bourgeoisie or of the reactionary elements in Britain. That was an illusion. Similarly he thought that British democracy was almost convinced that capitalism was dead and that the alternative to Fascist regimentation of the social economy which, of course, is detested was a new democratic

[1] *History of the Civil War in the U.S.S.R.*, Vol. II, p. 292.

approach (not in the old, formal sense) to the domestic, foreign and colonial problems with which it was confronted. That, again, was an illusion. I do not, however, deny that there is substance in Mr. Roy's contention that the racial composition of the capitalist structure in India has been transformed on a major scale, a thesis which he enunciated more than two decades ago. But one should not forget that the British Labour Party's historic role is one of compromise. They understand a Gandhi more than a Stalin ; a Nehru more than a Roy ; a Patel more than a Joshi. They are not used to thinking in terms of social revolutions of the Continental or Russian category. They know Birlas and Tatas more than the workers' councils or kishan sabhas which would in any event press for India's secession from the British political system which is the coercive symbol of the British bourgeoisie.

Even if the Labour Party were free from the prejudices, superstitions and complexes of the philosophy of gradualness, they could not all of a sudden rid themselves of the influence of the civil service and diplomatic corps which are manned by persons of proven respectability. The execution of policy rests with them and there is a good deal of difference between formulation of policy and its execution. Progress may be impeded and schemes sabotaged by dilatory or destructive tractics. In the formulation of policy, too, they exercise a measure of control, if not directly, at any rate by subtle suggestions. Therefore, however, lofty the ideals to which the Labour Party may proclaim their adherence, it is but natural that they should not make any orthodox departure from formal democracy. The Indian National Congress swept the polls in the "General" constituencies in 1945. The All-India Muslim League floored the non-Leaguers in the Muslim constituencies. In the approved democratic way it was for these two organisations to share power. Failing agreement, it was for the stronger of the two to assume authority. No exception could be taken to this line of argument on the basis of formal democracy.

But assuming that the formation of the Interim Government on the advice of the Congress President involved a breach of faith to the Muslim League, the explanation, first, is that the Labour Government could no longer afford to invite the civilised world's ridicule and contempt for their dogged persistence in "nothing doing" tactics ; and secondly, that in the opinion of the leaders of the Labour Party a political deal with the Congress was a better immediate, though not long-term, investment, Mr. Jinnah and the Muslim League say that the British have betrayed the Muslims of India. They allege a conspiracy between the British Government and the Congress directed against Muslims as a community. These are not sustainable charges. Events have only forced the British to change their strategy. Religious conflict is no longer their *forte*. That stage is over. It is now almost a broken reed to rely upon. It served them well in the early years of their rule when there was no Indian bourgeoisie. It stood them in good stead during the last forty years of the present century, especially during the first two decades. Now it is class collaboration of a particular type, on which they hope to build their future, and in such collaboration Mr. Jinnah and the Muslim League count but little. For the League leadership is dominantly feudal while that of the Congress basically national-bourgeois. Religious or communal tension is sought to be maintained by false promises or wily gestures not for the sake of such tension, but as a means to an end. The end is disruption of labour or kishan unity so that for the moment at least or for some time yet there may be no serious challenge to class collaboration. The Indian upper classes, Hindu as well as Muslim, join in the communalist chorus to drown the voice of the common man. Hindus shout for Akhand Hindusthan. Muslims clamour for Pakistan.

2. What is "Nation"?

A close examination of the Cabinet Mission's proposals will reveal that the problem of national self-determination or of nationalities or even of minorities has been deliberately shelved by them. The onus has been thrown on Indian peoples themselves to face and solve it, if they can. Rejecting Pakistan, the Mission have refused to give any consideration to the two-nation theory. Recommending what they call the "basic form" the constitution should take, they have laid down the principles of a three-tier structure to allay Muslim apprehensions. Sponsoring an Advisory Committee on minorities, they have given little or no indication of what they mean by *minorities*. All these omissions are significant. They do not augur well for the Constituent Assembly and its Sectional auxiliaries.

What is "nation"? What is "nationality"? What are

"minorities" in India? Are Muslims a nation? Are Hindus a nation ? Is there any Indian nation at all ? Where do Sikhs stand ? These questions are relevant because Mr. Jinnah and the Muslim League demand division of India into Pakistan and Hindusthan on the two-nation theory, because the Hindu Mahasabha and its protogonists take their stand on Akhand Hindusthan, because the Congress prepared, as it has ever been, to give minorities, including Muslims, the amplest measure of protection compatible with democracy, has set its face resolutely against the two-nation theory. "Nation" has been defined by textbook writers in endless ways at different times and in different countries. It has very often been used by politicians and statesmen with reference now to language and religion, now to race, now to common political organisation, now to distant common memory and sometimes to all these factors taken as a collective whole. Generally there is some vague, mystic idealisation. There are thinkers, too, who would imagine a perfect nation or a nation "in perfect form" and then draw a distinction between their idealistic chatter and the stark inexorable reality.

Burgess defines "nation" as a population having a common language and literature, inhabiting a given territory, sharing a common tradition, history and customs and bound together by a common consciousness of rights and wrongs.[1] Bluntschli says that a "nation" is a union of masses of men of different occupations and social strata in a hereditary society of common spirit, feeling and race, bound together specially by language and customs, in a common civilisation, which gives them a sense of unity and distinction from all foreigners, quite apart from the bond of the State. He seeks to make out a distinction between a ***nation*** so defined and a ***people***. A people, according to him, is, unlike a nation, a society of all the members of a State united and organised in the State. A nation is an ethnic concept while a people is a political concept. Affinity of race and community of language, habits, customs and religion are the elements which are held to constitute a nation. A common race consciousness is supposed to bring in a sense of kinship. A common language is supposed to provide the basis of common understanding. A common religion is supposed to bind men and women together by a common tradition,

[1] *Political Science and Constitutional Law*, Vol. I, p. 2.

a common heritage and unity of outlook.[1] Lecky rejects race as being a good criterion of the existence of a nation. It is much too obscure and deceptive. He regards language and religion as more decisive and important factors in determining national entities, although it is admitted that history furnishes examples of different religions and languages being blended into one nationality.

"A portion of mankind," writes John Stuart Mill, "may be said to constitute a nationality if they are united among themselves by common sympathies which do not exist between them and others—which make them coöperate with each other more willingly than with other people, desire to be under the same Government and desire that it should be government by themselves or a portion of themselves exclusively."[2] Is it, then, an identity of race and descent? Is it a geographical entity? Is it a community of language and of religion ? Is it expressed in common political hopes and aspirations and traditions ? All these, according to Mill, may each in its own way contribute to that sense of gregariousness, to that herd-instinct, which constitutes the quintessence of nationality. But in his view the most potent factor is the sense of political unity, the same idea of right and wrong, the same urge of survival against attacks by alien forces, the same sensation of exaltation over triumphs against trespassers or invaders. Other factors are neither indispensable nor sufficient by themselves. "It is in general a necessary condition," says Mill, "of free institutions that the boundaries of governments should coincide in the main with those of nationalities."[3] There is emphasis in Mill's thesis on the political aspect of that moral and psychological awareness which is held to weld individuals, groups or tribes into a common nationality.

Professor H. J. Laski agrees with Renan in insisting that the idea of nationality "is essentially spiritual in character."[4] It implies a sense of special unity emerging from a common history, from a common memory of victories and reverses, of customs and traditions. It is a kind of unity which distinguishes those who share in it from the rest of mankind. To the extent that this common memory emphasises kinship it tends to foster a spirit of

[1] *Democracy and Liberty*, Vol. I, p. 5.
[2] *Representative Government* (1861), pp. 359—60.
[3] Ibid pp. 296—298.
[4] A Grammar of Politics, pp. 219—220.

exclusiveness from others. The tension of this conflict of two opposite forces varies from country to country and from time to time. Sometimes it leads to a great creative effort in art, literature and architecture. Sometimes and in a different historical setting it creates conditions of war by tariff walls, colonial expansion, struggle for markets and the economics of self-sufficiency called autarchy. Now it leads to struggles for liberation from alien yoke ; now it offers an incentive to aggressive wars for pillage and conquest. Such a community is neither racial nor tribal. If it were so, the British would be a conglomeration of tribes and races rather than a nation. Similarly composite in texture is the German nation, the French nation, the Italian nation or the Swiss people.

So, as Stalin puts it, a nation is primarily a historically constituted, stable community of people. A national community, again, is not conceivable without a common language. It does not mean, however, that all those who speak a common language necessarily constitute one nation. At the present moment Englishmen and Americans speak the same language. But they are two separate nations. Therefore, a community of territory is another characteristic feature of a national community. That by itself, again, is not enough. To this commonness of territory should be added an internal economic bond, a sort of economic cohesion welding the people into a single whole. A Georgian himself, Stalin says that before the abolition of serfdom in 1861 the Georgians did not constitute a nation, although they inhabited a common territory and spoke the same language. And why ? Because during that period they pillaged each other and invoked the aid and assistance of the Turks and Persians against each other. They emerged as a nation with the fall of feudalism, the abolition of serfdom, the rise of capitalism, the development of means of communication, all these and other analogous developments shattering in the latter half of the nineteenth century the edifice of feudal economic self-sufficiency and giving in the process a sense of economic unity to disorganised and disunited Georgia.

Though an essential feature of a nation, the unity of economic life alone does not make up a complete national whole. The spiritual complexion of a people (not in the sense of religious forms or formularies), which expresses itself in the peculiarities of what is popularly known as its culture, is another important, perhaps a decisive factor. This psychological make-up is not a static concept. It changes and responds to new urges. But at a given moment it "leaves its imprint on the physiognomy of the nation". Thus Stalin defines "nation" as "a historically evolved, stable community of language, territory, economic life, and psychological make-up manifested in a community of culture". It is a social phenomenon belonging to a definite historical epoch, the epoch of rising capitalism, and is subject to the law of change and has its beginning and end. No single one of these characteristics of a national pattern or even a number of them makes a conglomeration of groups, tribes or races a nation. We have a nation when all these characteristics are present.[1] Stalin's definition of "nation", it will be seen, contains no reference to religion and political organisation as such. The omission of religion in the circumstances in which the presentation of the problem was attempted (1913) is understandable for the reason that at that stage religion not only formed no part of the programme of the Social-Democrats as they were called, but was detested and held in contempt. But it will be wrong to think that no importance was attached to the political aspect of the problem.

3. Historical Evolution of the National Problem

In presenting his thesis on the national problem to the Tenth Congress of the Russian Communist Party in 1921, Stalin explained in detail the different trends in national movements. Explaining the Marxist-Leninist doctrine that modern nations are the product of the epoch of rising capitalism, he said that the British, French, Germans and Italians had constituted themselves into nations during the victorious march of capitalism and its triumph over feudal disunity. So far as these peoples were concerned, they developed into independent bourgeois States. The boundaries of Governments coincided, more or less, with those of nationalities with the exception, in one typical instance, of Great Britain where Ireland was reduced to the position of an oppressed nationality. In Eastern Europe, however, the centralised States came into being for the purposes of defence before the overthrow of feudalism and the emergenc of full-fledged capitalism. The

[1] Stalin's *Marxism and the National and Colonial Question*, pp. 5—9.

result was that the machinery of the State was entirely under the control of one dominant nation while the weaker nationalities were subjected to all manner of tyranny and oppression. Such were, as Stalin points out, Austria, Hungary and Russia. During that period the question of national self-determination did not arise in Western Europe save for Ireland, as it did in Eastern Europe, which later was the scene of national oppression and the dominant ruling nation's chauvinistic approach to the national problem.

In the wake of capitalistic expansion came the search for new markets, raw materials and other requisites for exploitation. This led to the export of capital and the development of imperialism. In the process Western European mono-national States were transformed into multi-national States. The dominant nations of these States not only defended by all possible means their State boundaries but strove to extend them and conquer and acquire new territories. So there was, on the one hand, conflict between the dominant nations and, on the other, between these nations and the subject, oppressed nations. The war, for instance, between Britain and Germany in 1914-18 belonged to the first category while the conflict between Britain and Ireland was of the second category. Thus the capitalist epoch was followed by the epoch of finance-capital, of imperialism. The latter was slowly but steadily undermined by its inner contradictions—the conflict between workers and employers within municipal limits, the jealousy and rivalry between the dominant nations and the struggle in the colonial countries for emancipation from foreign imperialistic yoke. All these precipitated the World War of 1914-18.

The war ended in a military victory for the Allies, but the national conflict became more and more acute. Britain was shaken by the mobilisation of national forces in Ireland and India. The defeated multi-national States in Eastern Europe were completely dismembered. Britain sought to stabilise her position by the Anglo-Irish treaty of 1921, and the Mont-ford Reforms of 1919 for India. These paved the way for further conflicts taking concrete shape in revolutionary constitutionalism in Southern Ireland and in extra-legal movements in India initiated under the leadership of Gandhiji. In Eastern Europe the solution of the national problem was sought, on the basis of Woodrow Wilson's doctrine of self-determination, in the formation of bourgeois national States such as Poland, Czecho-Slovakia, Yugoslavia, Bulgaria, Finland etc., known as the Succession States of Europe. Stalin contended that the installation of these new States could not eliminate the fundamental causes of national conflict because they were in design and structure based on private property and class exploitation. For such States could not exist without (1) oppressing their own national minorities, (2) extending their territories at the expense of their neighbours, and (3) looking for financial and military aid to the Big Powers in Europe and America. It is true that the Minorities Guarantee Treaties were concluded with a view to the pro-protection of national minorities between the Succession States and the great victorious Powers.[1] But these were calculated to tackle the symptoms, and not the disease. The result was failure.

The League of Nations was inaugurated with the ostensible object of preventing wars of aggression and resolving conflicts arising out of the oppression of national minorities and their determination to achieve freedom to shape their own destinies. How and why the League failed to work out the ideals which had been proclaimed by Woodrow Wilson and European statesmen of "peace" offers lessons of history into which I need not go. Stalin has drawn the conclusion from these trials, experiments and failures that bourgeois society was utterly incapable of solving the national problem.[2] The Marxian thesis is interesting in this context. The nation is a necessary product, an inevitable form, in the bourgeois epoch of social development. Marx made it clear at the same time that the working classes "have no country". "Since the proletariat", he argued, "must first of all acquire political supremacy, must rise to be the leading class of the nation, must constitute itself the nation, it is, so far, itself national, though not in the bourgeois sense of the world."[3] What Marx meant was that the working class, while keeping constantly in mind its main and fundamental objective (classless society) and working for it, must assume the leadership of the nation, wresting power from the bourgeois elements, and identity itself with all colonial and national movements for liberation.

Lenin developed this thesis in more concrete terms by analysing the tasks of the proletariat. The nature and character of those tasks could not and should not be the same in all countries. In

[1] For fuller treatment read the author's *The Problem of Minorities*.
[2] Stalin's *Marxism and the National and Colonial Question*, pp. 88-90.
[3] *The Communist Manifesto* published in 1848.

this respect countries were divided into three main types in relation to the question of national self-determination, namely, (1) the advanced capitalist countries of Western Europe and the United States of America, (2) Eastern European countries and States, and (3) colonial and semi-colonial countries like China, Persia and India. In the first, the proletariat's role was to force the bourgeois democratic State to acknowledge the right of secession on the part of the oppressed colonial peoples such as Ireland and India. In the second, its task was to "merge the class struggle of the workers in the oppressing nations with the class struggle of the workers in the oppressed nations." In the third, it was for the proletariat to "render determined support to the more revolutionary elements in the buorgeois-democratic movements for national liberation . . . and assist their rebellion—and, if need be, their revolutionary war—against the imperialist Powers that oppress them."[1]

There should, however, be no confusion as to the meaning of the "right of national self-determination". It does not mean cultural autonomy. It means "the right to independence in a political sense, the right to be free, political secession from the oppressing nation." There must be no restriction on the freedom of agitation in favour of secession, no interference with the right of the oppressed nation to settle the question of secession by means of a popular democratic referendum. But, as Lenin explained, "this demand is by no means identical with the demand for secession, for the partition and for the formation of small States." Socialism does not aim at the formation of small States ; its aim is to bring the nations closer to each other and, in favourable circumstances, to merge them. But again to quote Lenin, just as mankind "can achieve the abolition of classes only by passing through the transition period of the dictatorship of the oppressed class, so mankind can achieve the inevitable merging of nations only by passing through the transition period of complete liberation of all the oppressed nations, i.e., their freedom to secede."[2]

4. Is India a "Nation"?

If Stalin's definition, which in the main follows the Marxist-Leninist line, is accepted, then India is not a nation, nor do Hindus

[1] *Lenin's Selected Works,* Vol. 5, pp. 275-276.

[2] Ibid, pp. 270-271.

or Muslims each separately constitute a nation. India cannot claim "a community of language" which, in his opinion, is an essential characteristic of a nation. Nor does it bind all Hindus together as distinguished from Muslims and Muslims as opposed to Hindus. A Bengali Muslim and a Bengali Hindu speak almost the same language and each differs in his speech from a Pathan Muslim and a Punjabi Hindu. About the other factors on which Stalin lays stress, such as the community of territory, economic cohesion, psychological make-up as manifested in a community of culture, it may be said that these are more or less present. So also is the fact that India is a historically evolved stable community. But Stalin says that there is no nation if a single one of all the characteristics, including the community of language, is absent. A definition was attempted as early as 1891 by Mr. Ananda Charlu in the course of his Presidential address to the Indian National Congress at Nagpur. The Congress President spoke with reference to the controversy then raised as to whether or not India was a nation. He observed :

> In the first place, it (nation) has for its central stock—like the trunk of a tree—the people who have for ages and generations settled and domiciled in a country, with more or less ethnic identity at bottom, and more or less unified by being continually subjected to identical environments and to the inevitable process of assimilation. In the next place, it gets added to, from time to time, by the accession of other peoples—like scions engrafted on the central stem, or like creepers attaching thereto—who settle in the country in a like manner, and come under the many unifying influences already referred to, though still exhibiting marks of separateness and distinctness. Affirm this standard and you have an Indian nation. Deny it and you have a nation nowhere on the face of the earth.

This looks like Stalin's picture of a historically evolved, stable community. But it is a community not so much of language as of ethnic unity at botton, and of identical environments, and subject to the same inevitable process of assimilation. Into this main central current flow other streams and a composite people comes into being by absorption, assimilation and adaptation. Thus a nation is formed and it may well be that the tributaries retain their individual existences except at the point where they merge themselves in the main central current. Mr. Ananda Charlu claimed that within the short period of seven years from 1885 to the end of 1891 the Congress had contributed to a sense of unity between Hindus and Muslims despite their long separation from one another and their sectarian jealousies and rivalries. He said that this was "a magnificent product of the Congress as a mighty nationaliser".[1]

Nobody can deny the fundamental basis of Mr. Ananda Charlu's thesis. Anyone whose outlook has not been vitiated by communal bias or fanatical slogans will admit that the Congress as an organisation has striven hard and long to bring the different communities in India on a common platform with a view to liberating the country from foreign rule and setting up what it has conceived to be an independent, democratic Indian State with guarantees in respect of the protection of minorities. But it is also a fact that with the increasing transfer of responsibilities from British to Indian hands Muslims have dissociated themselves more and more from the Congress and its policy and programme. Muslims alone are not to blame. The Congress and a section of its leadership cannot absolve themselves of their share of responsibility for this deplorable state of affairs. Notwithstanding pronouncements by individual Congress leaders like Pandit Nehru and vague official declarations of rights such as those embodied in the Karachi resolution adopted in 1931, the Congress has thought more in terms of the transfer of power than in terms of the much-needed reconstruction of the productive relations at least on the basis of democracy which alone may make an appeal to the Muslim masses and steal the thunder of a fanatical, reactionary Muslim leadership.

It is not enough to say that Mr. Jinnah and his colleagues are misleading the Muslim masses and driving them headlong into disaster. One must show where precisely they are wrong. It is not enough to say that they are wrong. One must offer an effective antidote to their wrong-doing not by pious platitudes and lyrical effusions, but by concrete measures of social reconstruction, of which the Muslim masses may be proud and worthy beneficiaries in common with other sections of the community. Suspicion is not dispelled or mutual understanding promoted by bitter attacks on the leadership of a great community or by calling its accredited spokesmen agents of British imperialism.

There has been much too mechanical, sometimes militant, in-

[1] A. C. Banerjee's *Indian Constitutional Documents*, Vol. II: 1858-1945, pp. 115-116.

sistence that British imperialism as the third party has fomented and fostered divisions by using the Muslim League leadership as a brake on Indian progress by false promises or clandestine deals. Apart from its unnecessarily provocative character, a charge of this sweeping nature is not sustainable on historical grounds. Even if it were well-founded, the way of statesmanship is not to force the Muslim League and its adherents into the camp of British imperialism, but to draw them into the opposite camp. It is rather amazing that many otherwise knowledgeable and intelligent people should be blind to the simple fact that the third party cannot have its way where there is no deep, abiding antagonism between the other two parties. The only way to silence and corner the third party is to create conditions, in disregard of its gestures, in which the other two parties can work in a spirit of mutual esteem, and not to promote alliances between the third party and one of the other two parties. Underneath the Muslim League's fanatical adherence to a historically wrong and utterly reactionary slogan there are deep social currents which one dare not ignore without throwing the whole country into mediæval religious convulsions. In the relatively upper strata of the Muslim community there is a desperate race for unequal competition with the militant Hindu bourgeoisie. At the lowest rung of the ladder the impoverished Muslim peasantry and proletariat are being irresistibily driven by historical forces to an anti-landlord and anti-bourgeois struggle. These social urges have not yet taken a definite shape and are not vocal. But things are changing very fast indeed.

Now, much may be said for and against Statlin's definition of "nation", the description generally found in text-books or Mr. Ananda Charlu's idea of "nation" quoted above. I myself wrote several years ago,[1] that "the essential factor of nationality . . . is a common political consciousness and a common ideal", that "nationalism may grow and develop among peoples differing from one another in race, language and religion." I am disposed to think, however, that we in this country have already outlived the controversy over this idea or concept of nation which has now become an irritant. Nationalism by its deification of a mystic entity has in our time become a reactionary slogan except in so far as it represents, as in colonial and dependent countries, a movement for the overthrow of the oppressing power. Mr. Jinnah's

[1] Read the author's *The Problem of Minorities*, p. 341.

two-nation theory is in this context as retrograde and fraught with dangerous and sinister potentialities as the slogan of Akhand Hindusthan corresponding at the psychological base to the metaphysical concept of one deified Indian nationalism. It is, of course, true that the national sentiment was acknowledged as a real political fact at the partition of Poland in 1772, that it "gave force to the Spanish resistance against the French Government from 1806 until 1813", that it "produced the defeat of Napoleon at Moscow and the revival of Germany."[1] In the nineteenth century in Europe it brought about the political emancipation of Greece, Roumania, Serbia and Bulgaria. It led also to the separation of Belgium from Holland. It exerted a tremendous influence in other directions.

But we are in the throes of wider and more far-reaching social crises. Let us not, therefore, make the so-called Indian unity or Indian nationalism the starting point of our consideration of the problems that face us. For apart from its lack of conformity to ethnic and other social facts which recent investigations have brought into bold relief,[2] this insistence on one nation, one State, irritates and repels large Muslim masses, and has already exposed itself to attacks by no inconsiderable body of the submerged Hindu masses statutorily called the scheduled castes. Let us not start with Mr. Jinnah's two-nation theory either, because apart from the absurd and preposterous claims it assumes, it will be resisted by Hindus, Sikhs and a large section of the scheduled castes. Let us instead start on the basis that there are communities, races and tribes, then proceed with the redistribution of Provinces and States after expert and impartial investigation, and finally frame and work out plans for our political and social reshaping in consonance with the express will of each territorial unit and the needs of democracy. In such readjustments there will be minorities or communities—whatever you may call persons or groups of persons who in race, religion or language may happen to differ from the majority of the population in the unit concerned. Legal and constitutional provisions susceptible of juridical treatment must be made for their protection along lines laid down in the Minorities Guarantee Treaties. For these purposes I reject the thesis that India is one single nation. I reject the Muslim League's

[1] Delisle Burns' *Political Ideals*, pp. 184-185.

[2] Read Ishawara Topa's *Facts about India*.

two-nation theory, too. If religion is accepted, as is implicit in the Muslim League's thesis, as the basis of a "nation", its logical end is not a separate, independent Muslim State or States in India, but pan-Islamism which can have no place in any scheme of India's political reconstruction.

Incidentally reference may be made to Stalin's idea of Indian "nationalities". In his report presented to the Twelfth Congress of the Russian Communist Party on April 23, 1923, he wrote that there are "no less than eight hundred nationalities in India".[1] It is, on the face of it, an astounding thesis. It is not clear whether a distinction is made between "nationality" and "nation" in his context. But throughout his writings on this question these are presumed for all practical purposes to be synonymous terms. When not used in the sense of citizenship or subjecthood based on the doctrine of allegiance to a State as distinguished from alienage, it is not easy to distinguish "nationality" from "nation". For the sake of convenience, however, a nation is sometimes construed to mean a population of the same race and language inhabiting the same territory and constituting a larger part of the whole, whereas nationality is one of several distinct ethnic groups scattered over the State's territory and constituting a comparatively small part of the whole population.[2] It is not quite clear whether Stalin holds this view unless it is assumed that a distinction was intended when in his speech on the Draft Constitution in 1935, he said that in the Soviet Union "there are about sixty nations, national groups and nationalities". If he has used "nationalities" in the sense of "nations" as defined by him, I can only say that his idea that there are "no less than eight hundred nationalities" in India sounds almost fantastic. It is necessary to repel the idea propagated in foreign lands that there are about three to four hundred language groups in India. The fact is that the main Indian languages vary between twenty and twentyfive.

5. The Basic Principle of Pakistan

The Muslim League's demand for Pakistan is traced to the apprehensions entertained by a large section of Muslims that with the transfer of power to India the Muslim community may be

[1] *Marxism and the National and Colonial Question*, p. 162.
[2] Burgess' *Political Science and Constitutional Law*, Vol. I, p. 5.

subjected to tyranny and repression by the great Hindu majority, and to their natural desire for a due share of power and authority in the management of public affairs. These apprehensions were aggravated by the alleged activities of the Congress Ministries in Provinces, where the Hindus are in a majority, after the inauguration of Provincial Autonomy under the Act of 1935. In the course of a statement made in 1939, Mr. Jinnah said that "since the inauguration of the new Provincial constitution it has been established beyond doubt, particularly by the way in which the Congress High Command has pursued its policies and programmes, that the sole aim and object of the Congress is to annihilate every other organisation and set itself up as a Fascist and authoritarian organisation of the worst type."[1] But the idea of independent Muslim political existence had been canvassed by Sir Mahommed Iqbal in his Presidential address to the Allahabad Session of the All-India Muslim League in 1930. He said that Muslims were entitled to full and free development on the lines of their own culture and tradition in their own Indian "homelands" on the basis of a permanent communal settlement whether within or without the British Empire. The formation of a consolidated North-West Indian Muslim State was to him "the final destiny of the Muslims at least of North-West India." Sir Mahommed wanted to see "the Punjab, the North-West Frontier Province, Sind and Baluchistan amalgamated into a single State."

The Iqbal thesis set a section of Muslims furiously thinking. In 1933, a secret circular was issued by several Muslim students at Cambridge which sought to propagate the theory that the Muslims of North-West India were a distinct nation and proposed the amalgamation of the Provinces mentioned by Sir Mohammad Iqbal and Kashmir into a separate, independent Federation without any federal tie with any All-India Federation. That was popularly known as the Rahmat Ali circular. In 1938, the Cambridge circular, which had been rejected by the Muslim representatives at the Round Table Conferences, formed the basis of a resolution adopted by the Sind Provincial Muslim League Conference. There were other attempts in this direction and the core was the existence of Muslims as a distinct national entity from the rest of India, which for some mysterious reason or other had

[1] A. C. Banerjee's *Indian Constitutional Documents*, Vol. II, p. 408.

hitherto escaped the attention of Hindus, Muslims and others. On March 23, 1940, the All-India Muslim League formulated its demand in these terms:

> That it is the considered view of this session of the All-India Muslim League that no constitutional scheme would be workable in this country or acceptable to Muslims unless it is designed on the following basic principle, viz., that geographically contiguous units are demarcated into regions which should be constituted with such territorial readjustments as may be necessary, that the areas in which the Muslims are numerically in majority, as in the north-western and eastern zones of India, should be grouped to constitute independent States in which the constituent units shall be autonomous and sovereign.
>
> That adequate, effective and mandatory safeguards should be specifically provided in the constitution for minorities in these units and in these regions for the protection of their religious, cultural, economic, political, administrative and other rights and interests in consultation with them ; and in other parts of India where the Mussalmans are in a minority, adequate, effective and mandatory safeguards shall be specifically provided in the constitution for them and other minorities for the protection of their religious, cultural, economic, political, administrative and other rights and interests in consultation with them.

The resolution authorised the League Working Committee to frame a scheme of constitution in accordance with these basic principles. It was contemplated that the respective Muslim zones or regions would assume all powers, including defence, external affairs, communications, customs and such other subjects as might be necessary for the purpose.

Both the President[1] and the General Secretary[2] of the Muslim League stated that Pakistan would embrace the North-West Frontier Province, Baluchistan, Sind and the Punjab in north-west, and in north-east Assam and Bengal, including "the rich industrial and port city of Calcutta". Mr. Jinnah is reported to have expressed the view in the course of an interview to a correspondent of *The New York Times* on February 6, 1943, that under his scheme the north-western and eastern zones of Pakistan would be "connected by a corridor running along the northern borders of the United Provinces and Bihar". This "corridor" business has not been officially canvassed during the last six years. But that it must have been in Mr. Jinnah's mind is supported by his insis-

[1] *The Amrita Bazar Patrika* (Calcutta Edition), of November 12, 1945.

[2] *The Statesman* (Calcutta Edition) of September 29, 1945.

tence that the principle of Pakistan should not only be recognised, but that approval should be accorded to such territorial adjustments as were essential to the strategic and economic requirements of a fully sovereign and independent Pakistan State or States, whatever their effect on Hindus and other communities in the areas in question. The case for inclusion of Assam in north-eastern Pakistan apparently rests on this ground.

I do not agree that there is no clear indication of the Muslim League's plan in the Lahore resolution or in the statements and pronouncements of its leaders. Speaking for myself, I find no difficulty in understanding what they demand. They believe that there are two nations in India—Hindus and Muslims. They demand partition of India in recognition of the Muslim right of self-determination. They claim the Provinces named above as their "homelands", where they must be free to settle their own affairs as an independent nation without interference by any outside authority. They claim Assam, which is a Muslim-minority Province, as part of their eastern zone on strategic and economic grounds. Within their zones they are prepared to provide constitutional guarantees for the protection of minorities on the basis of reciprocity. They are prepared as a free and independent State or States to consider the question of negotiating a treaty of alliance with Hindusthan on specific matters or subjects. Mr. Jinnah has repudiated the suggestion that Pakistan would be a satellite State or States of Britain. This in a nutshell is the Pakistan scheme. Whether one accepts or rejects it—I myself do not accept the scheme as it is—it cannot be said with truth that it is absolutely vague and nebulous. If there is nothing clear and definite in the scheme, why is there so much opposition from the non-Leaguers? If, as is evident, there is so much opposition, the charge of vagueness falls to the ground. One does not fight against an imaginary foe in the air.

The British Government's first attempt to meet the Muslim League's case was made by the Cripps Mission in 1942. They recognised the right of non-accession on the part of any existing British Indian Province. This right should not, however, be confused with the right of secession. Non-accession implies a pre-federation act while secession means a post-federation decision. While admitting that the Mission's concession was in response to the League's insistent demand for partition the

Muslim League Working Committee objected to the method and procedure laid down in the formula on the ground amongst others that a decision by the existing Legislative Assembly in each of the Provinces concerned, particularly in Bengal, Assam and the Punjab, was likely to negative the proposed plan of the British Government.[1] They reiterated their demand for Pakistan as foreshadowed in the Lahore resolution and called upon the British Government to accept unequivocally the principle of partition on the basis of their two-nation theory. The Congress Working Committee's reaction to the formula was incorporated in their resolution released to the Press on April 10, 1942. It was stated in the resolution *inter alia :*

> The Congress has been wedded to Indian freedom and unity and any break in that unity, especially in the modern world when people's minds inevitably think in terms of ever larger federations, would be injurious to all concerned and exceedingly painful to contemplate. Nevertheless, the Committee cannot think in terms of compelling the people in any territorial unit to remain in an Indian Union against their declared and established will. While recognising this principle the Committee feel that every effort should be made to create conditions which would help the different units in developing a common and co-operative national life. The acceptance of the principle inevitably involves that no changes should be made which result in fresh problems being created and compulsion being exercised on other groups within that area.

The propositions implicit in the Congress Working Committee's resolution were (1) that there should be a free and united India; (2) that in the context of the modern world a break in the unity would be disastrous; (3) that a federal Indian Union should be the basic form of the future constitutional arrangements ; (4) that if the people of any territorial unit (Hindus, Muslims and others) decide not to remain in such an Indian Union, they would not be compelled by force or any other analogous method to act contrary to their decision; and (5) that freedom to opt out of the non-acceding or seceding unit should be accorded to other substantial groups within the area should they desire separation.

Mr. C. Rajagopalachariar suggested a formula more or less in terms of this resolution and with a view to providing a basis for Congress-League agreement both for the tran-

[1] The League Working Committee's resolution adopted on April 11, 1942.

sition period and the post-war future. Gandhiji touched it up finally in his letter to Mr. Jinnah, dated September 24, 1944, in connection with the prolonged Gandhi-Jinnah negotiations held in Bombay for about three weeks. Gandhiji refused to accept the League's two-nation theory. He was, however, prepared to assume that Muslims in Baluchistan. Sind, the North-West Frontier Province and that part of the Punjab where they were in absolute majority, and in parts of Bengal and Assam where again they were in such majority, desired to live in separation from the rest of India. These areas should be demarcated by a Commission approved by the Congress and the League. Thereafter the wishes of the inhabitants of the areas so demarcated should be ascertained by adult vote or through some equivalent method. If the vote was in favour of separation, then on the attainment by India of full and complete independence these areas should form a separate State from the rest of India. There must be a treaty between these two parts concerning such matters as foreign affairs, defence, internal communications, commerce and the like. The treaty must contain safeguards for the protection of minorities in the two States.

The proposals made by Gandhiji on the basis of the C. R. Formula were not acceptable to Mr. Jinnah as "they neither meet the substance nor essence of the Lahore resolution".[1] They were, in his opinion, "calculated completely to torpedo the Pakistan demand of Muslim India". In his own way Mr. Jinnah was right. Gandhiji repudiated the League's two-nation theory. He did not accept its claim that it was the sole representative of Muslims and that once it made a demand it was to be conceded without putting it to a popular vote. He did not agree that areas should be assigned to Pakistan where Muslims were not in majority except on the basis of a democratic, popular verdict.

It should be remembered that at no stage of the proceedings or thereafter did the Congress officially accord its approval to the C. R. Formula or its amendment by Gandhiji. Until the Cabinet Mission's negotiations the Congress Working Committee's resolution of April, 1942, and the All-India Congress Committee's resolution of May, 1942,[2] stood, although the latter seemed to have

[1] Mr. Jinnah's letter to Gandhiji, dated September 26, 1944.

[2] "The A.-I.C.C. is of opinion that any proposal to disintegrate India by giving liberty to any component State or territorial unit to secede from

cancelled the former despite Maulana Azad's contention to the contrary. Obviously two opposite forces were working in the inner Councils of the Congress, the one sympathetic on principle to the Muslim League's case for self-determination and the other veering round to the Hindu Mahasabha's stand for Akhand Hindusthan.

The Cabinet Mission rejected the demand for Pakistan on grounds more or less similar to those urged in different quarters. They rejected the truncated form of Pakistan as suggested by Gandhiji in terms of Mr. Rajagopalachariar's formula on the ground that it was not acceptable to the Muslim League and, further, that it involved a radical partition of the Punjab and Bengal which would be contrary to the wishes and interests of a very large proportion of the inhabitants of these Provinces. In the north-west embracing the Punjab, the North-West Frontier Province, Sind and British Baluchistan the Muslim population, according to the census of 1941, is 62.07% and non-Muslim minorities 37.93%. In the Punjab the whole of the Ambala and Jullundar divisions is a Muslim minority area. This area could not be assigned to a sovereign Muslim State without obtaining a clear verdict from Sikhs and Hindus. In the north-east embracing Bengal and Assam the census puts the Muslim majority at 51.69% and non-Muslim minorities at 48.31%. Here, again, the whole of Assam except Sylhet is a Muslim minority Province and in the Province as a whole the Muslim proportion is only 33.72% against 66.28% for Hindus, including tribes and other non-Muslims. In Bengal a large part of Western Bengal, including Calcutta, is a Muslim minority area. In Calcutta the Muslim proportion of population is between 24% and 26%. The inclusion of these districts and areas in Assam and Bengal in the Muslim League's north-eastern Pakistan Zone without a general plebiscite was simply coercion, which would be bitterly resisted. About the force of these arguments there could be no doubt whatsoever.

But the Cabinet Mission's "weighty administrative, economic and military considerations", their special pleading for a successful defence in depth and their emphasis on the distance of seven hundred miles betwen the two halves of the Pakistan State seem

the Indian Union or Federation will be highly detrimental to the best interests of the people of the different States and Provinces and the country as a whole and the Congress, therefore, cannot agree to any such proposal."

impertinent. Certainly it did not lie in the mouth of these distinguished Missionaries of State to urge these points in rejecting the Muslim League's demand, particularly because they were unable to meet the point that Britain would for the same "weighty" considerations cease to be an independent sovereign State. They talked as if they were teaching lessons to naughty schoolboys. These were points which it was for the peoples of India to decide themselves. Lord Pethick-Lawrence and his colleagues, however, unconsciously betrayed an indecent anxiety over the future of India as a bastion of defence of the realm and it is rather surprising that these special pleadings on their part should have failed to provoke a fitting and well-merited rebuff from the leaders of political parties. But then it was a different story.

6. The Mission's Plan Repugnant To Democratic Centralism

The Cabinet Mission's scheme of a three-tier constitution is a negation of both democracy and centralism. It is a negation of democracy because it denies the right of free choice to the people of a territorial unit demarcated on a linguistic and cultural basis in the matter of their political and constitutional arrangements. It is a negation of centralism because the basic form the constitution is required to take with a Central Federal Union having powers of a restricted character cannot meet the requirements of the modern scientific age. Exposed to endless internal friction, the machinery may break down at the first unfriendly impact from outside. In their anxiety to appear as sincere upholders of a free united India the three Cabinet Ministers have abandoned the term "peoples" with reference to the "communities" or "nationalities" of India—a term which had been used from 1919[1] right up to 1942[2] in authoritative documents. They appealed to "the leaders and people of India" to accept their proposals embodied in the State Paper and avert by a co-operative endeavour the alternative of "a grave danger of violence, chaos and even civil war."[3] The assumption of the Mission's proposals is that the races, castes, communities of India, etc. constitute an organic whole and that these are either a majority or a minority with reference to the whole of India or with reference to the specified areas or zones according to their

[1] Preamble to the Government of India Act, 1919, paragraph 3.
[2] The Cripps scheme, clause (e).
[3] The Mission's statement of May 16, paragraph 24.

numerical strength in proportion to the total population country-wise or area-or zone-wise, as the case may be. To these are added inhabitants of the tribal and excluded and partially excluded areas.

Lord Pethick-Lawrence evaded the question put to him at a Press Conference which he addressed on May 17, 1946, whether Muslims were a minority or a nation. The Secretary of State said that they were "a great community". This difference between "minority" and "community" was sought to be made out in the Secretary of State's letter addressed on May 9 to the President of the Muslim League, in which reference was made to "large communities" and "small minorities". That a united India at least for ten years after the commencement of the new constitution is taken as the basis of political reconstruction in the State Paper is clear from an explanatory note issued a few hours after the Mission's Memorandum on the States was released on May 22. It is stated in the note that the expression "Succession Government or Governments of British India" used in the Memorandum should be read as having been withdrawn after their statement of May 16. The Mission would have the world believe that they changed their minds definitely in favour of a united India after their discussions with party leaders. There is, however, no explanation why the Commander-in-Chief should have permitted himself to refer to "three assemblies" in connection with constitution-making in his broadcast on May 17, and upon what weighty considerations.

An exact definition of "minorities" has not been attempted by the Mission. It may be that they deliberately kept the matter in the hands of the projected Advisory Committee and the Union Constituent Assembly and the "Sectional" representatives. It may as well be that the question was much too simple for elucidation in the State Paper. Nor does the Government of India Act, 1935, offer guidance unless reliance is placed on clause X of the Instrument of Instructions to the Provincial Governors which reads :

> Our Governor shall interpret his special responsibility for the safeguarding of the legitimate interests of the minorities as requiring him to secure, in general, that those racial or religious communities for the members of which special representation is accorded in the Legislature, and those classes of the people committed to his charge who, whether on account of the smallness of their number or their lack of educational or material advantages or from any other cause,

cannot as yet fully rely for their welfare upon joint political action in the Legislature, shall not suffer, or have reasonable cause to fear neglect or repression. But he shall not regard as entitled to his protection any body of persons by reason only that they share a view on a particular question which has not found favour with the majority.

The federal principle is the basic assumption of the Constitution Act of 1935. Accordingly within the defined area of their jurisdiction, but subject to certain specified reservations, the Provinces are as supreme and sovereign as the Centre is in its own field. In the Provinces of Bengal, the Punjab, the North-West Frontier and Sind, Hindus are a numerical minority whereas in the rest of the Governor's Provinces they are the majority. Muslims constitute the majority in the former group of Provinces ; in the latter group they are a minority. That is so in the literal sense of the terms. But despite the federal basis of the structure Hindus as such have been accorded no special representation even in the Legislatures of the Provinces where they are a minority, although as a matter of fact the seats allocated to "General" are mostly filled by members of that community.

The term "General"[1] includes every racial or religious community or group for which no special representation has been provided in the Legislature concerned. Provision for such representation varies from Province to Province. Sikhs, for instance, are treated as a minority in the Punjab and the North-West Frontier Province, but they come under "General" in the other Provinces. Europeans are a minority in all the Provinces except the North-West Frontier Province and Orissa where by implication they belong to "General". Anglo-Indians are part of the "General" community in Assam, the North-West Frontier Province, Orissa and Sind and in the rest constitute a minority. Indian Christians are treated as a minority in all the Provinces barring the Central Provinces and Berar, the North-West Frontier Province and Sind, where they are mixed up with the "General" community. There is no "Hindu" as such in the design and structure of the Act. Muslims are treated as a minority community, no matter whether they constitute a majority or a minority in one Province or the other. It has often been contended that on occasion opportunity has been taken of this legal or constitu-

[1] Fifth Schedule to the Government of India Act, 1935.

tional device to withhold from Hindus in the Hindu-minority Provinces the protection to which normally and in fact they were entitled notwithstanding the exercise by the Provinces of almost sovereign powers in legislation and administration in the demarcated sphere of their jurisdiction.

Now, the question has been raised whether the Indian States, Muslims or Sikhs can by their withdrawal from the constitution-making body suspend or veto the operation of the Cabinet Mission's long-term Plan. In the Plan itself there is no clear guidance. It is, of course, assumed that no party would keep out. But if any of these parties do keep out, what happens ? It is no part of the interim project that the States should be associated with the Central Government.[1] They are also left out of the preliminary meeting of the British Indian representatives in the Constituent Assembly at which stage their Negotiating Committee parley with a corresponding Committee to be set up by the Provincial representatives.[2] If as a result of negotiations which are in progress they refuse to send their representatives to the Union Constituent Assembly, I do not think that there is anything in the Mission's proposals which may be relied upon for declaring a breakdown of the constitution-making machinery solely on that ground.

With regard to Sikhs, the Mission have recognised them as one of the "three main communities" for the purposes of separate representation through the Punjab quota in Section B and the Union Constituent Assembly, the other two being "General" and Muslim. The "General" community includes all persons who are not Muslims or Sikhs. The numerical strength of Sikh representation in the constitution-making body is 4. It is not contemplated that this number, whatever the importance of the Sikh community, would have the right, by withdrawal or refusal to participate in the proceedings of the Union Constitution Assembly or of Section B, to upset or negative the whole Plan. Support is found for this view in the safeguard for paragraph 15 as well as in the special provision as to decisions on major communal issues, where Sikhs have been excluded from the category of "major communities".[3] These "major communities" are two and not three and they are Hindus and Muslims. I am only explaining what I consider to be

[1] The State Paper of May 16, paragraph 23.
[2] Ibid, paragraph 19 (II).
[3] Ibid, paragraph 19 (VII).

the legal bearings of the relevant clauses of the Mission's statement of May 16, for what they are worth. This does not mean that I believe that Sikhs have had no legitimate cause for grievance on this score.

The position of Muslims does not look as simple as that of the States or of Sikhs. Obviously some difficulty arises if, as a body, their representatives refuse to withhold their co-operation in constitution-making. They are in the majority in both B and C Sections. In four Provinces out of five in these two Sections (Assam being the only exception) the majority of representatives in the Constituent Assembly come from the Muslim community. The Muslim withdrawal would mean non-co-operation by the major community in these Provinces and the carrying on of proceedings of the Union Constituent Assembly without Muslim participation would be against the spirit of the Plan. This is, to a large extent, proved by the safeguards in paragraph 19 (vii) of the State Paper. Legally, however, there appears to be no bar unless the above-mentioned provisions are interpreted to mean that the major portion of the Muslim representatives must be present and that no alteration of paragraph 15 and no decision on a major communal issue shall be effective save with the assent of the majority of the Muslims present and voting in the Union Constituent Assembly. No quorum has been fixed for meetings of that Assembly. Obviously that is a matter to be decided at the preliminary meeting of the representatives of Provinces, whose function it is to settle the order of business. There is nothing in the Plan to prevent the majority of members of Section A and the minority of Sections B and C from sitting at the preliminary meeting and carrying on in terms of the State Paper without Muslim participation. If, again, the Interim Government could function, as it did at the beginning of the new set-up, in the absence of the Muslim League's quota of representation, there should be no bar to constitution-making being proceeded with merely on the ground of Muslim non-co-operation.

The Muslim League leaders do not rule out this possibility and it appears that in the event of the preliminary meeting being convened without prior agreement they may call upon their representatives to meet in Sections B and C and frame the constitutions of the Provinces concerned and "Group" constitutions so that the onus may be thrown upon the British Government to choose between the two diametrically opposite lines of approach and take their decision. For the success of both the short-term plan and the long-term project Hindu-Muslim agreement, and for the matter of that, agreement between Hindus, Muslims, Sikhs and the Indian States, is not only implied but expressly intended, although the Mission's intentions have not been clothed with sufficient legal precision so as to attract the intervention of a properly constituted Court. But what, one wonders, is the point in Mr. Clement Attlee's oft-quoted assurance in Parliament that a minority must not be allowed to veto the advance of the majority if for lack of Hindu-Muslim agreement or on the ground of Muslim non-co-operation the whole scheme is rendered null and void ? The Cabinet Mission had no answer. Maybe the British Government have none either.

7. Popular Misconceptions About The Soviet Union

In recent years public attention has been focussed on the Soviet Union and the machinery it has adopted to give expression to the principle of national self-determination and for the protection of national minorities. There is an impression in this country that it was Woodrow Wilson who for the first time in 1918 enunciated the principle of self-determination. That is clearly wrong. It had been earlier taken up by Karl Marx in connection with Ireland,[1] by Lenin in connection with the oppressed nationalities in Eastern Europe and all colonial peoples,[2] and by Stalin[3] in his elaborate thesis on the role of the social democrats and later of the Bolshevik Party in connection with the demand for political secession by oppressed peoples of the world.

There is another erroneous impression and it is that the Bolshevik leaders enunciated the principle as an absolute right and that in actual practice they have not hesitated to violate the principle. National self-determination, according to them, is not an end in itself ; it is a means to an end. It represents a particular phase of social evolution. The exercise of this right is a transitional arrangement just as the proletarian dictatorship was no more

[1] Read the resolution on the relations between the Irish and the English working classes drafted in 1869.

[2] Read Lenin's pamphlet on *Socialism and War* published in August, 1915, before the Zimmerwald Conference.

[3] Read Stalin's thesis on *Marxism and the National Question* published in 1913.

than a stepping-stone to a fuller and richer democracy. Writing about the role of the Socialists in 1915, Lenin said that "they cannot reach their great aim without fighting against every form of national oppression". It was for them to demand that the social democrats of the oppressing countries "should recognise and defend the right of the oppressed nations to self-determination in the political sense of the word, i.e. the right to political separation". But Lenin pointed out at the same time that to "defend this right does in no way mean to encourage the formation of small States, but, on the contrary, it leads to a freer, more fearless and, therefore, wider and more universal formation of larger Governments and Unions of Governments—a phenomenon more advantageous for the masses and more in accord with economic development." The Bolshevik approach to the problem is not formalistic ; it is dialectical. There is no dispute about the right of a nation freely to determine its own destiny. It has the right to arrange its life on autonomous lines ; it has the right to secede.

"But this does not mean," as Stalin observes, "that it should do so under all circumstances, that autonomy or separation will everywhere and always be advantageous for a nation, i.e. for the majority of its population, i.e. for the toiling strata".[1] Stalin then poses a practical problem. Suppose the Transcaucasian Tartars as a nation assemble in their Diet and, succumbing to the seductive gestures of the reactionary Mullahs, decide to secede from the State, and to restore the old order of things. Surely if the principle of national self-determination were an absolute right, they would be perfectly entitled to go their own way. That right not being absolute and its exercise not being mechanistic, the social democrats should come forward and interfere in the matter and offer a solution of the problem which would be most advantageous to the Tartar masses. This question does not arise today in view of so many developments, social and constitutional, that have taken place since Stalin wrote. The exact solution must depend on the historical conditions in which the nation finds itself. These conditions, like everything else, change, and it may well be that a solution which is correct at a given time may prove unsuitable at another. Hence the historical conditions which are in the process of constant change must be taken into consideration in any scientific treatment of the problem.

[1] *op. cit*, p. 20.

In 1920 Stalin explained at length the policy of the Soviet Government on the national question in Russia and the thesis thus developed was presented by the People's Commissariat of Nationalities. Certain observations were then made which require more than a passing notice not merely because of the principles therein enunciated but also for the reason that they have frequently been quoted in this country in condemnation of the alleged dual or opportunist role played by the Bolsheviks. Stalin said :

> The demand for the secession of the border regions from. Russia as the form that should be given to the relations between the centre and the border regions must be rejected not only because it is contrary to the very definition of the establishment of an alliance between the centre and the border regions, but primarily because it is fundamentally opposed to the interests of the masses of the peoples both of the centre and the border regions . . . . One has only to glance at Georgia, Armenia, Poland, etc., which have seceded from Russia but which have retained only the semblance of independence, while in reality they have been converted into unconditional vassals of the Entete ; one has only, finally, to recall the recent case of the Ukraine and Azerbaijan, the former of which was plundered by German capital and the latter by the Entete, in order to realise the counter-revolutionary nature of the demand for the secession of the border regions under present international conditions. When a life-and-death struggle is being waged, and is spreading, between proletarian Russia and the imperialist Entete, only two alternatives confront the border regions:
>
> Either they join forces with Russia, and then the toiling masses of the border regions will be emancipated from imperialist oppression ;
>
> Or they join forces with the Entete, and then the yoke of imperialism is inevitable.
>
> Of course, the border regions of Russia, the nations and tribes which inhabit these regions, just as all other nations, possess the inalienable right to secede from Russia and if any of these nations decided by a majority to secede from Russia, as was the case with Finland[1] in 1917, Russia, presumably, would be obliged to record

[1] When the Finnish Diet voted in favour of secession from Russia, the Council of People's Commissars issued a decree on December 18, 1917, recognising the independence of the Finnish Republic. On December 22, the All-Russian Central Executive Committee adopted "The Revolutionary Government's Declaration on the Independence of Finland". On December 29, the Council of Peoples' Commissars promulgated a decree declaring that "the Workers' and Peasants' Government of Russia supports the right of the Armenians in Turkish Armenia, which is occupied by Russia, to free self-determination."

> the fact and sanction the secession. But the question here is not of the indubitable rights of nations, but of the interests of the masses of the people both in the centre and in the border regions. . . . And the interests of the masses of the people render the demand for the secession of the border regions at the present stage of the revolution a profoundly counter-revolutionary one.[1]

I have reproduced these long extracts purposely. There has been wilful distortion of the Bolshevik stand on this question. There is a good deal of ignorance too. On the face of it, the assertion of a principle is cancelled by the exigencies of the State. But the contradictions are more apparent than real. This is typical dualism in practice in the Marxian dialectical solution of a great problem. What were the historical conditions of that time ? For only in the context of such conditions should the Stalinist thesis be examined. The first constitution, after the October-November revolution of 1917, was adopted on July 10, 1918. The new State was called the Russian Socialist Federated Soviet Republic (RSFSR). Its jurisdiction extended only to a part of the Tsarist territory or of the present USSR. Other parts were held by the armies of intervention represented by the Entete—British, French, Japanese, American—and also by Germany. These territories were under foreign occupation for about two years more and only as they were driven out some of these established with the RSFSR confederal relations and then on December 30, 1922, the delegates from the RSFSR, the Ukraine, White Russia and Transcaucasia sitting in the First Congress of Soviets declared the formation of a Union. The Union Constitution was confirmed by the Second Congress in 1924.

In 1920, when the article was written, the first experiment in revolutionary Soviet Government was being tried with Moscow as the centre, the foreign armies of intervention were holding vast regions in Russia and the administrative reconstruction of Russia was still incomplete. The central theme of the article was to show how to bring about "a revolutionary alliance between the centre and the border regions as a guarantee against intervention on the part of imperialism".[2] It was also a reply to the Entete who, while resisting the demand for secession by India, Egypt, Arabia

[1] *op. cit*, pp. 79-80.
[2] *op. cit*, p. 298.

and the other colonies, was working for the separation of the border regions from Russia to undermine the Soviet State. Stalin and the Bolsheviks supported the demand for secession by the colonies like India, Egypt and others because it meant their liberation from imperialism, "thus undermining the position of imperialism" and paving the way for revolution. They were against the secession of the border regions from Russia because it involved imperial servitude for them, "thus undermining the revolutionary power of Russia and strengthening the position of imperialism".

The question of secession was to be decided not with reference to some abstract, transcendental idea, but in the concrete setting of a given national and international situation and in the interests of the revolution. Secession for national development, progress and revolution must be supported. Secession for reaction, nationalist chauvinism and counter-revolution must be resisted. That in a nutshell was the Stalinist thesis in 1920, which has sometimes been distorted and very often misquoted. In concrete Indian terms the position may be put in this way. Suppose a free, democratic federal centre is established in India and Bengal as a constituent territorial national unit, succumbing to the influence of Mullahs or priests, or to the pleasing but sinister whispers of a reactionary bourgeoisie or a feudal aristocracy, demands secession in order that it may restore a regime of exploitation either itself or in alliance with any alien reactionary power. Viewing self-determination as an absolute right, there can be no objection to this demand for secession. But in the given objective conditions it must be opposed. Suppose, conversely, an authoritarian centre comes into existence under the control of an exploiting bourgeoisie or a feudal-bourgeois coterie of tyrants and Bengal proposes to assert the right of secession in order that the people or the nationality concerned may pursue democratic ways of life and maintain their freedom alike from central control or foreign exploitation. The demand for secession must then be supported by all lovers of democratic freedom. In the first case, the principle of self-self-determination is a counter-revolutionary slogan. In the second case, the demand is a revolutionary one.

Take the American Civil War to which reference is often made in defence of one Indian nation, one Indian State. In the United States it was a conflict between North and South over the question of slavery. The North was generally for its abolition and the South for its retention. In *Scott* v. *Sandford*[1] (Dred Scott Case) the Supreme Court in 1857 held slavery to be a national institution. Chief Justice Taney observed that the constitution had been made by and for white men, that when it was adopted the Negroes had for more than a century been "regarded as beings of an inferior order, and altogether unfit to associate with the white race, either in social or political relations", that "they had no rights which the white man was bound to respect".[2] A State (a constituent unit of the U.S.A.), according to the Chief Justice, could not make a citizen. The fact that Dred was a Negro was enough to dispose of his right to any standing in the court.

Before this case the struggle to get possession of Kansas had begun between "slavery" and "anti-slavery" men. The struggle for possession of Kansas, the controversy on the Dred Scott decision and the events that followed rapidly provoked such an atmosphere of bitterness between the "slavery" men of the South and the "abolitionists" of the North that the former thought that the only effective guarantee against abolition of slavery was secession from the United States. Their demand for separation was resisted to the bitter end and the issue was settled by Civil War. The result was the adoption of the Thirteenth Amendment in 1865, which forbade slavery within the United States, or any place subject to its jurisdiction. The demand for secession by the South on such an issue was a reactionary and dangerous slogan and the action taken against "slavery" men was historically justified. But it does not mean that because the "anti-slavery" men of the North in America fought tooth and nail to stop slavery any democratically disposed men and women would be justified in resisting a movement for secession directed against slave rule, foreign domination, national suppression or capitalistic or feudal exploitation. Every demand must be examined and scrutinised in a historical perspective.

If the principle of national self-determination is not an absolute right, if the demand for secession is a fight against a particular phase of social relations, that is, the phase of oppressing bourgeois nationalism, why, it may pertinently be asked, did Stalin in 1935

[1] 19 Howard 393 (1857).

[2] art. I, sec. 2, para 3 ; art. I, sec. 9, para 1 and para 4 ; art. IV, sec. 2, para 3.

oppose the proposed amendment seeking to strike out the right of secession reserved to each constituent republic under article 17, knowing as he did that the Soviet Union was not a national State but a proletarian democracy ? Stalin anticipated that question and gave his answer. He said that there was not a single union republic in the USSR that would want to secede. He said that in the USSR there was not a single union republic that would want to subjugate another union republic. Yet he opposed its deletion because it was necessary to emphasise the voluntary character of the Union and the equality of rights of the union republics.[1] Comparing the new Soviet constitution with what he called bourgeois constitutions (Britain, America etc.) Stalin observed that the latter "proceed from the premise that nations and races cannot have equal rights, that there are nations with full rights and nations without full rights, and that, in addition, there is a third category of nations or races, for example, in the colonies which have even fewer rights than the nations without full rights." At bottom all these constitutions, in his opinion, were nationalistic, that is, constitutions of ruling nations. On the other hand, the constitution of the USSR is profoundly internationalistic. It proceeds from the premise that all nations and races have equal rights, that on no ground can the national inequality of rights be justified, that they must be free to enjoy equal rights in all spheres of the economic, social, political and cultural life of society.[2]

In the formative period of the Soviet Union—and it was first formed in 1924—the relations among the peoples had not yet been properly adjusted, the survivals of distrust and suspicion against the Great Russians had not yet disappeared and the centrifugal forces had not ceased to operate. With a view to eliminating these disruptive forces the principles of equality between different nationalities and their voluntary association were asserted and provision was incorporated in the union constitution granting the union republics the right of secession. The withdrawal of this provision even in 1935, it was held, might give rise to suspicion and the proposed amendment was rejected. The antidote to centrifugal tendencies psychologically was ready and unqualified acknowledgment of the principle of division. To oppose them on this or the

[1] Read *Stalin on the Draft Constitution of the USSR*, pp. 37-38.
[2] Ibid, p. 21.

other ground would only strengthen the hands of reactionaries and disruptors. What was adopted in the Soviet Union as contrasted with bourgeois multi-national States was democratic centralism. It was multi-national in form but socialist in content.[1]

Yet another erroneous impression is that the basic form of the Soviet constitution was union first and, if necessary, division afterwards. In reply to certain conclusions Mr. Rajagopalachariar deduced from the "Russian Lesson" Sir N. N. Sircar wrote that the Madras Congress leader's thesis was the very opposite of the Russian pattern. The Soviet constitution, according to Sir Nripendra Nath, "starts with union, giving the right to separate, and not with division with separate States, which are not subordinate to any central authority." Continuing he added, "Working in union, each constituent republic getting the benefit of the entire strength and resources of the USSR is expected to make that union stronger and stronger than with which the start was made. The very opposite of this is starting with division, than which nothing will be more conducive to increasing disunity."[2]

It is not for me to adjudicate upon the controversy that Mr. Rajagopalachariar's article provoked at that time. But so far as this particular point is concerned, there is no doubt in my mind that Sir N. N. Sircar's interpretation was contrary to fact. When on July 10, 1919, the first Soviet constitution RSFSR was adopted after the revolution large tracts of Russian territory were left out. The Ukraine, White Russia and Transcaucasia joined with the RSFSR in 1922, and the union then decided upon began to function in 1924. These four original union republics—the RSFSR, the Ukraine, White Russia and Transcaucasia—were increased by the end of that year by two more, namely, Uzbekistan and Turkmenia. In 1929, the seventh—Tazikistan—came and acceded to the union. The constitution of 1936 split up Transcaucasia into Georgia, Armenia and Azerbaijan ; and Kirghizia and Kazakstan were formed out of a part of the RSFSR. In 1936, there were eleven union republics. To these were added five more union republics on the western borders of Russia in 1940—the Karelo-Finnish, Estonian, Latvian, Lithuanian and Moldavian republics.

It appears that Sir N. N. Sircar assumed that the USSR had

[1] *op. cit.* pp. 16-17.

[2] *The Amrita Bazar Patrika* (Calcutta Edition) of August 26, 1944.

been originally formed with these eleven (as in 1936) or sixteen (as in 1940) union republics and that they had been given the right to secede, which none of them exercised. That is not correct. What happened was that the RSFSR first came into existence, then the Soviet Union with some other republics in addition to the RSFSR, and thereafter gradually others came and the bigger ones were split up and constituted into union republics. As a matter of fact, before the formation of the union there were, in addition to the people's commissariat for Foreign Affairs of the RSFSR, corresponding commissariats in the Ukraine, Byelorussia (White Russia), Georgia, Armenia and Azerbaijan, which in certain definite cases maintained foreign relations with other States. A number of treaties and agreements were also concluded between individual Soviet republics and foreign States. In some cases, however, representatives of the RSFSR were specially empowered by other Soviet republics to represent them at international conferences and to conclude treaties or agreements with foreign States on behalf of all or several of the Soviet republics.

Nor was this procedure peculiar to the Soviet Union. In all known federations in modern times, for instance, in the U.S.A., Canada and Australia the same procedure had been followed. They all started with States or Provinces as sovereign units free to decide their own course of action, and then proceeded to settle terms of compact, some with a centrepetal bias and some with a bias in the opposite direction. Some States or Provinces formally acceded to the federal compact. The door was kept open for subsequent accession on the part of non-acceding ones. Thus these federations grew and developed.

Much of the existing misconception is apparently due to the fact that the right of secession has been confused with the right of non-accession. The first, as I have earlier shown, is a post-federal concept whereas the second is a pre-federal power. The power to withhold adhesion from the federation or to accede to it subsequently is the inherent right of States or Provinces. It has been acknowledged without reservation in the U.S.A., Canada, Australia and the USSR. But only in the last-named federation so far has the right to secede been conceded, as marking out the Soviet Union from the bourgeois federal constitutions. It has been claimed by the Soviet leaders that this peculiar feature of their union emphasises its voluntary character and the equality of rights of its component national units. What is more, the recognition of this right and its statutory incorporation have served more to bring the different nationalities together than to repel them from each other. This provision for separation, strange as it may sound, has for all practical purposes been a unifying factor rather than a disruptive force and the "Russian Lesson" is not without its lessons for us in India in the tense and exciting atmosphere of to-day. It does not mean, however, that there should be slavish adherence to the Soviet pattern. Here again, as Stalin insisted in a different context, the peculiar historical conditions and social and political environments must play an important role in the reconstruction of the Indian State.

It should not be forgotten that this right freely to secede from the USSR is reserved to every union republic,[1] and not accorded to other national units such as autonomous republics, autonomous regions and national areas.[2] Unlike the union republics these are not constituent units of the Soviet Union, although along with the union republics they have been given representation in the Soviet of Nationalities (Second Chamber) on the basis of twentyfive deputies from each union republic, eleven deputies from each autonomous republic, five deputies from each autonomous region, and one deputy from each national area.[3] An amendment was proposed in 1935 for abolition of this Chamber, which Stalin opposed. He said that the Soviet Union had a supreme body, the Soviet of the Union, (the Lower House as they call it in bourgeois countries), in which were represented the "common" interests of all the working peoples of the USSR irrespective of nationality. But in addition to common interests, "the nationalities of the USSR," observed Stalin, "have their particular, specific interests, connected with their specific national characteristics." A special supreme body was required to reflect precisely those specific interests and the Soviet of Nationalities was such a Chamber. A muti-national State like the USSR could not be properly administered, it was pointed out, except through such a bicameral legislature, both the Chambers enjoying equality of powers and one being constituted as

[1] art. 17.

[2] A detailed enumeration of the administrative territorial division of the union republics into these national categories is inserted in articles 22-29-b of the constitution.

[3] art. 35.

democratically as the other. The dual-chamber system was retained. But under the new constitution an equal number of members was given to both the Houses.[1]

An interesting point was raised in the debate on the proposal to raise the autonomous republics to the status of union republics on their reaching "the proper level of economic and cultural development". Stalin strenously repudiated the theory that economic and cultural maturity was the criterion of classification in respect of status, powers and functions. Such maturity, he argued, could no more be urged as the ground for transfering autonomous republics to the category of union republics than the lack of it could be urged as justification for leaving any particular republic in the list of autonomous republics. The one or the other quality was no consideration whatsoever. A republic on a lower level of economic and cultural development might be a union republic while a republic on a higher level might be listed an autonomous republic.

There are three tests for a union republic, whatever the level of its economic and cultural development. The first test is that it must be a border republic. And why ? Because as the right freely to secede is reserved to a union republic it must be so arranged that "it does not become a meaningless scrap of paper". If, for instance, an inland republic expresses its will to exercise the right of secession, where can it go, surrounded as it is on all sides by Soviet territory? Therefore, all union republics must be border republics. The second test is that even if a republic were a border republic, it must not be a union republic unless the nationality which gives it its name constitutes "a more or less compact majority within the republic". Stalin cites the case of the Crimean autonomous republic. It is a border republic, but the Crimean Tatars, after whom the republic is named, do not constitute the majority. They are a minority and the republic's promotion to the status of a union republic with the right of secession may give rise to complications which the Soviet constitution has sought to avoid. Therefore, a union republic must not only be a border republic, but one with a compact national majority which gives it its name. The third test is that the population of the republic must be of sufficiently large size so as to enable it, should it decide upon secession, to maintain its independent national existence and, if neces-

[1] Stalin on the *Draft Constitution of the USSR.*

sary, to repel attacks by any imperialist or despotic foreign power. Stalin puts the approximate population strength at not less than one million. That, however, depends on the strategic position of the republic in question. Therefore, a union republic must not only be a border republic, but a border republic whose name is derived from a compact national majority and with a population of considerable size from military and other points of view.[1]

The USSR is a federal State, formed on the basis of the voluntary association of Soviet Socialist Republics having equal rights, known as the union republics.[2] The jurisdiction assigned to the union is more or less specified[3] and the sovereignty of the union republics is limited only to the extent it has been transferred or delegated to the union under defined powers. Outside of these powers each union republic exercises its authority independently.[4] The residuary belongs, as in the U.S.A. and Australia, and not as in Canada, to the constituent units which, however, have the right, unlike the units in those bourgeois constitutions, freely to secede from the union. But in the event of discrepancy between the law of a union republic and an all-Union law, the latter prevails.[5]

By constitutional amendments effected in 1944, in the midst of the war, the status of the union republics was raised and their functions and powers considerably enlarged. In the first period after the revolution, that is, prior to the formation of the union only the Republican People's Commisariats for Foreign Affairs existed. In the second period, that is, on the inauguration of the union the subject was taken over by the All-Union People's Commissariat for Foreign Affairs. By the change now introduced that Commissariat has been "transformed into a more complex and more widely ramified organisation, into a Union-Republican People's Commissariat", a sort of machinery for the exercise of what may be called concurrent jurisdiction. The union republics have been empowered to enter into direct relations with foreign States and to conclude agreements with them. Of the twenty-three subjects assigned to the Union the first was described as "representation of the Union in international relations, conclu-

[1] Ibid, pp. 38-40.
[2] art. 13.
[3] art. 14.
[4] art. 15.
[5] art 20. Compare it with s. 109 of the Commonwealth of Australia Act, 1900; and s. 107 of the Government of India Act, 1935.

sion and ratification of treaties with them". To that has now been added "establishment of a uniform system in the relations between the union republics and foreign States".[1] A new article has been inserted[2] which lays down that "each union republic has the right to enter into direct relations with foreign States, conclude agreements with them and exchange diplomatic and consular representatives." An additional clause has been added to the article bearing on the enumerated, as distinguished from the residuary powers of the union republics and the clause reads, "establishes representation of the union republics in international relations."[3] This is the amendment relating to the conduct and administration of foreign affairs.

Then comes the amendment on troop formations. In Tsarist Russia certain nationalities and peoples were not called up for military service. The Uzbeks, Kazakhs, Tajiks, Turkmenians, Kirghiz and most of the peoples of the North Caucasus were excluded. They were not trusted by the Tsarist Government and were kept in a state of colonial or semi-colonial subjection. Nearer home, incidentally, one finds an appropriate analogy in the British Government's policy consistently pursued, particularly after the rebellion of 1857, in segregating areas and peoples for the purposes of military recruitment in India, and in the artificial distinction drawn between martial and non-martial races. But in Russia the situation changed fundamentally after the formation of the Union and the Tsarist policy of racial or national discrimination was abandoned once and for all. National military formations were organised under the Red Army, but it was not possible in the formative period, merely upon objective considerations, all at once to draw and attract contingents for the Red Army from all parts of the Soviet Union. The Second World War offered opportunities for the organisation of national military formations in the union republics.

The amendment was designed to enable the union republics to exploit the possibilities in this regard to the maximum possible extent. Accordingly, to article 14-G has been added "establishment of the guiding principles of organisation of the troop formations of the union republics". A new article has been inserted stating that

[1] art. 14-a.
[2] art. 60-e.
[3] art. 18-a.

"each union republic has its own republican troop formations".[1] Again, the enumerated powers of the union republics have been extended to establishment of "the system of organisation of the republican troop formations".[2] The People's Commissariat of Defence has been transformed from All-Union into a Union-Republican People's Commissariat. These changes and similar other changes had been foreshadowed by Stalin as long ago as 1923, when to the Party Congress he said :

> We shall discuss the national question more than once, because national and international conditions change and may change again. I do not reject the possibility that later on we shall have to divide some of the Commissariats which we are uniting in the Union of Republics.

What does this institutional transformation introduced in 1944 mean ? A word or two seem pertinent in connection with the organisation of the Commissariats. At the centre there are two categories of Commissariats—All-Union People's Commissariats and Union-Republican Commissariats. The former direct the branches of State administration entrusted to them throughout the territory of the USSR either directly or through bodies appointed by them.[3] The latter, as a rule, direct the branches entrusted to them through the corresponding commissariats of the union republics and administer directly only a limited number of enterprises.[4] Similarly the People's Commissariats of a Union Republic are of two kinds—Republican Commissariats and Union-Republican Commissariats.[5] It is through the latter that the Union-Republican Commissariats at the centre generally discharge their functions. It is a sort of dyarchy, but obviously where a conflict of jurisdiction arises the central direction supersedes the republican decision, if any.

It is clear from the exact terms of the relevant amendment that the principles of the military organisation are determined by the centre while the formation of national troops is entrusted to the union republics. Almost in the same way, although each union republic has the right to enter into direct relations with foreign States, the centre is competent to ensure a uniform system in the relations between union republics and foreign States. If there is

[1] art. 18-b.
[2] art. 60-f.
[3] art. 75.
[4] art. 76.
[5] art. 86.

no conflict, there is dualism. Where there is any discrepancy the decisions of the union republics must be subordinated to the paramount requirements of the Union. It is wrong to think that the USSR is a loose confederation. It is nothing of the kind. In economic matters and, subject to the new amendments in foreign policy and military affairs, the Union is for all practical purposes supreme whereas in the development of national culture, art and literature there is hardly any Union interference with the policy and programme formulated from time to time by the union republics. A considerable measure of autonomy is exercised in these respects by the autonomous republics and autonomous regions and national areas also.

But all these forms and procedures cannot be properly understood and appreciated except in the context of the basic, fundamental Soviet way of life. In the first stage it was a dictatorship not, of course, in the sense the term is used by bourgeois text-book writers, but in the sense that it was exclusively a Government of the workers. It was the dictatorship of the proletariat. That was a transition. Now it is a muti-national federal socialist State. It represents what Marx called the first or lower phase of communism. In communism the State ceases to exist, but the Soviet State is an imposing and impressive and gigantic reality. In communism, again, the formula of distribution is : "From each according to his abilities, to each according to his needs," but at the present moment the formula followed in the Soviet State is : "From each according to his abilities, to each according to his work." The present, therefore, is another phase of transition. The change envisaged will be from the Socialist State to Communistic Society. Whether the present trend will lead to this transformation or produce opposite results is a question with which it is not the object of this book to deal. But dialectically this grand Socialist State, according to the Soviet leaders, contains within itself the stirrings and urges of transformation into a higher form of social organisation, the phase of communism, of class-less society. Stalin claims that the USSR is not the "ordinary" and "universally recognised" democratism in the abstract, but socialist democratism. It does not merely proclaim democratic liberties, but provides the material means by which these can be exercised.[1] It guarantees free and

[1] *Stalin on the Draft Constitution of the USSR*, pp. 18-22.

unfettered enjoyment by appropriate legislative provisions of the rights declared in the constitution. The right to secession accorded to the union republics furnishes one example ; there are many others in the Organic Laws.

CHAPTER VII

CONCLUSION

1. Restatement of British Policy

I should now say a few words about the shape or form that the constitution of India should take and the procedure that should be adopted not for the purpose only of framing the constitution but also of enforcing it by all possible means. There are glaring gaps in the machinery that has been recommended by the Cabinet Mission or even in the proposals contained in the British Government's statement of February 20, 1947. The framing of a constitution on the capture of power by a people in revolt is different from the framing of a constitution by agreement between the ruling authority and the people concerned. For the moment at least the first procedure is excluded both by the Congress and the Muslim League, not to speak of the Princes. Hence it is a question of the British Government making the grant by a deed of transfer and the peoples of India taking it in pursuance of the policy to which the former stand solemnly committed. Curiously enough, nothing has been done so far by the British Government in this regard except for initiating certain formal steps taken by the Viceroy or the Provincial Governors in connection with the Constituent Assembly or Assemblies. In this kind of transfer of power there must be, in any event, a symbolic withdrawal of the British ruling power so that the necessary atmosphere of change may be generated. No such withdrawal has taken place. Only the elections to the Constituent Assembly have been completed and a Negotiating Committee set up by the Princes to parley with a corresponding British Indian Committee and, by way of gesture, an Interim Government has been formed at the Centre in terms of the Government of India Act, 1919.

The Viceroy remains with all his authoritarian powers. So do the Governors of Provinces. The Commander-in-Chief remains as representing the ultimate British authority over the armed forces of the State, although in form a Civilian Defence Member has been appointed to the Interim Government. The Princes remain where they have always been save for a declaration that on the attainment of independence by India the British Crown's paramountcy shall cease to operate. No concrete steps have been taken affecting the status and position of the British European community with particular reference to their interests in trade, commerce and industry in this country. These are the symbols of British suzerainty over India. With all these symbols in the background the Interim Government or the Constituent Assembly looks a tame and unimpressive show and no more than an experiment in reformism. What may be described as the British Government's "Quit India" statement of February 20, does not seem to have modified their policy except to the extent that they have undertaken to introduce legislation "in due course to give effect to the final transfer of power."

Obviously the statement referred to above is by way of reply to certain suggestions contained in the communications said to have been addressed, on the one hand, by Pandit Nehru and, on the other, by Mr. Liaquat Ali Khan to the Viceroy and the British Government. Pandit Nehru's first reaction to the document is that Mr. Attlee's Government have taken "a courageous and wise decision" and subject to reservations in regard to matters of procedure and detail, the Congress High Command have formally endorsed his view[1]. What the Vice-President of the Interim Government had in mind when he made his comment is the declaration to the effect that it is the intention of the British Government "to take necessary steps to effect he transference of power to responsible Indian hands by a date not later than June, 1948". The fixing of this deadline, the termination of Lord Wavell's appointment as the Viceroy and the appointment of Viscount Mountbatten as his successor are of the essence of this announcement of policy. These are definite commitments. The rest of the document is obscure. Before I proceed further I must say that the fixing of the dateline for British withdrawal marks a landmark just as the announcement made by Lord Linlithgow in 1940 stating that it was for Indians themselves to frame their own constitution was a welcome departure from the British Government's past policy.

Naturally one or two questions occur to the Indian mind. What, for instance, happens to the Constituent Assembly and, for

[1] Read the Congress Working Committee's resolution adopted on March 8, 1947.

the matter of that, to the entire long-term project of the Cabinet Mission? Is it written off or held in abeyance or left undisturbed? Do the British Government contemplate a change in the Interim Government, and if they do, what kind of change do they envisage? Will the present Interim Government continue or be allowed to continue upto the end of the prescribed period? Has Viscount Mountbatten been given instructions to reconstitute the Interim Government along certain lines? There are no definite answers in the statement itself to these legitimate questions.

As far as I can see, the declaration by no means amounts to revocation of the Cabinet Mission's Plan. That will be clear from the Secretary of State's speech in the Lords on January 26, in the course of which he said that it was intended to impress on Indian parties the British Government's sincerity in the promise to transfer power and the urgency of the parties' finding a solution of their differences among themselves. This point is confirmed by paragraph 9 of the White Paper where it is stated that it is essential that "all parties should sink their differences in order that they may be ready to shoulder the great responsibilities which would come upon them next year." Then in the next paragraph they proceed to point out that if it should appear that an agreed constitution will not have been worked out by a fully representative Assembly before the final date fixed for the transfer of power, they will have to consider to whom the power of the Central Government in British India should be handed over on the due date. Therefore, the British Government's declaration is an invitation to the Indian political parties, particularly the Congress and the Muslim League, to accept in its entirety and without reservation the Cabinet Mission's Plan and proceed on the basis of agreement to work out the proposals contained therein for the framing of the constitution or constitutions.

In the considered opinion of Mr. Attlee and his colleagues the Constituent Assembly, which is now in session, is not fully representative and as such does not fulfil the requirements contemplated in the Cabinet Mission's Plan. This view finds expression in paragraph 6 which says that they find that "there are still differences among Indian parties which are preventing the Constituent Assembly from functioning as was intended that it should." They go farther and remark that it is "of the essence of the Plan that the Assembly should be fully representative".

It means, as is made plain in paragraph 4, that unless the future constitution of India was settled by a Constituent Assembly "composed of representatives of all communities and interests in British India and of the Indian States"[1] the British Government would consider themselves relieved of any undertaking or pledge to recommend to Parliament that steps should be taken to implement the decisions of the Constituent Assembly. The position precisely is that the Assembly now in session cannot bind the British Government. But it does not mean its dissolution.

The British Government's declaration is an intimation to the Congress that the latter would be well advised in making it fully representative by seeking the co-operation of the Muslim League and, in a vague and distant way, of the Indian States. Recognising the urgency of the problem and the implications of the British Government's pronouncement and also bearing in mind that the initial hurdle has been negotiated in connection with the States' entry into the Constituent Assembly, Pandit Nehru and the Congress Working Committee have made an appeal to the Muslim League to come and join the Assembly and seek by compromise integrated solutions of the Indian problems. On the face of it, the Attlee Government's stand as revealed in their statement looks like giving the minority the power to veto the advance of the majority and, what comes to the same thing, to render the Cabinet Mission's Plan null and void by tactics of intransigence.

The challenge, however, is not held out to the Congress alone. There is an intimation, if not a note of warning, to the Muslim League, too, that if the machinery devised in the Cabinet Mission's Plan is not worked out in the spirit in which it has been offered, the British Government may decide to hand over the powers of the Central Government in British India as a whole to "some form of Central Government for British India, or in some areas to the existing Provincial Governments, or in such other way as may seem most reasonable and in the best interests of the Indian people".[1] Apparently the British Government's first preference is the machinery contemplated in the Cabinet Mission's Plan and they have accordingly invited the parties concerned to work out that plan fully on the basis of agreement and then present to them the proposals made by them. Should that fail—and the

[1] para 10.

Attlee Government think that there is no clear prospect that an agreed constitution will emerge—the British Government reserve to themselves the sole authority and discretion to choose any of the three alternatives indicated.[1] Nothing is clear or precise about any of these three alternative courses. I have my doubts whether the distinguished authors of the statement have themselves any clear idea. Their main objective has been to get together the major political parties and interests to frame an agreed constitution or constitutions in terms of the Cabinet Mission's Plan and these proposals have been made to keep the parties and interests guessing as to what may upon failure of agreement finally emerge.

Whether the alternative courses presented to the peoples of India would promote unity or cause further disruption is more than one can say at the present moment with any measure of confidence. The Muslim League may have ground for apprehension that if it persists in withholding co-operation from the Constituent Assembly, the authority of the State in British India may be handed over to some form of Central Government. It may not be just the Interim Government which is functioning today. It may well be that on the assumption of charge by the new Viceroy those members of the Interim Government, who refuse to work out the Cabinet Mission's scheme or who stand for a divided India, will be asked to vacate their offices and that the Interim Government will accordingly be reconstituted. Somewhere it has been suggested that the termination of the Viceroy's appointment leads automatically to the dissolution of the Governor-General-in-Council. That is a view which is not supported by the existing law or usage in India. Possibly the exponent of this doctrine has persuaded himself to think that in law and in fact the Viceroy holds a position analogous to that of the Prime Minister in England or in the Dominions. The fact is that, unique as the Viceroy's position is in the mechanism of the British Indian State, he does not exercise the functions of the Prime Minister as such. With his recall or with the termination of his appointment members of the Government of India are not *ipso facto* thrown out of their jobs legally or politically. Nevertheless it is open to the new Viceroy to call upon members in the name of the King to tender their resignations so that he may be enabled to seek reconstruction of his Executive Council in the

[1] Ibid.

execution of the British Government's policy. I shall not be surprised if by the compulsion of events Viscount Mountbatten should adopt this course.

On the other hand, the Congress and other parties or interests who for the moment stand by the Congress may have ground for apprehension that the second alternative may lead to the division of India. In some areas the powers of the Central Government may be handed over to the "existing Provincial Governments". That expression has reference to the time of the transfer and the existing Governments of today may cease to exist or change hands at that time. For instance, the Muslim League has succeeded in breaking the Punjab Coalition Ministry where the major community of the Province went unrepresented. Similarly there may be a change of the Congress Ministry in the North-West Frontier Province as a result of internal friction and of pressure from the tribes and the border regions. There is evidence that the Muslim League is planning its strategy to that end. If what the Muslim League expects will emerge in the course of the next few months materialises, it will have its ambition fulfilled in the whole of the so-called Pakistan zone with the exception of Assam in the north-east. With regard to Assam the Muslim League leaders seem to think that that Province, being thus isolated from the rest of Hindusthan, will not be able to hold its own for any length of time.

But there is a snag. The British Government mention "some areas" and not whole Provinces. This is significant. If it is not bluff, the natural conclusion is that areas in which there are compact groups of non-Muslims will be excluded from the Pakistan zone. In this view of the matter Muslim independent rule may not extend to large parts of Bengal, including Calcutta, and important areas in the Punjab. Already the Congress Working Committee have recommended what they consider a just and fair solution for the Punjab. Applying the same test to the Muslim-minority Province of Assam, the Surma Valley districts, particularly Sylhet, may get the right to opt out and join with Bengal partly on the ground of religion and partly for the reason that they speak practically the same language. The British Government's second alternative looks like a slightly revised version of the C. R. Formula. In any event, if this comes to materialise, India will be partitioned, though not exactly in the same way as the Muslim League envisaged at its Lahore resolution in 1940.

As to the third alternative course, discretion rests with the British Government. It follows that if finally the Cabinet Mission's Plan fails and if the first two alternative courses prove ineffective, the British Government will proceed to consider the question de novo and make such arrangements for the transfer of power as they may deem appropriate in the circumstances. But I take it that the British "quitting" will not be delayed longer than the deadline fixed, whatever the consequences. Quitting, however, does not necessarily mean complete evacuation. So far as the latter aspect of the problem is concerned, it will be the subject-matter of the proposed agreement or agreements. As regards the Indian States, the position as outlined in the Cabinet Mission's scheme and explained at length in the British Government's Memorandum on the States is not altered except to the extent that for the intervening period the relations of the Crown with individual States may be adjusted by agreement. To put it briefly, the Attlee Government's new declaration of policy is by no means a revocation or withdrawal of the Cabinet Mission's Plan. But it marks a change in attitude in that even at the initial stage it keeps the question of constitutional unity of India open. What is of special importance from the point of view of broad principle is their pledge to withdraw from the political scene, at least formally, by an appointed date.

2. Act of Succession Necessary

I deem it essential that the British Government should be called upon to sponsor immediately in Parliament a Bill of Succession declaring in precise and clear terms that the entire power and authority to govern India is transferred to the Indian peoples, and fixing up a specific date by which all symbols of British paramountcy shall be withdrawn. Despite the deadline the British Government's intentions in this regard are open to conflicting interpretations. An analogy in procedure, though not in content, is furnished by the statute known as the Government of India Act, 1935. The constitution which it replaced, after formally vesting in the Crown the Government of India and assuming for the King all the powers which, upto 1858, had been vested in the East India Company, proceeded to place in the hands of the Secretary of State in Council complete control over "all acts, operations and concerns which relate to the Government and revenues of India". It committed the civil and military government of India to the Governor-General in Council, and the government of each Province to a Governor acting with an Executive Council and Ministers, but at the same time placed the Provincial Governments in a position of subordination to the Governor-General in Council and the latter to the Secretary of State in Council. It further empowered the Secretary of State in Council, so far as the transferred subjects of the Provinces were concerned, by statutory rules to relax or remove his hitherto all-embracing powers of superintendence, direction and control. That was the position under the Government of India Act.

The Act of 1935 resumed into the hands of the King all powers exercisable in, or in relation to, India by any authority, and thereafter distributed to the various authorities created under it the exercise of the whole of these powers in so far as they were distributed by it, and to leave the King free to delegate such of those powers as were outside the strict ambit of the statute, as he thought fit, to the Governor-General or the Governors to be exercised on his behalf. It was a formal deed. The transfer was from certain authorities to the King and then there was retransfer from the King to authorities created under the statute but owning allegiance to the King. What I suggest is that the procedural part of this process should be adopted, thereby divesting the Crown and all other visible and invisible authorities of the powers hitherto exercisable by them either by delegation or in terms of the statute, and a declaration made that by a specific date they shall come to be exercised by Indian peoples. What instruments are to be devised for the exercise of these powers is a matter which is to be decided by the Constituent Assembly and its Sectional auxiliaries. But an Act of Succession is essential at this stage.

By this Act of Succession all British statutes, laws or regulations relating to India must be repealed, including the laws and statutes of nationality, and further a statutory provision incorporated to the effect that no other Act of the British Parliament nor any British law shall apply to India or any part thereof without the consent of the Constituent Assembly or Assemblies. I make special mention of the nationality laws and statutes because these have enabled the British European community in India to claim the rights of citizenship and, on the basis of such citizenship derived from the doctrine of allegiance to the Crown, to enjoy special privileges in respect of trade, commerce, industry and political representation.

It should be followed up by a treaty to be concluded between a properly constituted committee of the Constituent Assembly or the Provisional Interim Government and the British Government covering matters arising out of the transfer of responsibilities from the British to Indian hands. I have in a previous chapter indicated the lines along which the terms of the treaty should, on the Indian side, be insisted upon. This treaty should be ratified by the appropriate authority representing each of the two contracting parties. Immediately thereafter an Act should be passed by the British Parliament conferring upon the Interim Government powers analogous to those assumed by the Irish Provisional Government after the Irish Rebellion, and the Interim Government vested with such powers and suitably reconstructed should undertake the responsibility of enforcing the decisions of the Constituent Assembly or Assemblies. They shall continue in office until they are replaced by a new Government or Governments set up under the constitution or constitutions framed by the Constituent Assembly or Assemblies.

3. Formal Democracy Outmoded

When these preliminaries will have been gone through, it shall be for the Constituent Assembly and the Sectional auxiliaries to settle the fundamental principles of the structure of the new State. It shall decide, that is, whether the State shall be unitary or federal, a formal democracy in the western sense or a socialist democracy in the modern context, a united Indian State or an India divided into two or more States. There is, however, evidence of a strong bias in this country for western democracy and this is partly due to ignorance and partly to some sort of subtle propaganda carried on by its exponents through the press, text-books and long-winded declarations and statements. Events in the inter-war period have shown that formal democracy as evolved in Britain or America suffers miserably from its inherent lack of moral and material adequacy to the requirements of our time. It might have been—possibly it was—a useful instrument in the epoch of rising capitalism when it was in a position to reconcile somehow its inner contradictions. That epoch is now over.

In recent years there has been some vague fascination in certain circles for the Swiss model. I think, therefore, that a few words bearing on the Swiss constitution may not be out of place here. The three principal languages spoken in Switzerland—German, French and Italian—are treated as the national languages. The idea is that if these three distinct nationalities could agree to evolve a common machinery of government, without prejudice to the interests of any particular nationality, we in this country can do so, too, provided we follow the Swiss method and procedure for adjustment of claims and interests of the different communities.

Stress is particularly laid on the composition of the Federal Executive. It differs from the British Cabinet system in that it is elected by the Legislature for a fixed period of three years and that it is not collectively responsible to the Legislature for its acts. It is a collegiate form of Government rather than a Cabinet in the political sense of the term. It is laid down that not more than one person from each Canton may be chosen for the Federal Council, the total strength being seven members. It differs from the Presidential system prevalent in the United States in that members of the Federal Council are not appointed by the President and do not hold office during his pleasure. It is contended that the Swiss pattern of the Executive ensures not only fixity of tenure but representation of important Cantons and, through these Cantons, of the major nationalities in the country. Hence if we have on the Swiss analogy a Federal Executive with a fixed tenure and composed of a prescribed proportion of members from the major communities and interests in India, it is argued, there should be no reasonable ground for fear that any vital interest may be jeopardised. This, I am afraid, is taking a superficial view of the complicated situation in India. The background history of the two countries is not the same. Conditions are not similar. The claims advanced or the assertions made by the Muslim community in particular are more far-reaching in their implications than the problem that Switzerland had to face.

Besides, the Swiss approach was, in the context of modern events and social urges, rather formalistic than dynamic. An irremovable executive in our time may be tempted by internal arrangements to assume dictatorial control of a Fascist type. Even the democratic character of the British Cabinet system is open to doubt for the obvious reason that it has almost succeeded by various devices in paralysing the legislature and bypassing the electorate. What is essential is that the policy and programme of the executive as well as the activities of the legislature should be subjected to review and, if necessary, to censure by the peoples when they involve issues of national or social importance. I take the view that it is the content rather than the form that matters now and that the form is important in so far it makes the content real, substantial and vital. There is no doubt that religion continues to play an important, if somewhat crude, role in political alignments in this country. But I do maintain that beneath the surface there are deep undercurrents of social antagonism, irrespective of caste, community or religion. While it is necessary to eliminate religious or communal animosities by a bold and imaginative programme, builders of the future of India will have to concentrate more and more on the social foundations of the State. An attack on our problems from this angle will, with the passage of time, not only reconcile the religious conflicts but provide equal opportunities to the masses of different communities for full expression of their personalities in their day-to-day lives as well as in the management and control of public affairs. A nineteenth century structure evolved in the epoch of rising capitalism cannot by its very nature resolve the present crisis of human institutions.

Formal democracy, except perhaps for a time in the United States, is doomed. It must yield place either to Fascist regimentation or to some kind of socialist democracy ; and whatever the alignment of forces the proceedings of the International Conferences may reveal, the potential conflict lies in the antithesis between the American idea of freedom of enterprise and private property and the Soviet way of life as manifested in collective ownership and community control. With or without her will Britain will soon have to make her choice. With or without her will India, too, will have to decide one way or the other. It must be remembered that the late Mr. Wendell Wilkie's *One World* was by no means an oratorical flourish. It is a reality. Peace or war is indivisible. We cannot avoid war when war is abroad. Nor can we be deprived of the fruits or triumphs of peace, wherever it may reign. Pandit Nehru's broadcast from New Delhi on September 7, giving messages of goodwill and friendship in the name of India and on behalf of the Interim Government to the United States, the USSR,

China and all countries, far and near, was in a way a good gesture. But the time is soon coming when India will have to take sides, whether she likes it or not, not only in defence of freedom but also for the purposes of her own security and peace.

That being so, and also for the reason that the international conduct of a particular State is only a projection of its internal or domestic policy, I do suggest that the Constituent Assembly or Assemblies must proceed with socialist democracy as the basis of productive relations within the new Indian State or States. It does not necessarily mean socialism of the Soviet type. It does not mean what they call, sometimes scientifically and very often in a vulgar sense, communism. It is not British or American democracy. A living constitution must interpret in concrete terms the social urges and impulses of a people at a given time. Should it fail to do so it becomes an anachronism or produces friction which it cannot eliminate by any contrivance. We in this country have reached a stage of social development in which a feudal autocracy represented by the Princes and landlords is a liability, an encumbrance, a dead weight, which must be done away with. Not that the Princes or landlords should be thrown out into the streets, but the former's right or prerogative of governance and the latter's right to the fruits of the soil without toil or sweat must be liquidated. Provision may be made for some monetary allowance for the Princes for life in the proposed treaty in accordance with their status and position and the liability for payment thereof may be passed on to the Federal Government of India or to Provincial States, according as the territories of the Indian States are distributed. The talk of evolving in the Indian States a revised form of constitutional monarchy after the British pattern is unreal and contrary to the urges of the peoples of the States. Should the Negotiating Committee set up by the States refuse to abide by the decisions of the Constituent Assembly the alternative is to go to the peoples concerned and enable them to send their quota of representation by resort to democratic electoral procedure. This will be one of the important functions of the Provisional Interim Government.

So far as the Indian industrialists and capitalists are concerned, it seems to me that their progressive role has been exhausted by the impact of the war as manifested in the drastic racial transformation of the capitalist structure. They can no longer identify themselves with the progressive elements of the population and their hopes and aspirations. Hence it is necessary that provision should be made for the transfer of ownership of land, underground riches and transport services from private hands to the peoples as organised into political communities. The basic and key industries susceptible of collective ownership, control and management should be similarly socialised. Where private industries are permitted there may be a measure of freedom of enterprise. Banks and all credit institutions should belong to the whole community so that the power and authority of the community may not in fact come to be exercised by private financiers or groups of financiers as by the City of London in Britain or Wall Street in America.

4. Demarcation of National Units by Boundaries Commission

In the context of these necessary and urgent social changes the Constituent Assembly should proceed, either through a Boundaries Commission appointed by the Provisional Interim Government or through an *ad hoc* Committee set up by them, to take measures for delimitation of the Provinces and the existing Indian States on the basis of linguistic and cultural homogeneity. In their memorandum submitted to the Cabinet Mission on April 15, 1946, the Communist Party of India gave a list of the national units that may be formed out of the existing Indian territories embracing both British India and the Indian States. The list describes the national units as Tamilnad, Andhradesha, Kerala, Karnatak, Maharashtra, Gujrat, Rajasthan, Sind, Beluchistan, Pathanland, Kashmir, the Western Punjab, the Central Punjab, Hindusthan, Behar, Assam, Bengal and Orissa. It is a good basis to work upon, but obviously certain minor nationalities have not been taken into account. These are, for example, the Adibasis in Chotanagpur in Behar, the excluded areas in Assam and the North-West Frontier Province, the scheduled castes in certain compact areas in eastern and northern Bengal and several tribes both in north-west and north-east. Obviously these names are illustrative and in no sense exhaustive. It is just possible that the Communist Party did not mention these minorities or nationalities because they could not for various reasons constitute themselves into a territorial national unit with the right freely to secede from the Federal Union. I am disposed to think that side by the side with big Provincial units, or included therein, there should be smaller national entities more or less on the Soviet analogy. These units should be free to develop their culture, art and literature, but with no right of separation from the rest of India.

There is substance in the thesis that the framing of a free Indian constitution should be proceeded with on the basis of treating India as one constitutional unit. This is necessary, first, because there exist no territorial national units that can take the power on behalf of the whole of India and, secondly, because there is a strong feeling in this country against division of the country as the starting point of new constitutional arrangements of a free and independent India. The procedure suggested is, however, contrary to the basic form of almost all known federal compacts, where the right of non-accession on the part of each territorial unit was clearly implied. But the administrative development of India during these two hundred years of British rule has been in the direction of complete centralisation, although the Government of India Act, 1935, marks a mild departure from that trend. The result is that, whatever our past history, we have been accustomed to thinking in terms of Indian unity, ignoring the basic facts of our variegated cultures, languages and national forms. That prejudice or idealisation cannot be got rid of or eradicated all at once. Therefore, it is expedient, if not scientific, to start with India as one constitutional unit.

At the same time, it must be a socialist democratic federal India and, as indicated above, there must be adequate guarantees as to democracy and fundamental rights with effective material means to ensure that democracy and those rights. If, however, any territorial national unit demarcated on the basis of linguistic and cultural homogeneity refuses to accede to the federation, there should be no bar to such non-accession. Any non-acceding unit should be left free, if it so likes, to accede at a subsequent stage. Those units which adhere to the federation should be given the right freely to secede from it. But the decisions as to non-accession and secession must be taken democratically. If a particular party says "no", that "no" must not be decisive. If another party says "yes", that "yes" should likewise be tested by a popular referendum. The question of non-accession as well as of secession may be raised only after the new constitution has been set up and the Provincial Assemblies elected on the basis of adult suffrage. Meanwhile the provisional arrangements should continue. If, after the first election under the new constitution, a resolution is passed by a Provincial Assembly against accession, it should be submitted to a referendum of the entire adult population of the Province concerned. In the event of the majority ratifying it, non-accession must be accepted. Similarly if, after adhering to the federation, a national territorial unit expresses its desire to secede from the Union, the same procedure must be adopted. The exercise of the right of post-federal accession should be simple. Only a resolution to that effect by the appropriate Legislative Assembly should be decisive. It must be laid down in the constitution framed by the Constituent Assembly, as a measure of security in regard to the fundamental principles of democracy, that the non-acceding provinces, if any, must be governed by all the provisions of the constitution in so far as they have no federal bearing. While in principle it must be conceded that the people of each unit should have the right to fashion their own lives the exercise of that right must not be allowed to prejudice the interests of the toiling millions or interfere with the promotion of certain essential social objectives. No opportunity should be given to adventurers, social chauvinists or reactionaries to exploit the principle of self-determination for setting up authoritarian regimes or puppet governments virtually under the control of a foreign power.

If all these rights are, as is suggested, specifically guaranteed, the Indian Federation must not be a loose confederation as is contemplated in the Cabinet Mission's long-term project. The proposals made by them are repugnant to all modern social trends. Those units which want to keep out may do so. Those that want to secede may opt out if they like. But those who join now or hereafter must agree to a large measure of central discretion and control in the sphere of economic development, organisation of defence and conduct of foreign relations. As in the USSR there should be democratic centralism: economic and security centralisation exercised in a democratic way and complete decentralisation in the sphere of cultural development to be exercised by the constituent units equally in a democratic way. In no circumstances can there be secession by inland units or units which may not contain a population of considerable size so as to enable them to offer effective resistance against foreign aggression or exploitation by reactionary foreign States.

I consider proportional representation by means of the single transferable vote on the basis of universal adult suffrage the best and most effective machinery for ensuring adequate representation of minorities or smaller nationalities as well as for fostering a sense of class unity as distinguished from communalist separatism or chauvinism. I do not think that the substitution of joint electorates with reservation of seats for separate electorates is a practical proposition in India. Separate electorates divide the community into watertight religious or sectarian groups with what results one can see in India today. Separate electorates with reservation of seats tend to prejudice the interests of the minority community in the matter of representation in any electoral area and are looked upon with suspicion by them. Proportional representation, on the contrary, is an elastic method and may be used for national as well as for sectarian or group ends.

I have given only a bare outline of the constitutional framework. My object has been to state principles rather than to discuss details, to provoke thought rather than to give a full and complete picture of the India to be. I am convinced that nationalism is now an exploded and dangerous dogma. I have rejected the Muslim League's two-nation theory. India of the future must be a multi-national State. She is already multi-national, although the forms of the existing State do not conform to the different national patterns. In the interests of peace, freedom and progress this multi-national State of India must also be democratically organised not in the sense in which they understand the capitalist democracy of Britain or the American democratic capitalism. The settlement of the Congress-League controversy or the Hindu-Muslim-Sikh controversy lies neither in mechanical insistence on Indian nationalism nor in the persistent clamour for the division of India into two nations on the basis of religion. The solution lies in compromise, in the evolution of a democratically organised socialist multi-national State with equal rights for all the constituent nationalities and complete freedom on their part, if they so desire, to live their own lives without interference by a central machine whose authority they may repudiate, but without prejudice to the interests of the broad masses of people.

APPENDICES

APPENDICES

APPENDIX I

MONTAGU'S DECLARATION

(August 20, 1917).

British Decision Final

"The policy of His Majesty's Government, with which the Government of India are in complete accord, is that of the increasing association of Indians in every branch of the administration and the gradual development of self-governing institutions with a view to the progressive realisation of responsible government in India as an integral part of the British Empire. They have decided that substantial steps in this direction should be taken as soon as possible, and that it is of the highest importance as preliminary to considering what these steps should be that there should be a free and informal exchange of opinion between those in authority at Home and in India. His Majesty's Government have accordingly decided, with His Majesty's approval, that I should accept the Viceroy's invitation to proceed to India to discuss these matters with the Viceroy and the Government of India, to consider with the Viceroy the views of Local Governments, and to receive with him the suggestions of representative bodies and others.

"I would add that progress in this policy can only be achieved by successive stages. The British Government and the Government of India, on whom the responsibility lies for the welfare and advancement of the Indian peoples, must be judges of the time and measure of each advance, and they must be guided by the co-operation received from those upon whom new opportunities of service will thus be conferred and by the extent to which it is found that confidence can be reposed in their sense of responsibility.

"Ample opportunity will be afforded for public discussion of the proposals which will be submitted in due course to Parliament.

APPENDIX II

WHITE PAPER—1940

Change of Policy

The following statement by the Viceroy (Lord Linlithgow) on the new measures being taken in the hope of achieving greater national unity in India, published on August 8, 1940 as a White Paper entitled "India and the War" was read in the House of Commons on the same date by Mr. L. S. Amery, Secretary for India:

"India's anxiety at this moment of critical importance in the world struggle against tyranny and aggression to contribute to the full to the common cause and to the triumph of our common ideals is manifest. She has already made a mighty contribution. She is anxious to make a greater contribution still. H. M. Government are deeply concerned that that unity of national purpose in India which would enable her to do so should be achieved at as early a moment as possible. They feel that some further statement of their intentions may help to promote that unity. In that hope they have authorised me to make the present statement.

"Last October H. M. Government again made it clear that Dominion Status was their objective for India. They added that they were ready to authorise the expansion of the Governor-General's Council to include a certain number of representatives of the political parties and they proposed the establishment of a consultative committee.

"In order to facilitate harmonious co-operation it was obvious that some measure of agreement in the provinces *between the major parties* was a desirable prerequisite to their joint collaboration at the Centre. Such agreement was, unfortunately, not reached, and in the circumstances no progress was then possible.

"During the earlier part of this year, I continued my efforts to bring the political parties together. In these last few weeks I again entered into conversations with prominent political personages in British India and the Chancellor of the Chamber of Princes, the result of which have been reported to H. M. Government. H. M. Government have seen also the resolutions passed by the Congress Working Committee, the Moslem League, and the Hindu Mahasabha.

"It is clear that earlier differences which had prevented the achievement of national unity remain unbridged. Deeply as H. M. Government regret this, they do not feel that they should any longer, because of those differences, postpone the expansion of the Government-General's Council and the establishment of a body which will more closely associate India's public nopinion with the conduct of the war by the Central Government.

"They have authorised me accordingly to invite a certain number of representative Indians to join my Executive Council. They have authorised me further to establish a War Advisory Council which would meet at regular intervals and which would contain representatives of the Indian States and of other interests in the national life of India as a whole.

"The conversations which have taken place and the resolutions of the bodies which I have just mentioned made it clear, however, that there is still in certain quarters doubt as to the intentions of H. M. Government for the constitutional future of India, and that there is doubt, too, as to whether the position of minorities, whether political or religious, is sufficiently safeguarded in relation to any future constitutional change by assurances already given.

"There are two main points that have emerged. On those two points H. M. Government now desire me to make their position clear.

"The first is as to the position of minorities in relation to any future constitutional scheme. It has already been made clear that my declaration of last October does not exclude examination of any part either of the Act of 1935 or of the policy and plans on which it is based. H. M. Government's concern that full weight should be given to the views of minorities in any revision has also been brought out. That remains the position of H. M. Government.

"It goes without saying that they could not contemplate transfer of their present responsibilities for the peace and welfare of India to any system of government whose authority is directly denied by large and powerful elements in India's national life. Nor could they be parties to the coercion of such elements into submission to such a Government.

"The second point of general interest is the machinery for building within the British Commonwealth of Nations the new constitutional scheme when the time comes. There has been very strong insistence that the framing of the scheme should be primarily the responsibility of Indians themselves and should originate from Indian conceptions of the social, economic, and political structure of Indian life.

"H. M. Government are in sympathy with that desire and wish to see it given the fullest practical expression subjects to the due fulfilment of the obligations which Great Britain's long connection with India has imposed on her and for which H. M. Government cannot divest themselves of responsibility.

"It is clear that a moment when the Commonwealth is engaged in a struggle for existence is not one in which fundamental constitutional issues can be decisively resolved. But H. M. Government authorise me to declare that they will most readily assent to the setting up after the conclusion of the war, with the least possible delay, of a body representative of the principal elements in India's national life in order to devise the framework of the new Constitution, and they will lend every aid in their power to hasten decisions on all relevant matters to the utmost degree. Meanwhile they will welcome and promote in any way possible every sincere and practical step that may be taken by representative Indians themselves to reach a basis of friendly agreement, first, upon the form which the post-war representative body should take and the methods by which it should arrive at its conclusions, and, secondly, upon the principles and outlines of the Constitution itself.

"They trust, however, that for the period of the war (with the Central Government reconstituted and strengthened in the manner I have described and with the help of the War Advisory Council) all parties, communities, and interests will combine and co-operate in making a notable Indian contribution to the victory of the world cause which is at stake. Moreover, they hope that in this process new bonds of union and understanding will emerge and thus pave the way towards the attainment by India of that free and equal partnership in the British Commonwealth which remains the proclaimed and accepted goal of the Imperial Crown and of the British Parliament."

APPENDIX III

MR. CHURCHILL'S STATEMENT—1942

ANNOUNCEMENT OF MISSION

The following official statement on India was made in the House of Commons by Mr. Churchill on the 11th March, 1942:

"The crisis in the affairs of India arising out of the Japanese advance has made Britain wish to rally all the forces of Indian life to guard their land from the menace of the invader.

"In August 1940, a statement was made about the aims and policy which we are pursuing in India. This amounted in short to a promise that, as soon as possible after the war, India should attain Dominion Status in full freedom and equality with this country and other Dominions under a constitution to be framed by Indians by agreement amongst themselves and acceptable to the main elements in the Indian national life. This was, of course, subject to the fulfilment of our obligations for the protection of minorities, including the Depressed Classes, and our treaty obligations to the Indian States and to a settlement of certain lesser matters arising out of our long association with the fortunes of the Indian sub-continent.

"However, in order to clothe these general declarations with precision and to convince all classes, races and creeds in India of our sincere resolve, the War Cabinet have agreed unitedly upon conclusions for present and future action which, if accepted by India as a whole, would avoid the alternative dangers, either that the resistance of a powerful minority might impose an indefinite veto upon the wishes of the majority, or that a majority decision might be taken, which would be resisted to a point destructive of internal harmony and fatal to the setting up of a new constitution.

"We had thought of setting forth immediately the terms of this attempt by a constructive contribution to aid India in the realisation of full self-government. We are, however, apprehensive that to make a public announcement at such a moment as this might do more harm than good. We must first assure ourselves that our scheme would win a reasonable and practical measure of acceptance and thus promote concentration of all thoughts and energies upon the defence of the native soil. We should ill serve the common cause if we made a declaration which would be rejected by the essential elements in the Indian world and which would provoke fierce constitutional and communal disputes at a moment when the enemy is at the gates of India.

"Accordingly we propose to send a Member of the War Cabinet to India to satisfy himself on the spot by personal consultation that the conclusions upon which we are agreed and which we believe represent a just and final solution, will achieve their purpose. The Lord Privy Seal and Leader of the House, Sir Stafford Cripps, has volunteered to undertake this task. He carries with him the full confidence of His Majesty's Government and he will strive in their name, to procure the necessary measure of assent, not only from the Hindu majority, but also from those great minorities amongst which the Muslims are most numerous and on many grounds pre-eminent.

"The Lord Privy Seal will at the same time consult with the Viceroy and the Commander-in-Chief on the military situation, bearing always in mind the paramount responsibility of His Majesty's Government, by every means in their power, to shield the people of India from the perils which now beset them. We must remember that India has a great part to play in the world struggle for freedom and that her helping hand must be extended in loyal comradeship to the valiant Chinese people, who have fought along so long. We must remember also that India is one of the bases from which the strongest counter-blows must be struck at the advance of tyranny and aggression.

"Sir Stafford Cripps will set out as soon as convenient and suitable arrangements can be made. He will command in his task the heart-felt good wishes of all parts of the House, and meanwhile no words will be spoken or debates held here or in India which would add to the burden he has assumed in his mission or lessen the prospects of good result. During Sir Stafford Cripps' absence from Parliament, his duties as Leader will be discharged by the Foreign Secretary, Mr. Eden."

APPENDIX IV

BRITISH WAR CABINET'S PROPOSALS—1942

A Post-war Machinery Contemplated

The following are the conclusions of the British War Cabinet which Sir Stafford Cripps brought with him for discussion with Indian leaders in March-April, 1942:

His Majesty's Government having considered the anxieties expressed in this country and in India as to the fulfilment of promises made in regard to the future of India have decided to lay down in precise and clear terms the steps which they propose shall be taken for the earliest possible realisation of self-government in India. The object is the creation of a new Indian Union which shall constitute a Dominion associated with the United Kingdom and other Dominions by a common allegiance to the Crown but equal to them in every respect, in no way subordinate in any aspect of its domestic or external affairs.

His Majesty's Government, therefore, make the following Declaration:—

(*a*) Immediately upon the cessation of hostilities steps shalll be taken to set up in India in the manner described hereafter an elected body charged with the task of framing a new Constitution for India.

(*b*) Provision shall be made, as set out below, for the participation of Indian States in the Constitution-making body.

(*c*) His Majesty's Government undertake to accept and implement forthwith the Constitution so framed subject only to:—

(*i*) The right of any province of British India that is not prepared to accept the new constitution to retain its present constitutional position, provision being made for its subsequent accession if it so decide.

With such non-acceding provinces, should they so desire, His Majesty's Government will be prepared to agree upon a new Constitution giving them the same full status as the Indian Union and arrived at by a procedure analogous to that here laid down.

(*ii*) The signing of a treaty which shall be negotiated between His Majesty's Government and the Constitution-making body. This treaty will cover all necessary matters arising out of the complete transfer of responsibility from British to Indian hands; it will make provision, in accordance with undertakings given by His Majesty's Government, for the protection of racial and religious minorities; but will not impose any restriction on the power of the Indian Union to decide in future its relationship to other Member States of the British Commonwealth.

Whether or not an Indian State elects to adhere to the constitution it will be necessary to negotiate a revision of its arrangements so far as this may be required in the new situation.

(*d*) The Constitution-making body shall be composed as follows unless the leaders of Indian opinion in the principal communities agree upon some other form before the end of hostilities:

Immediately upon the result being known of provincial elections which will be necessary at the end of hostilities, the entire membership of the Lower Houses of Provincial Legislatures shall as a single electoral college proceed to the election of the Constitution-making body by the system of proportional representation. This new body shall be in number about 1/10th of the number of the electoral college.

Indian States shall be invited to appoint representatives in the same proportion to their total population as in the case of representatives of British Indian as a whole and with the same powers as British Indian members.

(*e*) During the critical period which now faces India and until the new Constitution can be framed His Majesty's Government must inevitably bear the responsibility for and retain the control and direction of the defence of India as part of their world war effort, but the task of organising to the full the military, moral and material resources of India must be the responsibility of the Government of India with the co-operation of the peoples of India. His Majesty's Government desire and invite the immediate and effective participation of the leaders of the principal sections of the Indian people in the counsels of their country, of the Commonwealth and of the United Nations. Thus they will be enabled to give their active and constructive help in the discharge of a task which is vital and essential for the future freedom of India.

APPENDIX V

RESOLUTION OF THE CONGRESS WORKING COMMITTEE, APRIL 2, 1942.

Doubts About British Policy

The Working Committee have given their full and earnest consideration to the proposals made by the British War Cabinet in regard to India and the elucidation thereof by Sir Stafford Cripps. These proposals, which have been made at the very last hour because of the compulsion of events, have to be considered not only in relation to India's demand for independence, but more especially in the present grave war crisis, with a view to meeting effectively the perils and dangers that confront India and envelop the world.

The Congress has repeatedly stated, ever since the commencement of the War in September, 1939, that the people of India would line themselves with the progressive forces of the world and assume full responsibility to face the new problems and shoulder the new burdens that had arisen, and it asked for the necessary conditions to enable them to do so to be created. An essential condition was the freedom of India, for only the realisation of present freedom could light the flame which would illumine millions of hearts and move them to action. At the last meeting of the All-India Congress Committee, after commencement of the War in the Pacific, it was stated that "only a free and independent India can be in a position to undertake the defence of the country on a national basis and be of help in the furtherance of the larger causes that are emerging from the storm of war."

The British War Cabinet's new proposals relate principally to the future upon the cessation of hostilities. The Committee, while recognising that self-determination for the people of India is accepted in principle in that uncertain future, regret that this is fettered and circumscribed and certain provisions have been introduced which gravely imperil the development of a free and united nation and the establishment of a democratic state. Even the constitution-making body is so constituted that the people's right to self-determination is vitiated by the introduction of non-representative elements. The people of India have as a whole clearly demanded full independence and the Congress has repeatedly declared that no other status except that of independence for the whole of India could be agreed to or could meet the essential requirements of the present situation. The Committee recognise that future independence may be implicit in the proposals, but the accompanying provisions and restrictions are such that real freedom may well become an illusion. The complete ignorance of the ninety millions of the people of the Indian States and their treatment as commodities at the disposal of their rulers is a negation of both democracy and self-determination. While the representation of an Indian State in the constitution-making body is fixed on a population basis, the people of the State have no voice in choosing those representatives, nor are they to be consulted at any stage, while decisions vitally affecting them are being taken. Such States may in many ways become barriers to the growth of Indian freedom, enclaves where foreign authority still prevails and where the possibility of maintaining foreign armed forces has been stated to be a likely contingency, and a perpetual menace to the freedom of the people of the States as well as of the rest of India.

The acceptance beforehand of the novel principle of non-accession for a province is also a severe blow to the conception of Indian unity and an apple of discord likely to generate growing trouble in the provinces, and which may well lead to further difficulties in the way of the Indian States merging themselves in the Indian Union. The Congress has been wedded to Indian freedom and unity and any break in that unity, especially in the modern world when people's minds inevitably think in terms of ever larger federations, would be injurious to all concerned and exceedingly painful to contemplate. Nevertheless the Committee cannot think in terms of compelling the people in any territorial unit to remain in an Indian Union against their declared and established will. While recognising this principle, the Committee feel that every effort should be made to create conditions which would help the different units in developing a common and co-operative national life. The acceptance of the principle inevitably involves that no changes should be made which result in fresh problems being created and compulsion being exercised on other substantial groups within that area. Each territorial unit should have the fullest possible autonomy within the Union, consistently with a strong national State. The proposal now made on the part of the British War Cabinet encourages and will lead to attempts at seperation at the very inception of a Union and thus create friction just when the utmost co-operation and goodwill are most needed. This proposal has been presumably made to meet a communal demand, but it will have other consequences also and lead politically reactionary and obscurantist groups among different communities to create trouble and divert public attention from the vital issues before the country.

Any proposal concerning the future of India must demand attention and scrutiny, but in to-day's grave crisis, it is the present that counts, and even proposals for the future are important in so far as they affect the present. The Committee have necessarily attached the greatest importance to this aspect of the question, and on this ultimately depends what advice they should give to those who look to them for guidance. For this present the British War Cabinet's proposals are vague and altogether incomplete, and it would appear that no vital changes in the present structure are contemplated. It has been made clear that the defence of India will in any event remain under British control. At any time defence is a vital subject; during war time it is all important and covers almost every sphere of life and administration. To take away defence from the sphere of responsibility at this stage is to reduce that responsibility to a farce and a nullity, and to make it perfectly clear that India is not going to be free in any way and her Government is not going to function as a free and independent Government during the pendency of the War. The Committee would repeat that an essential and fundamental pre-requisite for the assumption of responsibility by the Indian people in the present, is their realisation as a fact that they are free and are in charge of maintaining and defending their freedom. What is most wanted is the enthusiastic response of the people, which cannot be evoked without the fullest trust in them and the devolution of responsibility on them in the matter of defence. It is only thus that even at this grave eleventh hour it may be possible to galvanise the people of India to rise to the height of the occasion. It is manifest that the present Government of India, as well as its provincial agencies, are lacking in competence, and are incapable of shouldering the burden of India's defence. It is only the people of India, through their popular representatives, who may shoulder this burden worthily. But that can only be done by present freedom, and full responsibility being cast upon them.

The Committee, therefore, are unable to accept the proposals put forward on behalf of the British War Cabinet.

APPENDIX VI

RESOLUTION OF THE ALL-INDIA CONGRESS COMMITTEE.
(Bombay, August 8, 1942.)

"Quit India" Demand

The All-India Congress Committee has given the most careful consideration to the reference made to it by the Working Committee in their resolution, dated July 14, 1942, and to subsequent events including the development of the war situation, the utterances of responsible spokesmen of the British Government, and the comments and criticisms made in India and abroad. The Committee approves of and endorses that resolution and is of opinion that events subsequent to it have given it further justification and have made it clear that immediate ending of British rule in India is an urgent necessity both for the sake of India and for the success of the cause of the United Nations. The continuation of that rule is degrading and enfeebling India and making her progressively less capable of defending herself and of contributing to the cause of world freedom.

The Committee has viewed with dismay the deterioration of the situation of the Russian and Chinese people and records its high appreciation of their heroism in defence of their freedom. This increasing peril makes it incumbent on all those who sympathise with the victims of aggression, to examine the foundations of the policy so far pursued by the Allied Nations, which have led to repeated and disastrous failure. It is not by adhering to such aims and policies and methods that failure can be converted into success, for past experience has shown that failure is inherent in them. These policies have been based not on freedom so much as on the domination of subject and colonial countries and the continuation of the imperialist tradition and method. The possession of Empire, instead of adding to the strength of the ruling power, has become a burden and a curse. India, the classic land of modern imperialism, has become the crux of the question, for by the freedom of India will Britain and the United Nations be judged and the peoples of Asia and Africa be filled with hope and enthusiasm.

The ending of the British rule in this country is thus a vital and immediate issue on which depend the future of the war and the success of freedom and democracy. A free India will assure this success by throwing all her great resources in the struggle for freedom and against the aggression of Nazism, Fascism and Imperialism. This will not only affect materially the fortunes of the war, but will bring all subject and oppressed humanity on the side of the United Nations, and give these nations, whose ally India would be, the moral anl spiritual leadership of the world. India in bondage will continue to be the symbol of British imperialism and the taint of that imperialism will affect the United Nations.

The peril of today, therefore, necessitates the independence of India and the ending of British domination. No future promises or guarantees can affect the present situation or meet that peril. They cannot produce the needed psychological effect on the minds of the masses. Only the glow of freedom now can release that energy and enthusiasm of millions of people which will immediately transform the nature of the war.

The A.I.C.C., therefore, repeats with all emphasis the demand for the withdrawal of the British power from India. On the declaration of India's independence, a provisional Government will be formed and free India will become an ally of the United Nations, sharing with them in the trials and tribulations of the joint enterprise of the struggle for freedom. The provisional Government can only be formed by the co-operation of the principal parties and groups in the country. It will thus be a composite Government representative of all important sections of the people of India. Its primary functions must be to defend India and resist aggression with all the armed as well as non-violent forces at its command, together with its Allied Powers, and to produce the well-being and progress of the workers in the fields and factories and elsewhere, to whom essentially all power and authority must belong. The provisional Government will evolve a scheme for a Constituent Assembly which will prepare a Constitution for the Government of India acceptable to all sections of the people. This Constitution, according to the Congress view, should be a federal one, with the largest measure of autonomy for the federating units and with residuary powers vesting in these units. Freedom will enable India to resist aggression effectively with the people's united will and strength behind it.

The freedom of India must be the symbol of and prelude to the freedom of all other Asiatic nations under foreign domination. Burma, Malaya, Indo-China, the Dutch Indies, Iran and Iraq must also attain their complete freedom. It must be clearly understood that such of these countries as are under Japanese control now must not subsequently be placed under the rule or control of any other colonial power.

While the A.I.C.C. must primarily be concerned with the independence and defence of India in this hour of danger, the Committee is of opinion that the future peace, security and ordered progress of the world demand a world federation of free nations, and on no other basis can the problems of the modern world be solved. Such a world federation would ensure the freedom of its constituents, the prevention of aggression and exploitation by one nation over another, the protection of national minorities, the advancement of all backward areas and peoples, and the pooling of the world's resources for the common good of all. On the establishment of such a world federation, disarmament would be practicable in all countries ; their national armies, navies and air forces would no longer be necessary and a world federation defence force would keep the world peace and prevent aggression.

An Independent India would gladly join such a world federation and co-operate on equal basis with other countries in the solution of international problems.

Such a federation would be open to all nations who agree with its fundamental principles. In view of the war, however, the federation must inevitably, to begin with, be confined to the United Nations. Such a step taken now will have a most powerful effect on the war, on the peoples of the Axis countries, and on the peace to come.

The Committee regretfully realises, however, that despite the tragic and overwhelming lessons of the war and the perils that overhang the world, the Governments of few countries are yet prepared to take this inevitable step towards world federation. The reactions of the British Government and the misguided criticism of the foreign press also make it clear that even the obvious demand for India's independence is resisted, though this has been made essentially to meet them in their hour of need. The Committee is anxious not to embarass in any way the defence of China or Russia, whose freedom is precious, and must be preserved, or to jeopardise the defence capacity of the United Nations. But the peril grows both to India and these nations, and submission to a foreign administration at this stage is not only degrading India and reducing her capacity to defend herself and resist aggression but is no answer to that growing peril and is no service to the peoples of the United Nations. The earnest appeal of the Working Committee to Great Britain and the United Nations has so far met with no response and the criticisms made in many foreign quarters have shown an ignorance of India's and and the world's need and sometimes even hostility to India's freedom which is significant of a mentality of domination and racial superiority which cannot be tolerated by a proud people conscious of their strength and of the justice of their cause.

The A.I.C.C. would yet again, at this last moment, in the interest of world freedom renew this appeal to Britain and the United Nations. But the Committee feels that it is no longer justified in holding the nation back from endeavouring to assert its will against an imperialist and authoritarian Government which dominates over it and prevents it from functioning in its own interest and in the interest of humanity. The Committee resolves, therefore, to sanction, for the vindication of India's inalienable right to freedom and independence, the starting of a mass struggle on non-violent lines, on the widest possible scale, so that the country might utilise all the non-violent strength it has gathered during the last 22 years of peaceful struggle. Such a struggle must inevitably be under the leadership of Gandhiji and the Committee requests him to take the lead and guide the nation in the steps to be taken.

The Committee appeals to the people of India to face the danger and hardships that will fall to their lot with courage and endurance, and to hold together under the leadership of Gandhiji and carry out his instructions as disciplined soldiers of Indian freedom. They must remember that non-violence is the basis of the movement. A time may come when it may not be possible to issue instructions or for instructions to reach our people, when no Congress Committees can function. When this happens every man and woman who is participating in this movement must function for himself or herself within the four corners of the general instructions issued. Every Indian who desires freedom and strives for it must be his own guide urging him along the hard road where there is no resting place and which leads ultimately to the independence and deliverance of India.

Lastly, while the A.I.C.C. has stated its own view of the future governance under free India, the A.I.C.C. wishes to make it quite clear to all concerned that by embarking on a mass struggle it has no intention of gaining power for the Congress. The power, when it comes, will belong to the whole people of India.

APPENDIX VII

RESOLUTION OF THE WORKING COMMITTEE OF THE MUSLIM LEAGUE

(April 11, 1942.)

Pakistan Reiterated

The Committee appreciate that the British Prime Minister, in his pronouncement, made it clear that the Draft Declaration embodied only the proposals of His Majesty's Government and not their decision, and that they are subject to agreement between the main elements in India, thus maintaining the validity of the Declaration of August 8,1940, which had promised to the Mussalmans that neither the machinery for the framing of the constitution should he set up nor the constitution itself should be enforced without the approval and consent of Muslim India.

The Committee, while expressing their gratification that the possibility of Pakistan is recognised by implication by providing for the establishment of two or more independent Unions in India, regret that the proposals of His Majesty's Government, embodying the fundamentals, are not open to any modification and, therefore, no alternative proposals are invited. In view of the rigidity of the attitude of His Majesty's

Government with regard to the fundamentals not being open to any modification, the Committee have no alternative but to say that the proposals in their present form are unacceptable to them for reasons given below.

(1) The Mussalmans, after twenty-five years of genuine efforts for the reconciliation of the two major communities and the bitter experience of the failure of such efforts, are convinced that it is neither just nor possible, in the interest of peace and happiness of the two peoples, to compel them to constitute one Indian Union, composed of the two principal nations —Hindus and Muslims—which appears to be the main object of His Majesty's Government, as adumbrated in the Preamble of the Draft Declaration, the creation of more than one Union being relegated only to the realm of remote possibility and is purely illusory.

(2) In the Draft Declaration a constitution-making body has been proposed with the primary object of creating one Indian Union. So far as the Muslim League is concerned, it has finally decided that the only solution of India's constitutional problem is the partition of India into independent zones; and it will, therefore, be unfair to the Mussalmans to compel them to enter such a constitution-making body, whose main object is the creation of a new Indian Union. With conditions as they are, it will not only be futile but, on the contrary, may exacerbate bitterness and animosity amongst the various elements in the country.

Besides, the machinery which has been proposed for the creation of the constitution-making body, namely, that it will consist of members elected by the newly elected Lower Houses of the eleven provinces, upon the cessation of hostilities, as a single electoral college by the system of proportional representation, is a fundamental departure from the right of the Mussalmans, hitherto enjoyed by them, to elect their representatives by means of separate electorates, which is the only sure way in which true representatives of the Mussalmans can be chosen.

The constitution-making body will take decisions by a bare majority on all questions of most vital and paramount character involved in the framing of the constitution, which is a departure from the fundamental principles of justice and contrary to constitutional practice so far followed in the various countries and dominions; and the Mussalmans, by agreeing to this will, instead of exercising their right and judgment as a constituent factor, be at the entire mercy of the constitution-making body, in which they will be a minority of about twenty-five per cent.

(3) The right of non-accession to the Union, as contemplated in the Draft Declaration, has been conceded, presumably, in response to the inistent demands by the Mussalmans for the partition of India, but the method and the procedure laid down are such as to negative the professed object, for, in the draft proposals, the right of non-accession has been given to the existing provinces, which have been formed from time to time for administrative convenience and on no logical basis.

The Mussalmans cannot be satisfied by such a Declaration on a vital question affecting their future destiny and demand a clear and precise pronouncement on the subject. Any attempt to solve the future problem of India by the process of evading the real issues is to court disaster.

In the draft proposals no procedure has been laid down as to how the verdict of the province is to be obtained in favour of, or against, accession to one Union, but in the letter dated April 2, from the secretary of Sir Stafford Cripps, addressed to the President of the All-India Muslim League, it is stated that "a province should reach the decision whether or not to stand out of the Union by a vote in the Legislative Assembly on a resolution to stand in. If the majority for accession to the Union is less than sixty per cent., the minority will have the right to demand a plebiscite of the adult population." In this connection it must be emphasised that in the provinces where the Mussalmans are in a majority, as in the case of the major provinces of Bengal and the Punjab, they are in a minority in the Legislative Assemblies ; and in the Assemblies of Sind and the North-West Frontier Province, the total number, namely, sixty and fifty respectively, is so small and the weightage given to the non-Muslims so heavy that it can be easily manipulated and a decision under such conditions cannot be the true criterion of ascertaining the real opinion of the Mussalmans of those provinces.

As regards the suggested plebiscite in the provinces in which the Mussalmans are in a majority, in the event of the requisite majority not being available in the Legislative Assemblies the procedure laid down is that reference shall be made to the whole adult population of the provinces and not to the Mussalmans alone, which is to deny them the inherent right to self-determination.

(4) With regard to the Indian States, it is the considered opinion of the Committee that it is a matter for them to decide whether to join or not to join or form a Union.

(5) With regard to the treaties to be negotiated between the Crown and the Indian Union or Unions, the proposals do not indicate as to what would happen in case of disagreement on the terms between the contracting parties, nor in there any provision made as to what would be the procedure when there is a difference of opinion in negotiating a revision of treaty arrangements with the Indian States in the new situation.

(6) With regard to the interim arrangements, there is no definite proposal except the bare statement that His Majesty's Government desire and invite the effective and immediate participation of the leaders of the principal sections of the Indian people in the counsels of their country, of the Commonwealth and of the United Nations. The Committee are, therefore, unable to express their opinion until a complete picture is availabe. Another reason why the Committee are unable to express their opinion of the interim arrangements for participation in the counsels of the country, is that Sir Stafford Cripps has made it clear that the scheme goes through as a whole or is rejected as a whole and that it would not be possible to retain only the part relating to the immediate arrangements at the centre and discard the rest of the draft scheme, and as the Committee have come to the conclusion that the proposals for

the future are unacceptable, it will serve no useful purpose to deal further with the question of the immediate arrangements.

In conclusion the Committee wish to point out that the position of the Muslim League has been and is that unles the principle of Pakistan Scheme as embodied in the Lahore Resolution dated March, 1940, which is now the creed of the All-India Muslim League . . . . is unequivocally accepted and the right of the Mussalmans to self-determination is conceded by means of a machinery which will reflect the true verdict of Muslim India, it is not possible for the Muslim League to accept any proposal or scheme regarding the future.

APPENDIX VIII

THE WAVELL PLAN, 1945.

STATEMENT OF THE SECRETARY OF STATE, HOUSE OF COMMONS.
(June 14, 1945.)

1. During the recent visit of Field-Marshal Viscount Wavell to this country His Majesty's Government reviewed with him a number of problems and discused particularly the present political situation in India.

2. Members will be aware that since the offer by His Majesty's Government to India in March 1942 there has been no further progress towards the solution of the Indian constitutional problem.

3. As was then stated, the working out of India's new constitutional system is a task which can only be carried through by the Indian peoples themselves.

4. While His Majesty's Government are at all times most anxious to do their utmost to assist the Indians in the working out of a new constitutional settlement, it would be a contradiction in terms to speak of the imposition by this country of self-governing institutions upon an unwilling India. Such a thing is not possible, nor could we accept the responsibility of enforcing such institutions at the very time when we were, by its purpose, withdrawing from all control of British Indian affairs.

5. The main constitutional position remains therefore as it was. The offer of March 1942 stands in its entirety without change or qualification. His Majesty's Government still hope that the political leaders in India may be able to come to an agreement as to the procedure whereby India's permanent future form of Government can be determined.

6. His Majesty's Government are, however, most anxious to make any contribution that is practicable to the breaking of the political deadlock in India. While that deadlock lasts not only political but social and economic progress is being hampered.

7. The Indian administration, overburdened with the great tasks laid upon it by the war against Japan and by the planning for the post-war period, is further strained by the political tension that exists.

8. All that is so urgently required to be done for agricultural and industrial development and for the peasants and workers of India cannot be carried through unless the whole-hearted co-operation of every community and section of the Indian people is forthcoming.

9. His Majesty's Government have, therefore, considered whether there is something which they could suggest in this interim period, under the existing constitution, pending the formulation by Indians of their future constitutional arrangements, which would enable the main communities and parties to co-operate more closely together and with the British to the benefit of the people of India as a whole.

10. It is not the intention of His Majesty's Government to introduce any change contrary to the wishes of the major Indian communities. But they are willing to make possible some step forward during the interim period if the leaders of the principal Indian parties are prepared to agree to their suggestions and to co-operate in the successful conclusion of the war against Japan as well as in the reconstruction in India which must follow the final victory.

11. To this end they would be prepared to see an important change in the composition of the Viceroy's Executive. This is posible without making any change in the existing statute law except for one amendment to the Ninth Schedule to the Act of 1935. That Schedule contains a provision that not less than three members of the Executive must have had at least ten years' service under the Crown in India. If the proposals I am about to lay before the House meet with acceptance in India, that clause would have to be amended to dispense with that requirement.

12. It is proposed that the Executive Council should be reconstituted and that the Viceroy should in future make his selection for nomination to the Crown for appointment to his Executive from amongst leaders of Indian political life at the Centre and in the provinces, in proportions which would give a balanced representation of the main communities, including equal proportions of Moslems and Caste Hindus.

13. In order to pursue this object, the Viceroy will call into Conference a number of leading Indian politicians who are the heads of the most important parties or who have had recent experience as Prime Ministers of Provinces, together with a few others of special experience and authority. The Viceroy intends to put before this Conference the proposal that the Executive Council should be reconstituted as above stated and to invite from the members of the Conference a list of names. Out of these he would hope to be able to choose the future members whom he would recomment for appointment by His Majesty to the Viceroy's Council, although the responsibility for the recommendations must, of course, continue to rest with him, and his freedom of choice, therefore, remains unrestricted.

14. The members of his Council who are chosen as a result of this arrangement would, of course, accept the position on the basis that they would whole-heartedly co-operate in supporting and carrying through the war against Japan to its victorious conclusion.

15. The members of the Executive would be Indians with the ex-

ception of the Viceroy and the Commander-in-Chief, who would retain his position as War Member. This is essential so long as the defence of India remains a British responsibility.

16. Nothing contained in these proposals will affect the relations of the Crown with the Indian States through the Viceroy as Crown Representative.

17. The Viceroy has been authorised by His Majesty's Government to place this proposal before the Indian leaders. His Majesty's Government trust that the leaders of the Indian communities will respond. For the success of such a plan must depend upon its acceptance in India and the degree to which responsible Indian politicians are prepared to co-operate with the object of making it a workable interim arrangement. In the absence of such general acceptance existing arrangements must necessarily continue.

18. If such co-operation can be achieved at the Centre, it will no doubt be reflected in the provinces and so enable responsible Governments to be set up once again in those provinces where, owing to the withdrawal of the majority party from participation, it became necessary to put into force the powers of the Governors under section 93 of the Act of 1935. It is to be hoped that in all provinces these Governments would be based on the participation of the main parties, thus smoothing up communal differences and allowing Ministers to concentrate upon their very heavy administrative tasks.

19. There is one further change which, if these proposals are accepted, His Majesty's Government suggest should follow.

20. That is, that External Affairs (other than those tribal and frontier matters which fall to be dealt with as part of the defence of India) should be placed in the charge of an Indian Member of the Viceroy's Executive so far as British India is concerned, and fully accredited representatives shall be appointed for the representation of India abroad.

21. By their acceptance of and co-operation in this scheme the Indian leaders will not only be able to make their immediate contribution to the direction of Indian affairs, but it is also to be hoped that their experience of co-operation in Government will expedite agreement between them as to the method of working out the new constitutional arrangements.

22. His Majesty's Government consider, after the most careful study of the question, that the plan now suggested gives the utmost progress practicable within the present constitution. None of the changes suggested will in any way prejudice or prejudge the essential form of the future permanent constitution or constitutions for India.

23. His Majesty's Government feel certain that given goodwill and a genuine desire to co-operate on all sides, both British and Indian, these proposals can mark a genuine step forward in the collaboration of the British and Indian peoples towards Indian self-government and can assert the rightful position, and strengthen the influence, of India in the counsels of the nations.

APPENDIX IX

THE WAVELL PLAN, 1945.

(Broadcast by the Viceroy)

His Excellency the Viceroy, in a broadcast speech on 14th June 1945 on His Majesty's Government's proposals to ease the present political situation in India, said:

I have been authorised by His Majesty's Government to place before Indian political leaders proposals designed to ease the present political situation and to advance India towards her goal of full self-government These proposals are at the present moment being explained to Parliament by the Secretary of State for India. My intention in this broadcast is to explain to you the proposals, the ideas underlying them, and the method by which I hope to put them into effect.

This is not an attempt to obtain or impose a constitutional settlement. His Majesty's Government had hoped that the leaders of the Indian parties would agree amongst themselves on a settlement of the communal issue, which is the main stumbling block but this hope has not been fulfilled.

In the meantime, India has great opportunities to be taken and great problems to be solved, which require a çommon effort by the leading men of all parties. I therefore propose, with the full support of His Majesty's Government, to invite Indian leaders both of Central and Provincial politics to take counsel with me with a view to the formation of a new Executive Council more representative of organised political opinion. The proposed new Council would represent the main communities and would include equal proportions of Caste Hindus and Moslems. It would work, if formed, under the existing constitution. But it would be an entirely Indian Council, except for the Viseroy and the Commander-in-Chief, who would retain his position as War Member.

It is proposed that the portfolio of External Affairs, which has hitherto been held by the Viceroy, should be placed in charge of an Indian Member of Council, so far as the interests of British India are concerned.

A further step proposed by His Majesty's Government is the appointment of a British High Commissioner in India, as in the Dominions, to represent Great Britain's commercial and other such interests in India.

Such a new Executive Council will, you realise, represent a definite advance on the road to self-government. It will be almost entirely Indian, and the Finance and Home Members will for the first time be Indians, while an Indian will also be charged with the management of India's foreign affairs. Moreover Members will now be selected by the Governor-General after consultation with political leaders, though their appointment will, of course, be subject to the approval of His Majesty the King Emperor.

The Council will work within the frame-work of the present constitution; and there can be no question of the Governor-General agreeing not to exercise his constitutional power of control; but it will of course not be exercised unreasonably.

I should make it clear that the formation of this Interim Government will in no way prejudice the final constitutional settlement.

The main tasks for this new Executive Council would be:—

First, to prosecute the war against Japan with the utmost energy till Japan is utterly defeated.

Secondly, to carry on the Government of British India, with all the manifold tasks of post-war development in front of it, until a new permanent constitution can be agreed upon and come into force.

Thirdly, to consider, when the Members of the Government think it possible, the means by which such agreement can be achieved. The third task is most important. I want to make it quite clear that neither I nor His Majesty's Government have lost sight of the need for a long-term solution, and that the present proposals are intended to make a long-term solution easier.

I have considered the best means of forming such a Council; and have decided to invite the following to Viceregal Lodge to advise me:—

Those now holding office as Premier in a Provincial Government; and for provinces now under Section 93 Government, those who last held the office of Premier.

The Leader of the Congress party and the deputy leader of the Muslim League in the Central Assembly; the leaders of the Congress Party and the Muslim League in the Council of State; also the leaders of the Nationalist Party and the European group in the Assembly.

Mr. Gandhi and Mr. Jinnah as the recognised leaders of the two main political parties.

Rao Bahadur N. Siva Raj to represent the Scheduled classes. Master Tara Singh to represent the Sikhs.

Invitations to these gentlemen are being handed to them to-day and it is proposed to assemble the Conference on 25th June at Simla where we shall be cooler than at Delhi.

I trust that all those invited will attend the Conference and give me their help. On me and on them will lie a heavy responsibility in this fresh attempt to make progress towards a final settlement of India's future.

If the meeting is successful, I hope that we shall be able to agree on the formation of the new Executive Council at the Centre. I also hope that it will be possible for Ministries to ressume office and again undertake the tasks of Government in the provinces now administered under Section 93 of the Constitution Act and that these Ministries will be coalitions.

If the meeting should unfortuntely fail. we must carry on as at present until the parties are ready to come together. The existing Executive Council, which has done such valuable work for India, will continue if other arrangements cannot be agreed.

But I have every hope that the meeting will succeed, if the party leaders will approach the problem with the sincere intention of working with me and with each other. I can assure them that there is behind this proposal a most genuine desire on the part of all responsible leaders in the United Kingdom and of the British people as a whole to help India towards her goal. I believe that this is more than a step towards the goal, it is a considerable stride forward and a stride on the right path.

I should make it clear that these proposals affect British India only and do not make any alteration in the relations of the Princes with the Crown representative.

With the approval of His Majesty's Government, and after consultation with my Council, orders have been given for the immediate release of the members of the Working Committee of Congress who are still in detention. I propose to leave the final decision about the others still under detention as the result of the 1942 disturbances to the new Central Government, if formed, and to the Provincial Governments.

The appropriate time for fresh elections for the Central and provincial legislatures will be discussed at the conference.

Fially, I would ask you to help in creating the atmosphere of goodwill and mutual confidence that is essential if we are to make progress. The destiny of this country and of the many millions who live in it depend on the wisdom and good understanding of the leaders, both of action and of thought, British and Indian, at this critical moment of India's history.

India's military reputation never stood higher in the world than it does at present, thanks to the exploits of her sons drawn from all parts of the country. Her representatives at international conferences have won high regard for their statesmanlike attitude. Sympathy for India's aspirations and progress towards prosperity was never greater or more widespread. We have thus great assets if we can use them wisely. But it will not be easy, it will not be quick, there is very much to do, there are many pitfalls and dangers. There is on all sides something to forgive and forget.

I believe in the future of India, and as far as in me lies will further her greatness. I ask you all for your co-operation and goodwill.

APPENDIX X

LORD WAVELL'S STATEMENT ON SIMLA CONFERENCE (July 14, 1945.)

Unfortunately, the Conference was unable to agree about the strength and composition of the Executive Council, and on the 29th June I undertook, with the approval of the Conference, to endeavour to produce a solution not based on any formula agreed in advance. I asked the parties to let me have lists of names, and said I would do what I could to produce a solution acceptable to the leaders and to the Conference.

I received lists from all parties represented here except from the European Group, who decided not to send a list, and the Muslim League. I was, however, determined that the Conference should not fail until I had made every possible effort to bring it to a successful ending. I therefore made my provisional selections including certain Muslim League names, and I have every reason to believe that if these selections had been acceptable here they would have been acceptable to His Magesty's Government.

My selections would, I think, have given a balanced and efficient Executive Council, whose composition would have been reasonably fair to all parties.

I did not find it possible, however, to accept the claims of any party in full. When I explained my solution to Mr. Jinnah he told me that it was not acceptable to the Muslim League and he was so decided that I felt it would be useless to continue the discussion.

In the circumstances I did not show my selections as a whole to Mr. Jinnah, and there was no object in showing them to the other leaders. The Conference has, therefore, failed.

Nobody can regret this more than I do myself. I wish to make it clear that the responsibility for the failure is mine. The main idea underlying the Conference was mine. If it had succeeded its success could have been attributed to me and I cannot place the blame for its failure upon any of the parties.

APPENDIX XI

STATEMENT OF MAULANA ABUL KALAM AZAD AT PRESS CONFERENCE, SIMLA (July 14, 1945.)

The Congress was prepared to accommodate the Muslim League consistently with its national policy. This would be made clear when the panel submitted by the Congress was officially released. Failure of the Conference was due to the uncompromising attitude taken by the League.

The British Government must share the responsibility for the communal situation in the country to-day. Settlement would be possible either now or in future only on a reasonable and fair term.

Two points arise out of the present position ; the first is that the attitude of the Muslim League is responsible for the failure of the Conference and the second point which emerges from the situation is that after the refusal of the Muslim League the question naturally came before the Viceroy whether a forward step should be taken or not. The Viceroy decided not to take it for the present.

It was made clear to the Viceroy that the Congress was prepared to go forward and if a certain group wished to keep out it might be left out.

With a faltering step and wavering mind we cannot cover our destination.

It is good to think twice before taking a step forward. But when the step has already been taken hesitation is not virtue but weakness. If the British Government wished to give shape to things they should have realised the communal condition. They should have been prepared not to surrender the right of veto to any group and thus block the path of progress.

It should be emphasized that (1) the present arrangement was purely temporary and interim, (2) it was a preliminary step to the goal of independence, and (3) the Working Committee wished to co-operate in every reasonable way but their decision required ratification by the All-India Congress Committee.

Other points to be remembered are that (1) every effort should be made to give national character to the Indian Army and to bring about cordiality between the National Army and the National Government and the people, and (2) the India Government could not support any policy aimed at continuation of imperialist control of any of the countries in South-East Asia nor could it allow use of its resources in men and money.

APPENDIX XII

MR. JINNAH'S STATEMENT AT PRESS CONFERENCE, SIMLA (July 14, 1945.)

On a final examination and analysis of the Wavell plan, we found that it was a snare. There was the combination consisting of Gandhi Hindu Congress, who stand for India's Hindu national independence as one India, and the latest exponent of geographical unity, Lord Wavell, and Glancy-Khizr, who are bent upon creating disruption among the Mussalmans in the Punjab, and we were sought to be pushed into this arrangement, by which, if we had agreed to, as proposed by Lord Wavell, we would have signed our death warrant.

Next, in the proposed Executive we would be reduced to a minority of one-third. All other minorities, such as the Scheduled Castes, Sikhs and Christians, have the same goal as the Congress. They have their grievances as minorities, but their goal and ideology is and cannot be different from or otherwise than that of United India. Ethnically and culturally they are very closely knitted to the Hindu Society. I am not against full justice being done to all the minorities and they should be fully safeguarded and protected as such, wherever they may be, but in the actual working and practice, invariably their vote will be against us and there is no safeguard for us except the Viceroy's veto, which, it is well known to any constitutionalist, cannot be exercised lightly as everyday business against majority decisions with regard to the policy and the principles that will have to be laid down and measures adopted, both administrative and legislative.

On the top of this came the last straw on the camel's back, that even about the five members of the Muslim bloc which were allotted to us communalwise, which is the essence of the Wavell proposals, we were told that the Muslim League was not entitled to nominate all the Muslim representatives as our chosen spokesmen and there were two claimants—the Congress which claimed two, and Glancy-Khizr on behalf of the Punjab claimed one. This move on the part of these two went at the very root and the very existence of the Muslim League regarding its position, character and status. But finally we broke as Lord Wavell insisted upon his having one non-Leaguer, a nominee of Malik Khizr Hyat Khan, representing the Punjab Muslims.

APPENDIX XIII

MR. ATTLEE'S SPEECH ON THE BRITISH CABINET MISSION (March 15, 1946.)

In the course of his reply to Mr. Richard Butler who opened the debate on the British Cabinet Mission to India, Prime Minister Clement Attlee said:

I find from our friends in this House who had been out to India and returned, from letters received from Indians and from Englishmen in India of all points of view, complete agreement on the fact that India is to-day in a state of great tension and that this is indeed a critical moment. I am quite sure that everyone in this House realises the difficulty of the task which the members of the Mission have undertaken in conjunction with the Viceroy and that no one will desire to say anything whatever that will make that task more difficult.

I entirely agree with Mr. Butler in saying that the Mission should go out in a positive mood. That, indeed, is the mood in which they are undertaking this mission.

It is time emphatically for very definite and clear action. I do not intend to make a long speech. I do not think it would be wise to do so and in particular it would be most unhelpful to review the past. It is so easy to go back over the past, and in accordance with one's predilections to apportion blame for past failures in long drawn out discussions on this extraordinarily difficult problem—the problem of development of India to a completely self-governing nation.

In the long period of the past, it is so easy to point out and say that at this stage or that stage opportunities were missed by faults on one side or the other.

I have had very close connection with this problem for nearly twenty years and I say there have been faults on both sides, but this time, we should look to the future rather than harp back to the past. Thus I would say it is no good applying the formula of the past to the

17

present position. The temperature of 1946 is not the temperature of 1920, 1930 or even 1942. The slogans of earlier days are discarded. Sometimes, words that seemed at that time to Indians to express the height of their aspirations are now set on one side and other words and ideas thrust forward.

Nothing increases the pace and movement of public opinion more than a great war. Everyone who had anything to do with this question in the early days between the war knows what effect the war of 1914-18 had on Indian aspirations and ideas. The tide that runs comparatively slowly in peace, in wartime becomes vastly accelerated, and especially directly afterwards, because that tide is to some extent banked up during war. I am quite certain that at the present time the tide of nationalism is running very fast in India and indeed all over Asia.

One always has to remember that India is affected by what happens elsewhere in Asia. I remember when I was on the Simon Commission what effect the challenge that had been thrown out by Japan at that time had had on the Asiatic people and the tide of nationalism that at one time seemed to be canalised among a comparatively small portion of the people of India, mainly a few of the educated classes, has tended to spread wider and wider.

I remember that in the Simon Commission Report although there were great differences in expression of the nationalistic sentiment between what were called extremists and moderates and although in many instances there might be such stress of communal claims as may seem almost to exclude the conception of nationalism, yet we found that Hindus, Moslems, Sikhs and Marattahs, politicians or civil servants—among all of them—that conception of nationalism had been growing stronger and stronger and to-day I think that the national idea has spread right through, not the least perhaps among some of those soldiers who had done such wonderful service in the war.

I would like to-day, therefore, not to stress so much the differences between the Indians, but let us all realise that whatever the difficulties and divisions may be, there is this underlying demand among all the Indian people.

Mr. Butler did not suggest that the Government should publish any exact terms of reference of the Mission. We have set out the general purpose and it is our intention that they should be given as free a hand as possible.

There will be matters undoubtedly on which it is necessary to refer back for Cabinet decision, but in our fluid position at the present time when we desire to get the utmost co-operation and goodwill between all leaders of Indian opinion it would be unwise to try and tie down those who are going out too rigidly.

The obvious reason for sending out the Cabinet Ministers is that you send out persons of responsibility who are able to take decisions. Of course, there must be an area in which there may have to be a reference back.

Mr. Butler had stressed the great part India had played in the war. It is worth remembering that twice in 25 years India has played a great part in the defeat of tyranny. Therefore, is it any wonder that to-day she claims—a nation of four hundred million people that twice sent her sons to die for freedom—that she should herself have freedom to decide her own destiny?

My colleagues are going to India with the intention of using their utmost endeavours to help her to attain that freedom as speedily and fully as possible. What form of Government is to replace the present regime is for India to decide, but our desire is to help her to set up forthwith a machinery for making that decision.

There you have met with the initial difficulty of getting that machinery set up, but we are resolved that a machinery shall be set up and we seek the utmost co-operation of all Indian leaders to do so.

India herself must choose as to what will be her future situation and her position in the world. Unity may come through the United Nations, or through the Commonwealth, but no great nation can stand alone by herself without sharing what is happening in the world. I hope that India and her people may elect to remain within the British Commonwealth. I am certain that she will find great advantages in doing so, but if she does she must do it of her own free will, for the British Commonwealth and Empire is not bound together by chains of external compulsion. It is a free association of free peoples.

If on the other hand she elects for independence—and in our view she has a right to do so—it will be for us to help make the transition as smooth and easy as possible.

We have a united India and given her that sense of nationality which she largely lacked in the previous centuries and she has learnt from us principles of democracy and justice.

When Indians attack our rule, they base their attack, not on Indian principles, but on the basis of standards derived from Britain. I am well aware that when I speak of India I speak of a country containing congeries of races, religions and languages and I know well the difficulties thereby created but these difficulties can only be overcome by Indians.

We are mindful of the rights of the minorities and the minorities should be able to live free from fear. On the other hand, we cannot allow a minority to place their veto on the advance of a majority.

We cannot dictate how these difficulties shall be overcome. Our first duty is to get a machinery of decision set up and that is the main purpose of the Ministerial Mission and the Viceroy.

We want to see set up an interim government—one of the purposes of the Bill which has been discussed to-day—to give the Viceroy greater freedom in order that in the period which is to elapse while a constitution is being worked out, you may have a government enjoying the greatest possible support in India. I would not like to fetter the Viceroy's decision in any way in regard to the choice of portfolios.

In many Indian States, great advance has been made and there is a most interesting experiment in Travancore. Of course, feelings in

India with regard to nationalism the unity of India cannot be confined by boundaries that separate the States from the provinces.

I am hoping that statesmen of Britain and of Princely India will be able to work out a solution of the problem of bringing together in one great polity the various constituent parts, and there again we must see that Indian States find their due place. I do not believe for a moment that the Indian Princes would desire to be a bar in the forward march of India.

This is a matter which Indians will settle themselves. I am very well aware of the minority problem in India. I think all Indian leaders are realising more and more the need for getting a settlement of these minority problems if India is to have a smooth passage in future years and I believe that due provision will be made for them in the constitution.

The Mission will certainly not neglect this point. But you cannot make Indians responsible for governing themselves and at the same time retain over here the responsibility for treatment of minorities and powers of intervention on their behalf.

We are mindful too of the position of the services and of the men who have done great service to India. India should be sensible of the responsibility she has to those who have served her.

Any interim government which takes over the assets of the Government will also take over the liabilities. That again is a point to be dealt with later on. It does not concern the immediate setting up of the instrument of decision.

With regard to the treaty, we are not going to hang out for anything for our own advantage which would be to the disadvantage of India.

Let me stress again the crucial nature of the task before us. This problem is of vital importance not only to India and the British Commonwealth and Empire but to the world.

In the mass of Asia, an Asia ravaged by war, we have here the one country that has been seeking to apply the principles of democracy. I have always felt myself that political India might be the light of Asia. It is a most unfortunate circumstance that just at the time when we have to deal with these great political issues there should be grave economic difficulties. In particular, we have very grave anxiety over India's food supply.

The House knows that the British Government are deeply concerned in this problem and the Minister of Food is now in the United States with the Indian delegation. We shall do our utmost to help India.

I do not think I should refer to the social and economic difficulties except to say that I believe that these difficulties can only be solved by Indians themselves because they are so closely bound up with the whole Indian way of life and outlook. Whatever we can do to assist we shall do.

My colleagues are going out to India resolved to succeed and I am sure everyone will wish them god-speed.

APPENDIX XIV

THE CABINET MISSION'S DECLARATION
(May 16, 1946.)

1. On the 15th March last, just before the despatch of the Cabinet Mission to India, Mr. Attlee, the British Prime Minister, used these words:—

"My colleagues are going to India with the intention of using their utmost endeavours to help her to attain her freedom as speedily and fully as possible. What form of Government is to replace the present regime is for India to decide; but our desire is to help her to set up forthwith the machinery for making that decision . . .

* * * * * *

"I hope that the Indian people may elect to remain within the British Commonwealth. I am certain that she will find great advantages in doing so . . .

* * * * * *

"But if she does so elect, it must be by her own free will. The British Commonwealth and Empire is not bound together by chains of external compulsion. It is a free association of free peoples. If, on the other hand, she elects for independence, in our view she has a right to do so. It will be for us to help to make the transition as smooth and easy as possible."

2. Charged in these historic words we—the Cabinet Ministers and the Viceroy—have done our utmost to assist the two main political parties to reach agreement upon the fundamental issue of the unity or division of India. After prolonged discussions in New Delhi we succeeded in bringing the Congress and the Muslim League together in Conference at Simla. There was a full exchange of views and both parties were prepared to make considerable concessions in order to try to reach a settlement, but it ultimately proved impossible to close the remainder of the gap between the parties and so no agreement could be concluded. Since no agreement has been reached we feel that it is our duty to put forward what we consider are the best arrangements possible to ensure a speedy setting up of the new constitution. This statement is made with the full approval of His Majesty's Government in the United Kingdom.

3. We have accordingly decided that immediate arrangements should be made whereby Indians may decide the future constitution of India, and an interim government may be set up at once to carry on the administration of British India until such time as a new constitution can be brought into being. We have endeavoured to be just to the smaller as well as to the larger sections of the people; and to recommend a solution which will lead to a practicable way of governing the India of the future, and will give a sound basis for defence and a good opportunity for progress in the social, political and economic field.

4. It is not intended in this statement to review the voluminous evidence which has been submitted to the Mission ; but it is right that we should state that it has shown an almost universal desire, outside the supporters of the Muslim League, for the unity of India.

5. This consideration did not, however, deter us from examining closely and impartially the possibility of a partition of India ; since we were greatly impressed by the very genuine and acute anxiety of the Muslims lest they should find themselves subjected to a perpetual Hindu-majority rule. This feeling has become so strong and widespread amongst the Muslims that it cannot be allayed by mere paper safeguards. If there is to be internal peace in India it must be secured by measures which will assure to the Muslims a control in all matters vital to their culture, religion, and economic or other interests.

6. We therefore examined in the first instance the question of a separate and fully independent sovereign State of Pakistan as claimed by the Muslim League. Such a Pakistan would comprise two areas: one in the North-West consisting of the Provinces of the Punjab, Sind, North West Frontier, and British Baluchistan ; the other in the North-East consisting of the Provinces of Bengal and Assam. The League were prepared to consider adjustment of boundaries at a later stage, but insisted that the principle of Pakistan should first be acknowledged. The argument for a separate State of Pakistan was based, first, upon the right of the Muslim majority to decide their method of Government according to their wishes, and, secondly, upon the necessity to include substantial areas in which Muslims are in a minority, in order to make Pakistan administratively and economically workable.

The size of the non-Muslim minorities in a Pakistan comprising the whole of the six Provinces enumerated above would be very considerable as the following figures (latest census of 1941) show:—

NORTH-WESTERN AREA

		Muslim	Non-Muslim
Punjab	...	16,217,242	12,201,577
NWFP	...	2,788,797	249,270
Sind	...	3,208,325	1,326,683
Br. Baluchistan	...	438,930	62,701
		22,653,294	13,840,231
		62.07%	37·93%

NORTH-EASTERN AREA

		Muslim	Non-Muslim
Bengal	...	33,005,434	27,301,091
Assam	...	3,442,479	6,762,254
		36,447,913	34,063,345
		51.69%	48·31%

The Muslim minorities in the remainder of British India number some 20 million dispersed amongst a total population of 188 million.

These figures show that the setting up of a separate sovereign state of Pakistan on the lines claimed by the Muslim League would not solve the communal minority problem ; nor can we see any justification for including within a sovereign Pakistan those districts of the Punjab and of Bengal and Assam in which the population is predominantly non-Muslim. Every argument that can be used in favour of Pakistan can equally, in our view, be used in favour of the exclusion of the non-Muslim areas from Pakistan. This point would particularly affect the position of the Sikhs.

7. We, therefore, considered whether a smaller sovereign Pakistan confined to the Muslim majority areas alone might be a possible basis of compromise. Such a Pakistan is regarded by the Muslim League as quite impracticable because it would entail the exclusion from Pakistan of (a) the whole of the Ambala and Jullundur Divisions in the Punjab ; (b) the whole of Assam except the district of Sylhet ; and (c) a large part of Western Bengal, including Calcutta, in which city the percentage of the Muslim population is 23.6 per cent. We ourselves are also convinced that any solution which involves a radical partition of the Punjab and Bengal, as this would do, would be contrary to the wishes and interests of a very large proportion of the inhabitants of these Provinces. Bengal and the Punjab each has its own common language and a long history and tradition. Moreover, any division of the Punjab would of necessity divide the Sikhs leaving substantial bodies of Sikhs on both sides of the boundary. We have therefore been forced to the conclusion that neither a larger nor a smaller sovereign state of Pakistan would provide an acceptable solution for the communal problem.

8. Apart from the great force of the foregoing arguments there are weighty administrative, economic and military considerations. The whole of the transportation and postal and telegraph systems of India have been established on the basis of a united India. To disintegrate them would gravely injure both parts of India. The case for a united defence is even stronger. The Indian Armed Forces have been built up as a whole for the defence of India as a whole, and to break them in two would inflict a deadly blow on the long traditions and high degree of efficiency of the Indian Army and would entail the gravest dangers. The Indian Navy and Indian Air Force would become much less effective. The two sections of the suggested Pakistan contain the two most vulnerable frontiers in India and for a successful defence in depth the area of Pakistan would be insufficient.

9. A further consideration of importance is the greater difficulty which the Indian States would find in associating themselves with a divided British India

10. Finally, there is the geographical fact that the two halves of the proposed Pakistan state are separated by some seven hundred miles and

the communications between them both in war and peace would be dependent on the goodwill of Hindustan.

11. We are therefore unable to advise the British Government that the power which at present resides in British hands should be handed over to two entirely separate sovereign states.

12. This decision does not, however, blind us to the very real Muslim apprehensions that their culture and political and social life might become submerged in a purely unitary India, in which the Hindus with their greatly superior numbers must be a dominating element. To meet this the Congress have put forward a scheme under which Provinces would have full autonomy subject only to a minimum of Central subjects, such as Foreign Affairs, Defence and Communications.

Under this scheme Provinces, if they wished to take part in economic and administrative planning on a large scale, could cede to the Centre optional subjects in addition to the compulsory ones mentioned above.

13. Such a scheme would, in our view, present considerable constitutional disadvantages and anomalies. It would be very difficult to work a Central Executive and Legislature in which some Ministers, who dealt with compulsory subjects, were responsible to the whole of India while other Ministers, who dealt with optional subjects, would be responsible only to those Provinces who had elected to act together in respect of such subjects. This difficulty would be accentuated in the Central Legislature, where it would be necessary to exclude certain members from speaking and voting when subjects with which their Provinces were not concerned were under discussion. Apart from the difficulty of working such a scheme, we do not consider that it would be fair to deny to other Provinces, which did not desire to take the optional subjects at the Centre, the right to form themselves into a group for a similar purpose. This would indeed be no more than the exercise of their autonomous powers in a particular away.

14. Before putting forward our recommendation we turn to deal with the relationship of the Indian States to British India. It is quite clear that with the attainment of independence by British India, whether inside or outside the British Commonwealth, the relationship which has hitherto existed between the Rulers of the States and the British Crown will no longer be possible. Paramountcy can neither be retained by the British Crown nor transferred to the new Government. This fact has been fully recognised by those whom we interviewed from the States. They have at the same time assured us that the States are ready and willing to co-operate in the new development of India. The precise form which their co-operation will take must be a matter for negotiation during the building up of the new constitutional structure, and it by no means follows that it will be identical for all the States. We have not therefore dealt with the States in the same detail as the Provinces of British India in the paragraphs which follow.

15. We now indicate the nature of a solution which in our view would be just to the essential claims of all parties and would at the

same time be most likely to bring about a stable and practicable form of constitution for All-India.

We recommend that the constitution should take the following basic form:—

(1) There should be a Union of India, embracing both British India and the States which should deal with the following subjects: foreign affairs, defence, and communications; and should have the powers necessary to raise the finances required for the above subjects.

(2) The Union should have an executive and a legislature constituted from British Indian and States representatives. Any question raising a major communal issue in the legislature should require for its decision a majority of the representatives present and voting of each of the two major communities as well as a majority of all the members present and voting.

(3) All subjects other than the Union subjects and all residuary powers should vest in the Provinces.

(4) The States will retain all subjects and powers other than those ceded to the Union.

(5) Provinces should be free to form groups with executives and legislatures, and each group could determine the Provincial subjects to be taken in common.

(6) The constitutions of the Union and of the groups should contain a provision whereby any Province could, by a majority vote of its legislative assembly, call for a reconsideration of the terms of the constitution after an initial period of ten years and at ten-yearly intervals thereafter.

16. It is not our object to lay out the details of a constitution on the above programme but to set in motion the machinery whereby a constitution can be settled by Indians for Indians.

It has been necessary, however, for us to make this recommendation as to the broad basis of the future constitution because it became clear to us in the course of our negotiations that not until that had been done was there any hope of getting the two major communities to join in the setting up of the constitution-making machinery.

17. We now indicate the constitution-making machinery which we propose should be brought into being forthwith in order to enable a new constitution to be worked out.

18. In forming any Assembly to decide a new constitutional structure the first problem is to obtain as broad-based and accurate a representation of the whole population as is possible. The most satisfactory method obviously would be by election based on adult franchise, but any attempt to introduce such a step now would lead to a wholly unacceptable delay in the formulation of the new constitution. The only practicable course is to utilize the recently elected Provincial Legislative Assemblies as electing bodies. There are, however, two factors in their composition which make this difficult. First, the numerical strengths

of the Provincial Legislative Assemblies do not bear the same proportion to the total population in each Province. Thus, Assam, with a population of 10 million, has a Legislative Assembly of 108 members, while Bengal, with a population six times as large, has an Assembly of only 250. Secondly, owing to the weightage given to minorities by the Communal Award, the strengths of the several communities in each Provincial Legislative Assembly are not in proportion to their numbers in the Province. Thus the number of seats reserved for Muslims in the Bengal Legislative Assembly is only 48 per cent. of the total, although they form 55 per cent of the Provincial population. After a most careful consideration of the various methods by which these points might be corrected, we have come to the conclusion that the fairest and most practicable plan would be—

(a) to allot to each province a total number of seats proportional to its population, roughly in the ratio of one to a million, as the nearest substitute for representation by adult suffrage.

(b) to divide this provincial allocation of seats between the main communities in each province in proportion to their population.

(c) to provide that the representatives allotted to each community in a province shall be elected by the members of that community in its Legislative Assembly.

We think that for these purposes it is sufficient to recognise only three main communities in India, General, Muslim and Sikh, the "General" Community including all persons who are not Muslims or Sikhs. As smaller minorities would upon a population basis have little or no representation, since they would lose the weightage which assures them seats in Provincial Legislatures, we have made the arrangements set out in paragraph 20 below to give them a full representation upon all matters of special interest to minorities.

19. (i) We, therefore, propose that there shall be elected by each Provincial Legislative Assembly the following numbers of representatives, each part of the Legislative Assembly (General, Muslim or Sikh) electing its own representatives of the method of proportional representation with single transferable vote:—

TABLE OF REPRESENTATION

SECTION A

Province		General	Muslim	Total
Madras	...	45	4	49
Bombay	...	19	2	21
UP	...	47	8	55
Bihar	...	31	5	36
CP	...	16	1	17
Orissa	...	9	0	9
Total	...	167	20	187

SECTION B

Province		General	Muslim	Sikh	Total
Punjab	...	8	16	4	28
NWFP	...	0	3	0	3
Sind	...	1	3	0	4
Total	...	9	22	4	35

SECTION C

Province		General	Muslim	Total
Bengal	...	27	33	60
Assam	...	7	3	10
Total	...	34	36	70
Total for British India				292
Maximum for Indian States				93
Total				385

Note.—In order to represent the Chief Commissioner's Provinces there will be added to Section A the member representing Delhi in the Central Legislative Assembly, the member representing Ajmer-Merwara in the Central Legislative Assembly and a representative to be elected by the Coorg Legislative Council. To Section B will be added a representative of British Baluchistan.

(ii) It is the intention that the States would be given in the final Constituent Assembly appropriate representation which would not, on the basis of the calculation of population adopted for British India, exceed 93; but the method of selection will have to be determined by consultation. The States would in the preliminary stage be represented by a negotiating committee.

(iii) Representatives thus chosen shall meet at New Delhi as soon as possible.

(iv) A preliminary meeting will be held at which the general order of business will be decided, a chairman and other officers elected and an Advisory Committee (see paragraph 20 below) on the rights of citizens, minorities and tribal and excluded areas set up. Thereafter the provincial representatives will divide up into the three sections shown under A, B and C in the Table of Representation in sub-paragraph (1) of this paragraph.

(v) These sections shall proceed to settle the provincial constitutions for the provinces included in each section and shall also decide whether any group constitution shall be set up for those provinces and if so with what provincial subjects the group should deal. Provinces should have power to opt out of groups in accordance with the provisions of sub-clause (viii) below.

(vi) The representatives of the sections and the Indian States shall reassemble for the purpose of settling the Union constitution.

(vii) In the Union Constituent Assembly resolution varying the provisions of paragraph 15 above or raising any major communal issue shall require a majority of the representatives present and voting of each of the two major communities. The Chairman of the Assembly shall decide which, if any, resolutions raise major communal issues and shall, if so requested by a majority of the representatives of either of the major communities, consult the Federal Court before giving his decision.

(viii) As soon as the new constitutional arrangements have come into operation it shall be open to any province to elect to come out of any group in which it has been placed. Such a decision shall be taken by the legislature of the province after the first general election under the new constitution.

20. The Advisory Committee on the rights of citizens, minorities and tribal and excluded areas will contain due representation of the interests affected and their function will be to report to the Union Constituent Assembly upon the list of fundamental rights, clauses for protecting minorities, and a scheme for the administration of the tribal and excluded areas, and to advise whether these rights should be incorporated in the provincial, group, or Union constitutions.

21. His Excellency the Viceroy will forthwith request the provincial legislatures to proceed with the election of their representatives and the States to set up a negotiating committee.

It is hoped that the process of constitution-making can proceed as rapidly as the complexities of the task permit so that the interim period may be as short as possible.

22. It will be necessary to negotiate a treaty between the Union Constituent Assembly and the United Kingdom to provide for certain matters arising out of the transfer of power.

23. While the constitution-making proceeds the administration of India has to be carried on. We attach the greatest importance therefore to the setting up at once of an interim government having the support of the major political parties. It is essential during the interim period that there should be the maximum of co-operation in carrying through the difficult tasks that face the Government of India. Besides the heavy tasks of day-to-day administration, there is the grave danger of famine to be countered, there are decisions to be taken in many matters of post-war development which will have a far-reaching effect on India's future and there are important international conferences in which India has to be represented. For all these purposes a government having popular support is necessary. The Viceroy has already started discussions to this end and hopes soon to form an interim government in which all the portfolios, including that of War Member, will be held by Indian leaders having the full confidence of the people. The British Government, recognising the significance of the changes, will give the fullest measure of co-operation to the Government so formed in the accomplish-

ment of its tasks of administration and in bringing about as rapid and smooth a transition as possible.

24. To the leaders and people of India, who now have the opportunity of complete independence, we would finally say this. We and our Government and countrymen hoped that it would be possible for the Indian people themselves to agree upon the method of framing the new Constitution under which they will live. Despite the labours which we have shared with the Indian parties and the exercise of much patience and goodwill by all, this has not been possible. We, therefore, now lay before you proposals which, after listening to all sides and after much earnest thought, we trust will enable you to attain your independence in the shortest time and with the least danger of internal disturbance and conflict. These proposals may not, of course, completely satisfy all parties, but you will recognise with us that, at this supreme moment in Indian history, statesmanship demands mutual accommodation and we ask you to consider the alternative to acceptance of these proposals. After all the efforts which we and the Indian parties have made together for agreement, we must state that, in our view, there is small hope of a peaceful settlement by the agreement of the Indian parties alone. The alternative would, therefore, be a grave danger of violence, chaos and even civil war. The gravity and duration of such a disturbance cannot be foreseen, but it is certain that it would be a terrible disaster for many millions of men, women and children. This is a possibility which must be regarded with equal abhorrence by the Indian people, our own countrymen and the world as a whole. We, therefore, lay these proposals before you in the profound hope that they will be accepted and operated by you in the spirit of accommodation and goodwill in which they are offered. We appeal to all who have the future good of India at heart to extend their vision beyond their own community or interest to the interests of the whole four hundred millions of Indian people.

We hope that the new independent India may choose to be a member of the British Commonwealth. We hope, in any event, that you will remain in close and friendly association with our people. But these are matters for your own free choice. Whatever that choice may be, we look forward with you to your ever-increasing prosperity among the greatest nations of the world and to a future even more glorious than your past.

APPENDIX XV

GENERAL AUCHINLECK ON THE POSITION OF THE ARMED FORCES

(May 17, 1946)

Reference to Three Assemblies

Explaining the Cabinet Mission's proposals to the armed forces of India His Excellency the Commander-in-Chief, General Auchinleck in the course of a broadcast in Hindustani said:

As you have heard from H.E. the Viceroy, the British Government have put forward a scheme to enable Indians to make their own constitution and set up an independent Indian Government. As you all know, too, Members of the British Government and the Viceroy have for some time past been discussing with the leaders of the Muslim League and of the Congress. They have been trying to decide what kind of Government shall be set up in India. Their object is to make good the promise of the British Government that in future India shall be governed entirely by her own people, free from all control by Britain, and free to remain within the British Commonwealth or to go outside as she likes.

In spite of every attempt to find a form of Government which would be acceptable to the Congress and the Muslim League, no agreement has been reached.

The Muslim League considers that there must be two independent and separate Governments in India, Pakistan for the Muslims and Hindustan for the Hindus. The Congress thinks that India must not be divided and that there should be one Central Government with the provinces controlling their own affairs to the greatest possible extent.

This, very briefly, is the position taken up by the two main political parties.

It was hoped that between the two points of views some compromise acceptable to both parties might be found. This has, however, not been found possible, although both parties have, for the sake of good will, modified their views to a considerable extent.

The British Government, therefore, having failed to get the two principal political parties to agree, has decided that it is their duty to the people of India to lay down that everything shall be done in order to give India her independence as soon as possible in an orderly and peaceful manner so that the mass of the people may be put to the least inconvenience and disturbance.

In making these arrangements, the British Government has tried to ensure justice and freedom for the smaller as well as for the large sections of the people of India.

The British Government realises that the Muslims have a real fear that they may be forced to live for always under a Hindu Government and that any new form of government must be such as to make this fear groundless for all time.

With this in view, the possibility of setting up a completely separate and independent Muslim State of Pakistan has been most carefully considered from every point of view and without any partiality at all.

As a result of this examination the British Government has been forced to conclude that the setting up of completely independent states not linked together in any way would not result in a settlement of the differences between Hindu and Muslim.

The setting up of two or more independent Governments would, in their opinion, result in great loss and danger to India in the future.

They, therefore, cannot agree to divide India into separate states, though they do think that some way must be found for the predominantly

Muslim areas to govern themselves if they wish to do so and to live their own lives. This is also recognised by the Hindus and the Congress Party.

The British Government, therefore, have approved neither the setting up of completely separate states nor the retention of all power at the Centre. They consider that although the different areas should have a large measure of independence if the people desire it, the responsibility for the Army, Navy and Air Force and for the defence of the whole of India in war, must rest with one authority for the whole of India.

Apart from this, they have accepted the principle that each province or group of provinces may have powers to manage its own affairs as desired by its own people without interference from the Centre.

These proposals are meant to ensure that all creeds and classes shall have their say in how they are to be governed and also to prevent any one section of the people being forced to live under the rule of any other section, without being sure that they will have the right to live their lives in their own way without fear or persecution.

The details of this new system of government for India must be worked out by the people of India themselves. It is not the task of the British Government to do this.

To carry on the administration of the country while a new system of government is worked out, the Viceroy proposes to form an interim government composed of himself and of leaders of political opinion who have the confidence of the people.

In this temporary Government, the post of War Member which is at present held by the Commander-in-Chief (that is myself) will be held by a civilian who will be an Indian. I shall continue to be responsible for the command and welfare of the Army, Navy and Air Force but all political matters will be in the hands of the new War Member under whom I shall serve, just as the Commanders in Britain serve under civilian ministers.

While this temporary Government carries on the daily business of governing the country, it is proposed that there should be set up three assemblies composed of representatives of all parties and creeds and classes, and elected by the Provincial Legislatures.

It will be the task of these three Assemblies together with representatives from the Indian States to decide how India will be governed in the future.

The British Government hopes that in this way peace and security will come to India under the rule of her own leaders and that she will become great and prosperous as she deserves.

While these discussions and meetings are going on, it is the duty of the Navy, Army and Air Force to continue to serve the Government and to carry out its orders.

As I have said, this temporary Government will be an Indian Government composed of members chosen from the leaders of the main political parties in the country who have full confidence of the people.

There is no doubt that today there is danger of strife and disorder in the country. Whether you are in the Army, the Navy or the Air Force, you all know the good that comes from discipline and toleration. You have also learned to live together, Hindu, Muslim, Sikh and Christian, in the service of your country without quarrelling or jealousy.

You have learned each to respect the other and to work side by side for one object—the good of your country.

In this you have set an example to all India.

I trust you, as I have always trusted you, to go on setting this example and to do your duty, as you have always done it in war and peace.

I for my part shall do the same. So long as I am here you may rely on me to safeguard your interest in the future as in the past.

APPENDIX XVI

THE CABINET MISSION'S STATEMENT

(May 25, 1946)

The Delegation have considered the statement of the President of the Muslim League dated May 22 and the resolution dated 24th May of the Working Committee of the Congress.

2. The position is that since the Indian leaders, after prolonged discussion, failed to arrive at an agreement, the Delegation put forward their recommendations as the nearest approach to reconciling the view of the two main parties. The scheme stands as a whole and can only succeed if it is accepted and worked in a spirit of co-operation.

3. The Delegation wish also to refer briefly to a few points that have been raised in the statement and resolution.

4. The authority and the functions of the Constituent Assembly, and the procedure which it is intended to follow are clear from the Cabinet Delegation's statement. Once the Constituent Assembly is formed and working on this basis there is no intention of interfering with its discretion or questioning its decisions. When the Constituent Assembly has completed its labours, His Majesty's Government will recommend to Parliament such action as may be necessary for the cession of sovereignty to the Indian people, subject only to two matters which are mentioned in the statement and which, we believe, are not controversial, namely: adequate provision for the protection of the minorities (paragraph 20 of the statement) and willingness to conclude a treaty with His Majesty's Government to cover matters arising out of the transfer of power (paragraph 22 of the statement).

5. It is a consequence of the system of election that a few Europeans can be elected to the Constituent Assembly. Whether the right so given will be exercised is a matter for them to decide.

6. The representative of Baluchistan will be elected in a joint meeting of the Shahi-Jirga and the non-official members of the Quetta Municipality.

7. In Coorg the whole Legislative Council will have the right to vote but the official members will receive instructions not to take part in the election.

8. The interpretation put by the Congress resolution on paragraph 15 of the statement to the effect that the Provinces can in the first instance

make the choice whether or not to belong to the Section in which they are placed, does not accord with the Delegation's intentions. The reasons for the grouping of the Provinces are well known and this is an essential feature of the scheme and can only be modified by agreement between the parties. The right to opt out of the groups after the constitution-making has been completed will be exercised by the people themselves, since at the first election under the new provincial Constitution this question of opting out will obviously be a major issue and all those entitled to vote under the new franchise will be able to take their share in a truly democratic decision.

9. The question of how the States representatives should be appointed to the Constituent Assembly is clearly one which must be discussed with the States. It is not a matter for decision by the Delegation.

10. It is agreed that the interim Government will have a new basis. That basis is that all portfolios including that of the War Member will be held by Indians and that the members will be selected in consultation with the Indian political parties. These are very significant changes in the Government of India and a long step towards independence. H.M.G. will recognise the effect of these changes, will attach the fullest weight to them and will give to the Indian Government the greatest possible freedom in the exercise of the day-to-day administration of India.

11. As the Congress statement recognizes, the present Constitution must continue during the interim period; and the interim Government cannot, therefore, be made legally responsible to the Central Legislature. There is, however, nothing to prevent the members of the Government, individually or by common consent, from resigning if they fail to pass an important measure through the Legislature, or if a vote of no-confidence is passed against them.

12. There is, of course, no intention of retaining British troops in India against the wish of an independent India under the new Constitution; but during the interim period, which it is hoped will be short, the British Parliament has under the present Constitution the ultimate responsibility for the security of India and it is necessary, therefore, that British troops should remain.

APPENDIX XVII

THE CABINET MISSION AND THE VICEROY ON INTERIM GOVT.
(June 16, 1946)

1. H. E. the Viceroy, in consultation with the members of the Cabinet Mission, has for some time been exploring the possibilities of forming a coalition Government drawn from the two major parties and certain of the minorities. The discussions have revealed the difficulties which exist for the two major parties in arriving at any agreed basis for the formation of such a Government.

2. The Viceroy and the Cabinet Mission appreciate these difficulties and the efforts which the two parties have made to meet them. They consi-

der, however, that no useful purpose can be served by further prolonging these discussions. It is indeed urgently necessary that a strong and representative Interim Government should be set up to conduct the very heavy and important business that has to be carried through.

3. The Viceroy is, therefore, issuing invitations to the following to serve as members of the Interim Government on the basis that the constitution-making will proceed in accordance with the statement of May 16:—

Sardar Baldev Singh, Sir N. P. Engineer, Mr. Jagjiwan Ram, Pandit Jawaharlal Nehru, Mr. M. A. Jinnah, Nawabzada Liaquat Ali Khan, Mr. H. K. Mahtab, Dr. John Matthai, Nawab Mohammad Ismail Khan, Khawaja Sir Nazimuddin, Sardar Abdur Rab Nishtar, Mr. C. Rajagopalachari, Dr. Rajendra Prasad and Sardar Vallabhbhai Patel.

If any of those invited is unable for personal reasons to accept, the Viceroy will, after consultation, invite some other persons in his place.

4. The Viceroy will arrange the distribution of portfolios in consultation with the leaders of the two major parties.

5. The above composition of the Interim Government is in no way to be taken as a precedent for the solution of any other communal question. It is an expedient put forward to solve the present difficulty only, and to obtain the best available coalition Government.

6. The Viceroy and the Cabinet Mission believe that Indians of all communities desire to arrive at a speedy settlement of this matter so that the process of consttitution-making can go forward and that the Government of India may be carried on as efficiently as possible in the meantime.

7. They, therefore, hope that all parties especially the two major parties will accept this proposal so as to overcome the present obstacles, and will co-operate for the successful carrying on of the Interim Government. Should this proposal be accepted the Viceroy will aim at inaugurating the new Government about the 26th of June.

8. In the event of the two major parties or either of them proving unwilling to join in the setting up of a coalition Government on the above lines, it is the intention of the Viceroy to proceed with the formation of an Interim Government which will be as representative as possible of those willing to accept the statement of May 16.

9. The Viceroy is also directing the Governors of the Provinces to summon the Provincial Legislative Assemblies forthwith to proceed with the elections necessary for the setting up of the constitution-making machinery as put forward in the statement of May 26.

APPENDIX XVIII

CONGRESS STRESS ON DEFECTS

The following is the full text of the resolution of the Congress Working Committee adopted on June 26, 1946:

On May 24, the Working Committee passed a resolution on the statement dated May 16 issued by the British Cabinet Delegation and the

Viceroy. In this resolution they pointed out some defects in the statement and gave their own interpretation of certain parts of it.

Since then the Committee have been continuously engaged in giving earnest consideration to the proposals made on behalf of the British Government in the statements of May 16 and June 16 and have considered the correspondence in regard to them between the Congress President and the members of the Cabinet Delegation and the Viceroy.

The Committee have examined both these sets of proposals from the point of view of the Congress objective of immediate independence and the opening out of the avenues leading to the rapid advance of the masses, economically and socially, so that their material standards may be raised and poverty, malnutrition, famine and the lack of the necessaries of life may be ended, and all the people of the country may have the freedom and opportunity to grow and develop according to their genius. These proposals fall short of these objectives. Yet the Committee considered them earnestly in all their aspects because of their desire to find some way for the peaceful settlement of India's problem and the ending of the conflict between India and England.

The kind of independence Congress has aimed at is the establishment of a united, democratic Indian federation, with a Central authority, which would command respect from the nations of the world, maximum provincial autonomy and equal rights for all men and women in the country. The limitation of the Central authority as contained in the proposals, as well as the system of grouping of provinces, weakened the whole structure and was unfair to some provinces such as the N. W. F. Province and Assam, and to some of the minorities, notably the Sikhs. The Committee disapproved of this. They felt, however, that, taking the proposals as a whole, there was sufficient scope for enlarging and strengthening the Central authority and for fully ensuring the right of a province to act according to its choice in regard to grouping, and to give protection to such minorities as might otherwise be placed at a disadvantage. Certain other objections were also raised on their behalf, notably the possibility of non-nationals taking any part in the constitution-making. It is clear that it would be a breach of both the letter and spirit of the statement of May 16 if any non-Indian participated in voting or standing for election to the Constituent Assembly.

In the proposals for an Interim Government contained in the statement of June 16 the defects related to matters of vital concern to the Congress. Some of these have been pointed out in the letter dated June 25 of the Congress President to the Viceroy. The Provisional Government must have power and authority and responsibility and should function in fact, if not in law, as a *de facto* independent Government leading to the full independence to come. The members of such a Government can only hold themselves responsible to the people and not to any external authority. In the formation of a provisional or other Government Congressmen can never give up the national character of the Congress, or accept an artificial and unjust parity, or agree to the veto of a communal group. The Committee are unable to accept the proposals for the formation of an Interim Government as contained in the statement of June 16.

The Committee have, however, decided that the Congress would join the proposed Constituent Assembly, with a view to framing the constitution of a free, united and democratic India.

While the Committee have agreed to Congress participation in the Constituent Assembly, it is in their opinion essential that a representative and responsible provisional national Government be formed at the earliest possible date. A continuation of authoritarian and unrepresentative Government can only add to the suffering of famishing masses and increased discontent. It will also put in jeopardy the work of the Constituent Assembly, which can only function in a free environment.

The Working Committee recommend accordingly to the All-India Congress Committee, and for the purpose of considering and ratifying this recommendation they convene an emergent meeting of the A.-I.C.C. in Bombay on July 6 and 7.

APPENDIX XIX

MUSLIM LEAGUE'S ANXIETY

The full text of the resolution passed by the Council of the All-India Muslim League on June 6, 1946 is as follows:

This meeting of the Council of the All-India Muslim League, after having carefully considered the statement issued by the Cabinet Mission and H. E. the Viceroy on May 16 and other relevant statements and documents officially issued in connection therewith, and after having examined the proposals set forth in the said statement in all their bearings and implications, places on record the following views for the guidance of the nation and direction to the Working Committee:

That the reference made and the conclusions recorded in paragraphs 6, 7, 8, 9, 10 and 11 of the statement concerning the Muslim demand for the establishment of full sovereign Pakistan as the only solution of the Indian constitutional problem are unwarranted, unjustified and unconvincing and should not, therefore, have found place in a state document issued on behalf and with the authority of the British Government.

These paragraphs are couched in such language and contain such mutilations of established facts that the Cabinet Mission have clearly been prompted to include them in their statement solely with the object of appeasing the Hindus in utter disregard of Muslim sentiments. Furthermore, the contents of the aforesaid paragraphs are in conflict and inconsistent with the admissions made by the Mission themselves in paragraphs 5 and 12 of their statement which are to the following effect:—

First, the Mission "were greatly impressed by the very genuine and acute anxiety of the Muslims lest they should find themselves subject to perpetual Hindu majority rule."

Second, "this feeling has become so strong and widespread amongst the Muslims that it cannot be allayed by mere paper safeguards."

Third, "if there is to be internal peace in India, it must be secured by measures which will assure to the Muslims a control in all matters vital to their culture, religion, economic or other interests."

Fourth, very real Muslim apprehensions exist that "their culture and political and social life might become submerged in a purely unitary India, in which Hindus with their greatly superior numbers must be a dominating element."

In order that there may be no manner of doubt in any quarter, the Council of the All-India Muslim League reiterates that the attainment of the goal of complete sovereign Pakistan still remains the unalterable objective of the Muslims of India for the achievement of which they will, if necessary, employ every means in their power and consider no sacrifice or suffering too great.

That notwithstanding the affront offered to Muslim sentiments by a choice of injudicious words in the preamble of the statement of the Cabinet Mission the Muslim League, having regard to the grave issues involved, and prompted by its earnest desire for a peaceful solution, if possible, of the Indian constitutional problem, and inasmuch as the basis and the foundation of Pakistan are inherent in the Mission's Plan, by virtue of the compulsory grouping of the six Muslim provinces, in Sections B and C, is willing to co-operate with the constitution-making machinery proposed in the scheme outlined by the Mission, in the hope that it would ultimately result in the establishment of complete sovereign Pakistan and in the consummation of the goal of independence for the major nations, and all the other people inhabiting this vast sub-continent.

It is for these reasons that the Muslim League is accepting the scheme and will join the constitution-making body and will keep in view the opportunity and the right of secession of provinces or groups from the Union which have been provided in the Mission's plan by implication.

The ultimate attitude of the Muslim League will depend on the final outcome of the labours of the constitution-making body and on the final shape of the constitutions which may emerge from the deliberations of that body jointly and separately in its three sections.

The Muslim League also reserves the right to modify and revise the policy and attitude set forth in this resolution at any time during the progress of deliberations of the constitution-making body or the Constituent Assembly or thereafter if the course of events so require, bearing in mind the fundamental principles and details hereinbefore adumbrated to which the Muslim League is irrevocably committed.

That with regard to the arrangements for the proposed Interim Government at the Centre, this Council authorises its President to negotiate with H.E. the Viceroy and to take such decisions and actions as he deems fit and proper.

APPENDIX XX

CHANGE IN LEAGUE'S ATTITUDE

The following is the full text of the resolution adopted by the Muslim League Council at Bombay on July 30, 1946, withdrawing acceptance of the Cabinet Mission's proposals:

On June 6, 1946, the Council of the All-India Muslim League accepted the scheme embodied in the statement of the Cabinet Delegation and the Viceroy dated May 16, 1946, and explained by them in their statement dated May 25, 1946. The scheme of the Cabinet Delegation fell far short of the demand of the Muslim nation for the immediate establishment of an independent and fully sovereign State of Pakistan comprising the six Muslim provinces, but the Council accepted a Union Centre for 10 years strictly confined to three subjects, viz., defence, foreign affairs and communications, since the scheme laid down certain fundamentals and safeguards and provided for the grouping separately of the six Muslim provinces in Sections B and C for the purpose of framing their provincial and Group constitutions unfettered by the Union in any way; and also with a view to ending the Hindu-Muslim deadlock peacefully and accelerating the attainment of the freedom of the peoples of India.

In arriving at this decision the Council was also greatly influenced by the statement of the President, which he made with the authority of the Viceroy, that the Interim Government, which was an integral part of the Mission's scheme, was going to be formed on the basis of the formula: five Muslim League, five Congress, one Sikh and one Indian Christian or Anglo-Indian, and the most important portfolios to be distributed equally between the two major parties, the Muslim League and the Congress. The Council authorized the President to take such decision and action with regard to further details of setting up the Interim Government as he deemed fit and proper. In that very resolution, the Council also reserved the right to modify and revise this policy, if the course of events so required.

The British Government have committed a breach of faith with the Muslim League in that the Cabinet Delegation and the Viceroy went back on the original formula of 5: 5: 2 for the setting up of the Interim Government to placate the Congress.

The Viceroy, having gone back on the original formula upon the faith of which the Muslim League Council came to their decision of June 6, suggested a new basis of 5: 5: 3 and, after carrying on considerable negotiations with the Congress and having failed to get the Congress to agree, intimated to the parties on June 15 that he and the Cabinet Delegation would issue their final statement with regard to the setting up of the Interim Government.

Accordingly, on June 16, the President of the Muslim League received a statement embodyng what was announced to be the final decision for setting up the Interim Government by the Viceroy, making it clear that, if either of the two major parties refused to accept the Statement of June 16, the Viceroy would proceed to form the Interim Government with the major party accepting it and such other representatives as were willing to join. This was explicitly laid down in Paragraph 8 of the Statement of June 16.

Even this final decision of the Cabinet Mission of June 16 with regard to the formation of the Interim Government was rejected by the Congress, whereas the Muslim League definitely accepted it—although it was different from the original formula i.e., 5: 5: 2—because the Viceroy provided safeguards and gave other assurances in his letter dated June 20, 1946.

The Viceroy, however, scrapped the proposal of June 16 and postponed the formation of the Interim Government on the plea concocted by the legalistic talents of the Cabinet Mission putting a most fantastic and dishonest construction upon Paragraph 8 of the Statement to the effect that, as both the major parties, i.e., the Muslim League and the Congress, had accepted the Statement of May 16, the question of the Interim Government could only be taken up in consultation with the representatives of both the parties *de novo*.

Even assuming that this construction was tenable, for which there is no warrant, the Congress, by their conditional acceptance with reservations and interpretations of their own, as laid down in the letter of the President of the Congress dated June 25 and the resolution of the Working Committee of the Congress passed at Delhi on June 26, repudiating the very fundamentals of the scheme had, in fact, rejected the Statement of May 16, and, therefore, in no event was there any justification, whatsoever, for abandoning the final proposals of June 16.

As regards the proposal embodied in the Statement of May 16 and 25 of the Cabinet Delegation and the Viceroy, the Muslim League alone of the two major parties had accepted it.

The Congress have not accepted it because their acceptance is conditional and subject to their own interpretation which is contrary to the authoritative statements of the Delegation and the Viceroy issued on May 16 and 25. The Congress have made it clear that they do not accept any of the terms or fundamentals of the scheme, but that they have agreed only to go into the Constituent Assembly and to do nothing else; and that the Constituent Assembly is a sovereign body and can take such decisions as it may think proper in total disregard of the terms and the basis on which it is to be set up. Subsequently they made this clear beyond doubt in the speeches that were made at the meeting of the AICC in Bombay on July 6 by prominent members of the Congress and in the statement of Pandit Nehru, the President of the Congress, to a Press conference on July 10 in Bombay and then again, even after the debate in Parliament, at a public speech by him at Delhi on July 22.

The result is that, of the two major parties, the Muslim League alone has accepted the Statements of May 16 and 25 according to the spirit and letter of the proposals embodied therein. In spite of the attention of the Secretary of State for India having been drawn to this situation by the statement of the President of the Muslim League on July 13 from Hyderabad (Dn.), neither Sir Stafford Cripps in the House of Commons nor Lord Pethick-Lawrence in the House of Lords, in the course of the recent debate, has provided or suggested any means or machinery to prevent the Constituent Assembly from taking decisions which would be *ultra vires* and not competent for the Assembly to do. The only reply to this matter that the Secretary of State gave was the mere expression of a pious hope when he said 'that would not be fair to the other parties who go in.'

Once the Constituent Assembly has been summoned and meets, there is no provision or power that could prevent any decision from being taken by the Congress with its overwhelming majority, which would not be competent for the Assembly to take, or which would be *ultra vires* of it, and, however repugnant it might be to the letter or spirit of the scheme, it would rest entirely with the majority to take such decisions as they may think proper or suit them ; and the Congress had already secured by sheer number an overwhelming Caste Hindu majority, and they will be in a position to use the Assembly in a manner which they have already declared, i.e., that they will wreck the basic form of the grouping of provinces, and extend the scope, powers and subjects of the Union Centre which is confined strictly to three specific subjects as laid down in Paragraph 15 and provided for in Paragraph 19 of the Statement of May 16.

The Cabinet Delegation and the Viceroy collectively and individually have stated several times that the basic principles were laid down to enable the major parties to join the Constituent Assembly and that the scheme cannot succeed unless it is worked in a spirit of co-operation. The attitude of the Congress already shows that these conditions precedent for the successful working of constitution-making do not exist. This fact, taken together with the policy of the British Government of sacrificing the interests of the Muslim nation and some other weaker sections of the peoples of India, particularly the Scheduled Castes, to appease the Congress, and the way in which they have been going back on their oral and written solemn pledges and assurances given from time to time to the Muslims, leave no doubt that, in these circumstances, participation by Muslims in the proposed constitution-making machinery is fraught with danger ; and the Council, therefore, hereby withdraws its acceptance of the Cabinet Mission's proposals which was communicated to the Secretary of State for India by the President of the Muslim League on June 6, 1946.'

APPENDIX XXI

MEMORANDUM ON STATES' TREATIES AND PARAMOUNTCY

The following is the full text of the Memorandum on States' Treaties and Paramountcy presented by the Cabinet Delegation to the Chancellor of the Chamber of Princes on May 22, 1946:

1. Prior to the recent statement of the British Prime Minister in the House of Commons an assurance was given to the Princes that there was

no intention on the part of the Crown to initiate any change in their relationship with the Crown or the rights guaranteed by their treaties and engagements without their consent. It was at the same time stated that the Princes' consent to any changes which might emerge as a result of negotiations would not unreasonably be withheld. The Chamber of Princes has since confirmed that the Indian States fully share the general desire in the country for the immediate attainment by India of her full stature His Majesty's Government have now declared that if the Succession Government or Governments in British India desire independence, no obstacle would be placed in their way. The effect of these announcements is that all those concerned with the future of India wish her to attain a position of independence within or without the British Commonwealth. The Delegation have come here to assist in resolving the difficulties which stand in the way of India fulfilling this wish.

2. During the interim period, which must elapse before the coming into operation of a new constitutional structure under which British India will be independent or fully self-governing, paramountcy will remain in operation. But the British Government could not and will not in any circumstances transfer paramountcy to an Indian Government.

3. In the meanwhile, the Indian States are in a position to play an important part in the formulation of the new constitutional structure for India, and H.M.G. have been informed by the Indian States that they desire in their own interests and in the interests of India as a whole, both to make their contribution to the framing of the structure, and to take their due place in it when it is completed. In order to facilitate this they will doubtless strengthen their position by doing everything possible to ensure that their administrations conform to the highest standard. Where adequate standards cannot be achieved within the existing resources of the State they will no doubt arrange in suitable cases to form or join administrative units large enough to enable them to be fitted into the constitutional structure. It will also strengthen the position of States during this formulative period if the various Governments which have not already done so take steps to place themselves in close and constant touch with public opinion in their States by means of representative institutions.

4. During the interim period it will be necessary for the States to conduct negotiations with British India in regard to the future regulation of matters of common concern, especially in the economic and financial field. Such negotiations, which will be necessary whether the States desire to participate in the new Indian constitutional structure or not, will occupy a considerable period of time, and since some of these negotiations may well be incomplete when the new structure comes into being, it will, in order to avoid administrative difficulties, be necessary to arrive at an understanding between the States and those likely to control the Succession Government or Governments that for a period of time the then existing arrangements as to these matters of common concern should continue until new arrangements are completed. In this matter, the British Government and the Crown Representative will lend such assistance as they can, should it be so desired.

5. When a new fully self-governing or independent Government or Governments come into being in British India, H.M.G.'s influence with these Governments will not be such as to enable them to carry out the obligations of paramountcy. Moreover, they cannot contemplate that British troops would be retained in India for this purpose. Thus, as a logical sequ ence and in view of the desires expressed to them on behalf of the Indian States, His Majesty's Government will cease to exercise the powers of paramountcy. This means that the rights of the States which flow from their relationship to the Crown will no longer exist and that all the rights surrendered by the States to the Paramount Power will return to the States. Political arrangements between the States on the one side and the British Crown and British India on the other will thus be brought to an end. The void will have to be filled either by the States entering into a federal relationship with the Succession Government or Governments in British India, or failing this, entering into particular political arrangements with it or them.

An explanatory note issued a few hours after the Memorandum said:

The Cabinet Delegation desire to make it clear that the document issued today entitled "Memorandum on States' Treaties and Paramountcy presented by the Cabinet Delegation to His Highness the Chancellor of the Chamber of Princes" was drawn up before the Mission began its discussions with party leaders and represented the substance of what they communicated to the representatives of the States at their first interviews with the Mission. This is the explanation of the use of the words "succession Government or Governments of British India," an expression which would not of course have been used after the issue of the Delegation's recent statement.

APPENDIX XXII

PRINCES ACCEPT WHITE PAPER

The following statement was issued by the Nawab of Bhopal, Chancellor of the Chamber of Princes, on behalf of the Standing Committee on June 10, 1946:

The Standing Committee of the Chamber of Princes have in consultation with the Committee of Ministers and the Constitutional Advisory Committee given careful consideration to the statement issued by the Cabinet Delegation and His Excellency the Viceroy on May 16, 1946. They have also examined the Delegation's memorandum on States' treaties and paramountcy, and the further statement of May 26. They are of the view that the plan provides the necessary machinery for the attainment by India of independence as well as a fair basis for further negotiations. They welcome the declaration of the Cabinet Mission in regard to paramountcy, but certain adjustments for the interim period will be necessary.

There are, however, a few points in the plan which still require elucidation. There are also several matters of fundamental importance which are left over for negotiation and settlement. The Standing Committee have therefore accepted the invitation of His Excellency the Viceroy to set up a negotiating committee and have authorised the Chancellor to arrange discussions as contemplated in the plan. It is proposed to place the results of these negotiations before a general conference of Rulers and representatives of States.

. As regards the arrangements for the interim period, the Standing Committee confirm the following proposals made by the Chancellor:—

(*a*) That a special committee may be set up consisting of representatives of the States and of the Central Government to discuss and reach agreement on, matters of common concern during the interim period ;

(*b*) That disputes on justiciable issues and on fiscal, economic, or financial matters should be referable to courts of arbitration as a matter of right ;

(*c*) That in personal and dynastic matters the agreed procedure should be implemented in letter and spirit, and the Crown Representative should ordinarily consult the Chancellor and a few other Princes if not objected to by the States concerned ;

(*d*) That in agreement with the States, a machinery may be provided for the early settlement of the pending cases and for the revision, at the instance of the States concerned, of the existing arrangements in regard to such subjects as railways, ports and customs.

The Committee have, therefore, authorised the Chancellor to conduct further negotiations with a view to reaching early decisions.

The Standing Committee endorse the suggestion made by the Cabinet Delegation that the States will doubtlessly strengthen their position by doing everything possible to ensure that their administrations conform to the highest standard. Where adequate standards cannot be achieved within the existing resources of the State they will no doubt arrange in suitable cases to form or join administrative units large enough to enable them to be fitted into the constitutional structure. It will also strengthen the position of the States during this formulative period if the various Governments, which have not already done so, take active steps to place themselves in close and constant touch with public opinion in their states by means of representative institutions.

The Standing Committee wish to emphasise the necessity for the States, which have not done so, to declare immediately their decision to follow the lines of internal reforms laid down in the declaration made by the Chancellor at the last session of the Chamber of Princes and to take necessary steps to implement that decision within 12 months.

APPENDIX XXIII

CONGRESS APPEAL FOR COOPERATION

The following is the text of the resolution adopted by the Congress Working Committee on July 10, 1946:

The Working Committee regret to note that the Council of the All-India Muslim League, reversing their previous decision have decided not to participate in the Constituent Assembly. In this period of rapid transition from dependence on a foreign Power to full independence when vast and intricate political and economic problems have to be faced and solved, the largest measure of co-operation among the people of India and their representatives is called for, so that the change-over would be smooth and to the advantage of all concerned.

The Committee realize that there are differences in the outlook and the objective of the Congress and the Muslim League. Nevertheless in the larger interests of the country as a whole and the freedom of the people in India, the Committee appeal for the co-operation of all those who seek freedom and the good of the country, in the hope that co-operation in the common tasks may lead to the solution of many of India's problems.

The Committee further note that criticisms have been advanced on behalf of the Muslim League to the effect that the Congress acceptance of the proposals contained in the statement of May 16 was conditional. The Committee wish to make it clear that, while they did not approve of all the proposals contained in this statement, they accepted the scheme in its entirety. .

They interpreted it so as to resolve the inconsistency contained in it and fill the omissions in accordance with the principles laid down in that statement. They hold that provincial autonomy is a basic provision and each province has the right to decide whether to form or join a group or not. The question of interpretations will be decided by the procedure laid down in the statement itself and the Congress will advise its representatives in the Constituent Assembly to function accordingly.

The Committee have emphasized the sovereign character of the Constituent Assembly, that is its right to function and draw up the constitution for India without interference of any external Power or authority, but the Assembly will naturally function within the internal limitations which are inherent in its task, and will further seek the largest measure of co-operation in drawing up the constitution of free India, allowing the greatest measure of freedom and protection for all just claims and interests.

It was with this objective and with the desire to function in the Constituent Assembly and make it a success that the Working Committee passed the resolution of June 26, 1946, which was subsequently ratified by the A.-I.C.C. on July 7. By that decision of the A.-I.C.C. they must stand, and they propose to proceed accordingly with their work in the Constituent Assembly.

The Committee hope that the Muslim League and all others concerned will in the wider interests of the nation as well as of their own join in this great task.

APPENDIX XXIV

LEAGUE'S CRITICISM

The following is the full text of Mr. Jinnah's statement of September 12, 1946, criticising the resolution of the Congress Working Committee:

The entire scheme of the British Cabinet Mission consisted of the long-term plan statement of May 16 and May 25 and the short-term proposal of setting up an Interim Government, and these two formed integral parts of the whole scheme and were interdependent and indivisible. The Muslim League accepted both whereas the Congress rejected the Interim Government proposal of June 16 and accepted the statement of May 16 conditionally with reservations and their own interpretations.

The Cabinet Delegation and the Viceroy scrapped the Interim Government proposal of June 16 and treated the Congress decision communicated to them on June 25 and 26 wrongly as acceptance. The so-called acceptance was, in fact, a rejection

After that the Viceroy declined to postpone the elections for the Constituent Assembly on the plea that arrangements for it had gone too far ahead, although the arrangements with regard to the Interim Government were complete and the resignations of his then members of the Executive Council were held by him, and according to the statement of June 16 the Interim Government was to be set up on or about June 26. Yet it was scrapped. After this the Muslim League was free to take such decision as they thought proper as the entire basis of the scheme had fallen through. It was only the Council of the All-India Muslim League that could finally have decided our attitude, and in these circumstances we summoned the Council of the All-India Muslim League at Bombay on July 27-29 and they decided to withdraw our acceptance formally.

In the meantime, we decided to contest the elections to the Constituent Assembly in order to prevent undesirable people getting in as Muslim representatives, and we captured 95 per cent of Muslim seats. Meanwhile, before the Council of the League had met Congress leaders, including the President, in their speeches at the A.-I.C.C. meeting on July 6 and 7 made pronouncements which created grave apprehensions in League circles which were expressed by Mr. Liaquat Ali Khan, Secretary of the All-India Muslim League, in his statement from Delhi, and in my statement from Hyderabad on July 13, notably with regard to the pronouncement of Pandit Nehru on July 10 at a Press Conference, which left no doubt as to the intentions of the Congress. Both these statements were given in the Press by news agencies.

The debate in Parliament, which took place on July 18, showed that the British Government approved of the scrapping of the Interim Government by the Cabinet Delegation and the Viceroy, and paid no attention whatever to the new situation that had arisen, not only by pronouncements and clarifications and interpretations given by the Congress leaders which were published throughout the country, but also by the fact that the Assam Assembly, while electing its representatives to the Constituent Assembly, had under instructions of the Congress High Command, passed a resolution giving a mandate not only to the Congress members but also to the representatives of the Muslims elected by a separate bloc of Muslim members, to have nothing to do with the C Group from the very start.

This clearly repudiated one of the fundamental terms of the statement of May 16 and this is an instance of how the majority acted, although it is highly doubtful whether the Assam Assembly was competent to give such a mandate to the representatives to the Constituent Assembly.

The latest resolution of the Congress Working Committee passed at Wardha on August 10 does not carry us anywhere, because it is only a repetition of the Congress stand taken by them from the very beginning. only put in different language and phraseology.

This is what they say with regard to their decision on the long-term plan:

> 'The Committee further noted that criticisms have been advanced on behalf of the Muslim League to the effect that Congress acceptance of the proposals contained in the statement of May 16 was conditional. The Committee wish to make it clear that, while they did not approve of all the proposals contained in this statement, they accepted the scheme in its entirety.'

The resolution further continues:

> 'They interpreted it so as to resolve the inconsistency contained in it, and fill the omission in accordance with the principle laid down in that statement.'

Therefore, to start with, they are free to resolve the inconsistency and fill in the omissions. How can that be in accordance with the principle laid down in that statement? What is the inconsistency and what are the omissions?

> The resolution further says: 'They hold that provincial autonomy is a basic provision and each province has the right to decide whether to form, or join a group or not.'

Therefore, they maintain that it is open to the Congress to decide whether any particular province could join the group or not. But they go on to say:

> 'The question of interpretations will be decided by the procedure laid down in the statement itself and the Congress will advise its representatives to the Constituent Assembly to function accordingly.'

Who will decide this question of interpretations and by what procedure and what is the procedure laid down in the statement for the purpose of interpreting the Statement or any clause thereof, except by the brute majority?

The resolution then says that the Committee have emphasized the sovereign character of the Constituent Assembly, that is, the right to function and draw up the constitution for India without the interference of any external power or authority. But the Assembly will naturally function within the internal limitations which are inherent in its task, and will further seek the largest measure of co-operation in drawing up the Constitution of a free India, allowing the greatest measure of freedom and protection for all just claims and interests.

Therefore it is obvious that they still hold that this constitution-making machinery is a sovereign Constituent Assembly but they resent any interference of any external power and authority. The question is how this Assembly will function and they make it clear that it will do so with the internal limitations in the Statement of May 16, which could not be overruled by a sovereign Constituent Assembly.

If any decisions are taken by this Assembly which are repugnant, *ultra vires* or incompetent for the Assembly to adopt, what is the check either internally or externally except again the brute majority in the Assembly?

They conclude by saying that the resolution of the Working Committee passed on June 26 and confirmed by the A.-I.C.C. must stand and they propose to proceed accordingly with their work in the Constituent Assembly.

Therefore, it is quite clear that there is no change on the part of the Congress except the startling expression that they had accepted the scheme in its entirety, whicd is immediately contradicted by what follows in the resolution, and they have reiterated their repudiation of grouping and emphasized once more the sovereign character of the Constituent Assembly, which can only mean that it will not be bound by anything laid down in the Statement of May 16 and would be free to decide every question by a majority.

I need not deal with the rest of the resolution, which is nothing but verbiage and an appeal to the League to join in the battle of India's independence. But there is no doubt left as to India's independence now because the Statement of May 16, at any rate, makes it clear on the part of the British and Mr. Patel, in his recent speech in Bombay, said there was no need any longer to fight the British and that the only revolution that was needed was an internal revolution.

With whom does the Congress ask us to join hands and for what purpose? I am afraid the situation remains as it was and we are where we were.

APPENDIX XXV

LORD WAVELL'S BROADCAST

APPEAL TO LEAGUE

(September 24, 1946)

You must have heard the announcement of the names of the members of the new Interim Government which will come into office very shortly. You will all realise that a very momentous step forward has been taken on India's road to freedom. Some of you who listen to me may feel that the step should not have been taken in this way or at this time. It is to these that I want principally to address myself tonight.

Those of you who were opposed to the formation of the new Government are not, I assume, opposed to the main policy of H.M.G., namely, to fulfil their pledges by making India free to follow her own destiny. You will also, I think, all agree that we need at once a Government of Indians as representative as possible of political opinion in the country.

This is what I set out to secure. But though five seats out of 14 were offered to the Muslim League, though assurances were given that the scheme of constitution-making would be worked in accordance with the procedure laid down, and though the new Interim Government would operate under the existing Constitution, it has not been possible at present to secure a coalition.

No one could be sorrier about the failure than I am. No one could be more sure that it is a Coalition Government in which both the main parties are represented that is needed at this moment in the interests of all parties and communities in India. This is a view which I know the President of the Congress, Pandit Nehru, and his colleagues hold as strongly as I do. His efforts, like mine, will still be directed towards persuading the League to join the Government.

Let me state clearly the offer which has been made and is still open to the League. They can propose to me five names for places in a Government of 14 of which six will be nominees of Congress and three will be representatives of the minorities. Provided these names are acceptable to me and approved by His Majesty, they will be included in the Government, which will at once be re-formed. The Muslim League need have no fear of being outvoted on any essential issue. A Coalition Government can only exist and function on the condition that both the main parties in it are satisfied. I will see that the most important portfolios are equitably distributed. I hope that the League will reconsider their policy and decide to participate in the Government.

Meanwhile, however the administration of India has to go on and there are large issues which have to be decided. I am glad that the representatives of a very large body of political opinion in the country will be my colleagues in carrying on the Government. I welcome them to my Council. I am also glad that the Sikhs have now decided to participate in the Constituent Assembly and the Interim Government. I have no doubt that their decision is a wise one. As I made it clear I shall implement fully H.M.G's policy of giving to the new Government the maximum freedom in the day-to-day administration of the country.

In the field of provincial autonomy, the Provincial Governments have a very wide sphere of authority in which the Central Government cannot intervene. My new Government will not have any power, or indeed any desire, to trespass on the field of provincial administration.

The recent terrible occurrences in Calcutta have been a sobering reminder that a much greater measure of toleration is essential if India is to survive the transition to freedom. I appeal most earnestly not only o sober citizens but to the young and to the discontented to recognise that no conceivable good either to themselves or to their community, or to India, can come from violent words and violent deeds.

It is essential that in all provinces law and order is maintained and the protection of the ordinary peaceful citizen is assured with a firm and impartial hand.

The Army had to be called in at Calcutta to restore order, and rightly so. But I must remind you that to suppress civil disturbances is not the normal duty of the Army but of the Provincial Government. The use of the Army is the last resort only. A general recognition of this basic principle is essential both from the point of view of the civil population and of the Army itself. I heard much praise of the discipline and efficiency of the troops employed in Calcutta, and I will here add my own tribute of admiration to my own Service for their behaviour in their duty which is the most exacting and unpleasant on which troops may be employed.

The War Member in the new Government will be an Indian, and it is a change which both the C-in-C and I warmly welcome. But the constitutional position of the Armed Forces is in no way changed. They still owe allegiance in accordance to their oath to the King-Emperor, to whom and Parliament I am still responsible.

In spite of all immediate appearances, I believe there is still a chance of agreement between the two principal parties. I am quite sure that there is a very large body of opinion in both parties and of non-party men who would welcome such agreement, and I hope they will work for it.

I would appeal to the Press to use its very great influence on the side of moderation and compromise. Remember that the Interim Government can be re-formed tomorrow if the League decides to come in.

Meanwhile, it will be administered in the interest of the country as a whole and not in the interest of one party or group. It is desirable also that the work of the Constituent Assembly should begin as early as possible. Here again I can assure the Muslim League that the procedure laid down in Para 15 of the Cabinet Mission's statement of May 16 regarding the framing of provincial and group constitutions will be strictly adhered to and that there can be no question of any change in the fundamental principles of the Constituent Assembly or of a decision on a main communal issue without a majority of both major communities; and that the Congress are ready to agree that any dispute of interpretation may be referred to the Federal Court.

I sincerely trust that the Muslim League will reconsider their decision not to take part in the plan which promises to give them so wide a field in which to protect the interest and decide the future of the Muslims of India.

We have come to another critical and solemn issue in the affairs of India. Never was tolerance and soberness in thought and action so necessary, never were the wild speaking and rash deeds of a few fraught with greater danger to so many millions. Now is the time for all Indians of any authority, with any influence, to show by their good sense and restraint that they are worthy of their country and that their country is worthy of the freedom it is to receive.

APPENDIX XXVI

LEAGUE'S REACTION TO VICEROY'S STATEMENT

The following is the full text of Mr. Jinnah's statement of the 26th August, 1946, commenting on the Viceroy's statement.

My reaction to the Viceroy's broadcast is that he has struck a severe blow to the Muslim League and Muslim India, but I assure that Mussalmans of India will bear this up with fortitude and courage and learn lessons from our failure to secure our just and honourable position in the Interim Government and the Constituent Assembly.

I once more repeat my question why has the Viceroy gone back on what was announced in the statement of the Cabinet Delegation and the Viceroy on the 16th of June as final, and the assurances given to the Muslim League in his letter dated 20th June? What had happened between the 16th of June and 22nd July that he was pleased to change that formula vitally and substantially and what has happened between the 22nd of July and the 24th of August that he has gone ahead and jammed in a one-party Government?

He says in his broadcast that he was addressing those who advised him that this step should not have been taken in this way or at this time I was one of those unfortunate persons and I still maintain that the step should not have been taken in this way or at this time. I was one of those unfortunate persons and I still maintain that the step that he has taken is most unwise and unstatesmanlike and is fraught with dangerous and serious consequences and he has only added insult to injury by nominating 3 Muslims who, he knows, do not command either respect or confidence of Muslim India and two more Muslim names still remain to be announced.

He is still harping that we are not opposed to the main policy of His Majesty's Government to fulfil their pledges by making India free to follow her own destiny. Of course we are not opposed to the freedom of the peoples of India and we have made it clear that the only solution of India's problem is a division of India into Pakistan and Hindustan which would mean real freedom for the two major nations and every possible safeguard for the minorities in the respective States.

I am sorrier than the Viceroy is about his failure to secure a Coalition Government but my sorrow springs from a different fountain and for different reasons from those of his. I am glad that the Viceroy realises that what is needed is a Coalition Government in which both the main parties are represented and I am glad that he is also speaking on behalf of Pandit Jawaharlal Nehru and the Congress that they hold this view as strongly as he does and that their efforts will still be directed to persuade the League to join the Government. I don't know what the Viceroy means when he says, in his broadcast, of his offer that has been made and which is still open. It is so vague except that the Muslim League will have 5 seats. Nothing else is clearly stated.

He has referred to many other things into which I need not go at present. As regards the Constituent Assembly I do not know what he means when he says that "here again let me remind you that assurances have been given to the League that the procedure laid down in the statement of May 16 regarding the framing of provincial and group constitutions will be faithfully adhered to." It is not a procedure. It is fundamental and basic. The question is whether it can be changed in any way whatsoever.

Then he proceeds to say that there can be no question of any change in the fundamental principles proposed for the Constituent Assembly in Paragraph 15 of the statement of May 16 and he echoes that the Congress are ready to agree that any dispute or interpretation may be referred to the Federal Court. But how can we expect an agreement on the terms and fundamentals of the statement of the 16th of May when one party puts one interpretation contrary to the authoritative statement of the Mission dated the 25th of May and the other party puts a different interpretation which is more in accord with the statement of the 25th of May? But he complacently goes on to say that any dispute or interpretation may be referred to the Federal Court. To begin with, there is no provision for such a dispute being referred to the Federal Court and secondly on the very threshold the parties fundamentally differ in their interpretations regarding the basic terms. Are we going to commence the proceedings of the Constituent Assembly with litigation and lawsuits in the Federal Court? Is this the spirit in which the future Constitution can be framed affecting 400 millions of this sub-continent? If the Viceroy is sincere and if he is in earnest he should translate it into concrete proposals and by his deed and actions.

APPENDIX XXVII

INTERIM GOVERNMENT'S ANNOUNCEMENT OF POLICY

The following is the full text of Pandit Nehru's first broadcast as Vice-President of the Interim Government on July 7, 1946:

Six days ago, my colleagues and I sat on the chairs of high office in the Government of India. A new Government came into being in this ancient land, the Interim or Provisional Government we called it, the stepping stone to the full independence of India. Many thousands of messages of greeting and good wishes came to us from all parts of the world and from every nook and corner of India. And yet we asked for no celebration of this historic event and even restrained our people's enthusiasm. For we wanted them to realize that we were yet on the march, and the goal had still to be reached. There were many difficulties and obstacles on the way, and our journey's end might not be so near as people thought. Any weakness now, any complacency, would be fatal to our cause.

Our hearts were heavy also with the terrible tragedy of Calcutta and because of the insensate strife of brother against brother. The freedom we had envisaged and for which we had laboured, through generations of toil and suffering, was for all the people of India, and not for one group or class or the followers of one religion. We aimed at a co-operative commonwealth in which all would be equal sharers in opportunity and in all things that give meaning and value of life. Why then this strife—this fear and suspicion of each other?

I speak to you today not much of high policy of our programme for the future—that will have to wait a while—but to thank you for the love and affection which you have sent us in such abundant measure. That affection and spirit of co-operation are always welcome, but they will be needed more than ever in the difficult days ahead of us. A friend sent me the following message: 'May you weather every storm, first pilot of the Ship of State, bon voyage.' A cheering message, but there are many storms ahead and our Ship of State is old and battered and slow-moving and unsuited to this age of swift change ; it will have to be scrapped and give place to another, but, however old the ship and however old the pilot there are so many millions of willing hearts and hands to help ; we can brave the high seas and face the future with confidence.

That future is already taking shape and India, this old and dear land of ours, is finding herself again through travail and suffering. She is youthful again with the bright eyes of adventure, and with faith in herself and her mission. For long years she had been narrowly confined, and had lost herself in brooding. But now she looks out on the wide world and holds out her hands in friendship to the other peoples of the world, even though that world may still be full of conflict and thoughts of war.

The Interim National Government is part of a larger scheme which includes the Constituent Assembly which will meet soon to give shape to the Constitution of a free and independent India. It is because of this expectation of an early realization of full independence that we have entered this Government, and we propose to function progressively to achieve that independence in action both in our domestic affairs and our foreign relations. We shall take full part in international conferences as a free nation with our own policy, and not merely as a satellite of another nation. We hope to develop close and direct contacts with other nations and to co-operate with them in the furtherance of world peace and freedom.

We propose, as far as possible, to keep away from the power politics of groups, aligned against one another, which have led in the past to world wars and which may again lead to disasters on an even vaster scale. We believe that peace and freedom are indivisible, and denial of freedom anywhere must endanger freedom elsewhere and lead to conflict and war. We are particularly interested in the emancipation of colonial and dependent countries and peoples, and in the recognition in theory and practice of equal opportunities for all races.

We repudiate utterly the Nazi doctrine of racialism, wheresoever and in whatever form it may be practised. We seek no dominion over others, and we claim no privileged position over other peoples. But we do claim equal and honourable treatment for our people wherever they may go, and we cannot accept any discrimination against them.

The world, in spite of its rivalries and hatreds and inner conflicts, moves inevitably towards closer co-operation and the building up of a world commonwealth. It is for this one world that Free India will work, a world in which there is the free co-operation of free peoples, and no class or group exploits another.

In spite of our past history of conflict, we hope that an independent India will have friendly and co-operative relations with England and the countries of the British Commonwealth. But it is well to remember what is happening in one part of the Commonwealth today. In South Africa racialism is the State doctrine, and our people are putting up a heroic struggle against the tyranny of a racial minority. If this racial doctrine is going to be tolerated, it must inevitably lead to vast conflicts and world disaster.

> We send our greetings to the people of the U.S.A. to whom destiny has given a major rôle in international affairs. We trust that this tremendous responsibility will be utilized for the furtherance of peace and human freedom everywhere. To that other great nation of the modern world, the Soviet Union, which also carries a vast responsibility for shaping world events, we send greetings. They are our neighbours in Asia, and inevitably we shall have to undertake many common tasks and have much to do with each other.

We are of Asia, and the peoples of Asia are nearer and closer to us than others. India is so situated that she is the pivot of Western, Southern and South-East Asia. In the past, her culture flowed to all these countries. They came to her in many ways. Those contacts are being renewed, and the future is bound to see a closer union between India and South-East Asia on the one side, and Afghanistan, Iran and the Arab world on the west. To the furtherance of that close association of free countries, we must devote ourselves. India has followed with anxious interest the struggle of the Indonesians for freedom and to them we send our good wishes.

China, that mighty country, with a mighty past, our neighbour, has been our friend through the ages and that friendship will endure and grow. We earnestly hope that her present troubles will end soon and a united and democratic China will emerge, playing a great part in the furtherance of world peace and progress.

I have not said anything about our domestic policy, nor at this stage do I wish to do so.

> But that policy will inevitably have to be governed by the principles by which we have stood all these years. We shall look to the common and forgotten man in India, and seek to bring him relief and raise his standard of living. We shall continue our fight against the curse of untouchability and other forms of enforced inequality, and shall especially try to help those who are economically

or otherwise backward. Today millions lack food and clothing and houses, and many are on the verge of starvation. To meet this immediate need is an urgent and difficult task, and we hope other countries will help us by sending foodgrains.

An equally urgent and vital task for us is to conquer the spirit of discord that is abroad in India. Out of mutual conflict we shall never build the house of India's freedom, of which we have dreamt so long. All of us in this land have to live and work together, whatever political developments might take place. Hatred and violence will not alter this basic fact, nor will they stop the changes that are taking place in India.

There has been much heated argument about Sections and Groupings in the Constituent Assembly. We are perfectly prepared to accept, and have accepted, the position of sitting in Sections, which will consider the question of the formation of Groups. I should like to make it clear, on behalf of my colleagues and myself, that we do not look upon the Constituent Assembly as an arena for conflict or for the forcible imposition of one viewpoint over another. That would not be the way to build up a contented and united India. We seek agreed and integrated solutions with the largest measure of goodwill behind them, we shall go to the Constituent Assembly with the fixed determination of finding a common basis for agreement on all controversial issues. And so, in spite of all that has happened and the hard words that have been said, we have kept the path of co-operation open, and we invite even those who differ from us to enter the Constituent Assembly as equals and partners with us with no binding commitments. It may well be that when we meet and face common tasks, our present difficulties will fade away.

India is on the move and the old order passes. Too long have we been passive spectators of events, the play-things of others. The initiative comes to our people now, and we shall make the history of our choice. Let us all join in this mighty task and make India, the pride of our heart, great among nations, foremost in the arts of peace and progress. The door is open and destiny beckons to all. There is no question of who wins and who loses, for we have to go forward and together as comrades, and either all of us win or all go down together. But there is going to be no failure. We go forward to success, to independence, and to the freedom and wellbeing of the 400 millions of India.—Jai Hind.

APPENDIX XXVIII

MEMORANDUM OF THE AKALI PARTY TO THE CABINET MISSION

[This Memorandum was submitted by Master Tara Singh, leader of the Akalis, to the Cabinet Mission.]

The position of the Minorities has changed since the Cripps Mission. As conceded by Major Attlee, Indians cannot be made responsible for governing themselves and at the same time power retained in the hands of an authority outside India for intervention on behalf of such Minorities for ensuring their proper treatment by the majority.

This makes it all the more necessary for the Sikhs to safeguard in the Constitution itself their political status in the future policy of the country.

The draft declaration provides for the right of non-accession of provinces. The Sikhs make it plain that they are opposed to any possible partition of India as envisaged in the draft declaration. As stated above, the Sikhs form a compact cultural nationality of about six millions.

They further maintain that, judged by any definition or test, the Punjab is not only their homeland, but their holy land. They were the last rulers of the Punjab and before the advent of the British they enjoyed in the Punjab independent economic and political status which has gradually deteriorated under British rule.

They wish, however, to point out that, with the inauguration of Provincial Autonomy on the basis of the Communal Award, they have been reduced to a state of complete helplessness. If the existing provincial political set-up is continued, the transference of power to the people would perpetuate the coercion of the Sikhs under what in practice has come to be Muslim rule.

That set-up is unjust to the Sikhs. Its working has meant Muslim communal rule in the Punjab which has almost exasperated the Sikhs to the point of revolutionary protest. The intervention of war conditions alone has been responsible for the Sikhs acquiescing temporarily in this communal tyranny. They cannot be expected to continue to submit to it as a permanent arrangement in any new scheme of Indian polity.

Akali Demands:

The statutory Muslim majority in the Legislature of the Province must go and the position of the Sikhs must be strengthened by increased representation therein so as to ensure to the Sikhs an effective voice in the administration of the country.

In the alternative, out of the existing province of the Punjab a new province may be carved out as an additional provincial unit in the United India of the future in such a way that all the important Sikh Gurdwaras and shrines may be included in it as also a substantial majority of the Sikh population in the existing province of the Punjab.

The Sikhs cannot, however, blind themselves to the fact that the Muslims have declared that they are a separate nation as distinct from the Sikhs, the Hindus and others, and that on that basis they are entitled to Pakistan. We have already expressed unequivocally our opposition to the establishment of such a State.

In view of the rumours that are current we are obliged to take note of the possibility of the Cabinet Mission giving serious consideration to the Muslim League claim.

Before the Mission arrives at a decision on this question, we would emphasise that the Sikhs have as good a claim for the establishment of a separate sovereign Sikh State as the Muslims for Pakistan and that the Mission should not concede the claim for Pakistan without conceding at the same time the claim for a separate State made on behalf of the Sikhs.

The Sikhs are in favour of a single constitution-making body in which they should be represented as already indicated above.

In case the Mission should think of taking into serious consideration the proposal that has been made for two constitution-making bodies, one for Pakistan and the other for the rest of India, we wish, in the light of what has been said by us above, to make our position clear that there should be a separate constitution-making body also for the Sikh State.

APPENDIX XXIX

MEMORANDUM OF THE HINDU MAHASABHA TO THE CABINET MISSION

1. Declaration of Independence:

As all sovereignty in respect of India vests in the Indian people, it is the right of the Indians to be fully and completely free like all the free peoples in the world.

It is only absolutely unfettered freedom that will enable India to be a front-line nation in the world, and to play her rightful role in the maintenance of world-peace and world-order. It is independence, coupled with India's natural resources, man-power and strategic position in the geography of the world, that will enable her to hold the scales even between the West and the East. There are also several other considerations which require that India should be free from any external obligation and control.

The Hindu Mahasabha, therefore, urges that India should be fully free and independent, and that a declaration to that effect should be immediately made by the British Cabinet through proper channel.

The Mahasabha is of the opinion that it is alliance on equal terms with, rather than membership of, the British Commonwealth of Nations, that will be in tune with the time-spirit, and will also prove beneficial to both in the long run.

2. India's Integrity and Indivisibility:

Be the modes of living and worship of the Indian people what they may, there can be no doubt that geographically, historically, enthnologically, politically, and even culturally India is one, whole and indivisible, and it must remain so in future. This integrity and indivisibility must be maintained whatever the cost and sacrifice be.

No community in India can rightfully claim to constitute a nation, much less a sovereign nation, with a separate homeland of its own. Partition of India into two or more sovereign nations under any guise or disguise will be economically unsound and disastrous; and politically unwise and suicidal.

3. Territorial self-determination:

The Hindu Mahasabha is opposed to the new-fangled principle of territorial self-determination, as in theory it is vicious and in practice will prove more dangerous than Pakistan itself.

4. Indian Union:

India's Constitution should be of a federal type with the Indian

Union at the Centre and the Provinces and the Indian States as its federating Units.

The Constitution should leave no room for any Province or an Indian State not to accede to the said Union or to secede therefrom.

5. Provincial Autonomy and Residuary powers:

The Constitution should provide for the grant of the utmost possible measure of autonomy to the federating Units, but with the residue of powers vested in the Centre.

The Union Government should have the power of superintendence and control in cases where the federating Units go wrong in respect of national policy or interest and should be strong enough to exercise this power effectively.

6. Rule of Majority:

The Constitution should contain no provision which will tend directly or indirectly, to reduce a majority into a minority by the grant of special concessions to minorities such as weightage, excessive representation, parity and so forth. The governing principle of the Constitution should be democracy, which means the rule of the majority. The so-called "parity of representation" should not be recognised even with joint electorates, as it would amount to penalising the Hindus for no fault of theirs but for the mere reason that they constitute a majority.

The Constitution shall guarantee adequate safeguards for the protection of religion, culture and language for all, including minorities.

7. Joint Electorates and Adult Franchise:

The representation both in the Federal and Provincial Legislatures should be on the principle of adult franchise and one man one vote. The electorate should be joint with reservation of seats for minorities according to the population basis, wherever necessary.

The Hindu Mahasabha is of the opinion that it will be highly imprudent to frame India's Constitution on principles other than those as envisaged above, as such a Constitution will not fail to be a perennial source of political irritation and strife.

8. Interim Government:

An Interim Central Government should be formed immediately composed of representatives of the political parties willing to shoulder responsibility. The formation of such a Government should not be delayed on the plea of non-co-operation on the part of any particular party. During the period of transition, the Viceroy will act as the Constitutional Head and will not exercise his power of veto.

There should take place complete transfer of power and authority of the Government of India to the Interim Government.

It should be one of the primary functions of this Government to provide adequate facilities to the Constituent Assembly to carry on its work without let or hindrance.

9. Constituent Assembly:

The Constituent Assembly will consist of representatives of all political parties in proportion to their voting strength as shown in the last elections.

The Constituent Assembly will be the sovereign body which will decide the terms of treaty with Great Britain.

The Constituent Assembly will decide all matters by majority vote, and the decisions so taken should be binding on all.

The Constitution framed by the Constituent Assembly will be the Constitution of India.

These are broadly the main principles which the Hindu Mahasabha stands for, in so far as India's Constitution is concerned.

APPENDIX XXX

THE COMMUNIST PARTY OF INDIA'S MEMORANDUM TO THE CABINET MISSION

1. Declaration of Independence

The foremost desire of all Indians today is the immediate ending of British rule which has meant for them economic degradation and political slavery. Two centuries of British rule with its record of brutal suppression of the Indian people and of famine, destitution and poverty for the mass of people, has convinced every Indian that there is no decent existence possible for him unless the British overlordship over India is ended. Successive British Governments, who have not hesitated to break their pledged word, have shattered the faith of the Indian people in the willingness of Britain to transfer power.

The Communist Party, therefore, will judge the Cabinet Mission only by its practice and the first proof of sincerity that they demand is an unequivocal and unambiguous declaration recognising Indian independence and Indian sovereignty.

In further proof of its sincerity, the British Government should declare its determination to effect within six months the total withdrawal of British troops from all Indian territory, including the States.

Such a declaration should be made and implemented irrespective of the fact whether India's political parties have settled their differences. The question of Indian unity is an internal question to be settled by the people themselves. It cannot be made an excuse for the refusal of Britain to transfer power. The withdrawal of British troops and the recognition of India's sovereignty must begin forthwith and the following measures should be taken to achieve the same:

2. Transfer of Power

Establishment of a Provisional Government, based on main popular parties. We think that the best course would be an agreement between the Congress and the League for parity in the Government and for adequate representation to minorities.

All the powers vested in the British Government and the King Emperor as the paramount and sovereign power *vis-a-vis* the Indian States and the present Indian Government as well as all special powers vested in the Viceroy and the Governors must be forthwith ended. This alone will enable the Provisional Government freely to negotiate with the British Government on the basis of equality and to be in a position to deal with the question of the Indian Princes and the States and their future place in a free India.

3. FUNCTION OF THE PROVISIONAL GOVT.

(i) The main task of the Provisional Government will be to convene a Constituent Assembly within six months of its establishment and ensure that the elections to the Assembly are free and democratic

(ii) The Provisional Government would be responsible to the Constituent Assembly when the latter comes into existence, as stated below and in the meanwhile it would not lie within its competence to commit India to any political, economic or military treaty with any power.

(iii) The Provisional Government should prepare a treaty to be negotiated with the British Government for the prompt payment of sterling balances and mutual trade relations, subject to its final ratification by the all-India Constituent Assembly.

4. CONSTITUENT ASSEMBLY

It is the right of the Indian people to frame their own constitution and it is in the Indian people alone that full sovereignty is vested.

The constitution-making body envisaged by the British Government is undemocratic, as it will be formed by election of delegates by the members of the Provincial Assemblies, on the basis of indirect election. The existing Provincial Assemblies based on a narrow franchise keep the vast majority of the people out of power.

5. SELF-DETERMINATION

The acute differences between the Congress and the League on the issue of Constituent Assembly can only be settled by the just application of the principle of self-determination.

We suggest that the Provisional Government should be charged with the task of setting up a Boundaries Commission to redraw the boundaries on the basis of natural ancient homelands of every people, so that the redemarcated Provinces become as far as possible linguistically and culturally homogeneous National Units, e.g., Sind, Pathanland, Baluchistan, Western Punjab, etc.*. The people of each such unit should have the unfettered right of self-determination, i.e. the right to decide freely whether they join the Indian Union or form a separate sovereign state or another Indian union.

The elections to the Constituent Assembly should, therefore, be based on recognition of this fundamental right and during the elections the question of separation or union should be put by the political parties to the

* The following is the comprehensive list of the National Units that will come into existence as suggested above and after the dissolution of the Indian States as contemplated under section 6—vis: Tamilnad, Andhradesha, Kerala, Karnatak, Maharastra, Gujerat, Rajasthan, Sind, Baluchistan, Pathanland, Kashmir, Western Punjab, Central Punjab, Hindustan, Bihar, Assam, Bengal, Orissa.

people. The delegates elected from each National Unit shall decide by a majority whether they will join the all-India Constituent Assembly to form an Indian Union or remain out and form a separate sovereign state by themselves or join another Indian Union.

The Communist Party stands for a free, voluntary democratic Indian Union of sovereign units. It is firmly convinced that the best interests of the Indian masses will be served by their remaining together in one common union in a common brotherhood to defend the freedom and solve the problems of poverty which require the co-operation of all. It is only on the basis of the application of the principle of self-determination as indicated above that Indian unity can be preserved.

6. States

The Indian people are determined to put an end to the Princes' autocracy which holds sway over one-third of India. Indian freedom and Indian democracy will have no meaning, in fact they will be constantly endangered, if one-third of India is allowed to remain under the yoke of these medieval autocrats. The Princes are the creation of the British Government, and have been in the past and are today maintained by British bayonets as a useful prop to British rule. India regards the so-called treaties and obligations of the British Government as merely a conspiracy against Indian democracy. There should be, therefore, no question of inviting the Princes to share power in the interim government or of allowing them any share in determining the decisions of the Constituent Assembly.

The peoples of the Indian States should, therefore, have the same rights and franchise as the rest of the Indian people. The peoples of each state should have the full right to decide through a freely-elected Constituent Assembly whether they should join the Indian Union as a separate Province or join any particular reconstituted Province, inhabited by people of the same nationality.

7. Civil Liberties

Normally when the independence of a country is to be discussed, an essential precondition to the opening of discussions should be the restoration of complete civil liberties and a general amnesty for all political prisoners. The Communist Party has noted that whatever is being done at present, is full of hesitation and discrimination.

The Communist Party, therefore, demands:

(i) the immediate release of all political prisoners including those convicted of terrorist offences and in particular the Bengal pre-reform prisoners, many of whom have been in jail for more than fifteen years ;

(ii) the immediate release of all Indians belonging to the Army, Navy and Air Force who have been imprisoned or convicted in connection with the recent strikes ;

(iii) the immediate release of all soldiers of the AZAD HIND FAUJ (Indian National Army) still in prison and of all Indians in the

Armed Forces who during the past six years have been convicted or detained on account of their political activities ;

(iv) the immediate lifting of the ban on all political parties (e.g. Congress Socialist Party, Forward Bloc, etc.) that still remain illegal ;

(v) the immediate restoration of full civil liberties to the entire people, including the cessation of arrest of political workers and of demands from newspapers for security, etc. actions which, in particular, are being increasingly directed at members and newspapers of the Communist Party.

8. Conclusion

The Communist Party is of the opinion that only if the British Government proceeds along the lines laid down in this Memorandum, will it be able to achieve stable democratic settlement between the Indian people and the British people on the basis of equality, thus solving one of the knottiest problems of world security and peace among peoples.

Any attempt, however, to exploit the differences among the Indian people, to impose an arbitrary partition, and to retain the Princes in order to perpetuate British domination will be resisted by the Indian people with all the strength at their command.

APPENDIX XXXI

MR. M. N. ROY'S OPEN LETTER TO THE CABINET MISSION

You came to this country as ambassadors of British democracy to negotiate a treaty which would end India's political subjugation and usher in a new era of voluntary and mutually beneficial co-operation between our two peoples. It was a noble mission, and you came with high hopes—with a firm determination to succeed. That certainly was the proper spirit with which a difficult task should be tackled. But one may well wonder if your sense of responsibility was as keen as your missionary zeal ; if facile optimism did not make you overestimate your power of persuasion and underrate the difficulty of the task.

The idea of coming to give freedom to four hundred million human beings is so very intoxicating as to turn the wisest of heads. In such a state of emotional exuberance, amounting to self-hypnosis, one tends to lose sight of realities, preferring to live in a world of make-believe. Whatever might have been the reason, you and the British Government certainly over-simplified the problem of setting India free, and suggested a solution which amounted to a negation of freedom for the vast bulk of the people, and therefore a betrayal of democracy. It is, indeed, a cruel irony that ambassadors of British democracy should undertake such a shameful mission.

The none too encouraging experience of the last few weeks might put you in a realistic frame of mind, and make you conscious even now of the sinister significance of your mission. For the same reason, you might now be inclined to cultivate a measure of humility and pay some heed to voices of caution and intelligence. With that hope, it may be a forlorn hope, I am addressing this open letter.

It was not necessary for you to come all the way to this country to learn what you have learned since you came. The talks during these three weeks have been mere repetition of the well known views of the heir-designates of dying Imperialism, whom the Labour Government also recognise as the trustworthy custodians of the Indian masses. The gift of freedom is to be made to the fortunate few of a privileged minority. But the chosen elite cannot agree about the division of the legacy of autocratic power.

A political regime controlled by a minority may be glorified as the National Government; but it will be an autocracy. A minority rule cannot be anything else. A constitution framed by the "elected representatives" of the enfranchised twelve per cent of the population may be fraudulently called the Charter of Indian Independence; but in effect, it will be a loadstone round the neck of Indian democracy, which thus will be exposed to the danger of being strangled to death.

The disagreement between the two upper-class communal organisations, euphemistically called the major political parties, has been deepening all these years. Their imperialist patrons made repeated efforts for a settlement as the basis of their taking over power. Experience showed that the communal difference was irreconcilable. Power could not be transferred to Indians, if India was to be identified with two groups of politicians thirsting for totalitarian power and exploiting the backwardness of their respective communities for promoting their ambition. India could not be free if there was no other way for freedom coming to her than an undemocratic procedure of pseudo-constitutionalism.

There was absolutely no reason to assume that the vicious atmosphere created by the negative politics of reactionary nationalism and by its imperialist patrons would clear, as soon as three well-meaning British Ministers came to India with the firm determination to succeed.

Gentlemen, you could not make a miracle. However, I still wish that you succeed in the mission of placing India on the road to freedom. If you fail, the honesty of your purpose and the sincerity of your mission will be disputed by those to whom exclusively you want make the gift of power; and you will have to thank your own conventionalism and conceit for that irony of fate.

Even on the face of it the liberal policy of British Socialism is not beyond doubt and criticism. It would hand over the fate of the Indian masses to the tender mercies of a coterie of nationalist politicians on the specious plea that the outstanding question of India's future Constitution is for the Indians to settle, the present British rulers only want some Indian government to take over, and you have come with the mission of negotiating the instrument of that proposed transfer.

The fallacy of this apparent liberalism is evident. If the British Government are really not concerned with what will happen after they hand over, why then this insistence that there should be an agreement between the two communal organisations which amongst themselves have created the present vicious circle? Are you not tying a string to your gift of freedom by making the condition? One can legitimately doubt the sincerity of your professed liberalism.

To obviate that plausible doubt about the sincerity of the British Government, you should not have come to this country. Instead of sending an obviously unnecessary mission, the Labour Government should have ordered the British rulers of this country to pack up and quit without any further delay. The heir-designates of dying Imperialism want the nominal British rulers to quit, so that they may take possession of the legacy without any let or hindrance. You have come to say that the quit notice has been duly received and will be acted upon. Was it at all necessary for you to come? Having come, perhaps by mistake, the most graceful thing for you to do will be to go back immediately, taking along all the hypocritical representives of a dead past, whose professed liberalism can only do harm to Indian democracy and the cause of Indian freedom.

Gentlemen, if you are sincere in your sloppy sentimentality and wooden constitutionalism, then, please do quit this country without any further ado. What will happen thereafter, is none of your business, according to your own profession. Your officiousness, the vain effort to do the impossible, does not prove good faith. On the contrary, it stigmatise you and your principal at home as hypocrites. And the shame and discredit of your bungling and conventionalism besmirch the fair name of British democracy.

If, on the other hand, you want to act as Socialists, as faithful ambassadors of British democracy, then don't any longer persist in your futile efforts to persuade reactionaries thirsting for totalitarian power, to be reasonable. The duty of British Socialists in power is not to practise fatuous liberalism, but to liberate the Indian masses from colonial slavery, and help them ascertain the democratic right of self-determination. If you do not have the courage to do that duty, please do us the favour of quitting soon.

Your practice contradicts the profession that you do not want to encroach upon the Indian people's sovereign right to determine their future. You are interfering, only to back up an upper class minority as against democracy. You are admittedly pursuing the policy of placing an upper-class minority in power—a policy which has no democratic justification nor even any conventional constitutional sanction. To recognise the right of an upper-class minority enfranchised by the grace of Imperialism, to usurp the sovereignty of the people, is a parody of constitutionalism.

It is not convincing for you to plead that pure idealism cannot be pursued in political practice; that one must be practical. The given Indian situation allows more than one line of practical politics. If to begin with, power must be transferred to an *ad hoc* government, why prefer an upper-class minority? A conservative British Government, naturally could not conceive of any alternative. The Viceroy's approach to the problem is also naturally determined by the social sympathies. Scion of a dying order, he cannot see beyond the narrow circle of conventional respectability. He believes that the upper-classes are destined to rule. He may belong to the curious breed which calls itself liberal conservatives; but he cannot be expected to believe in democracy. Representatives of British democracy in power and particularly when they profess Socialism, should have a broader outlook, and the boldness to prefer democratic practice to conventional constitutionalism, which often deceives democracy.

The situation being as it is, what do you, gentlemen, now propose to do? If the heir-designates agree, about the division of the legacy, a minority government will take over, and you will return home with the feeling that you have done your duty by India. But for the moment, that happy consummation of your misconceived liberal policy does not appear to be very promising. Your conventional approach to the problem can yield two alternative solutions, both of which will be equally disastrous from the point of view of Indian democracy. Either you will have to go back defeated, leaving the Indian situation to drift; or you must give up the pretence of non-interference. Choosing the latter alternative, you will confer your favour on the more powerful of the two communal organisations, and thereby throw India into the vortex of communal riots. You appear to shrink before the other alternative, which may plunge the country in an orgy of lawlessness and violence. Haunted by that spectre, you might decide to hand over to the larger party backed by the power of vested interests. But don't deceive yourselves about the consequence of your "practical politics". Firstly, there will be no guarantee against the spread of violence and lawlessness; and secondly, democracy will be thrown to the wolves. There is no reason to take Nehru's stage-thunder more seriously than Jinnah's threat of civil war. Both may be bluffing. But both are equally ominous. The unhappy country thus stands between the devil and the deep sea. You will do no good to anybody by tipping the scale one way or the other. Only a bold policy of democratic practice can extricate India from her present precarious position and place her firmly on the road to freedom.

Gentlemen, the pseudo-liberalism inherited from the Tory predecessors, having failed, the Labour Government should now be advised to get out of the beaten track of conventional constitutionalism and blaze the new trail of bold democratic practice. That will be taking a realistic view of the situation and pursuing practical politcs.

Now it is almost a foregone conclusion that the British Government must abandon the pretence of non-intervention, and propose a solution of the baffling problem. What will be the proposal? That is the crucial question. The fate of Indian democracy hangs in the balance. You, gentlemen, are in a position to tip it one way or the other—deliver India to the totalitarian nationalism of the Congress, or help Indian democracy assert herself.

Let there be no illusion about whom the Congress represents. It is the political instrument of big business. A political regime dominated by the Congress, therefore, will be a willing tool of Indian capitalism, which makes no secret of its fascist ambition. The national-capitalist plan of economic development frankly postulates a dictatorial political regime and regimentation of public life.

Gentlemen, haunted by the threat of the Congress leaders to do terrible things, should you help the rise of Fascism in India? Is that the liberating mission with which you came to this country? If there was really no alternative to that dreadful perspective, why compromise and discredit British democracy? The most honourable thing for you to do, in that case, is to quit this unhappy country immediately.

But there is a clear alternative. It has been repeatedly pointed out by the Radical Democratic Party. None can claim to be a Socialist, and yet fail to admit that the Radical Democratic Party has indicated the only practical approach to the problem of India's political future, if that is to be democratic freedom. Parliamentary democracy has not been such an unqualified success as to require no improvement whatsoever. In the post-war world, democracy must become social democracy, if it is to survive the shock of Fascism. The tendency is clearly to that direction. India's march to freedom must be in step with the rest of the world. Antiquated formal democracy of parliamentarism does not offer any solution of the problem of India's political progress. That has been made amply evident by experience Democratic practice must be adjusted to the peculiarities of the situation. Wooden conventionalism will lead not to democracy, but of fascism.

To advance towards genuinely democratic freedom, India needs a Constitution which will disrupt the reactionary social *status quo*, and invest the people with effective power. The Constitution is to be so framed as to enable the people to wield political power. Whoever will sponsor and promulgate such a Constitution, will promote Indian freedom. There is absolutely no reason why British democracy in power should not play that liberating role. But it is not necessary for the Labour Government to interfere more than they are doing at present through your mission.

Experience is driving you to the position where you must make recommendations for the solution of the problem of Indian Constitution. True to the commitment of transferring power to the Indian people, the British Labour Government is entitled to outline a Constitution such as will establish genuine democratic freedom in India. Having done that, it should proceed to the next step of helping the formation of a Provisional Government which will undertake the task of leading the Indian people through the successive stages of the process of framing the Constitution and its promulgation by a Constituent Assembly elected by universal suffrage. For the interim period, all power will be transferred to the Provisional Government.

The procedure obviously will be fair, impartial and fully democratic. There will be no discrimination against anybody. The Provisional Government can be an all-party government, if the old parties will abandon the claim to totalitarian power, and be prepared to co-operate in a democratic practice. Otherwise, the Provisional Government will be a no-party government, composed of individuals ready to undertake the task of enabling the people to take the initiative in the solution of the hitherto baffling problem of India's political progress.

Gentlemen, let not the threat of politicians playing the dog in the manger, scare you out of wits. The practical procedure outlined above will immediately lead to the formation of a Provisional Government which, by virtue of a bold democratic practice, will in no time rally the people. Should the older parties still not fall in line and co-operate with the process of the people themselves shaping the future of the country, they would do so at their own cost. Demagogy would no longer help them. The people feel that their destiny is in their own hand. The causes of racial animosity, distrust, bitterness, frustration will progresssively disappear. The political atmosphere of the country will be normalised and the people will apply themselves to the great task of building up the noble structure of democratic freedom.

Gentlemen, is it too much to hope that, having learnt from bitter experience, you would at last get out of the blind-alley of the beaten track, and take a realistic, practical view of the situation? Preconceived notions and conventionalism may persuade you to brush aside novel ideas, particularly when they come from modest quarters. But defeat may promote some humility, and consequently you may be prone to discuss new ideas with people who sincerely want you to succeed in the mission of placing India on the road to freedom. Otherwise, your mission will either be a dismal failure, or no more glorious than Chamberlain's mission to Munich.

APPENDIX XXXII

BRITISH GOVERNMENT'S INTERPRETATION

The following is the British Government's statement after the Tripartite Conference at 10, Downing Street on December 6, 1946:

The conversations held by His Majesty's Government with Pandit Jawaharlal Nehru, Mr. M. A. Jinnah, Mr. Liaquat Ali Khan and Sardar Baldev Singh came to an end this evening as Pandit Nehru and Sardar Baldev Singh are returning to India tomorrow morning.

The main difficulty that has arisen has been over interpretation of Para 19 (5) and (8) of the Cabinet Mission's statement of May 16, relating to meetings in sections, which runs as follows:

Para 19 (5):—These sections shall proceed to settle provincial constitutions for the provinces included in each section and shall also decide whether any group constitution shall be set up for those provinces and, if so, with what provincial subjects the group should deal. Provinces should have power to opt out of the groups in accordance with the provisions of Sub-Clause (8) below.

Para 19 (8):—As soon as the new constitutional agreements have come into operation, it shall be open to any province to elect to come out of any group in which it has been placed. Such a decision shall be taken by the legislature of the province after the first general election under the new Constitution.

The Cabinet Mission have throughout maintained the view that the decisions of the sections should, in the absence of an agreement to the contrary, be taken by a simple majority vote of the representatives in the sections. This view has been accepted by the Muslim League, but the Congress have put forward a different view. They have asserted that the true meaning of the statement, read as a whole, is that the provinces have the right to decide both as to grouping and as to their own constitutions.

HMG have had legal advice which confirms that the statement of May 16 means what the Cabinet Mission have always stated was their intention. This part of the statement, as so interpreted, must, therefore, be considered an essential part of the scheme of May 16 for enabling the Indian people to formulate a constitution which HMG would be prepared to submit to Parliament. It should, therefore, be accepted by all parties in the Constituent Assembly.

It is, however, clear that other questions of interpretation of the statement of May 16 may arise and HMG hope that if the Council of the Muslim League are able to agree to participate in the Constituent Assembly, they will also agree, as have the Congress, that the Federal Court should be asked to decide matters of interpretation that may be referred to them by either side and will accept such a decision, so that the procedure, both in the union Constituent Assembly and in the sections, may accord with the Cabinet Mission's plan.

On the matter immediately in dispute, HMG urge the Congress to accept the view of the Cabinet Mission in order that a way may be opened for the Muslim League to reconsider their attitude. If in spite of this reaffirmation of the intention of the Cabinet Mission the Constituent Assembly desires that this fundamental point should be referred for a decision to the Federal Court, such reference should be made at a very early date. It will then be reasonable that the meetings of the sections of the Constituent Assembly should be postponed until the decision of the Federal Court is known.

There has never been any prospect of success for the Constituent Assembly except upon the basis of agreed procedure. Should the constitution come to be framed by a Constituent Assembly in which a large section of the Indian population had not been represented, HMG could not, of course, contemplate—as the Congress have stated they would not contemplate—forcing such a constitution upon any unwilling parts of the country.

APPENDIX XXXIII

CONGRESS REACTION TO INTERPRETATION

The following is the full text of the resolution pased by the A.I.C.C. on January 6, 1947:

The A.I.C.C. having considered the events that have taken place in the country since the Meerut session, of the Congress in November last, the statement issued by the British Government of December 6, 1946 and the statement of the Working Committee of December 22, 1946, advises Congressmen as follows:—

The A.I.C.C. endorses the statement of the Working Committee of December 22, 1946, and expresses its agreement with the view contained therein.

While the Congress has 'always been' agreeable to making a reference to the Federal Court on the question of interpretation in dispute, such a reference has become purposeless and undesirable owing to recent announcements made on behalf of the British Government. A reference could only be made on an agreed basis, the parties concerned agreeing to abide by the decision given.

The A.I.C.C. is firmly of opinion that the constitution for a free and independent India should be framed by the peoples of India on the basis of as wide an agreement as possible. There must be no interference whatsoever by any external authority, and no compulsion of any province or part of a province by another province. The A.I.C.C. realises and appreciates the difficulties placed in the way of some provinces, notably Assam and the N.W.F.P. and the Sikhs in the Punjab and Baluchistan by the British Cabinet's scheme of May 16, 1946 and more especially by the interpretation put upon it by the British Government in their statement of December 6, 1946. The Congress cannot be a party to any such compulsion or imposition against the will of the people concerned, a principle which the British Government have themselves recognised.

The A.I.C.C. is anxious that the Constituent Assembly should proceed with the work of framing a constitution for free India with the goodwill of all parties concerned and, with a view to removing the difficulties that have arisen owing to varying interpretations, agree to advise action in accordance with the interpretation of the British Government in regard to the procedure to be followed in the sections.

It must be clearly understood, however, that this must not involve any compulsion of a province and that the rights of the Sikhs in the Punjab should not be jeopardised. In the event of any attempt at such compulsion, a province or part of a province has the right to take such action as may be deemed necessary in order to give effect to the wishes of the people concerned. The future course of action will depend upon the developments that take place and the A.I.C.C. therefore directs the Working Committee to advise upon it, whenever circumstances so require, keeping in view the basic principle of provincial autonomy.

APPENDIX XXXIV

THE LEAGUE ACCEPTS INTERPRETATION

The following is the full text of the resolution which the League Working Committee adopted at Karachi on January 31, 1947:

The Working Committee of the All-India Muslim League has given careful consideration to the statement issued by HMG on Dec. 6, 1946, the resolution passed thereafter by the Congress Working Committee on Dec. 22, 1946, and by the All-India Congress Committee on Jan. 6, 1947, the speeches delivered by responsible leaders of the Congress at the A.I.C.C. session referred to above, and the proceedings of the Constituent Assembly during its two sessions so far held, and record their views as follows:

By their statement of Dec. 6, HMG admitted that the interpretation which the Muslim League had always put on paragraphs 19 (V) and 19 (VIII) of the Cabinet Mission's statement of May 16 was the correct one and accorded with the intention of the Cabinet Mission and HMG.

By that statement it was also proved that the Congress, on the other hand, had "put forward a different view" and, therefore, had not accepted what HMG themselves described as "this fundamental point," namely, that decision in the Sections, including questions relating to the framing of the constitutions of Provinces included in each Group, "should, in the absence of agreement to the contrary, be taken by a simple majority vote of the representatives in the Sections."

HMG, furthermore, added that "this statement, as so interpreted, must, therefore, be considered an essential part of the scheme of May 16 for enabling the Indian people to formulate a constitution which HMG would be prepared to submit to Parliament." Accordingly, in their statement of Dec. 6 they urged the Congress to accept "this reaffirmation of the intention of the Cabinet Mission" or in the alternative to refer the point to the Federal Court at a very early date.

In their statement of Dec. 6 HMG also affirmed that the Congress had agreed that other questions of interpretation of the statement of May 16 which might arise might be referred by either side to the Federal Court whose decisions should be accepted, and, on the assumption that the Congress had agreed to this procedure, HMG asked the Muslim League also to agree to it in order to ensure that "the procedure both in the Union Constituent Assembly and in the Sections may accord with the Cabinet Mission's plan."

HMG, in the last paragraph of their statement of Dec. 6, reiterated the fact that "there has never been any prospect of success for the Constituent Assembly except upon the basis of the agreed procedure," and they repeated the assurance: "Should the constitution come to be framed by a Constituent Assembly in which a large section of the Indian population had not been represented, HMG would not, of course, contemplate—as the Congress has stated it would—forcing such a constitution upon any unwilling parts of the country."

The meaning and the application of this assurance were further clarified by Sir Stafford Cripps in his speech in the House of Commons on Dec. 12, 1946, when he said: "But the Government also had to envisage the possibility in the clause in the final paragraph of the statement. This was, perhaps, a statement of the obvious—that, if the Muslim League could not be persuaded to come into the Constituent Assembly, then parts of the country where they were in a majority could not be held to be bound by the results."

The situation created by the issue of this statement by HMG is that the onus of taking the next step fell on the Congress and it was called upon:—

1. To accept honestly and unequivocally the correct interpretation of paragraphs 19 (V) and 19 (VIII) of the Cabinet Mission's statement of May 16, which interpretation has been already accepted by the Muslim League, or to refer the point to the Federal Court.

2. To reaffirm that it has accepted the procedure for the settling of other questions or interpretations that might arise, so that the decision should accord with the basic and fundamental principles of the scheme of May 16, 1946, namely, that either side could refer such questions to the Federal Court whose decisions would be binding on all concerned; and

3. To postpone the session of the Constituent Assembly which had been called for Dec. 9, 1946, pending settlement of the dispute over the fundamental points of principle and procedure which had been brought to the fore by the statement of Dec. 6 and the correct interpretation of which the Congress has not accepted, as was made clear in that statement, there being no prospect of success for the Constituent Assembly without such agreement, particularly on the part of the Congress.

The Working Committee of the All-India Muslim League regrets to note that the Congress has reacted to the situation created by the statement of Dec. 6 in a manner which shows that it is determined to adhere to its own views and interpretations of the fundamental provisions in the Cabinet Mission's statement of May 16, which militate against the clearly expressed intentions and interpretations of the authors of that statement as well as of HMG as a whole and which destroy the very basis on which the constitutional plan set forth in that statement has been drawn up.

By its resolution of Dec. 22 the Congress Working Committee rejected the suggestion that the point in dispute should be referred to the Federal Court if the Congress did not accept "this re-affirmation of the intention of the Cabinet Mission," and the Committee decided to convene a meeting of the A.I.C.C. for the purpose of giving a decision on the issues raised by the statement of Dec. 6.

The Working Committee of the Congress, however, in its resolution indulged in an attack on the British Government for their renewed interpretation and clarification, which had called the Congress bluff, and on the Muslim League for no other fault than that its stand had been at last vindicated.

The A.I.C.C. by its resolution passed on Jan. 6, purported "to agree to advise action in accordance with the interpretation of the British Government in regard to the procedure to be followed in the Sections," about which there never was any doubt in the mind of any sane and honest person, but it immediately added the following qualifying clauses:

It must be clearly understood, however, that this must not involve any compulsion on a Province and that the rights of the Sikhs in the Punjab should not be jeopardized.

. In the event of any attempt at such compulsion, a Province or part of a Province has the right to take such action as may be deemed necessary in order to give effect to the wishes of the people concerned.

The future course of action will depend upon the developments that take place and the A.I.C.C., therefore, directs the Working Committee to advise upon it, whenever circumstances so require, keeping in view the basic principle of provincial autonomy.

These qualifying clauses, in the considered opinion of the Working Committee of the All-India Muslim League, confer the right of veto within the Section on "a Province" and, what is more absurd, on "a part of a Province," as well as on the Sikhs in the Punjab, and, therefore, they completely nullify the advice or so-called "acceptance" by the Congres of the Dec. 6 statement, and this A.I.C.C. resolution is no more than a dishonest trick and jugglery of words by which the Congress has again attempted to deceive the British Government, the Muslim League, and public opinion in general.

The question at issue was a very simple one. What was required was a straight and honest annswer and not these evasions, equivocations, and camouflage from one of the two major contracting parties to the questions whether the Congress honestly and sincerely agreed to the proposals of May 16 as clarified by HMG on Dec 6, 1946, and whether it was prepared to honourably abide by them and carry out the letter and spirit of the proposals which were put before the two major parties by the British Government, who were merely acting as mediators as, unfortunately, the two major parties had failed to come to any agreement at Simla and the conference at Simla had broken down.

Of the second point in HMG's statement of Dec. 6, namely, the procedure whereby either side could refer other questions of interpretation to the Federal Court, the resolution of the A.I.C.C. makes no mention, but the mover of the resolution, Pandit Nehru, on being questioned on the second day of the A.I.C.C.'s deliberations as to whether the Congress had agreed to this procedure, categorically answered in the negative and declared:

Apart from this, in view of the recent developments and the statement of Dec. 6, which produces a new situation, I am not prepared to admit for an instant that we have agreed to any future procedure about references. Whatever the future brings, we shall have to consider it. I should like to make it perfectly clear that we are giving no assurance about any references in regard to any other matters to the Federal Court. . . . . . We are not going to commit ourselves at the present moment to any reference to the Federal Court or to any other authority. We shall decide—or the Constituent Assembly shall decide—as we think best in the circumstances.

With regard to the third point, namely, "that if a constitution comes to be framed by a Constituent Assembly in which a large section of the Indian population has not been represented," such a constitution would not be forced upon any "unwilling parts of the country," the A.I.C.C. resolution, in paragraph 3, completely distorts the meaning and application of this principle and makes this an excuse to instigate a section of the population of Assam, the NWFP, the Sikhs and even Baluchistan, to revolt against decisions that might be taken by the relevant Sections sitting as a whole and by a simple majority vote. In the opinion of the Working Committee of the All-India Muslim League the subsequent decision of the Assam Provincial Congress not to abide by the procedure laid down for Sections and its reiteration that "the constitution for Assam shall be framed by her own representatives only" is a direct result of this instigation and is a step taken by Assam Congressmen in collusion with the all-India leaders of the Congress.

The Constituent Assembly met on Dec. 9 and subsequent dates and thereafter on Jan. 20 and subsequent dates and has already taken decisions of vital character so far, as it is known to the public: and as some of the sittings were held in camera it is very difficult to get correct information as to what other resolutions it has passed or what decisions it has already taken. It has passed a resolution, known as the independent sovereign republic resolution, laying down the objectives.

It is not only a proclamation of India as an independent sovereign republic but it lays down fundamentals of the Constitution as was admitted by Pandit Nehru, the mover of the resolution. It is a very vital resolution. It lays down the essentials of the next Constitution ; several things which are mentioned there are fundamentals of the Constitution. It speaks of a republic or Union, functions and powers vested in the Union or as are inherent or implied in the Union and resulting therefrom, and talks of present boundaries, States and present authorities, the residuary powers, powers being derived from the people, minority rights and fundamental rights.

These are undoubtedly fundamentals of the Constitution and they are beyond the limit of the powers and the terms of the scheme of the Cabinet Mission's statement of May 16 and the resolution is therefore illegal, *ultra vires* and not competent to the Constituent Assembly to adopt.

Next, it has appointed several committees and has proceeded to elect an Advisory Committee, referred to in paragraph 20 of the statement of the Cabinet Mission and the Viceroy on the rights of citizens, minorities, tribal and excluded areas. Further it has appointed a Steering Committee and various other committees and as some of the decisions have been taken in camera it is very difficult to say what resolutions it has passed or decisions it has taken. It has also passed the rules of procedure and assumed control of Sections by means of these rules for which there is no warrant or justification, particularly rule 63 which runs as follows:

"1. The Assembly shall, before finally setting the Union Constitution, give an opportunity to the several provinces and States through their legislatures to formulate, within such time as it may fix, their views upon the resolutions of the Assembly outlining the main features of the Constitution or, if the Assembly so decides, upon the preliminary draft of the Constitution.

"2. Before the Constitution of any province is finally settled or the decision to set up a Group Constitution for the Section in which the province is included is finally taken, an opportunity shall be given to the province concerned through its legislature to formulate, within such time as may be fixed for the purpose its views (a) upon the resolution outlining the main features of the Constitution or, if the majority of the representatives of the province in the Assembly so desire, upon the preliminary draft of such Constitution, and (b) upon the preliminary decision of the Section concerned as to whether a Group Constitution shall be set up for the provinces included in the Section and, if so, with what provincial subject the Group should deal."

It has also appointed a committee to define the scope of the Union subjects, whereas the position was made quite clear, immediately after the statement of May 16 was issued by the Secretary of State for India in his broadcast and by Sir Stafford Cripps at his Press conference where he read out an explanatory statement. Both of them stated in the clearest possible terms of the time and manner in which the Group Constitution were to be framed by the Sections concerned before the Union Constitution was taken up.

The Secretary of State said: "After a preliminary meeting in common, these representatives of the provinces will divide themselves up into three Sections. These Sections will decide upon provincial and Group matters. Subsequently they will reunite to decide upon the Constitution for the Union."

Sir Stafford Cripps at his Press conference said: "So the three Sections will formulate the provincial and Group Constitutions and when that is done they will work together with the States' representatives to make the Union Constitution. That is the final phase, and the Union is strictly confined to three subjects."

It is clear from the above that the Constituent Assembly in which only the Congress Party is represented, has taken decisions on principles and procedure, some of which exceed the limitations imposed by the statement of May 16 on the Constituent Assembly's functions and powers at the preliminary stage and which further impinge upon the powers and functions of the Sections. By taking these decisions in the Constituent Assembly and by appointing a committee consisting of individuals chosen by the Congress, the Congress has already converted that truncated Assembly into a rump and something totally different from what the Cabinet Mission's statement had provided for.

In view of these facts and circumstances the Working Committee of the Muslim League is definitely of opinion that the Congress, by rejecting this final appeal of HMG to accept the correct interpretation of the fundamental procedure of the Cabinet Mission's statement of May 16, and by having already, by the resolutions and decisions taken in two sessions, converted the Constituent Assembly into a body of its own conception and destroyed all fundamentals of the statement of May 16 and every possibility of compromise on the basis of the Cabinet Mission's constitutional plan. The Working Committee accordingly calls upon HMG to declare that the constitutional plan formulated by the Cabinet Mission, as announced on May 16 has failed because the Congress after all these months of efforts has not accepted the statement of May 16, not have the Sikhs, nor the Scheduled Castes.

The proposals of May 16 could only be given effect to and carried out if the two major parties agreed to accept them. The Congress had not, and has not accepted and does not accept them although the Muslim League had accepted, by its resolution, the statement of May 16 as far back as June 6, 1946. But in view of the fact that the Congress refused to accept the proposals in toto and unequivocally, the Muslim League had to withdraw its acceptance on July 29, 1946.

The Working Committee of the Muslim League is, therefore, emphatically of opinion that the elections to, and thereafter the summoning of the Constituent Assembly, in spite of strong protests and most emphatic objections on the part of the League, were *ab initio* void, invalid and illegal as not only the major parties had not accepted the statement but even the Sikhs and the Scheduled Castes had also not done so and that the continuation of the Constituent Assembly and its proceedings and decisions are *ultra vires*, invalid and illegal and it should be forthwith dissolved.

APPENDIX XXXV

PRINCES' TERMS FOR ENTRY INTO INDIAN UNION

The following is the text of the resolution adopted by the Chamber of Princes at New Delhi on Jan. 29, 1947:

This meeting reiterates the willingness of the States to render the fullest possible co-operation in framing an agreed constitution for, and in the setting up of, the proposed Union of India, in accordance with the accepted plan ; and declares that the following fundamental propositions form the basis for the States' acceptance of the Cabinet Mission's plan :—

(1) The entry of the States into the Union of India, in accordance with the accepted plan, shall be on no other basis than that of negotiation, and the final decision shall rest with each State. The proposed Union shall comprise, so far as the States are concerned, the territories of only such States or groups of States as may decide to join the Union, it being understood that their participation in the constitutional discussions, in the meantime, will imply no commitments in regard to their

ultimate decision, which can only be taken after consideration of the complete picture of the constitution.

(2) The States will retain all subjects and powers other than those ceded by them to the Union. Paramountcy will terminate at the close of the interim period, and will not be transferred to, or inherited by, the new Government of India. All the rights surrendered by the States to the Paramount Power will return to the States. The proposed Union of India will, therefore, exercise only such functions in relation to the States in regard to Union subjects as are assigned or delegated by them to the Union. Every State shall continue to retain its sovereignty except in regard to rights and powers that have been expressly delegated by it. There can be no question of any powers being vested, or inherent or implied in the Union in respect of the States unless specifically agreed to by them.

(3) The constitution of each State, its territorial integrity, and the succession of its reigning dynasty in accordance with the custom, law and usage of the State, shall not be interfered with by the Union or any unit thereof, nor shall the existing boundaries of a State be altered, except by its free consent and approval.

(4) So far as the States are concerned, the Constituent Assembly is authorized only to settle the Union constitution in accordance with the Cabinet Mission's plan, and is not authorized to deal with questions bearing on the internal administrations or constitutions of individual States or groups of States.

(5) HMG have made it clear in Parliament that it is for the States to decide freely to come in or not as they choose. Moreover, according to the Cabinet Mission's memorandum of May 12, 1946, on States treaties and paramountcy, political arrangements between the States on the one side, and the British Crown and British India on the other, will be brought to an end after the interim period. "The void will have to be filled either by the States entering into a federal relationship with the successor Government in British India, or failing this, entering into particular political arrangements with it."

APPENDIX XXXVI

DECLARATION OF CONSTITUENT ASSEMBLY'S OBJECTIVES

The following is the text of Pandit Nehru's resolution on "Objectives" which was unanimously passed by the Constituent Assembly on Jan. 22, 1947:

Wherein this Constituent Assembly declares its firm and solemn resolve to proclaim India as an independent sovereign republic and to draw up for her future governance a constitution the territories that now comprise British India, the territories that now form the Indian States, and such other parts of India as are outside British India and the State as well as such other territories as are willing to be constituted into the independent sovereign India shall be a Union of them all;

And wherein the said territories, whether with their present boundaries or with such others as may be determined by Constituent Assembly and thereafter according to the law of the constitution, shall possess and retain the status of autonomous units, together with residuary powers, and exercise all powers and functions of government and administration, save and except such powers and functions as are vested in or assigned to the Union, or as are inherent or implied in the Union or resulting therefrom: and wherein all power and authority of the sovereign independent India, its constituent parts and organs of government, are derived from the people;

And wherein shall be guaranteed and secured to all the people of India justice, social, economic and political: equality of status, of opportunity, and before the law: freedom of thought, expression, belief, faith, worship, vocation, association and action, subject to law and public morality;

And wherein adequate safeguards shall be provided for minorities, backward and tribal areas, and depressed and other backward classes;

And whereby shall be maintained the integrity of the territory of the republic and its sovereign rights on land, sea and air according to justice and the law of civilised nations, and this ancient land attain its rightful and honoured place in the world and make its full and willing contribution to the promotion of world peace and the welfare of mankind.

APPENDIX XXXVII

A NEW STATEMENT OF BRITISH POLICY

The following is the full text of Mr. Attlee's statement made in Parliament on Feb. 20, 1947:

1. It has long been the policy of successive British Governments to work towards the realization of self-government in India. In pursuance of this policy, an increasing measure of responsibility has been devolved on Indians, and today the civil administration and the Indian Armed Forces rely to a very large extent on Indian civilians and officers. In the constitutional field the Acts of 1919 and 1935, passed by the British Parliament, each represented a substantial transfer of political power. In 1940 the Coalition Government recognized the principle that Indians should themselves frame a new constitution for a fully autonomous India, and in the offer of 1942 they invited them to set up a Constituent Assembly for this purpose as soon as the war was over.

2. HMG believe this policy to have been right and in accordance with sound democratic principles. Since they came into office they have done their utmost to carry it forward to its fulfilment. The declaration of the Prime Minister on March 15 last, which met with general approval in Parliament and the country, made it clear that it was for the Indian people themselves to choose their future status and constitution,

and that, in the opinion of HMG, the time had come for responsibility for the Government of India to pass into Indian hands.

3. The Cabinet Mission, which was sent to India last year, spent over three months in consultation with Indian leaders in order to help them to agree upon a method for determining the future constitution of India, so that the transfer of power might be smoothly and rapidly effected. It was only when it seemed clear that, without some initiative from the Cabinet Mission, agreement was unlikely to be reached that they put forward propsals themselves.

4. These proposals, made public in May last, envisaged that the future constitution of India should be settled by a Constituent Assembly composed, in the manner suggested therein, of representatives of all communities and interests in British India and of the Indian States.

5. Since the return of the Mission, an Interim Government has been set up at the Centre, composed of the political leaders of the major communities, exercising wide powers within the existing constitution. In all the provinces, Indian Governments responsible to legislatures are in office.

6. It is with great regret that HMG find that there are still differences among Indian parties which are preventing the Constituent Assembly from functioning as it was intended that it should. It is of the essence of the plan that the Assembly should be fully representative.

7. HMG desire to hand over their responsibility to authorities established by a constitution approved by all parties in India in accordance with the Cabinet Mission's plan. But, unfortunately, there is at present no clear prospect that such a constitution and such authorities will emerge. The present state of uncertainty is fraught with danger and cannot be indefinitely prolonged. HMG wish to make it clear that it is their definite intention to take necessary steps to effect the transference of power to responsible Indian hands by a date not later than June, 1948.

8. This great sub-continent now containing over 400 million people has, for the last century, enjoyed peace and security as a part of the British Commonwealth and Empire. Continued peace and security are more than ever necessary today if the full possibilities of economic development are to be realized and a higher standard of life attained by the Indian people.

9. HMG are anxious to hand over their responsibilities to a Government which, resting on the sure foundation of the support of the people, is capable of maintaining peace and administering India with justice and efficiency. It is, therefore, essential that all parties should sink their differences in order that they may be ready to shoulder the great responsibilities which will come upon them next year.

10. After months of hard work by the Cabinet Mission, a great measure of agreement was obtained as to the method by which a constitution should be worked out. This was embodied in their statements of May last. HMG then agreed to recommend to Parliament a constitution worked out in accordauce with the proposals made therein by a

fully representative Constituent Assembly. But if it should appear that such a constitution will not have been worked out by a fully representative Assembly before the time mentioned in Paragraph 7 (June, 1948) HMG will have to consider to whom the powers of the Central Government in British India should be handed over, on the due date, whether as a whole to some form of Central Government for British India, or in some areas to the existing Provincial Governments, or in such other way as may seem most reasonable and in the best interests of the Indian people.

11. Although the final transfer of authority may not take place until June, 1948, preparatory measures must be put in hand in advance. It is important that the efficiency of the civil administration should be maintained and that the defence of India should be fully provided for. But inevitably as the process of transfer proceeds it will become progressively more difficult to carry out to the letter all the provisions of the Government of India Act, 1935. Legislation will be introduced in due course to give effect to the final transfer of power.

12. In regard to the Indian States, as was explicitly stated by the Cabinet Mission, HMG do not intend to hand over their powers and obligations under Paramountcy to any Government of British India. It is not intended to bring Paramountcy, as a system, to a conclusion earlier than the date of the final transfer of power, but it is contemplated that, for the intervening period, the relations of the Crown with individual States may be adjusted by agrement.

13. HMG will negotiate agreements in regard to matters arising out of the transfer of power with representatives of those to whom they propose to transfer power.

14. HMG believe that British commercial and industrial interests in India can look forward to a fair field for their enterprise under the new conditions. The commercial connexion between India and the United Kingdom has been long and friendly and will continue to be to their mutual advantage.

15. HMG cannot conclude this statement without expressing, on behalf of the people of this country, their goodwill and good wishes towards the people of India as they go forward to this final stage in their achievement of self-government. It will be the wish of everyone in these islands that, notwithstanding constitutional changes, the association of the British and Indian peoples should not be brought to an end, and they will wish to continue to do all that is in their power to further the well-being of India.

16. The House will wish to know of an announcement which is being made public today. FM the Rt. Hon. Viscount Wavell was appointed Viceroy in 1943, after having held high military command in the Middle East, S-E Asia and India with notable distinction since the beginning of the war. It was agreed that this should be a war-time appointment. Lord Wavell has discharged this high office during this very difficult period with devotion and a high sense of duty. It has,

however, seemed that the opening of a new and final phase in India is an appropriate time to terminate this war appointment.

17. His Majesty has been pleased to approve, as successor to Lord Wavell, the appointment of Adm. the Viscount Mountbatten, who will be entrusted with the task of transferring to Indian hands responsibility for the government of British India in a manner that will best ensure the future happiness and prosperity of India. The change of office will take place during March. The House will be glad to hear that His Majesty has been pleased to approve the conferment of an Earldom on Viscount Wavell.

18. Viscount Mountbatten will remain on the active list, in accordance with his wishes that his future employment in the Royal Navy shall not be prejudiced.

19. I am sure the House will wish him well in his task. The change of office will take place during March.

APPENDIX XXXVIII

CONGRESS APPROVAL OF BRITISH DECLARATION

The following resolution on HMG's statement of Feb. 20 was adopted by the Congress Working Committee at New Delhi on March 8, 1947:

The Congress Working Committee welcome the declaration made on behalf of the British Government of their definite intention to transfer power finally by a date not later than June 1948, and to take steps to that end in advance.

The transfer of power, in order to be smooth, should be preceded by the recognition in practice of the Interim Government as a Dominion Government with effective control over the Services and administration, and the Viceroy and Governor-General functioning as the constitutional head of the Government. The Central Government must necessarily function as a Cabinet with full authority and responsibility. Any other arrangement is incompatible with good government and is peculiarly dangerous during a transitional period full of political and economic crises.

The Congress has already expressed its acceptance of the British Cabinet Mission's scheme of May 16, 1946, and has further accepted the interpretations put upon it by the British Cabinet on Dec. 6, 1946. In accordance therewith, the Constituent Assembly has been functioning and has appointed various committees to carry on its work. It has become all the more essential now to expedite this work so that the constitution for an Indian Union and the constituent units should be finally prepared and given effect to well within the stated period to facilitate the final transfer of power.

The Working Committee welcome the decision of a number of States to join the Constituent Assembly and trust that all the States and their peoples will be effectively represented in this task of making a constitution for an Indian Union. The Committee invite afresh the representatives of the Muslim League, who have been elected to the Constituent Assembly, to join in this historic undertaking.

The work of the Constituent Assembly is essentially voluntary. The Working Committee have frequently stated that there can or should be no compulsion in the making of a constitution for India. It is the fear of compulsion or coercion that has given rise to distrust and suspicion and conflict. If this fear goes, as it must, it will be easy to determine India's future so as to safeguard the rights of all communities and give equal opportunities to all.

It has been made clear that the constitution framed by the Constituent Assembly will apply only to those areas which accept it. It must also be understood that any province or part of a province which accepts the constitution and desires to join the Union cannot be prevented from doing so. Thus, there must be no compulsion either way, and the people will themselves decide their future. This peaceful and co-operative method is the only way to make democratic decisions with the maximum of consent.

In this hour when final decisions have to be taken, and the future of India has to be shaped by Indian minds and hands, the Working Committee earnestly call upon all parties and groups, and all Indians generally, to discard violent and coercive methods, and co-operate peacefully and democratically in the making of a constitution. The time for decision has come and no one can stop it or stand by and remain unaffected. The end of an era is at hand and a new age will soon begin. Let this dawn of the new age be ushered in bravely, leaving hates and discords to the dead past.

APPENDIX XXXIX

APPEAL FOR LEAGUE CO-OPERATION

The following resolution inviting the League for talks with the Congress was adopted by the Congress Working Committee at New Delhi on March 8, 1947:

In view of new developments which are leading to a swift transfer of power in India, it has become incumbent on the people of India to prepare themselves jointly and co-operatively for this chance, so that this may be effected peacefully and to the advantage of all. The Working Committee, therefore, invite the All-India Muslim League to nominate representatives to meet representatives of the Congress in order to consider the situation that has arisen and to devise means to meet it.

The Working Committee will keep in close touch with the representatives of the Sikhs and other groups concerned, with a view to co-operating with them in the steps that may have to be taken and in safeguarding their interests.

APPENDIX XL

DIVISION OF PUNJAB RECOMMENDED

The following is the full text of the Congress Working Committee's resolution on the Punjab adopted at New Delhi on March 8, 1947:

During the past seven months India has witnessed many horrors and tragedies which have been enacted in an attempt to gain political ends by brutal violence, murder and coercion. These attempts have failed, as all such attempts must fail, and have only led to greater violence and carnage.

The Punjab, which had thus far escaped this contagion, became six weeks ago, the scene of an agitation, supported by some people in high authority, to coerce and break a popular Ministry which could not be attacked by constitutional methods. A measure of success attended this, and an attempt was made to form a Ministry dominated by the group that had led the agitation. This was bitterly resented and has resulted in increased and widespread violence. There has been an orgy of murder and arson and Amritsar and Multan have been scenes of horror and devastation.

These tragic events have demonstrated that there can be no settlement of the problem in the Punjab by violence and coercion, and that no arrangement based on coercion can last. Therefore, it is necessary to find a way out which involves the least amount of compulsion. This would necessitate a division of the Punjab into two provinces, so that the predominantly Muslim part may be separated from the predominantly non-Muslim part.

The Working Committee commend this solution, which should work to the advantage of all the communities concerned and lessen friction and fear and suspicion of each other. The Committee earnestly appeal to the people of the Punjab to put an end to the killing and brutality that are going on, and to face the tragic situation, determined to find a solution which does not involve compulsion of any major group and which will effectively remove the causes of friction.

APPENDIX XLI

PRINCES' PLEA FOR AGREED CONSTITUTION

The following is the full text of the resolution adopted at the Conference of the Rulers of Indian States on April 2, 1947:

This conference reiterates the support of the States to the freedom of the country and their willingness to render the fullest possible co-operation in framing an agreed Constitution and towards facilitating the transfer of power on an agreed basis.

It re-confirms the resolution adopted by the general conference of Rulers and representatives of States on Jan. 29, 1947.

It ratifies the general understanding reached between the States' Negotiating Committee and the corresponding committee set up by the Constituent Assembly, in regard to the allocation of the States' quota of seats in and the method of selection of the States' representatives to the Constituent Assembly and on the fundamental points discussed at their meetings held on Feb. 8 and 9 and March 1 and 2, 1947, subject to acceptance of the aforesaid understanding by the Constituent Assembly, provided that this acceptance must precede the participation of the representatives of such States as may decide to do so in the work of the Constituent Assembly at the appropriate stage.

This conference is glad to note that Mr. Attlee's statement of Feb. 20, 1947, further confirms the declaration made by the Cabinet Mission that paramountcy will cease at the close of the interim period. This means that all the rights surrendered by the States to the Paramount Power will revert to them and they will be in a position as independent units to negotiate freely in regard to their future relationship with others concerned.

This conference reaffirms its previous recommendations in regard to internal reforms, and emphasizes the urgency and importance of suitable action being taken without delay, where needed, with due regard to local conditions.

In view of the element of urgency introduced by Mr. Attlee's statement of Feb. 20, 1947, this conference authorizes the Chancellor and the Standing Committee of the Chamber of Princes to conduct further negotiations, through the States' Negotiating Committee, or such other sub-committees as the Standing Committee may appoint, in regard to questions affecting the States in general:

(I) With the Crown Representative in regard to matters relating to the lapse of paramountcy and those arising out of the proposed transfer of power so far as they affect the States;

(II) With the new Central Government and the competent British Indian authorities in regard to matters referred to in Paragraph 4 of the Cabinet Mission's memorandum of May 12, 1946, on the States' treaties and paramountcy; provided that—(A) These negotiations will be conducted in accordance with the resolution adopted by the general conference of Rulers on Jan. 29, 1947, and the instructions and resolutions of the States' Constitutional Advisory Committee as endorsed by the Standing Committee of Princes and the Committee of Ministers; (B) The results of these negotiations will be subject to the approval of the aforesaid States' committees and ratification by the States.

This conference requests His Highness the Chancellor to address His Excellency the Crown Representative with a view to ensuring an early and satisfactory settlement by HMG of questions relating to individual States prior to the transfer of power.

APPENDIX XLII

C. R. FORMULA

These were the proposals presented to Mr. Jinnah by Gandhiji in 1944:

Basis for terms of settlement between the Indian National Congress and the All-India Muslim League to which Gandhiji and Mr. Jinnah agree and which they will endeavour respectively to get the Congress and the League to approve:

(1) Subject to the terms set out below as regards the constitution for Free India, the Muslim League endorses the Indian demand for Independence and will co-operate with the Congress in the formation of a provisional interim government for the transitional period.

(2) After the termination of the war, a commission shall be appointed for demarcating contiguous districts in the north-west and east of India, wherein the Muslim population is in absolute majority. In the areas thus demarcated, a plebiscite of all the inhabitants held on the basis of adult suffrage or other practicable franchise shall ultimately decide the issue of separation from Hindustan. If the majority decide in favour of forming a sovereign state seperate from Hindustan, such decision shall be given effect to, without prejudice to the right of districts on the border to choose to join either State.

(3) It will be open to all parties to advocate their points of view before plebiscite is held.

(4) In the event of seperation, mutual agreements shall be entered into for safeguarding defence, and commerce and communications and for other essential purposes.

(5) Any transfer of population shall only be on an absolutely voluntary basis.

(6) These terms shall be binding only in case of transfer by Britain of full power and responsibility for governance of India.

APPENDIX XLIII

GANDHIJI'S REVISED TEXT

The C. R. formula as revised by Gandhiji in his final offer to Mr. Jinnah on Sept. 24, 1944, reads as follows:

The areas should be demarcated by a commission approved by the Congress and the League. The wishes of the inhabitants of the areas demarcated should be ascertained through the votes of the adult population of the areas or through some equivalent method.

If the vote is in favour of separation it shall be agreed that these areas shall form a separate state as soon as possible after India is free from foreign domination and can therefore be constituted into two sovereign independent states.

There shall be a treaty of separation which should also provide for the efficient and satisfactory administration of foreign affairs, defence, internal communications, customs, commerce and the like, which must necessarily continue to be matter of common matters between the contracting parties.

The treaty shall also contain terms for safeguarding the rights of minorities in the two States.

Immediately on the acceptance of this agreement by the Congress and the League the two shall decide upon a common course of action for the attainment of independence of India.

The League will however be free to remain out of any direct action to which the Congress may resort and in which the League may not be willing to participate.

APPENDIX XLIV

LEAGUE'S RESOLUTION ON PAKISTAN

The Muslim League adopted the following resolution on March 23, 1940, at Lahore:

Resolved that it is the considered view of this session of the All-India Muslim League that no constitutional scheme would be workable in this country or acceptable to Muslims unless it is designed on the following basic principle, viz., that geographically contiguous units are demarcated into regions which should be constituted with such territorial readjustments as may be necessary, that the areas in which the Muslims are numerically in majority, as in the north-western and eastern zones of India, should be grouped to constitute independent states in which the constituent unit shall be autonomous and sovereign.

That adequate, effective and mandatory safeguards should be specifically provided in the constitution for minorities in these units and in these regions for the protection of their religious, cultural, economic, political, administrative and other rights and interests in consultation with them; and in other parts of India where the Mussalmans are in a minority, adequate, effective and mandatory safeguards shall be specifically provided in the constitution for them and other minorities for the protection of their religious, cultural, economic, political, administrative and other rights and interests in consultation with them.

INDEX